FRIENDS

UNTIL THE

END

FRIENDS

UNTIL THE

END

EDMUND BURKE AND CHARLES FOX

IN THE AGE OF REVOLUTION

JAMES GRANT

W. W. NORTON & COMPANY

Independent Publishers Since 1923

For information about permission to reproduce selections from this book, write to
Permissions, W. W. Norton & Company, Inc., 500 Fifth Avenue, New York, NY 10110

For information about special discounts for bulk purchases, please contact
W. W. Norton Special Sales at specialsales@wwnorton.com or 800-233-4830

Manufacturing by Lakeside Book Company
Book design by Chris Welch
Production manager: Louise Mattarelliano

Library of Congress Cataloging-in-Publication Data is available.

ISBN: 978-0-393-54210-3

W. W. Norton & Company, Inc., 500 Fifth Avenue, New York, NY 10110
www.wwnorton.com
W. W. Norton & Company Ltd., 15 Carlisle Street, London W1D 3BS

10 9 8 7 6 5 4 3 2 1

for Patricia,
who else?

So sweet and voluble is his discourse.

—WILLIAM SHAKESPEARE,

LOVE'S LABOUR'S LOST, ACT 2, SCENE 1

CONTENTS

FRIENDS

UNTIL THE

END

Charles James Fox and Edmund Burke, the greatest English orators of the eighteenth century, made common political cause for twenty-five years. They supported the rebellious American colonies, opposed Lord North, and did their best to shield Britain's public credit from the ungainly, crisis-prone East India Company.

Improbably, the two were friends as well as political allies—the compulsively gambling and mistress-collecting Fox loved and admired Burke, feelings that the clean-living, deep-thinking Burke warmly reciprocated. The French Revolution ended their political union and shattered their friendship.

It wasn't a shared social position that brought the two together. Burke (1729–97) was the son of an Irish lawyer, Fox (1749–1806) the cosseted heir of a rich English political family. Nor did their friendship spring from a shared piety or an ambition for the approval of King George III or his friends. Fox, who seemed to have had not one religious bone, married late and then to a courtesan; the doctors who performed his autopsy especially marked the damage to his overtaxed liver. Burke, a professed Christian who held that the established English church was the bedrock of civil soci-

ety, was a homebody and monogamist. They jointly opposed what they
regarded as the overreaching crown.

What the two friends shared was fellowship, a love of language and
literature, and long careers in opposition. They moved easily together in
the London intellectual and literary world. Knowledge of the classical languages as well as familiarity with the English poets were standard furnish-
ings in that rarefied circle. To shine in conversation meant matching Latin
tag for Latin tag and one Shakespearean quotation for another. Presiding
over literary London was the formidable lexicographer Samuel Johnson,
who, with the portraitist Sir Joshua Reynolds, founded the famous Literary
Club in 1764. Said Johnson of Burke, "His stream of mind is perpetual."
And of Fox, he is "a most extraordinary man."[1]

Burke attained no governmental post higher than the lusterless paymaster of the forces. Fox held high ministerial office on two brief occasions, but he, like Burke, was best in opposition. What did they oppose?
Principally, the incursion of royal power on the prerogatives of the House
of Commons.

"There is no man who hates the power of the crown more, or who
has a worse opinion of the person to whom it belongs than I," wrote Fox
to Burke about their principal antagonist, the king himself.[2] George III
detested Fox in turn, as a father might; his son, the Prince of Wales, and
Fox were boon companions, the prince holding the unwanted distinction of owing even larger gambling debts than the dice-rolling and horse-
playing parliamentarian.

Speechmaking was the principal occupation of an opposition member
of Parliament. Fluency, wit, and self-command were essential to a speaker's success. Prepare as he might, the member must affect an air of spon-
taneity. He would memorize what he could, improvise for the rest. In the
galleries, reporters raced to record those words on the wing. They caught a
good many of Burke's in a speech in 1780 to stop wasteful public spending
on tumbledown royal palaces that time and "the restless tide of manners"
had passed by. To waste money on the preservation of such derelicts, said
Burke, "is to embalm a carcass not worth an ounce of the sums that are
used to preserve it. It is to burn precious oils in the tomb; it is to offer meat

and drink to the dead—not so much an honour to the deceased as a disgrace to the survivors."[3]

Burke demanded, in the same vein, the abolition of Britain's sleepy Board of Trade, which paid a handful of sinecurists a great deal of money for very little work. In a rare success, he garnered high praise from Edward Gibbon, whose £750 a year no-show job Burke had legislatively snatched away. He really didn't mind, said Gibbon; hearing "that diffuse and ingenious orator, Mr. Burke," was worth the personal cost.[4]

Conservative is the word with which posterity has chosen to identify Burke, and he indeed opposed even the mildest program of English parliamentary reform. His anti-revolutionary tract, *Reflections on the Revolution in France*, stands as one of the seminal works of political philosophy of any age. As to religion, he would brook no relaxation of the obligation of the clergy of the Church of England to attest to the truth of the Thirty-nine Articles of Religion, a doctrine that was finalized in 1571.

But it was the same Burke who rose to the defense of pilloried sodomists, who advocated for the liberation of Ireland and of all British Catholics from the chains of repressive English law, and who devoted unrequited years to the cause of the salvation of the Indian people from the misgovernance of the East India Company.

The Whig party was the political home that Burke and Fox eventually came to share. The Whigs stood for government by the enlightened few, chiefly the landed aristocracy—that is, themselves—whose forebears had led the Glorious Revolution of 1688. As to "Church and King," the Tories' motto, Fox wanted as little as possible to do with either. Burke favored both, though he and Fox were as one in impugning tyrannical motives to George III.

Fox was born a Whig. Burke rather came to those colors through reason and personal loyalty. The social divide between the son of Lord Holland (as Fox's father came to be styled) and the bookish son of a Dublin lawyer was unbridgeable, a fact that Burke accepted without envy. Nor, eventually, did Burke begrudge Fox, his junior by twenty years, Fox's position as leader of the party.

Such self-made men as himself Burke likened to "annual plants that perish with our season and leave no sort of traces behind us." Properly set above them in politics and society were the noble "great oaks that shade a country and perpetuate [their] benefits from generation to generation" (though, late in his parliamentary career, Burke had to remind his idle, putative betters how much they owed to such annual plantings as himself).[5]

"I pay no regard whatever to the voice of the people," said the insolent young Fox; "it is their duty to do what is proper, without considering what may be agreeable."[6] It was a very different Fox who, in 1780, won election to Westminster, England's most democratic borough, and who, during the French Revolution, raised the toast: "May ancient Nobility of England ever think it their highest honor to support the Rights of the People!"[7]

Fox, said Burke, was "born to be loved," and contemporaries bore witness to the personal charm of both men but especially Fox's. The novelist Frances Burney, who met Burke at a dinner given by Sir Joshua Reynolds in 1782, decided she was in love with him.

Thorns in the side of the Tories, Burke and Fox were fair game for the Tories' newspapers. Political cartoonists rendered Burke as Don Quixote, or as a thin, bespectacled priest in biretta and cassock with a partiality for whiskey and potatoes—an Irishman who supported Catholic emancipation was obviously a papist, let the facts to the contrary be what they may. There was no need to take visual liberties with Fox. He really was swarthy, fat, ungroomed, and hirsute. Even his onetime lover, the Duchess of Devonshire, affectionately called him "the Eyebrow."

Fox's friends loved him the more for his foibles, while his adversaries, not looking beyond his dissipation, underestimated his talents. It was Fox who attacked the slave trade and who, in 1783, introduced a bill into the House of Commons to bring under government regulation the quasi-private company that monopolized English trade with India and ruled over millions of its inhabitants. Though financially unstable, the East India Company was politically powerful, and its parliamentary allies were certain to be lying in wait for the bold mover of the legislation. To anticipate their attack, Burke rose to defend his friend's intentions and seriousness of purpose. "He has put to hazard his ease," said he of Fox, his security, his interest, his power, even his darling popularity, for the benefit of a people he has never seen. This is the road that all heroes have trod before him. He is traduced and abused for his supposed motives. He will remember that obloquy is a necessary ingredient in the composition of all true glory; he will remember that it is not only in the Roman customs, but it is in the nature and constitution of things, that calumny and abuse are essential parts of triumph.[8]

Neither could Fox's more perceptive enemies deny his formidable talents. "Charles," Lord North once cheerfully greeted Fox in the House of Commons, "I am glad you did fall on me today, for you were in full feather."[9] When a visiting French politician disparaged Fox in the presence of William Pitt, the long-serving Tory prime minister replied, "You have never seen the wizard within the magic circle."[10] (Pitt, Fox, and Burke, though divided by politics, were united in money. Each lived his life in debt, and each died broke.)

THIS NARRATIVE TREATS THE FRIENDSHIP BETWEEN BURKE AND FOX through three great events, of which the first is the American Revolution. Burke, as the London agent of the New York Assembly in the years leading up to the Declaration of Independence, took a sympathetic view of the American side, urging that Britain relinquish power, including the power to tax, rather than risk a fruitless war. He told the House of Commons: "I do not know the method of drawing up an indictment against an whole people."[11]

Fox literally wore his politics on his sleeve by sporting George Washington's colors, buff and blue, as he made his rounds of London. "Above all, my dear Lord," Fox addressed a Whig colleague after Washington's defeat at the Battle of Long Island in 1776, "I hope that it will be a point of honor among us all to support the American pretensions in adversity as much as we did in their prosperity, and that we will never desert those who have acted unsuccessfully upon Whig principles, while we continue to profess our admiration for those who succeeded in those principles in the year 1688."[12]

The impeachment of Warren Hastings, governor-general of the East India Company, on grounds of mismanagement and personal corruption, is the second of our three events. It was the first impeachment in Britain since 1725, it involved what was then among the largest business enterprises on earth, and it lasted for seven years. Burke and Fox were prime movers of the prosecution, Burke leading off the trial in 1788 with a speech that lasted for four days.

The business before the House, he said, "is not solely whether the prisoner at the bar be found innocent or guilty, but whether millions of mankind shall be made miserable or happy." Throughout, Burke spoke up in defense of India's ancient civilization against the venal assault of the British chartered monopoly: "Faults this nation may have; but God forbid we should pass judgment upon people who framed their laws and institutions prior to our insect origin of yesterday!"[13]

Over the long course of the trial, one-third of the Hastings jury pool, members of the House of Lords, died. When the time came to render a verdict, scarcely more than two dozen of the members had heard enough evidence to allow them in conscience to pass judgment. "Not guilty" on all counts was their verdict. Nearly everyone involved in this judicial marathon had long since become heartily sick of it, Fox not least, though Burke seemed never to flag. His reply to the summation of the arguments of the defense spanned nine days.

Long before the end of the trial, Burke and Fox had irrevocably split over the French Revolution, our third point of focus. To Fox, the overthrow of the ancien régime was something sublime: "How much the greatest event it is that ever happened in the World! & how much the best."[14] Burke wrote his masterpiece, *Reflections on the Revolution in France*, to denounce it. To Fox, a Francophile with extensive political and social connections in France, the revolution was nothing less than France's version of Britain's (and specifically of the Whigs' own) Glorious Revolution. To Burke, "this monstrous tragedy" was about not liberty but nihilism—and financial malpractice, too. Burke's critique of the revolutionists' monetary inventions anticipated debate over the justice and efficacy of modern central banking practice.

Fox and Burke each wondered if the other had lost his mind. Fox couldn't bear even to open *Reflections*. In the House of Commons, on May 6, 1791, Burke rose to condemn Fox's stand on France and to announce an end to their friendship. Fox, "though still applauding the French," a witness reported, burst into tears. Burke, also weeping, stood fast. There could be no sacrifice of principle, even for the sake of friendship.

The two never reconciled. On his deathbed, Burke refused to see Fox. In 1800 Fox refused to subscribe to a national memorial to Burke: "If I were to say that I have quite forgiven it, it would be boasting a magnanimity which I cannot feel."[15] Each died in disappointment, Burke on account of the death of his only child, Richard, and of his long years of seemingly futile opposition, Fox for his failure to prevent Britain's long war with France and because he would rather have been known for his amateur studies of Greek and Latin literature than for his verbal assaults on the government of William Pitt.

Both men arguably succeeded more in death than in life. Burke's writings form the intellectual core of modern conservatism, and Fox's ideals and oratory inspired generations of nineteenth-century English Whigs and Liberals. As for me, I love them for what they said and the way they said it; for what they believed and for what they did.

CHAPTER 1

An Irish education

The effect of genius is not to persuade the audience, but rather to
transport them out of themselves.

—LONGINUS

Ireland was poor and oppressed, and now, in the wake of a short harvest, it was starving. What to do with the burdensome children of the destitute Irish Catholics? Why, Jonathan Swift immortally suggested, let the English Protestant overlords cook them and eat them. Swift's "Modest Proposal" was published in Dublin in October 1729.

Edmund Burke was born in Dublin earlier the same year,* the son of a successful Protestant lawyer who was by no means starving. It mattered deeply whether his father, Richard, was born into the Protestant Church of Ireland or, if a cradle Catholic, he had abjured that faith and cast his lot with the religious establishment.

Whether Richard's infant son was baptized a Protestant or Catholic is similarly uncertain and likewise significant. The suspicion that he was indeed a Catholic, possibly a Jesuit, would dog the great orator throughout his parliamentary career. Burke chafed at the rumors, though not because he resented the imputation that the fundamental doctrine of the Catholic

---

* January 1, 1729, new style, is a frequently cited possibility.

Church was somehow abhorrent to him. He believed in the divinity of Jesus Christ with all his heart.

There is a record of someone named Richard Burke converting from Catholicism to the Church of Ireland in 1722—renouncing the "superstitious" and "idolatrous" worship of the saints, including the Virgin Mary, and renouncing, too, the doctrine that, in the sacrament of communion, the elements of bread and wine are actually transformed into the body and blood of the son of God. But there were plenty of Richard Burkes in Ireland.

Under British colonial rule, no Catholic could enter the professions, vote, buy land, own a firearm, possess a militarily suitable horse (the authorities living in fear of a repeat of the great Irish Rebellion of 1641), study abroad, or teach school, to name but a few of the myriad legislated "disabilities" on the Irish and English statute books. The preamble to the 1698 act to prohibit Catholics from joining the bar conveys a general flavor of what are known as the Penal Laws:

> Whereas by experience in this kingdom papist solicitors are the common disturbers of the peace of his Majesty's subjects in general, and whereas there are great number of papist solicitors practising within the several courts of law and equity, by whose numbers and the daily increase of them, great mischiefs are likely to ensue, no person shall practice as a solicitor or gent in any suit in law or equity, who has not taken the [prescribed oaths] and subscribed to the declaration against transubstantiation.[1]

Such laws accumulated like sediment, starting in the English Reformation of the sixteenth century and persisting through the rule of Oliver Cromwell (1653–58) and into the reign of George II (1727–60). The heyday of enactment, the 1690s, brought proscriptions on the Catholic majority involving church, family, and civil life. It was by leave of the Protestant Ascendancy that a Catholic congregation might build a church, but then only of wood and only if that eyesore were hidden off the main roads. The Penal Laws, by Edmund Burke's time, may have been more ferocious in the statute books than they were in the courts, but inconsistent enforcement could not efface the intent of the English lawmakers from the minds of the stigmatized, brutalized, transplanted, humiliated, and destitute Catholic majority.

The Richard Burke who converted to the Anglican Church of Ireland, whoever he might have been, was far from alone in choosing accommodation with Ireland's civil authority over loyalty to the Church of Rome. "The practice of the law, from the top to the bottom, is at present mostly in the hands of new converts," lamented the head of the Church of Ireland in 1727.[2] Not that all in the Protestant ruling class deigned even to take notice of such conversions. To Sir Richard Musgrave, 1st Baronet (1755–1818), a Catholic baptism was ineradicable. A man could no more abjure it by oath than attain the height of six feet by swearing to his seventy-two inches.[3]

For a politician destined for the English parliamentary opposition, few schools of statecraft would have been more instructive than that of Ireland during the Protestant Ascendancy. Coming of age in Dublin under British misrule, Burke could form his political philosophy by the simple principle of inversion. As the English, since the reign of Queen Elizabeth I (1533–1603), had devoted themselves to the suppression and impoverishment—sometimes to the extirpation—of Irish Catholics, he would champion their freedom, happiness, and prosperity. He would seek the same for all the ill-used subjects of English power, including the American colonists and the victims of the depredations of the British East India Company.

"My dear friend Burke leads a very unhappy life from his father's temper," a college friend of Edmund's named William Dennis reported in 1747; "and what is worse, there is no prospect of bettering it. He must not stir out at night by any means, and if he stays at home there is some new subject for abuse."[4] Dennis neglected to speculate on how much more amiable the elder Burke might have been without a teenage son under foot.

Though the grown Edmund Burke would use the word *splenetic* to describe his aging parent, he said more to his father's credit.[5] There was, for instance, the paternal "care," "tenderness," and "indulgence" in dissuading the youthful Ned (as Burke was known to friends and family) from venturing to America.[6] And the son remembered a father "not only in the first Rank" of the Dublin legal profession, "but the very first man of his profession in point of practice and credit." He died "worth very near £6,000."[7]

The elder Burke's last will and testament, dated November 4, 1761, suggests no such handsome estate, rather one closer to £2,000 (an amount perhaps reduced by losses in one or more of the bank failures that plagued Dublin between 1755 and 1760). The testator peremptorily directed that the lease interest on the family house, along with most of its contents, be auctioned within "one month, at most, next after my decease."

In those days, under the law, a woman could own nothing, so it seems more pedantic than cruel that Richard Burke left his wife her own clothes, her own jewelry, a little silver, a claim on a small unpaid loan, and five pounds for mourning, along with the interest on capital of £600.*

Burke's mother, Mary, a Catholic who remained one, was descended from the Nagles of County Cork, people of the "well-established subgentry" around Shanballymore, in the center of what to this day is known as Nagle country. They were swiftly disestablished under the conqueror Oliver Cromwell. Sir Richard Nagle (1635–99), one of the ornaments of the maternal family tree, was a little boy when Cromwell ordered the forfeit of lands in the possession of Irish Roman Catholics, his father's estate included. Intended for the priesthood, "probably the Jesuits,"[8] Richard became a lawyer instead. He prospered, was drawn to politics, and served King James II as private secretary and attorney-general before James's exile to France in 1688 (and he continued to stand by the Pretender in exile). It was this Catholic sovereign, an exponent of the divine right of kings, whom Parliament deposed to make way for the Protestants William and Mary (who happened to be King James II's daughter) in the Glorious Revolution of 1688. It was the very revolution that lifted Parliament over the crown and to which the Whig party, where Burke would make his political career, owed its founding. And it was this King William under whom Richard Nagle was presently outlawed and stripped of *his* property.

Surviving correspondence speaks to a deep mutual love between mother and son. When, in July 1746, some illness brought her close to death, Burke

* Which funds, however, the testator did not then possess but expected to receive in a legal judgment. Burke, *Early Life Correspondence*, 405. As to Edmund Burke's inheritance, there was little money, only "good principles, good instruction, good example, which I have not departed from," Burke told the House of Commons in 1771. Prior, *Life of Burke*, 69.

told a friend that he could scarcely function. But she lived to see him receive the Freedom of the City of Galway twenty years later for his advocacy of Irish interests in the British House of Commons. The pealing of the Galway bells in his honor filled her with joy, though not in a boastful way, she told a niece: "I assure you it is not the honors that are done him that make me vain of him but the goodness of his heart, than which I believe no man living has a better."[9]

Her fifteen or so pregnancies, spaced over the course of twenty years, produced only four adult children, a not-unusual outcome then. Ned was the middle son. Each boy, including the eldest, Garrett (1725–65), and the youngest, Richard (1733–94), his father's favorite, was raised a Protestant. Juliana (1728–90), like her mother, was brought up Catholic, as was customary for a daughter in a mixed marriage. Burke's first biographer, James Prior, quotes a contemporary of Juliana as recalling that Richard Burke's only daughter would have made as great an orator as Ned—hearing her talk, you wouldn't have changed a word.[10]

Visitors to Dublin attested to the city's grand houses, vibrant musical life,* magnificent university, and open heart but the residents had to cope with smoky air, damp basements, stinking cesspools, overfilled cemeteries, recurrent epidemics, and endemic drunkenness. Piped water was a luxury in even the better parts of town. As for the beggars, they repelled even Dean Swift—"Thieves, Drunkards, Heathen, and Whoremongers," he called them—who blamed Irish poverty not on the Irish character but on English oppression.[11]

Little Ned Burke was redheaded, nearsighted, and sickly. For the sake of his health, he was dispatched, at the age of six,[12] to live with his maternal uncle, Patrick Nagle, in picturesque Ballyduff, 140 miles to the southwest in County Waterford. Or perhaps, as Conor Cruise O'Brien proposes, it was for the sake of the boy's soul, not his health, that Mary Burke removed him from Dublin. By this line of conjecture, she determined to give him

---

* George Frederick Handel could not "sufficiently express the kind treatment I receive" in Dublin in November 1741 on the occasion of the first performance of his *Messiah*. Maxwell, *Dublin Under Georges*, 123.

a proper Roman Catholic upbringing, including a surreptitious Catholic baptism and Catholic schooling as well as the opportunity for faithful attendance at mass. The Penal Laws bit sharpest in anglicized Dublin but lightly in southern Ireland and in Blackwater Valley. At Ballyduff, Catholics conversed in Gaelic as well as English and French and worshipped openly. For the careful conduct of this cultural and religious agenda, Uncle Patrick filled the bill.[13]

At Ballyduff, Ned sat under the instruction of a Mr. O'Halloran,* master of a hedge school. In a nod to the letter of the law against Catholic education, the teacher kept no classroom but conducted school outdoors, not literally at a hedgerow in this case but by the ruins of a Norman castle called Monanimy. Ned would have learned that the castle had belonged to Richard Nagle, the forebear who had lost his estate to King William, as James Nagle had done to Cromwell.

Lifting his eyes from his first Latin book, Ned could peek at life on the north bank of the River Blackwater, as far as his short vision allowed. To the south, he could scan the mountains that bore the Nagle name. It was the same fetching Blackwater landscape that had earlier inspired the author of *The Faerie Queen*, Edmund Spenser.[14]

Edmund's immersion in the mores of Catholic Ireland ended in his eleventh year, with his relocation, along with that of his brothers Garrett and Richard, to a Quaker boarding school at Ballitore, County Kildare, forty miles outside Dublin. "He made the reading of the classics his diversion rather than his business," attested the headmaster, Abraham Shackleton, about his star student.[15] Bible reading, too, was a pleasure as well as an obligation. Ned's brother Richard concurred with the headmaster. When the other boys were at play, Ned was "always at work."[16]

In Shackleton, Burke found a more even-tempered father figure than the one he was born with, and in the headmaster's son Richard Shackleton, three years his senior, he formed the basis of what would prove a lifelong

---

* Encountering O'Halloran on a visit to Ireland in 1766, Burke took him eagerly by both hands and demanded that he stay the "whole day with me" to reminisce. At their parting, O'Halloran is supposed to have recounted, "Didn't he put five golden guineas into my hand as I was coming away?" Prior, *Life of Burke*, 6–7.

friendship. Having thus rubbed shoulders with Protestants, Catholics, and members of the Society of Friends, Burke completed his impromptu education in the living practice of religious tolerance.

Arriving at Magdalen College, Oxford, at the age of fifteen, Edward Gibbon found a university at rest with a wineglass at its elbow. The dons made few demands, and the students did little work, the author of *The History of the Decline and Fall of the Roman Empire* recorded. A very different experience awaited Burke, also age fifteen, on his arrival at Trinity College, Dublin, in the spring of 1744.[17] Only after construing passages from Horace, Virgil, and Homer to the satisfaction of the Rev. Dr. John Pellissier was he allowed to matriculate.

Trinity, which Queen Elizabeth I founded in 1592 to furnish an educated clergy for the Protestant Church of Ireland, was that country's only institution of higher learning. There was one course of study, the classical one, and every fellow was required to teach every subject. In Burke's time, the day began with six a.m. chapel. There was another chapel at ten a.m. and a third at four p.m. Students and fellows dined together at midday in a hall open to the weather at both ends, "the coldest room in Europe."

The undergraduates attended three or four classes a day plus special lectures and—for all but freshmen—disputations, the kind of formalized, scholastic debates that had engaged medieval divines. Logic, astronomy, geography, physics, mathematics, metaphysics, and ethics made up the "science" offerings. Student trustees took attendance at chapel and morning lectures.

Latin was the lingua franca of instruction, composition, and examination. Burke, who complained about the stiltedness of Latin prose, found much to love in Latin poetry. He kept his dog-eared copy of the Delphin edition of Virgil close at hand as late as the opening year of the French Revolution.

He carried on no comparable lifetime love affair with Greek poetry, though he found a kindred spirit in a first-century Greek essayist whose name has come down to us as Longinus.[18] Emulate the greats, Longinus counseled his readers, by trying to imagine Plato or Demosthenes or Thucydides looking over your shoulder as you write. "Great, indeed, is the ordeal," Longinus conceded, "if we propose such a jury and audience as this to listen to our utterances and make believe that we are submitting our work to the scrutiny of such superhuman witnesses and judges. Even more stimulating would it be to add, 'If I write this, how would all posterity receive it?'"[19]

"On the Sublime" is the title of Longinus's essay. *A Philosophical Enquiry into the Origin of Our Ideas of the Sublime and Beautiful* (1757) is the title of Burke's second book, on which he began work while still enrolled at Trinity. And if Longinus did not directly inspire Burke to delve into the connection between psychology and culture, the ancient critic uncannily anticipated the mixed effects that Burke's rhetorical flights would later have on the House of Commons. The MPs would marvel, laugh, cheer, yawn, and cough (in unison, by way of protest), but only rarely would they change their minds. Then again, wrote Longinus, "The effect of genius is not to persuade the audience, but rather to transport them out of themselves. Invariably what inspires wonder casts a spell upon us and is always superior to what is merely convincing and pleasing."[20]

As for the scientific portion of the curriculum, it began with the ordeal of *Institutiones logicae*, a hundred-year-old text by the Dutch logician Franco Burgersdijk. Everyone hated it. "The Scum of Pedantry," Burke denounced this Trinity rite of passage to his friend Shackleton. More to Ned's liking was the course in natural law for which the reading was Samuel Pufendorf's *Of the Law of Nature and Nations* (1672), an immense universal guide to the whole of human conduct. Later, as the prime parliamentary mover of the impeachment of Warren Hastings for crimes against the Indian people, Burke, recalling Pufendorf, could refute the East India Company's contentions that the Christian canons of right and wrong somehow did not run in Bengal.

It was not all work and no play for the Trinity collegians. Rioting filled odd hours not devoted to worship and study. Sometimes the undergraduates faced off against the town dwellers, at other times against the faculty and administration. The long-lingering antipathy between the Tory adherents of James II and the Whiggish defenders of the Glorious Revolution provided only one pretext for drinking, fighting, window-breaking, and monument-smashing.

In 1747, Burke's third year on campus, the arrest of a student for non-payment of debt incited an undergraduate assault on the foul "Black Dog" prison where the captive was held. Two people died in the melee, and five student ringleaders were expelled. The name of the father of modern conservatism does not appear on the list of the guilty student riot-makers,* but Burke did join a self-mobilized student force to protect Thomas Sheridan, actor-manager of the Smock Alley Theater (and father of the playwright Richard Brinsley Sheridan) against one of the mobs that had invaded the theater, destroyed his scenery, and made themselves at home in his greenroom.[21]

It was the city setting of Trinity College that tempted the students into sin, Burke, the freshman, professed. The charms and snares of Dublin were Satan's doing: "I am in the enemies' country," he advised Shackleton. "O how happy are you that you live in the country."[22]

And how the fifteen-year-old wished he could concentrate: "I am too giddy, this is the bane of my life, it hurries me from my studies to trifles and I am afraid it will hinder me from knowing any thing thoroughly. I have a superficial knowledge of many things, but scarce have the bottom of any." But he was not so flighty as to be unaware that the purpose of living was to secure salvation.[23]

The great flood of the River Liffey in Dublin in January 1745 soaked the Burke house on Arran Quay, less than a mile from the college, while recalling to Ned's mind the weakness of human flesh: "Let it shew me how low I am, and of myself how weak how far from an independent being, given as a Sheep into the hands of the great Shepherd of all, on whom let us Cast all our Care for he Careth for us!"[24]

Successful completion of a two-day oral examination on Greek and Roman authors won Burke a scholarship in 1746 along with free room and board—and a ticket out from under his father's roof. The obligatory purchase of a better grade of scholastic gown was a small price to pay.[25]

---

* Oliver Goldsmith, the future author of *The Vicar of Wakefield* and member, along with Burke and other Georgian luminaries, of Samuel Johnson's famous Literary Club, was among the students hauled up for disciplinary action over the Black Dog proceedings. He was named a "lesser offender."

Dr. Johnson said that the young Milton's writing won praise but did not excite "wonder."[26] Similarly with Burke's B-grade academic work ("barely in the top half of his class")[27] and of his teenage correspondence more generally: it was "not much more vivid or interesting than other people's undergraduate letters."[28]

Burke did not study as the "A" students did, with the object of shining in class rankings. His approach was rather one of serial, self-directed total immersion. He would do nothing but read or write poetry—his "poetical madness."* Then it was on to natural philosophy, which "employed me incessantly, this I call my furor mathematicus." To be followed by "furor historicus."[29]

At the magnificent new college library, he could curl up with the seventeenth-century heroic couplets of Edmund Waller ("tis surprizing how so much softness and so much grandeur could dwell in one Soul")[30] or with *Il Penseroso* of John Milton ("the finest poem in the English language").[31] At the other end of the spectrum of literary gravitas, he reveled in the lowbrow romance novels at which Cervantes poked fun in *Don Quixote*.[32] Down from the top of the stacks peered the busts of Aristotle, Demosthenes, Plato, and Cicero. Recalling Longinus, a student might have imagined those immortals proofreading his compositions.

In 1747, the spring of his junior year, Ned and a few friends organized a college debating society.† Seriousness of purpose was the guiding spirit of this "Academy of Belles Lettres." It was not enough to read books and hear lectures, the rising parliamentarians agreed; one must go forth into society to propagate that knowledge, expressing it "with readiness, justness, force and proper grace."[33]

"Decency and good Manners, virtue and religion, must guide their

---

* Not much of his own poetry excites wonder, except, perhaps, a translation that Burke made of Book 2 of Virgil's *Georgics*. John Dryden, too, had translated that classical work into English from Latin, but Burke bested the great English poet by his closer adherence to Virgil's text. So judges Lock, *Edmund Burke*, 53.

† It was the first such college debating club of which any record exists in the United Kingdom and survives as the Trinity College Historical Society. Burke, *Early Life Correspondence*, 203.

whole behavior, and no word, gesture, or action, contrary thereto pass uncensur'd,"[34] the first of the bylaws stipulated. The members, of whom there were presently seven, were expected to speak extemporaneously, to attend regularly, to read what was assigned, and to write when so directed. Transgressors earned fines and rebukes.[35]

The young orators took naturally to verbal sparring. In the meeting of Friday, April 24, Burke laid into his roommate, William Dennis, for failing to speak his oration. Dennis parried by observing that the bylaws reserved Tuesdays, not Fridays, for the speaking of orations. Burke stepped forward to read his "Essay on Society," a composition that might have foreshadowed the biting attack on the Deistic philosophy of Henry St. John, Viscount Bolingbroke, that formed the subject of Burke's first book, *A Vindication of Natural Society*, published in 1756.[36]

On May 30 we find the young critic apologizing to his fellows. "Burke says that he is sorry to be so frequent in his accusations," wrote Burke, the recording secretary, about himself, but his "love of the society overbears all other considerations."[37] The office of recording secretary, like that of president, shifted from member to member, but Burke, who in later life seemed never to lay down his pen, was the invariable minute-taker.[38]

Burke earned his bachelor's degree in February 1748, but his first postcollegiate move was decided before he graduated. Come 1750, he would begin legal studies at the Middle Temple in London. His father had seen to it.

Ned seemed a little less decided than his father. Rumors had reached him, as he told Shackleton, that a writing man could make a good living in London—"I heard the other day of a gentleman who maintained himself in the study of law by writing pamphlets in favor of the ministry."[39]

Technically, Burke was already a kind of professional author, being a contributor to a new weekly periodical called the *Reformer*, loosely styled on Joseph Addison and Richard Steele's *Spectator* of 1711–12. The tyro journalist drew confidence from the thousand-copy sale of the first *Reformer*, dated January 28, 1748.

Burke threw down the gauntlet in the lead sentence on page one: "There is a certain period when *Dulness* being arrived to its full Growth, and spreading over a Nation becomes so insolent that it forces men of *Genius* and *Spirit* to rise up, in spite of their natural Modesty, and work that Destruction it is ripe for."

"Destruction"? The familiar conserving spirit of the mature Edmund Burke was not much in evidence in these angry columns. Little seemed to please him about his hometown, which, perhaps, was so surprising in a young classics student. "The people here," he complained to Shackleton, "are the very reverse of the Description St Paul gives of the Athenians, that their whole business is to hear or relate something new—they have no sort of curiosity that way further than party Leads them, and no wonder—for books either in prose or verse seldom enter the Conversations of even people of fortune and those who have leisure enough—so that an Authors first cries cannot be heard but he is stiffled in his birth."[40] Ancient Greece, or even contemporary London, Dublin was not.*

The *Reformer* condemned the local theater, literature, and taste. It denounced the "senseless encouragement" that the city gave to "wretched" English plays, novels, and poems that it mindlessly imported. Irish poverty, its columns held, "can be no Excuse for not encouraging men of Genius, one tenth of what is expended on Fiddlers, Singers, Dancers and Players, would be able to sustain the whole Circle of Arts and Sciences."

It was a good thing, Burke and his fellows acknowledged, that a certain unnamed theater proprietor had made the actors learn their lines and told the drunks to pipe down, but those improvements were a far cry from the theatrical renaissance that the *Reformer* demanded. The editors wanted more Shakespeare ("who had a genius perhaps excelling any thing that ever appeared"). They denounced kissing on stage, and hissing from the pits, and ad-libbing, self-regarding actors.[41]

---

* In 1745 the bookseller George Faulkner and the king's printer, George Grierson, issued a satirical pamphlet to give vent to their frustration at the slow pace of book sales. Granted, the authors allowed, reading was a "useless drudgery," but reading was only one purpose for which their versatile products were suited. You could furnish a room with books or, having ripped out the unread pages, use them to wrap candles or make kites. An address to the "Nobility, Gentry, and Clergy of the City of Dublin" quoted in Maxwell, *Dublin Under Georges*, 166.

A typical issue of the *Reformer* ran to two thousand words or fewer, not including the advertisements, of which there were too few. Now and then the editors paid homage to the light and witty style of Addison and Steele's *Spectator*, but they were all business in the Easter edition:

> The practice of virtue and religion is indispensable at all Times; but never more than at this, when we commemorate the Time our Creator became our Redeemer, and for our sake manifested in the highest manner the highest attributes of his Divinity, his *Love* and his *Power*, the one in dying for us, and the other in conquering Death, by giving that glorious Proof of our Immortality, and being himself the first Fruits of the Resurrection.

Burke himself wrote with palpable rage in *Reformer* no. 7, which he devoted to the plight of the indigent Irish peasant:

> As for their Food, it is notorious they seldom taste Bread or Meat; their Diet, in Summer, is Potatoes and sour Milk; in Winter, when something is required comfortable, they are still worse, living on the same Root, made palatable only by a little Salt, and accompanied with Water: Their Cloaths is ragged, that they rather publish than conceal the Wretchedness it was meant to hide; nay, it is no uncommon Sight to see half a dozen Children run quite naked out of a Cabin, scarcely distinguishable from a Dunghill, to the great Disgrace of our Country with Foreigners, who would doubtless report them Savages, imputing that to choice which only proceeds from their irremediable Poverty. Let any one take a Survey of their Cabins, and then say, whether such a Residence be worthy any thing that challenges the title of a human creature.

Inequality by design was the social system in place in Ireland and England, and the *Reformer* entered no objection to it: "That some should live in a more sumptuous manner than others, is very allowable." However, the editors proceeded, "sure it is hard, that those who cultivate the Soil, should have so small a Part of its Fruits; and that among Creatures of the same Kind there should be such a disproportion in their manner of living; it is kind of a Blasphemy on Providence."

Before long Burke would stand with Adam Smith on the point that economic growth spread its blessings throughout society and that the man who succeeded did not do so at the expense of the one who failed. But colonial Ireland was a special case, a country impoverished by design. Over the century and a half prior to Burke's birth, the English had made war on Catholic Irishmen. They had commandeered the Catholics' land, moved them (on pain of death) from the richest Irish provinces to Connacht, which was, following the failed Irish Rebellion of 1641–50, the poorest. They had destroyed the incentives to economic well-being through punitive tariffs, the abridgment of property rights, and an educational system that virtually condemned the children of Catholic parents to lives of ignorance and poverty. Indeed, the Catholic majority can be said to have lived or died by the weather, so small was the surplus on hand to tide them over a poor harvest.[42] "Whoever travels through this country and observes the face of nature, or the faces and habits and dwellings of the natives," wrote Jonathan Swift in 1720, "would hardly think himself in a land where either law, religion, or common humanity was professed."[43]

The money behind the *Reformer*, which was never identified, seemed to run out at the end of volume one, number thirteen. At least, the temporary shutdown that Burke announced at the close of April 1748 (supposedly on account of the imminent emptying of the city in advance of the summer) proved permanent.

Early in 1750, Burke, en route to London to begin his legal studies, marveled at the gaiety, wealth, and vitality of the English countryside: "What a contrast between our poor country where you'll scarce find a cottage ornamented with a chimney!"[44]

CHAPTER 2

"A very sensible little boy"

Perhaps nobody except a royal infant has had a
better documented childhood.

—CHRISTOPHER HOBHOUSE, *FOX*

"How like a monkey he look'd before he was dressed," said Henry
Fox, father of Charles James Fox, on the occasion of Charles's
birth. The date was January 24, 1749.[1]
It was one of the few disparaging remarks ever heard from the elder Fox
about his hairy second son. Within a year, the father was doting on "the
eclat of his beauty," within three years on the delights of Charles's dinner-
table companionship, and within five on his "pert" and "argumentative"
temper. "All life, spirit, motion and good humor" was the paternal verdict
in year seven.[2]

Try as he might, Charles could do no wrong. "Well! If you must, I suppose you must," said Henry Fox in response to the child's announced plan
to destroy a watch. "Let nothing be done to break his spirit," the elder Fox
would say. "The world will do that business fast enough."

Little Charles seemed to regard himself as a third adult partner in his
own upbringing. It was he, at the age of seven, not his father or his mother,
Lady Caroline, who decided that the Wandsworth school was where he
should polish his French. At nine, he announced his determination to enter
Eton College. Duly enrolled, he excelled in the classics, French, Italian, and

mathematics, not in the grade-grubbing way but for the pleasure of reading and writing and problem-solving for their own sakes. Charles urged
his father and mother to impress on his Eton-bound cousin and soulmate,
George FitzGerald, the need to become "exceedingly perfect in Greek
grammar," as that skill is "of more consequence towards making learning there [at Eton] than can be imagined."[3] At the age of eleven, he was
requesting books by "the noble authors" and a history of Arabia.

The Foxes made their home in Holland House, originally known as
Cope Castle, which sprawled on sixty-four acres in Kensington, two miles
outside smoky London. Built in the early seventeenth century, it was the
home of Joseph Addison who arrived in 1716. Henry Fox and family moved
in late in the 1740s, the place having by this time become ramshackle. The
decorators and builders were still on the job when baby Charles first saw
the light of day at temporary quarters on Conduit Street, Mayfair.

There was little in Holland House, presently renowned for its "fantastic
gables, endless vista of boudoirs, libraries and drawing-rooms," to instill
in the pert and precocious child the idea of economic scarcity.[4] For all
Charles could tell, guineas grew on trees and had so blossomed since the
time of his paternal grandfather, founder of the family wealth and reverse
role model for his famed grandson.

Sir Stephen Fox (1627–1716) had risen from ordinary beginnings to
become "the richest commoner in three kingdoms."[5] He loyally attended
the future king Charles II through domestic political upheaval and long
exile in Europe during the English civil wars of the 1640s. Entering Parliament shortly after the king reclaimed his throne,[6] Sir Stephen earned what
proved to be the most lucrative office in his sovereign's gift, paymaster of
the guards and garrisons.

King Charles had lived from hand to mouth in Europe (it was Sir Stephen's husbanding of his scant funds that had sustained him there), but the
bags of gold that welcomed him home to Dover in 1660 proved no omen
of a well-financed reign. Chronically short of cash, the restored court
required an intermediary between itself and its creditors. Fox, who had
entered the royal service as a page boy only twenty years before, became
that indispensable factotum.

As paymaster, Sir Stephen discharged the essential service of paying the troops who guarded the king. And when Parliament neglected to vote the necessary funds, Fox had to borrow them.*

There was no such thing, just yet, as "the bond market," no established standing pool of capital on which a government could draw to finance a deficit or make war. A needy sovereign rather approached the London goldsmiths, the bankers of the day. In exchange for a loan, the king's agent would present the creditor with a tally stick. Notched pieces of wood, inscribed with data in "barbarous" Latin, the sticks committed the government to pay the bearer a specific sum of money on a certain date. They had served as sovereign securities since the 1100s.†

Sir Stephen had a deep appreciation of the power of compound interest and of the value of delayed gratification, gifts only sparingly bestowed on his male descendants. Yes, of course, Sir Stephen would reply to the improvident courtiers who asked him to add unpaid interest to the outstanding principal of their debts. He at least understood how much higher the future interest bill would be, paid on the enlarged principal balance, than it would have been on the originally contracted one.

"Good-looking, likeable, polished in his manners, kind-hearted, pious, honest, and of course immensely capable and hard working," a modern biographer records, before asking, "was Sir Stephen a man without flaws?"‡

* "Better a mortgage on a garden than on a kingdom" was a Frenchman's acid comment on the capricious position of a creditor to a sovereign state. The remark was directed to Louis XVI but could equally have pertained to Charles II, whose attitude toward financial obligations disastrously presaged that of Charles James Fox.

† With a push from Edmund Burke, Parliament in 1783 enacted a law to replace tallies with printed receipts, thus abolishing "several useless, expensive and unnecessary offices." However, because the tenants of those offices were allowed to hold them until death or retirement, and because the young incumbents proved stubbornly long-lived, the final tally was not cleft until 1826. Another eight years elapsed before the government disposed of its inventory of sticks by feeding them into the parliamentary furnace, an operation carried out with such "imprudent zeal" that the resulting fire destroyed Westminster Hall. Jenkinson, "Exchequer Tallies," 368.

‡ Christopher Clay could scrape up only a few examples—for instance, "he was easily offended, . . . slow to forgive and would nurse his grievance for years." Clay, *Public Finance*, 315.

"A wonderful child of providence," Sir Stephen described himself, and it was true.[7]

Sir Stephen's first wife, Elizabeth, bore him three daughters and seven sons, but they produced not one grandson named Fox. A widower at sixty-nine, the old paymaster remarried at seventy-seven to the twenty-four-year-old Christiana Hope,[8] a clergyman's daughter, who was to serve as the rich gentleman's conversational companion but furnished more than talk. The two were married in 1703,[9] and she bore him four children, the last in his eightieth year.

There were two sons, Stephen, his heir and namesake, and Henry, who would follow his father into Parliament and the gold mine of the paymastership; and two daughters, Christiana, a toddler who died from a fall out a window, and Charlotte, who married Edward Digby, a Tory politician and third son of William, Lord Digby, with whom she had seven children.

Sir Stephen was seventy-five years old in 1702, the year of Queen Anne's coronation and the sixty-third year of his royal service. He could look back on a storied career in politics, administration, investment, and philanthropy. As to the latter, he was a founding visionary and the principal financier of Royal Chelsea Hospital, the home for old soldiers that continues in operation to this day.* He occupied offices from first lord of the Treasury to member of Parliament for Westminster (the prestigious borough that Charles James Fox would later represent) to commissioner of the stables. It was in this last-named position—in fact, as first commissioner, out of a total of three—that Sir Stephen performed his final official act.

His duty was to escort the gouty, newly crowned queen down the steps from her throne at Westminster Abbey. Sir Stephen dreaded the steep stairs that tested the balance and agility of most elderly people, even that of a septuagenarian bridegroom, and Sir Stephen "thanked God [the duty] was happily performed."[10]

---

* "For the first time, the crown and the army authorities unequivocally assumed responsibility for at least those veterans who were most desperately in need," writes Sir Stephen's biographer, who properly counts the Christopher Wren–designed institution as "one of the great humanitarian feats of the age." Clay, *Public Finance*, 139.

It was with relief that he stepped into his new £500 coach, specially built for the coronation procession of great officers and peers of the realm, to lead those notables through the festive streets of London.

Christiana survived Sir Stephen by only two years. She died in 1718, but not before issuing a final maternal injunction to her children. "Having a less fortune," she addressed Henry, who faced the second son's dilemma of earning a living, "[you] won't be subject to so many temptations; but withstand those you have when you grow up. Then you'll learn to swear, rake about, to game and at last be ruined by those you unhappily think your friends." If she delivered the final sentence with a twinkle in her eye, it nonetheless proved prescient.[11]

Educated at Eton College and Christ Church, Oxford, Henry absorbed the Tory-Anglican doctrines of his time and family, but the ruling deism of fashionable London pushed aside Christian devotion. When he finally entered Parliament at thirty, it was as a Whig for whom "the consolations of friendship came to replace those of religion."[12]

Debts to Charles II ran deep in the Fox family. The Merry Monarch was the father of an illegitimate son by the enchanting Louise de Kérouaille, whom the French court had allegedly dispatched to spy on the British king. Charles, head over heels for Louise, gave the boy all that a natural child could hope for, including a title, the Duke of Richmond.

A generation later, in 1744, the eldest daughter of the 2nd Duke of Richmond, Lady Georgiana Caroline Lennox, twenty-one, eloped with the thirty-eight-year-old Henry Fox. It was immaterial to the parents of Lady Caroline that the groom was a lord of the Treasury, a gifted parliamentary debater, and descendant of the richest commoner in Charles II's Great Britain. He was a parvenu, and London gasped in sympathy with the desolated duke and duchess.[*][13]

But love prevailed, and the royal blood of Charles II presently flowed in the veins of the infant Charles James Fox, who bore the Christian names

---

* "At the opera the news ran along the front boxes 'exactly like fire in a train of gunpowder.'" Trevelyan, *Early History of Fox*, 9.

of the final two Stuart kings, as it had in those of his brother, firstborn Stephen, or "Ste," in 1745, and would in Henry, born in 1755.

When Charles was ten, their mother wrote appraisingly and comparatively:

> Tho' I love Ste better, I could with much more ease part with his company for some time, and Harry's too, than Charles's; you can have no idea how companionable a child he is, nor how infinitely engaging to us he is. If Mr. Fox and I are alone, either of us, or only us two, he never leaves one, enters into any conversation going forwards, takes his book if we are reading, is vastly amused with any work going on out of doors or indoors . . . will sit and read by me when my stomach is bad and I lie down between sleeping and waking, and is in every respect the most agreeable companion. I know you'll make allowances for my partiality, for these same qualities so pleasing to us often makes him troublesome to other people. He will know everything, watches one if one wants to speak to anybody, and is too apt to give his opinion about everything, which tho' generally a very sensible one, makes him appear pert to other people.[14]

Stephen suffered from birth from chorea, or Saint Vitus' dance, whose twitches and spasms tormented him, haunted his father, and upset Richard Rigby, a political friend of his father's and visitor to Holland House one evening when Stephen was eight.

Though he drank claret with his host till two in the morning, Rigby recalled, "I could not wash away the sorrow he is in at the shocking condition his eldest son is in, a distemper they call *Sanvitoss dance* (I believe I spell it damnably) but it is a convulsion that I think must kill him."[15]

Charles had the capacity to sit still for hours on end with a book in his hand, as Stephen did not. "Do you know," Lady Caroline related, "that Charles never leaves his Papa when there are any of the lawyers . . . with him, and is au fait of it as much as anybody but the law people are. Is this not an odd turn at his age?"[16]

"I will not deny that I was a very sensible little boy," admitted the grown

Charles James Fox, "a very clever little boy."[17] Likewise a consequential one, as he had the pleasure of reading about himself as early as the age of twelve. Thus, from the *London Chronicle*: "On Tuesday Charles James Fox, Esq.; son to the Right Hon. Henry Fox, had the misfortune to break his arm as he was hunting at the Duke of Richmond's at Goodwood."[18]

"The boy is a great deal better beloved than his father is," reported the senior Fox.[19]

HENRY FOX COMBINED A DEEP KNOWLEDGE OF PARLIAMENTARY PROCE-dure with a ferocious skill at debate. He passed down to his favorite son the barrister's gift for making, and parrying, arguments on the fly. Unlike that amiable son, however, the father cultivated his grudges as conscientiously as he ever did his friendships. He was a Whig within the narrow mean-ing of one who stood for aristocratic government on behalf of the people (though, as it hardly needed to be said, not by them). Complaining about the political situation in 1762, Fox emitted a Whiggish lament: "To this pass are we brought by newspapers & libels, & the encouragement given to the mob to think themselves the Government."[20]

The Glorious Revolution of 1688 had dispatched not only England's final Catholic king, and not only James's outmoded notions about the divine right of kings, but also the centrality of religion in English politics. What mattered to Henry Fox was not doctrinal disputes but "the loaves and fishes" of office, that is, money and royal preferment. Heaped up with the former, he felt cheated of the latter and for that reason died embittered.*

Fox loved the House of Commons and wanted to lead it. And though he held ministerial office, and indeed was now and then encouraged to seek the highest office, his most burning ambition was to secure a peerage for Lady Caroline, on whom he doted as fully as he did on his beloved Charles.

---

* Henry Fox poured out his disappointment over unbestowed favors to his sixteen-year-old son. "Don't ever, Charles, make any exception, or trust as I did," and quoted an instructive couplet:

"Of all court service know the common lot
To-day 'tis done, to-morrow 'tis forgot."

Trevelyan, *Early History of Fox*, 128.

In politics, Henry's forte, as he was the first to admit, was following, not leading: "Though I see how fatally ill things are going, as I don't know how to mend them I am not unreasonable enough to wish for what I could not conduct," he confessed in 1756 in response to urgings that he form a government to succeed the one in which he was unhappily serving as secretary of state and leader of the Commons.[21]

This was the administration of the overmatched Duke of Newcastle. All too ready to leave policy making to others, Fox had become the reluctant defender of Newcastle's strategic errors and maddening indecision. In 1756, two dispiriting years into the Seven Years' War, few imagined the ultimate glorious outcome for British arms in a worldwide struggle for control of North America, India, and Europe. Certainly, Fox did not foresee that victory, still less that his rival William Pitt would gather the laurels for it.

From the deck of this sinking ship, Henry Fox gingerly stepped to political safety in October 1756. The Paymaster's Office, so profitably occupied by his father, was now his refuge, "a place as retired as a hermitage, where I see nobody, meddle with no business nor stand in any body's way."[22] It was—along with a peerage for Lady Caroline—all he wanted.

The Seven Years' War (1754–63) brought Fox no honor, but it bathed him in wealth. By 1761, the government was borrowing "more millions in one day than our ancestors even in this century would have thought of voting in three Sessions," as he observed.[23]

However, unlike Sir Stephen, Henry bore small financial risk in the discharge of his duties, except in the speculations that he undertook for himself. The institutions of English public finance had matured in the half century since Sir Stephen was putting out Charles II's fiscal fires. The government may have tested the market's lending capacity, but it never defaulted. The funds that Henry Fox requisitioned from the Treasury were his to invest until the government needed to spend them. Interest on such balances, and profits on their timely investment, were his to keep, provided that he produced the money when called for. He was within his rights to operate in this fashion, even if the elder Pitt, a predecessor in that office, had chosen the self-denying course of allowing the funds consigned to his care to lie fallow at the Bank of England.

The Paymaster's Office paid its occupant £3,000 a year, but that salary, for Fox during his eight years on the job, was a trifle compared to his average annual unofficial income of £23,657. In the bumper year of 1766, he walked away with no less than £54,851 in investment income, or more than 18 times his salary.

Millions of pounds passed through Fox's hands, a sum enhanced by the fact that the paymaster's remit extended to Chelsea Hospital. To assure the smooth functioning of that monument to Sir Stephen's generosity and patriotism, his son was able to procure tens of thousands of additional investable pounds from the Treasury.[24]

It was the privilege of the paymaster not only to invest the cash entrusted to him but also to decide how much money to requisition and when to receive it. "This was a situation of some delicacy," to quote Lucy Sutherland and J. Binney, co-authors of a detailed investigation into Fox's career at the Paymaster's Office, "and it is not difficult to believe that the temptation to apply for more than was really necessary continually presented itself to Fox and his successors, up until the regulation of the Paymaster's office in 1782."[25]

Not one to let funds sleep at the bank, Fox invested actively and, as far as the records show, profitably. In buying the securities of the British Crown, Fox was lending the government its own money while pocketing the interest, and such was his right.

The concluding years of the war, 1761–62, presented an especially ripe field of opportunity. Peace rumors reached well-placed ears first, and Fox booked trading profits in the grand total of £159,000.[26]

The paymaster did not confine himself to government securities. He bought mortgages and common equities as well, including shares in the East India Company, the giant trading enterprise that was half investor-owned business enterprise, half quasi-sovereign colonial power. He eclectically committed the public funds in his possession to turnpikes, to a vessel employed in the East India trade, and to a privateer. He employed them in mortgages and real estate, including the seaside folly he built for himself in his retirement at Kingsgate, Kent, at a cost of more than £14,000.*

Individuals, too, figured among the recipients of Henry Fox's wealth. Edmund Burke and his speculating kinsman, William Burke, borrowed £500, which they seem not to have repaid. To his two elder sons, Charles James and Stephen, Henry advanced near-dynastic sums—in Charles's case, more than £100,000—to settle gambling debts, again, unrepaid. Neither did the paymaster deny assistance to the children he fathered out of wedlock, nor to the widow of his embezzling agent, John Ayliffe, who was hanged in 1759 for forging Fox's name.

The seventeenth-century diarist John Evelyn, who reckoned Sir Stephen's wealth at the staggering sum of £200,000, judged it to be "honestly gotten and unenvied, which is next to a miracle."[27] Henry Fox's winnings earned no such encomium. On the contrary, their sheer size raised questions of taste if not of law, and suspicion was rife that Fox had dealt in inside information concerning the peace negotiations that concluded the Seven Years' War (though there was no law against insider trading, either).[28] In any case, the paymaster denied the rumors.

"Obloquy generally attends money so got," Fox protested.

> The Government borrows money at 20 per cent disc[ount], I am not consulted or concern'd in making the bargain. I have as Pay Master great sums in my hands, which, not applicable to any present use, must either lye dead in the Bk, or be employ'd by me. I lend this to the Government in 1761. A peace is thought certain. I am not in the least consulted, but my very bad opinion of Mr. Pitt makes me think it will not be concluded: I sell out, & gain greatly. In 1762, I lend again; a peace comes, in which I again I am not consulted, & I again gain greatly.[29]

---

* Designed in the manner of a Roman villa and stuffed with the statues, busts, vases, and other antiquities that Lady Holland and he had brought home from a 1763 tour of Italy, the house spread to the right and the left from the center of a grand Doric portico. Lava stone, imported from Mount Vesuvius, lined the drive to encourage passing carriages to keep their distance.

CHARLES JAMES FOX WAS STILL AT ETON IN 1762 WHEN BELLIGERENTS IN
the Seven Years' War opened peace talks. Pitt's comprehensive victories—in North America, Europe, and India—had primed the British public
for a glorious peace, but George III rather favored a prompt one. To push
a satisfactory treaty through Parliament required a leader both persuasive
and ruthless. "We must call in bad men to govern bad men," said the king,
turning to Henry Fox, who seized the chance, perhaps his last, to "reward
friends, punish enemies, make a figure in the Commons and perhaps
secure an earldom." The earldom was not to be, but in the opportunity to
punish, Fox had all his heart could desire.

Now the king's fixer, Fox wheedled and bribed in his unique capacity as
"His Majesty's Minister in the House of Commons."* Members holding office
conferred by the crown came to know that continued employment depended
on an affirmative vote. To buy the cooperation of the grandson of his old mentor, Sir Robert Walpole, Fox offered Lord Orford the rangership of the London
parks, a sinecure paying £2,000 a year. Fox's letter to Orford's uncle, Horace
Walpole, conveys the spirit of the project. "Such an income," Fox wrote,

> might, if not prevent, at least procrastinate your nephew's ruin. I find
> nobody knows his Lordship's thoughts on the present state of poli-
> tics. Now, are you willing, and are you the proper person, to tell Lord
> Orford that I will do my best to procure this employment for him, if
> I can soon learn that he desires it? . . . This is offering you a bribe, but
> 'tis such a one as one honest good-natured man may without offense
> offer to another.[30]

So thoroughly did Fox succeed that a motion to delay the vote on the
peace went down to defeat, 213–74, while an address in support of the

---

* A title never before conferred in Georgian England. Functionally, Fox was "the King's
special 'minister' for the corruption of the Commons," thereby "enacting a new and most
insidious phase of Toryism. He was, in effect, proclaiming the right of the King (through
his efficient agent) to supervise the Commons." Charles James Fox would devote his career
to curbing the power of the crown. Riker, *Fox, First Lord Holland*, 2:318–19.

peace won by 319–65. The treaty was signed, sealed, and delivered with the royal assent on February 10, 1763.

There was nothing magnanimous about the parliamentary victor. The lash of Fox's vengeance stung any and all who had stood with Pitt and Newcastle to oppose the treaty, and against George III and the government of Lord Bute to conclude it. Foremost among the vanquished were the very Whig politicians with whom Fox had made common cause for the preceding thirty years. Placeholders and sinecurists down to fifty-pound-a-year custom clerks lost their stipends.

The author of these reprisals is the same Henry Fox whose devotion to Lady Caroline and their children was proverbial. "He plundered the many," in the words of Sir George Trevelyan, "whom he neither hated nor loved, in order to load with wealth, and surfeit with pleasure, the few human beings for whom he would have laid down his life, as readily and lightly as he sacrificed his conscience and reputation."[31]

For directing the passage of the Peace of Paris through Parliament, Fox settled for a barony rather than an earldom to complement the peerage that he had earlier secured for Lady Caroline. And the man who aspired to no high ministerial office had the pleasure of declining Bute's invitation to succeed him as prime minister. How much better, Holland decided, was retirement by the sea. But neither success nor money nor place nor revenge brought him contentment.

Bute and the king had mistakenly assumed that the paymaster would be prepared to surrender his office as he entered the House of Lords, in 1763. Fox, now Lord Holland of Foxley, was prepared to do no such thing. He could hardly afford to, spending, as he did, £6,000 a year on "housekeeping" alone,[32] and the misunderstanding became the source of throbbing rancor. A series of heated personal confrontations over who was responsible for misinforming the crown about his intentions toward the Paymaster's Office cost Lord Holland Rigby's friendship and made an implacable enemy of Lord Shelburne, the source of the misinformation. Holland relinquished the paymastership in 1765.

Bute, in conversation with Fox, tried to excuse Shelburne on the ground that, without Fox conniving so expertly on the floor of the Commons, the treaty would surely have failed. By way of pardoning Shelburne, Bute called Shelburne's untruth a "pious fraud."

"I see the fraud well enough, my Lord," Fox replied, "but where is the piety?"[33]

AT ETON, CHARLES JAMES FOX HAD MUSED TO HIS FATHER OVER THE impossibility of earthly happiness. Life "is a troublesome affair," the nine-year-old sighed, "and one wishes one had this thing or that thing, and then one is not the happier, and then one wishes for another thing, and one's very sorry if one don't get it, and it does not make one happy if one do so."

In 1763, the year of the signing of the Peace of Paris, Henry Fox, now Lord Holland, may or may not have been unhappy, but he was surely unpopular. Poets and politicians vied to excoriate him for his absurd wealth and his treachery to former friends.* Holland professed to be inured against unpopularity—certainly he had had long experience with it—and he had always disdained public opinion. "Thus happy in private life, am I not in the right to leave the public?" the new baron rhetorically asked a friend.[34]

Charles, fourteen years old, was in his fifth year at Eton when his father removed him from school for a few months' vacation in Europe. They visited Paris and Spa, in Belgium, where Charles received his early instruction in gambling.

"He talked French admirably," an Eton schoolfriend recorded of this formative educational experience, "& employd it in declaiming against Religion with a fashionable grace that would have charmed Voltaire himself. He gamed deep; had an arranged intrigue with a certain Mad. De Quallens, of high fashion, came back to Eton, & was whipped with me for stealing out Church, to play at Tennis."[35]

---

* In 1769 the Lord Mayor of London, in an address to George III, decried Henry Fox as a "Public Defaulter of unaccounted millions." Sutherland and Binney, "Fox as Paymaster," 229. The accusation was wrong in fact (he had not defaulted; indeed, his voluminous accounts were still undergoing the customary audit, which would vindicate him) and in law (he had broken none). Fox turned up in the satirical poetry of Thomas Gray and Charles Churchill, Gray writing him off as "abandoned by each venal friend." It will be recalled that his mother had warned him about that very possibility. Trevelyan, *Early History of Fox*, 37.

Lord Holland's favorite son became an inveterate gambler—a "deep player"—whose titanic losses required the paymaster's continual subsidy. "If you must, I suppose you must," the indulgent father had resignedly told his little boy. Now the father was goading the adolescent into life's bad habits.

The boy of the world returned to Eton flaunting Parisian style. That his classmates seem not to have ripped his red heels from his feet, or set his blue-powdered hair on fire, was testament to Charles's amiability. His friends would love him even as a foreign fop.

Not all were charmed, and among the disapproving minority was Lord Chatham. Said the elder Pitt of the father of the precocious Etonian: "He educated his children without the least regard to morality, and with such extravagant vulgar indulgence, that the great change that has taken place among our youth has been dated from the time of his sons' going to Eton."[36]

Father and son, the best of friends, corresponded almost as peers. In company with Lord Holland, Charles attended parliamentary debates, including the one of November 15, 1763, in which the House of Commons condemned the famous forty-fifth issue of *The North Briton*, John Wilkes's radical newspaper, as "a false, scandalous and seditious libel."* Three years later, in March 1766, Charles was again present at Westminster Hall to hear the fateful debate over the repeal of the Stamp Act.

"TOO WITTY," AND "A LITTLE TOO WICKED" FOR ETON, CHARLES FOX, AT fifteen, went up to Oxford, matriculating at Hart Hall, now Hertford College,[37] in the autumn of 1764. He remained there for two years, not taking a degree. "To a man who reads a great deal," pronounced the very young man, "there cannot be a more agreeable place."

Charles fell into the wholesome bookish company of William Dickson, an Eton schoolmate who owed his later consecration as the Bishop of Down and Connor to Fox's influence. At Oxford, the two friends frequented the bookshops together to read the pre-Restoration playwrights.

---

* Wilkes had attacked the "odious" and "ignominious" peace that Holland had helped procure and that George III had praised in a royal speech.

Fox later claimed that there was no such play, written and published before the return from exile of Charles II, that he hadn't read.[38]

The hirsute infant was by now coming into his full adult coat of hair. For the luxuriant growth ranging, unbroken, over both eyes, Charles would be known as "The Eyebrow." Edward Gibbon, marking his swarthy, often unwashed, complexion, called him a "black collier."[39]

The young Fox, though fat, was anything but sedentary. He played tennis and cricket, shot partridges, and walked prodigious distances. One hot day, Dickson and he resolved to tramp the fifty-three miles between Oxford and Holland House. Arriving home breathless late the same day, Charles announced to his father, "You must send half a guinea, or a guinea, without loss of time, to the alehouse-keeper at Nettlebed, to redeem the gold watch you gave me some years ago, and which I left in pawn there for a pot of porter." In that small matter, as later, in much larger ones, money was Charles's for the asking for as long as it lasted.[40]

In March 1765, Charles left Oxford to join his family on a long vacation in France. His tutor wished him Godspeed: "Application like yours requires some intermission, and you are the only person with whom I have ever had connection, to whom I could say this."[41] It was a Fox that few, besides the tutor, Dr. William Newcome, had ever met before, or would ever encounter again.

It was a self-aware Fox who thanked his friend Sir George Macartney for setting a shining example of application. It helped him, said Fox, to conquer "my natural idleness, of which Lady Holland will tell you wonders. Indeed, I am afraid it will in the end get the better of what little ambition I have, and that I shall never be anything but a lounging fellow."[42]

But few lounged as Fox did. He feasted on poetry and threw himself into amateur theatricals. "For God's sake learn Italian as fast as you can," he urged his soulmate Richard FitzPatrick, "if it be only to read Ariosto. There is more good poetry in Italian than in all other languages that I understand put together. In prose too it is a very fine language. Make haste and read these things that you may be fit to talk to Christians."[43]

When the Foxes traveled, they made certain to pack their money. Their sons' gambling debts (for Stephen, too, had contracted the betting habit) would alone have required the kind of sums that could raise eyebrows at the Bank of England. Besides, there were servants to house and transport, equipage to hire, first-class lodging to rent, fine dining to partake of. Between 1763 and 1769, they laid out more than £31,000 in Europe.

Charles left Oxford for good in the spring of 1766, two years short of a degree. The bibliophile lamented that Oxford had left him with no "useful knowledge," though Fox, like many a future unemployed student of the humanities, spoke too soon.[44] The plays in which he had acted, the poetry he had memorized, and the Latin and Greek he had translated made up the intellectual capital on which he would build his reputation as Burke's rival for the unconferred title of the greatest political talker of the age.

The school leaver did not confront the age-old problem of how to eat. For Fox, the idea of finding a job was as unimaginable as the thought of taking holy orders. France was his principal alma mater, as historian L. G. Mitchell observes, and the scholar availed himself of all that that beckoning school had to offer.*

IN THE AUTUMN OF 1766, FOX EMBARKED ON WHAT WOULD PROVE TO BE a two-year grand tour. The object was pleasure: sex, gambling, the humane letters, friendship. Beginning with Italy, in company with his family, he passed the winter in Naples. His father reported that Charles was "beyond Measure kind and attentive to me, he has a good heart & more to be admired for that than his head, which you know is no bad one."[45]

In April, Lord and Lady Holland returned to England while Charles lin-

---

* In the spring of 1765, Charles met with the secretary to the British embassy in Paris, none other than David Hume. A mutual friend of Hume and Holland reported on the philosopher's impression of the young traveler: "David is extremely surpriz'd by his knowledge, force of mind, and manly ways of thinking at his age. At the same time he has insinuated his fears to me, that the dissipation of this kind of Parisian life might check his ardor after useful knowledge, and lose in all appearance a very great acquisition to the publick. I told Charles this conversation between me and Hume, and that I was obliged to own that the risk would be very great, 99 times in a hundred, but that I trusted to a noble and worthy ambition, which I thought I saw very strong in him, and which gave me the strongest assurance that he would neither disappoint the public nor his friends. Tho' Charles won't promise anything positively upon this subject, yet he acknowledges himself to be entirely of my opinion." Clotworthy Upton to Holland, May 17, 1765, quoted in Mitchell, *Fox*, 9.

gered in Italy. The dullness of Turin was relieved by news that "there has been a woman of fashion put in prison lately for f—g (I suppose rather too publicly) a piece of unexampled tyranny."[46] With Uvedale Price, budding landscape designer, Fox summered in Venice and Florence. November 1767 found him in Paris, then on to the South of France with his Eton friend, Lord Carlisle, whose "freezing reserve" melted in Fox's ebullient company. The family reconnected at Nice (where there were "no whores")[47] in mid-December.

Advising James Boswell on what to do while touring in Europe, Dr. Johnson urged him to seek out cultivated minds as much as beautiful art. Fox did as Johnson commanded. He charmed Gibbon in Lausanne and listened to Voltaire in Ferney prescribe the books with which to rid himself of religious prejudices (the author of each being Voltaire).[48] Pope Clement XIV granted an audience to the young English visitor: "Fox put on so rueful a countenance, looked so like a disarmed Culprit that it was impossible to resist laughing, which his Holiness was too good-natured to be offended with."[49]

Fox returned to England early in August 1768, paused, packed his bags once more, and the following month, accompanied by William Dickson, his brother Stephen and Lady Mary, dashed back to Italy.

The nineteen-year-old was now a member of Parliament for the rotten borough of Midhurst. He had won his election, on May 10, 1768, while still in Europe, with the only vote that counted, Lord Holland's. Jointly with his brother, Lord Ilchester, Holland secured the borough for their sons, as a kind of rental, at a cost of £3,000.[50] Young Fox chose not to rush home to take up his life's work but lingered—in Parma, Cento, Venice, Bologna—to cultivate friends, lovers, belles lettres, and blessed idleness.

* Caring little for what others thought of him, Fox was hard to intimidate. Denied an invitation to the Parisian salon of Marie Thérèse Rodet Geoffrin, he blamed not his age (sixteen) but the famous *salonnière*. "Do you not think Mme Geoffrin a very silly Woman, not to cultivate so agreeable acquaintance as I am," he asked of his father. Mitchell, *Fox*, 9.

CHAPTER 3

Burke goes to Parliament

It is hard to say whether the Doctors of Law or Divinity have
made the greater Advances in the lucrative Business of Mystery.

—EDMUND BURKE, *A VINDICATION OF NATURAL SOCIETY*

E dmund Burke made no impetuous leap into his life's work. Pointed
for the law, he arrived in London in May 1750, more than two years
after graduating from Trinity College. Obedient to parental command, he looked up John Burke, a London lawyer, whom Richard, his
father, "did sometimes call Cousins."[1] It was under John's roof that Edmund
met Will Burke, John's son, another would-be lawyer and the product of
Westminster School and Christ Church, Oxford. The young men became
inseparable.

Edmund and Will began their legal studies together at Middle Temple,
one of the four London Inns of Court and the one especially favored by
Irish students. It was here that Edmund would learn the law, though Middle Temple would scarcely teach it.

Dinner comprised the Middle Temple's principal structured activity.
Apart from that pleasant daily ritual, an aspiring barrister was on his own.
There were no classes, examinations, or grades. There were no textbooks.
(Publication of volume one of Blackstone's pioneering *Commentaries on
the Laws of England* was fifteen years in the future.)[2] A student could haunt
the courts or seat himself in a law office to copy wills and deeds. As for the

stated obligation to perform nine academic exercises over the course of a six-year enrollment, one could pay a fee to skip it.[3]

The temptation to confine his studies to daily dining pressed hard on Edmund. The Middle Temple Hall was a charming place in which to eat and read, but Fleet Street, James Boswell's idea of the liveliest and happiest thoroughfare in the world, bustled nearby. Watercraft coursed the River Thames, a three-minute walk from the Middle Temple library. The law could hardly compete with teeming London. Nor could it hold a candle to the world of books and authors.

By 1751, Richard Shackleton, Burke's boon companion from school days at Ballitore, was already a father. Edmund could report only scant progress in the career that he didn't want to pursue. At least, Edmund wrote Shackleton, "tho a middling Poet cannot be endured there is some quarter for a middling Lawyer."

"I read as much as I can," Burke went on,

(which is however but a little,) and am but just beginning to know something of what I am about, which till very lately I did not; this Study carries no difficulty to those who already understand it and to those who never will understand it, and for all between those extreams, (God knows) they have a hard task of it.[4]

"Live pleasant," Burke entreated a friend years many later, and the underachieving law student now conducted himself in the anticipation of that future counsel. Winters found him in London, summers in the English countryside, generally with Will at his side.

Wherever they went, people wondered why they had come. Pairs of able-bodied, idle, respectable young men were no common sight in the Welsh village of Monmouth, where Edmund and Will turned up in the summer of 1751. Curious villagers suspected they were fortune hunters until the eligible bachelors left town without wives. More likely, then, they were spies for the French king.[5]

In Turleigh, a west Wiltshire textile-making town where Edmund and Will took up summertime residence in 1752, the locals pegged them for authors or perhaps—as they received more than their share of mail—merchants. Their landlady could see they were gentlemen, "but I ask no questions."[6]

Edmund Burke's health was problematical, or so he believed, and in 1750 he put himself under the care of Dr. Christopher Nugent (1698–1775), a French-trained Irish physician in Bath.[7] Nugent, who would write a book about the treatment of rabies, be elected a fellow of the Royal Society, and become one of nine original members of Samuel Johnson's Literary Club, was no ordinary doctor. Nor was he just any father: his daughter, Jane, was the future Mrs. Edmund Burke.

The physician and his daughter proved a tonic, each in his or her own way. "An Epistle to Doctor Nugent," which Edmund composed in September 1752 while taking his ease at Turleigh, included these lines:

'Tis now two Autumns, since he chanc'd to find,
A youth of Body broke, infirm of mind,
He gave him all that man can ask or give,
Restor'd his Life, and taught him how to Live,
But what, and when and How this youth shall pay,
Must be discuss'd upon a Longer day.[8]

All the while, Richard Burke was footing the bills, including an allowance of £100 a year, which was about what an Oxford fellow or a country curate earned.[9] In 1755, with the cumulative parental outlay rising to £1,000, word reached Dublin that Edmund had laid aside his law books and applied for a vacant post in the British colonial service. Unmasked, the guilty son wrote home to apologize for the mere contemplation of such an ill-conceived, ungrateful, and indeed, cruel step:

"I have nothing nearer my heart than to make you easy," he assured his father, "and I have no Scheme or design, however reasonable it may seem to me that I would not gladly Sacrifice to your Quiet and submit to your Judgment, you have surely had trouble enough with a Severe disorder without any addition from uneasiness at my Conduct." All he wanted in life was "to shew myself to you and my Mother a dutiful affectionate and obliged Son."[10]

IN 1755 OR EARLY 1756, BURKE WAS WALKING THROUGH ST. JAMES'S PARK with a certain Mr. Bodly. A hapless young traveler from India named Joseph Emin watched the two men at a distance. It was Emin's dream to liberate his native Armenia from the tyranny of the conquering Persians and Turks, and he had run away to England to begin his quest. The would-be liberator was making ends meet as a laborer. He was deeply discouraged and his back ached.[11]

Emin recognized Bodly from Calcutta but chose to address the man with the friendlier face. Removing his hat, he poured out his troubles to the "very tall and well made" stranger.

They walked and talked, stopping for a while to eat. As darkness fell, Burke invited Emin to continue their conversation at his apartment, "up two pair of stairs, at the sign of Pope's Head, at a bookseller's near the Temple."

"Sir," Emin's new friend introduced himself, "my name is Edmund Burke, at your service; I am a runaway son from a father, as you are.

"Upon my honor," Burke continued, producing a half guinea from his pocket and offering it to Emin, "this is what I have at present, please to accept it."

Emin, whose net worth was only slightly greater than Burke's proffered coin, declined. "If you will continue your kind notice towards me, that is all I want; and I shall value it more than a prince's treasure."

Burke put Emin to work copying his manuscripts. He introduced him to well-placed friends, helped him to enter the Royal Military Academy at Woolwich, and wrote to him when, as a volunteer in the British Army, he was posted to Europe on active service during the Seven Years' War.

Writing in the third person, Emin later attested, "Had not Mr. Burke consoled him now and then, he might have been lost for ever through despair; but his friend always advised him to put his trust in God; and he never missed a day without seeing Emin."[12]

AFTER ALL, THE TURLEIGH BUSYBODIES KNEW AN AUTHOR WHEN THEY saw one. *A Vindication of Natural Society** by Edmund Burke, a parody of the fashionable deistic doctrines of the philosopher and Tory statesman Henry St. John, 1st Viscount Bolingbroke, was published in 1756.

A literary lark, *A Vindication* mimics Bolingbroke's rich style and solemnly adapts his anti-Christian arguments to Burke's mock agenda of toppling nations, laws, and governments. How much better, runs the argument of which Burke believed not one word, a state of nature to the violence and corruption of "political society."

Bolingbroke, who died in 1751, was an intimate of Alexander Pope, a guiding light to such American founders as John Adams and a friend of Jonathan Swift and Voltaire. He was likewise a charming, handsome, ruthless, whoring, silver-tongued opportunist. In life, he supported the Church of England as a pillar of state. In death, too, his support of the institutional church was unwavering. What came to light in his *Works* that appeared in 1754, three years after his death, was his contempt for Christianity.

Publication triggered an anti-Bolingbroke outcry. William Warburton, the bishop of Gloucester, led the attack of the clergy with a four-part broadside. In the same cause, Burke deployed brevity and satire, the latter almost too successfully. So accomplished a parodist was he that readers mistakenly thought they were reading the dead infidel rather than the anonymous newcomer. In a subsequent edition of the *Vindication*, Burke was reduced to explaining his own joke.[13]

The miscast law student shines brightest in his top-to-bottom indictment of the profession for which he was ostensibly training. "New Laws were made to expound the old," writes Burke-as-Bolingbroke:

> and new Difficulties arose up on the new Laws; as Words multiplied, Opportunities of cavilling upon them multiplied also. Then Recourse was had to Notes, Comments, Glosses, Reports, *Responsa Pruden-*

---

* In full: *A Vindication of Natural Society: Or, A View of the Miseries and Evils Arising to Mankind from Every Species of Artificial Society.*

tum, learned readings: Eagle stood against Eagle: Authority was set
up against Authority. . . . Our Inheritances are become a Prize for Dis-
putation; and Disputes and Litigations are become an inheritance.[14]

In his zestful scourging of lawyers and the law, Burke writes from the
heart. Otherwise *A Vindication* can be read as a preview of the ideas that
the great conservative would spend his life denouncing. "It is hard to say,"
Burke has his Bolingbroke remark, "whether the Doctors of Law or Divinity have made the greater Advances in the lucrative Business of Mystery."
The faithful Burke knew the answer.[15]

A Vindication, which Burke, conforming to eighteenth-century custom,
presented to the world unsigned, ran to just 106 pages, octavo.[16] His next
production was the full-bodied survey of the psychology of human perception that he had begun in college. The leading critic of the Georgian age,
Dr. Johnson, pronounced it a triumph, and a new generation of romantic
poets, including Samuel Taylor Coleridge, would ponder and quote from it.

*The Sublime and the Beautiful** explores the nature of perception and
the power of emotion. Burke surveys the gamut of feelings from pain and
pleasure to joy and grief, sympathy and ambition. At one point he observes
how very different grief is from physical pain: "The person who grieves,
suffers his passion to grow upon him; he indulges it, he loves it; but this
never happens in the case of actual pain, which no man ever willingly
endure for any considerable time."[17]

He investigates the concepts of power, privation, light, darkness, smell,
and taste and "the cries of animals." He explains the power of language,
"how words influence the passions."

Burke writes and reasons like a scientist but with the certain knowledge
that God designed the world. Humbly seeking truth, he says, "we may be
admitted, if I may dare to say so, into the counsels of the Almighty by a
consideration of his works."[18]

For Burke, the "sublime" is the strongest feeling in the human repertoire.

---

* *A Philosophical Inquiry into the Origins of the Sublime and Beautiful with an Introduc-
tory Discourse Concerning Taste and Several Additions*, 1757.

Coleridge, later drawing on Burke, neatly defined it as "a suspension of the powers of comparison";[19] Burke himself likens it to terror. "I say the strongest emotion," Burke writes, "because I am satisfied the ideas of pain are much more powerful than those which enter on the part of pleasure."[20] Nobody would exchange a charmed life for a certain death by drawing and quartering.*

Beauty, he contends, "is no creature of our reason" but rather a phenomenon of the senses. It is what excites love. For Burke's money, beautiful objects are small and vulnerable.[21] "I need here say little of the fair sex," he boldly proceeds, "where I believe the point will be easily allowed me. The beauty of women is considerably owing to their weakness or delicacy, and is even enhanced by their timidity, a quality of mind analogous to it."[22] Later, the doomed queen of France, Marie Antoinette, resigned to her fate, ethereal in her movements, "glittering like the morning-star," became, for Burke, the quintessence of female beauty.[23]

The feminist writer Mary Wollstonecraft rolled her eyes but withheld her fire until 1790, when, in her *Vindication of the Rights of Woman*, she incorporated her condemnation of Burke's idea of female beauty into her repudiation of his view of the French Revolution.

Critics of both sexes have paused, wide-eyed, over Burke's solemn description of "the physical cause of love." Thus, the bachelor writes:

> When we have before us such objects as excite love and complacency, the body is affected, so far as I could observe, much in the following manner: the head reclines something on one side; the eyelids are more closed than usual, and the eyes roll gently with the inclination of the object; the mouth is a little opened, and the breath draws slowly, with now and then a low sigh.[24]

The budding orator is on firmer ground in dealing with the power of language. How much greater is the force of the written word, he argues,

---

* The would-be French regicide Robert-François Damiens met exactly that gruesome end in 1757 as would, nine years later, in Ireland, Father Nicholas Sheehy, a relative of Burke's by marriage.

than that of a painted image. Contrast an angel on canvas with a line of Milton's invoking the identical image: "the angel of the *Lord*."

"What painting can furnish out anything so grand as the addition of one word?"[25]

Besides earning its young author twenty guineas from the sale of the copyright, *Sublime and Beautiful* was Burke's ticket to the high table of Georgian culture. The book sold some seven thousand copies over thirty years, won the admiration of the orientalist Sir William Jones, of a pair of chaired Scottish university philosophy professors, James Beattie (1735–1803) and Hugh Blair (1718–1800), of the German philosopher Immanuel Kant (1724–1804), and of the chief editor of the French *Encyclopédie*, Denis Diderot (1713–84).[26]

Boswell describes Samuel Johnson holding forth in 1769 on the nature of literary criticism. The great lexicographer flicks away the pretensions of Mrs. Elizabeth Montagu, author of a well-received work on Shakespeare.* "No, sir, there is no real criticism in it: none shewing the beauty of thought, as formed on the workings of the human heart." Other critics come in for short shrift until Johnson turns to Burke: there, says he, of *Sublime and Beautiful*, "we have an example of true criticism."[27]

BURKE AND JANE NUGENT WERE MARRIED ON MARCH 12, 1757, A MONTH before the publication of *Sublime and Beautiful*. Careful readers of that work could form a mental picture of the bride. Delicate, of course, she was no careerist, but rather one of those "persons who creep into the hearts of most people, who are chosen as the companions of their softer hours, and their reliefs from care and anxiety, are never persons of shining qualities or strong virtues. It is rather the soft green of the soul on which we rest our eyes, that are fatigued with beholding more glaring objects."[28]

An undated anniversary gift, husband to wife, entitled "The Character of _____," left it up to Jane to fill in the missing name in the title of a nearly seven-hundred-word prose poem. The subject is his ideal woman. "If it at all answers any Original, I shall be pleased," he teasingly says; "for

---

* Elizabeth Montagu, *An Essay on the Writings and Genius of Shakespear* (1769).

if Such a person really exists as I would describe, she must be far Superior to my Description."

She's "handsome," of course, though not conventionally so; "it is all that Sweetness of Temper, Benevolence, Innocence and Sensibility, which a face can express, that forms her beauty."

"Her Eyes have a mild light, but they awe you when she pleases; they command like a good man out of office, not by Authority but by virtue." As for her smiles, they are "inexpressible," her voice is "low, Soft musick."

"To describe her body, describe her mind, one is the transcript of the other. Her understanding is not Shewn in the Variety of matters it exerts itself on, but in the goodness of the Choice she makes. She does not Shew it so much in doing or Saying striking things, as in avoiding such as she ought not to say or do."*[29] In any case, Burke knew she was too good for him.[30]

Richard Burke, their first child, was born in 1758; a second, Christopher, died in infancy. There were no others.

The newlyweds presently moved in with Dr. Nugent on Wimpole Street in Marylebone, then a semirural London suburb. Will, the groom's inseparable friend, joined them, as did Richard Burke, Edmund's younger brother. Edmund, Will, and Richard had already become "the Burkes," a unit that shared quarters, finances, dreams, writing assignments, and— unfortunately for Edmund—reputations.†

Edmund had lent a hand with Will's history of the New World, *An Account of the European Settlements in America*, which was published

---

* Burke had also conceived the ideal of a gentleman, which he committed to writing in a notebook long before his marriage. What distinguishes the gentleman is not his accomplishment in business but his attainments in society: "its Basis is politeness, whose essence is Ease; & hence it is that there is no Character more rarely found; for easy behavior, easy conversation & easy writing are the hardest things in the world." Though hardly ignorant, the gentleman is no scholar; "he seems rather to slight books, than not to know them." He smiles rather than laughs and is sparing with his wit; "there is a sort of concealed Irony that tinges his whole conversation. he entertains no extremes of opinion; he scarcely ever disputes." *W&S*, 1:61–64. An amateur scholar, a born disputant and chronic punster, Burke— whose laughter could be explosive—might thus be denoted a gentleman in spite of himself.

† In remarks to the House of Commons in 1782, Burke made reference to his "pretty large family." Presumably, he was including his relations in Ireland as well as his brother Richard, his "cousin" Will, his only child Richard, and his wife Jane. PH, 24:182.

in 1757 and by 1777 had gone through six editions. Will attested to the strength of the bond they had formed in a couple of lines of verse:

Your word, Dear friend, has been my guiding Line,
Your Conduct was, and is, the Rule of mine.[31]

Edmund, generously taking the measure of Will, confided his conclusions to a notebook. His friend was subject to short-lived bursts of passion. He was quick both to comprehend and to forget. Personable and gentlemanly, he would make a fine ambassador.[32]

Will did, in fact, land a kind of diplomatic post in 1759. It was apparently through the offices of Henry Fox that he was appointed secretary and register of Guadeloupe, a Caribbean sugar island that British forces had recently seized from the French. Will saw the elder Fox as his mentor, "my Great North Star to direct my political opinions," while the paymaster judged Will to be "a very clever fellow, and I believe a very honest one."[33]

All could see he was clever—"He is one of the few comforts in this dissolving climate," attested the English governor, Campbell Dalrymple[34]— but few, besides Henry Fox, noticed his honesty. To get rich quick was his approach to earning a living, and he conducted an unauthorized sketchy side business in Guadeloupe of which Dalrymple was known to disapprove.[35]

Encouraged by the critical success of the *Vindication* and *Sublime and Beautiful*, Edmund in February 1757 signed a contract to produce an *Abridgement of English History* but got no further than the reign of King John. Perhaps he quit from exhaustion, or in deference to the illustrious David Hume, who was completing his own history of England.[*]

Robert Dodsley, the jilted publisher, next proposed an "annual register,"

---

[*] "If we may believe the story that Burke desisted from the undertaking because Hume had taken up the same subject," remarked Lord Acton, "it must ever be regretted that the reverse did not occur." Burke had contracted to deliver 400,000 words by Christmas Day 1758, which committed him to write more than 200,000 words a year for two years, not counting time out for research. All told, it was the equivalent of three books of the length of this one. Lock, *Edmund Burke*, 1:143.

a magazine-like compendium of the year's notable events. Compiler, editor, and author, Burke would produce a combination almanac, anthology, and historical narrative, complete with poetry, book reviews, and biographical sketches, more or less single-handedly. The lapsed historian started work on the first edition of the *Annual Register* in 1758.

It was a stroke of luck all around—for the publisher (the *Register* became a bestseller), for the founding editor, and it is not too much to say, for the quality of British politics. To start, the *Register* paid its author £100 per annual volume, a premium to the standard hack rate,[36] and it thrust the future statesman into the stream of contemporary political, social, and economic events. The mighty labor of compiling, interpreting, and narrating the top occurrences of the year compensated Burke with an immense store of knowledge.

"Burke," Johnson once marveled in Boswell's earshot, "is the only man whose common conversation corresponds with the general fame which he has in the world. Take up whatever topic you please, he is ready to meet you."[37]

The first *Register*, covering 1758, appeared in May 1759. Unsigned, Burke introduced his work with a swipe at the snobs, "the Learned," who would look down their noses at it. The *Register* would inform, amuse, and astonish. Yearly publication, not the usual monthly frequency, would allow for deep discussion of weighty topics. It was no easy thing to produce, the editor wanted his readers to know, "and if we have performed what we intended in any sort to the reader's satisfaction, we may lay claim to some merit."[38]

The notable event of 1758 was the war, to which, from its 1756 inception through the campaign of 1758, Burke contributed an evenly balanced 42,000-word history. He did not withhold condemnation of Britain's defeats, nor of the public's "shameful" trembling over the threat of a cross-Channel invasion.[39] Neither did he stint praise for the personal conduct of the overconfident loser of the Battle of the Monongahela, General Edward Braddock, who, "after having five horses killed under him, was mortally wounded; wiping away all the errors of his conduct by an honorable death for his country."[40]

The *Register* detailed the growing wartime debt on which Paymaster

Fox was fattening his wealth. It described the "Particularities that attended a Lady after the Small Pox" and a "Description of the court and person of Queen Elizabeth." It quoted from John Holwell's account of the horrors of death by suffocation and dehydration in the Black Hole of Calcutta in 1756 and the "wonderful preservation of three persons buried above five weeks in the snow."

An Estimate of the Manners and Principles of the Times, John Brown's indictment of the supposed enfeeblement and decline of British society, was the first book to be reviewed in the first *Register*. "Exorbitant trade and wealth" produced luxury, the author contended, which fostered avarice and created a state of things that corrupted even the arts. Music, in that age of Handel and Haydn, was nothing more than "a eunuch's effeminate trill." Why, Brown wrote, debauched youth would rather play the horses than read great books.

The *Register* gently reproved the kind of author who would "throw virtue as far backward as possible" in service of the debatable proposition that the world is "continually degenerating."[41]

IN MARCH 1759, DAVID HUME, IN COMPANY WITH HIS FELLOW SCOTSMAN Alexander Wedderburn, was distributing copies of Adam Smith's new *Theory of Moral Sentiments* to a handful of influential Londoners.[*] Among these opinion makers was a certain "Burke, an Irish gentleman, who wrote lately a very pretty treatise [the new second edition] on the sublime."

Smith, too, was much taken with Burke's *Sublime*—indeed, the professor of moral philosophy at the University of Glasgow remarked that its author deserved a university chair.[42] Burke might well have jumped at the

---

[*] A formidable group, beginning with the jurist Wedderburn (1733–1805), a future lord chancellor who, at the age of twenty-one, had chaired the first meeting of Edinburgh's Select Society, among whose founding members were Hume, Smith, and the historian William Robertson. Other recipients included George Lyttelton (1709–73), Whig politician, gentleman author, and dedicatee of Henry Fielding's novel *Tom Jones*; Horace Walpole (1717–97), son of Robert Walpole, Britain's longest-serving prime minister, himself a Whig politician as well as a memoirist, diarist, historian, publisher, and gossip; and Soame Jenyns (1704–87), politician, author, and conversationalist, who scintillated at Mrs. Montague's bluestocking salon evenings.

opportunity, had it been offered (which it apparently was not). To bandy compliments with Smith was well and good,* but it couldn't support a family. The former law student and aspiring colonial officer, age thirty, was still unemployed.

To Shackleton, in 1757, Burke had characterized his life as "checquerd with various designs, sometimes in London, sometimes in remote parts of the Country, sometimes in France, and shortly please God, to be in America."†43

But by 1759, Burke had his eye on Spain. For help in securing the open position of British consul in Madrid, he applied to Mrs. Montagu, a keen admirer of his and a supporter, too, of Will Burke, but she could not, or at least did not, deliver.44

A SPONSOR OF A VERY DIFFERENT KIND, WILLIAM GERARD HAMILTON, now appeared in Edmund's life. Handsome, cultivated, and duplicitous, Hamilton was a member of Parliament whose dazzling maiden speech in 1755 overshadowed all subsequent efforts. Known thereafter as "Single-Speech," Hamilton was another protégé of Henry Fox, who found him a place at the Board of Trade and Plantations. In 1759, Edmund Burke signed on as Hamilton's private secretary or, as Burke informally styled himself, "companion to your studies." To others, he was Hamilton's "jackal."

In 1761 the reshuffling of English colonial government in Ireland caused a chain reaction of political advancement. Lord Halifax, the new viceroy, tapped Hamilton to be his chief secretary, and Hamilton named Burke his factotum. The three set off for Dublin, with Burke in the vanguard.

The hedge school alumnus was now a cog, albeit a passive, humane, and reluctant one, in the British machinery of Catholic suppression. He was in Dublin during the Irish parliamentary sessions in the winters of 1761 and 1763, the time of the Levellers, or Whiteboys, secret clans in the southern province of Munster whose members swore an oath to attack their Protes-

---

* In a letter to Smith, Burke qualified the praise he heaped on the *Theory of Moral Sentiments* with the demurrer that "you are in some few Places, what Mr Locke is in most of his writings, rather a little too diffuse. This is however a fault of the generous kind." C., 1:130.

† Evidently a hope rather than a fact.

tant oppressors. The name Whiteboy derived from the bright smocks that the clansmen wore to help them distinguish friend from foe in moonlight. Raging against the enclosure of land once commonly held for grazing and potato farming, the Whiteboys dug up fields, cut down orchards, filled in ditches, and knocked down walls (hence, with respect to the latter harassing tactic, "Levellers"). They harried the tithe farmers, tax collectors for the established Church of Ireland, where, of course, the Catholic Whiteboys would not be found at Sunday worship.

Burke was no disinterested observer of either the Whiteboys' lawlessness or the bloody repression of such crimes by Irish courts and magistrates. No known record of his official duties survives, but the Halifax-Hamilton administration in May 1762 was offering a fifty-pound reward for information leading to the arrest and conviction of

> any of the persons concerned in unlawfully assembling themselves in arms, and digging up several acres of land, and levelling several perches of walls and ditches in different parts of the kingdom, and committing many other outrages to the great annoyance of many of his Majesty's subjects, and to the disturbance of the publick peace and quiet of this kingdom.[45]

Boyhood friends and maternal relatives were among the agents of those outrages. Father Nicholas Sheehy, whose sister, Catherine, was married to a first cousin of Burke's, was the repeated target of prosecutors and grand juries for his open support of Whiteboy causes. The priest's hanging, drawing, and quartering, on March 15, 1766, on a murder charge proven to the satisfaction only of the Protestant judicial authorities, seeded generations of hatred and reprisals, including, in 1770, the stoning to death of Sheehy's executioner and the coining of the phrase "Sheehy's jury" to connote perjured and miscarried justice.[46]

Burke checked himself, even with Charles O'Hara, the friend with whom he was least guarded, in describing the injustices to which he was an official witness. He would say no more—save to revile "the unfeeling Tyranny of a mungril Irish Landlord" or the "Horrors of a Munster Circuit"—because it is "impossible to preserve ones Temper on the view of so detestable a scene."[*][47]

To the credit of the Halifax and Hamilton administration, it refused to give credence to baseless Protestant claims that the Whiteboy uprising was a French-inspired threat to national security, even as the Seven Years' War still raged. Halifax rather saw those troubles for the things they were, namely, armed protests against the legislated "disabilities" that had seeded pauperism-by-policy in the green Irish countryside.

Generosity was one of Halifax's most appealing traits. He spent heavily out of his own pocket to maintain his Dublin establishment while declining to accept a proffered raise in salary. He did not, however, begrudge his successor that bump up in pay. Neither did he oppose the sinecure that Hamilton obtained in 1763, nor, evidently, the £300 per annum pension, drawn on the Irish treasury, that Hamilton helped to procure for Burke, also in 1763.

Burke's gratitude to Hamilton was heartfelt—here, at last, was a glimpse of financial security—but the recipient qualified his thanks with a reminder of the value he attached to the leisure he needed to write. "Whatever advantages I have acquired," Burke addressed his benefactor, "have been owing to some small degree of literary reputation." As for the details of the working arrangements, they "may be very easily settled by a good understanding between ourselves, and by a discreet liberty, which I think you would not wish to restrain, or I to abuse."[48]

But there was no such understanding. From late 1764 into 1765, Hamilton, now returned to the British House of Commons, was pressing Burke to pledge to remain on the job indefinitely. Burke would do nothing of the kind—the sheer presumption of the idea enraged him—and he bade good riddance to Hamilton and farewell to his pension.

---

[*] Burke's incomplete "Tracts Relative to the Laws against Popery in Ireland," which was unpublished in his lifetime, presents a thoroughgoing arraignment of the anti-Catholic body of Irish law. "The happiness or misery of multitudes can never be a thing indifferent," Burke affirms. "A law against the majority of the people is in substance a law against the people itself." The dating of this essay is uncertain, but it would be surprising if Burke had ever not framed the question in terms as generous as these. O'Brien, *Great Melody*, 41.

Hamilton had not just hired him but had stolen "six of the best years of my Life," while from behind the bars of his gilded cage, Burke could see his contemporaries passing him by.[49] But even that was not the worst of it. Some people, listening to Hamilton's side of the story, had had the temerity to question his conduct. "I never can, (knowing, as I do, the principles upon which I always endeavour to act) submit to any sort of compromise on my Character," Burke wrote to a sympathetic college friend:

> and I shall never therefore look upon those, who after hearing the whole story, do not think me *perfectly* in the right, and do not consider Hamilton as an infamous Scoundrel,* to be in the smallest degree my friends, or even to be persons for whom I am bound to have the slightest Esteem, as fair or just estimaters of the Characters and Conduct of men.[50]

BY THIS TIME, BURKE HAD EARNED A DISTINCTION THAT NEITHER Hamilton nor time could efface. Along with his father-in-law, Dr. Nugent, he had become a founding member of the Club, later known as the Literary Club, along with such worthies as the artist Sir Joshua Reynolds, who had proposed the idea; Dr. Johnson; Oliver Goldsmith, author of *The Vicar of Wakefield*; Topham Beauclerk, man-about-town and, secretly, collector of books of sermons; Bennet Langton, classicist and country gentleman; Anthony Chamier, wealthy retired stockbroker; and Sir John Hawkins, "a Middlesex magistrate with a taste for music who at last proved unclubbable." The nine agreed to meet at the Turk's Head, in Gerrard Street, Soho, one evening a week, at seven o'clock, to drink and dine and converse. With the passing years, the weekly meetings became fortnightly (and only when Parliament was in session); and the nine expanded to thirty-five.[51]

---

* Fanny Burney agreed, though Hamilton indisputably had an eye for talent. For Burke's successor as "companion to his studies," he selected Samuel Johnson, whose friendship and loyalty he long retained. Lock, *Edmund Burke*, 207.

RALPH VERNEY, A WEALTHY BUCKINGHAMSHIRE LANDOWNER AND
member of Parliament, had made no great success in politics, but his loyalty to the Whig party did yield him some returns. Among such dividends
was the unexpected elevation of a protégé to the post of undersecretary of
state in the Rockingham administration of 1765. Will Burke was that lucky
man, and Verney presently offered him one of the parliamentary seats that
was in his gift.[52]

The close of the Seven Years' War left Will jobless, as Britain
returned Guadeloupe to its former owner, the King of France (despite
Will's arguments, published in pamphlets, that Britain would be better
off keeping the rich sweet island while ceding vast, barren, frigid Canada to France).

As Will blinked in this unfamiliar limelight, Edmund searched for a
new patron. Charles Townshend, one of the wittiest, most talented, and
flightiest members of the House of Commons, was one candidate, but not
even the obvious brilliance of Edmund Burke could persuade Townshend
to relinquish the office that was absorbing most of his time, and for which
he would have no need of Hamilton's former right-hand man. This was
Henry Fox's old gold mine, the Paymaster's Office.

Burke next turned to Charles Watson-Wentworth, 2nd Marquess of
Rockingham, a man as dull as he was rich, and as rich as he was noble;
for years, the only English peer to hold the rank of a marquess as his
principal title, he was, to his friends, simply "the marquess." Rockingham led one of the main elements of the Whig party. Its leading lights
were, like Rockingham himself, heirs to the Glorious Revolution of
1688. They were jealous of parliamentary prerogatives, suspicious of the
crown, and happiest while improving their estates or racing their horses.
Entitled to govern and desiring to lead, they were not always sure how to
go about it. Still less were they capable of explaining what they wanted.
Edmund Burke would supply the words, the pen, and the organization
they lacked. In the House of Commons, he would be Rockingham's
tongue and brains.

Scarcely had Burke and Rockingham shaken hands when the Duke of

Newcastle warned the marquess that Burke was, in fact, O'Bourke, a Catholic, indeed a Jacobite* and therefore unfit for any office of trust. Burke, when summoned to respond to the allegations, denied each one but nonetheless submitted his resignation—innocent though he was, he would not burden Rockingham with controversy. Nor, on hearing this, would Rockingham flinch, and the two again shook hands, sealing a political partnership that would last for the rest of Rockingham's life.

Only one thing remained to be settled: Rockingham's representative in the House of Commons needed a parliamentary seat. Will stepped forward with the solution. He would relinquish the seat that Lord Verney had procured for him—Edmund's talents were greater than his own—while Verney, in his generosity, would find another for Will.

So it was that Edmund Burke awakened on December 24, 1765, with a pounding headache on top of a heavy cold.[53] Elected to Parliament as the member for Wendover on the twenty-third, he had joined in the evening's victory party, which culminated with a toast to the absent John Wilkes, the guests falling to their knees on command of the happy proposer, Lauchlin Macleane. "All the Dishes were broken in the same Instant," as Macleane reported to Wilkes, then cooling his heels in Paris to escape the reach of British justice over charges of seditious libel against George III; "in a few minutes the Room was cleared of Smoke and full of—Liberty. Wilkes and Liberty, Burke and Wilkes, Freedom and Wendover; Empty Bottles, broken Glasses, Rivers of Wine, Brooks of Brandy, Chairs overturned, with the Men that sat upon them, while others in rising from their Knees fell under the Table."[54]

The new member for Wendover mailed his Christmas greetings the next day with a parliamentary frank.[55] Edmund Burke was a politician.

---

* One who opposed the Glorious Revolution, supported the notion of the divine right of kings, and yearned for the restoration of the senior line of the House of Stuart to the British throne. In short, one who held the opposite views of Edmund Burke. *Jacobite* derives from *Jacobus*, the Latin rendering of James, James II being the Stuart king who abandoned the throne and fled to France in 1688. It was Parliament's invitation to William and his wife, Mary II (James's daughter), to succeed the exiled James that established the principle of a contract between the sovereign and the people or, at least, between the sovereign and Parliament.

CHAPTER 4

Wilkes and liberty

[Burke] made two speeches in the House for repealing the Stamp-
act, which were publickly commended by Mr. Pitt, and have filled
the town with wonder.

—SAMUEL JOHNSON QUOTED IN BOSWELL, *LIFE OF JOHNSON*

The high cost of victory in the Seven Years' War turned the pockets of the British Exchequer inside out. Robert Walpole, Britain's
longest-serving prime minister (1721–42), had laid it down that
£100 million in public debt meant national ruin,[1] but now, at the close of
the Seven Years' War, Britain owed £132.6 million. Peering west across the
Atlantic, Prime Minister George Grenville thought he saw what his government needed: revenue.

The American colonists, by themselves, were in no position to fill the
gaping British fiscal hole, nor would Grenville demand that of them. But
they could surely contribute their fair share to the upkeep of the empire
within which they prospered. British Redcoats, after saving the colonists
from the French and Indians, had lately fought Chief Pontiac to a standstill
along the northwestern American frontier. It would be simple justice, and
no financial hardship, for the beneficiaries of that protection to share in
its cost. To this just and reasonable end, Grenville proposed a stamp tax.

Englishmen had uncomplainingly borne such imposts for seventy years.
The litigious colonists would scarcely notice the additional cost of the legal
documents to which they had all too frequent recourse. Nor would the

readers of colonial newspapers, the proprietors of colonial ale houses, the owners of colonial merchant ships, or the graduates from colonial colleges object to the trifling inconvenience of the British stamps, which, under the Grenville scheme, would be affixed to colonial licenses, diplomas, etc. (without which they would be legally void). In March 1765, with little debate and scarcely a dissenting vote, Parliament enacted the tax.

The colonists wondered what in the world the king and his ministers were thinking. The same George Grenville, a year earlier, had saddled them with the Sugar Act, an irksome tariff on imported molasses that, to hear the Americans tell it, ruined their commerce, enmeshed them in red tape, and incited the Royal Navy to an all-too-conscientious enforcement of the heretofore neglected laws against smuggling.[2] Molasses was the raw material that New England distilleries turned into rum—the rum that found a ready market in North American taverns and in the West African slave trade. Not a little of the cash thereby produced returned to Britain in payment for the English imports that filled the closets and parlors of well-to-do New England merchants and slave traders.

By the lights of American patriots, the Stamp Act was a worse provocation than the molasses tax. It was the first British attempt to lay a tax for the purpose of raising revenue rather than regulating commerce. Another repugnant novelty was that British admiralty courts would deal with suspected tax cheats. Far better, the patriots demanded, for the undoubtedly innocent accused to be judged by juries composed of sympathetic Boston neighbors.

A century or more separated the anti-tax colonists from their Puritan forebears, but not a few of John Adams's contemporaries saw in the Stamp Act the prelude to religious, as well as political and fiscal, subjugation. The Church of England, whose persecutions and errant theology had sped the early Puritan settlers on their way to the New World, was now invading New England under the banner of the Society for the Propagation of the Gospel in Foreign Parts, the king's American critics charged. Bishops and archbishops would surely follow.

The contention that taxation without representation was nothing short of enslavement would perhaps have amused the average member of

Parliament as much as it startled him; anticipated stamp tax revenue of as little as £60,000 a year worked out to just one shilling per American subject, or one-third of an average day's wages.[3]

The Reverend Jonathan Mayhew of Boston, an intellectual and spiritual mentor of, among other colonial leaders, John Adams, contended that the stamp tax was worse than the plagues, droughts, famines, earthquakes, fires, and wars that God had chosen to visit upon on the Pilgrim fathers and their descendants. "It may be questioned," preached Mayhew from the pulpit at West Church, "whether the ancient Greeks or Romans, or any other nation in which slavery was allowed, carried their idea of it much further than this."[4]

Britain's fiscal straits presented a different kind of threat. At eighteen pounds per subject, the national debt of the mother country towered over the colonists' public debt of a mere eighteen shillings per person. (Recall that twenty shillings made one pound sterling.)[5] The lopsidedness of the comparison only invited suspicion that Grenville intended to make the relatively lightly burdened Americans pay for the extravagance of the British court and for the war-making proclivities of British ministers.

Rarely have two peoples, united by language, consanguinity, and a shared body of law, misunderstood one another so thoroughly as did the mother country and her American subjects in 1765. Nor did the English ministry hold a monopoly on misjudgment of the consequences of a seemingly minor colonial impost.

In London, Benjamin Franklin, Pennsylvania's newly appointed colonial agent, opposed the Stamp Act but suspended his resistance once that legislation had gained the king's assent. "We might as well have hindered the sun's setting," he shrugged to an American correspondent. "That we could not do. But since 'tis down, my friend, and it may be long before it rises again, let us make as good a night of it as we can." Franklin thereupon set about finding well-paying jobs for his friends in the envisioned stamp tax collection bureaucracy.[6]

In Boston, the bare news that Parliament was considering such a levy sparked demands for a boycott of imported British merchandise, including customary black mourning garb. Better to grieve in homespun, the radicals cried, than to put money in the pockets of English tailors and weavers. In vain did the royal governor of Massachusetts, Francis Bernard, attempt to mollify hot tempers with appeals to distant authority. "In an empire," the governor addressed the colonial assembly on May 30, 1765, after receipt of news that the rumored tax had, in fact, become law,

> extended and diversified as that of Great Britain, there must be a supreme legislature, to which all other powers must be subordinate. It is our happiness that our supreme legislature is the sanctuary of liberty and justice, and that the prince who presides over it, realizes the idea of a patriot king.

Parliament was that "supreme legislature" and Bernard's "prince," King George III, of course personified Bolingbroke's idealized monarch. "Surely, then," Bernard continued, "we should submit our opinions to the determinations of so august a body, and acquiesce, in a perfect confidence that the rights of the members of the British empire will ever be safe in the hands of the conservators of the liberties of the whole."[7]

British Army officers in America had carried home wondrous stories of the fortunes that colonial contractors had extracted from His Majesty's paymasters during the Seven Years' War. Cousin Jonathan's reputed wealth only sharpened the appetite of the Grenville ministry for a slice of American revenue.[8]

John Adams beheld no such Golconda in the Boston of the mid-1760s. His clients and he were rather fellow sufferers in a postwar depression, and no new tax would ease the pain of plunging real estate values and mounting commercial bankruptcies.[9] Indeed, Adams contended, the stamp tax would drain the country (as young and poor and sparsely settled as it was) of every shilling of its hard cash, consigning "Multitudes of the poorer People of all their Property and reduce them to absolute Beggary."[10] Adams's legal practice stopped cold on the very date, November 1, 1765, when the stamp tax took effect.

British ears might or might not perk up to the colonists' respectful petition for redress, but at least the petition would not provoke the king's wrath. Mounting a direct challenge to British authority in America was a very different thing, and this was the fateful step that Patrick Henry, a freshman member of the Virginia House of Burgesses, urged on his fellow legislators in May 1765. Ignoring the warnings of the speaker of the House that he was uttering treason, Henry put forward his seven famous "Resolves," the burden of which was that Virginians alone had the right to tax themselves and that unjustly taxed citizens had the right to slap the hand that would reach into their pockets. Further in the service of colonial liberty, Henry cried, any person who contended to the contrary, in writing or conversation, "shall be deemed an enemy to His Majesty's Colony."[11] James Otis of Massachusetts, a political ally of Adams and no truckler to British authority, agreed with the speaker of the House of Burgesses that the hot-headed Henry had stepped over the line.[12]

If Virginia was first in constitutional argument against the Stamp Act, as the historian John C. Miller remarked, Boston "took the lead in rioting."[13] It presently became apparent that Franklin had done his friends no favors by nominating them for positions as colonial stamp agents; he might as well have mailed them bull's-eyes to sew onto the back of their coats. The Boston mob attacked Andrew Oliver, collector for Massachusetts, and pulled down the house of his brother-in-law, Thomas Hutchinson, lieutenant governor of the colony, whom the patriots wrongly and maliciously accused of championing the Stamp Act. (Hutchinson had in fact opposed it for reasons that he partially shared with Adams.)

Obsequiousness was no part of the broad American response to the arrival of the stamps from England or to the unwelcome appearance of the royal stamp tax gatherers. Dropping their ledgers to run for their lives, the would-be collectors took in a grand total of £4,000, or about £56,000 less than the low end of a year's projected receipts. The yield was a mere "Pepper-Corn," as some later taunted Grenville, for which his government had foolishly risked "millions" in colonial trade.[14]

Freeborn English subjects, the Americans, too, were heirs to the rights enshrined in the Magna Carta. On this most could agree, but to the merchants and manufacturers of Bristol and Manchester, the colonists were valued customers, first and foremost. English commercial interests had not asked for a stamp tax, and now they wished it would go away. Alluding to the North American customer base, a British pamphleteer put the matter simply: "They will never consent to enrich us, while they think we oppress them."[15]

So to many a Briton, repeal of the failed Grenville impost was the obvious way forward. On this point, the new ministry of Charles Watson-Wentworth, 2nd Marquess of Rockingham, installed in July 1765, was as one with British commercial sentiment. But first came the necessary legislative business of reminding the Americans that they were far from self-governing, except perhaps in the narrow sphere of taxation. Like the rest of His Majesty's subjects, they were bound by the laws that Parliament made and in which making they had no part. Nor did they deserve one, according to the new MP for the borough of Wendover. As slave owners, the Americans disqualified themselves from any such consideration.

"Common sense, nay self-preservation," Burke, some months before entering Parliament, had contended in the pages of the 1765 *Annual Register*, "seem to forbid, that those who allow themselves an unlimited right over the liberties and lives of others, should have any share in making laws for those who have long renounced such unjust and cruel distinctions. It is impossible that such men should have the proper feelings for such a task."[16]

Burke had more to do than extemporize brilliant speeches on the floor of the Commons. He was Rockingham's "man of business," the role in which he had served Hamilton, and it fell to him to deal with such problems as that of the troublesome, scintillating John Wilkes, MP, whose motto, "Wilkes and Liberty," Burke had merrily joined with others in roaring at the dinner to celebrate his election to Parliament before Christmas 1765.

Wilkes was a man of the people and a thorn in the side of established authority, both temporal and ecclesiastic. A journalist, squire, scholar, militia officer, and parliamentarian, he had been jailed for seditious libel and blasphemy. Boasting that he had "no small vices," Wilkes was the co-author of "Essay on Woman," a shockingly dirty, privately printed send-up of Alexander Pope's famous "Essay on Man" in which he had insulted God, church, and Bishop Warburton. The personage whom he libeled, in the forty-fifth number of his weekly newspaper, *The North Briton*, was none other than George III.

Wilkes was born in London in 1725 and excelled at his schoolboy lessons in Greek and Latin. Few men of his day were so brave or charming, and few so ugly. A confessed libertine, he said he loved every woman except his wife, and not a few women loved him right back again, his crossed eyes notwithstanding. As to his improbable attraction to the opposite sex, he was wont to say, "I need only half an hour to talk away my face." His scholarship was sound enough to win him entry into the Royal Society, and his religious scruples were loose enough to gain him admittance to the Order of the Knights of St. Francis of Wycombe, a fraternal body devoted to sex, drinking, conversation, and God-mocking. In Parliament, as member for Aylesbury, Wilkes was a follower of William Pitt, whose successful conduct of the war against France and devotion to the common man he cheered.

Wilkes did not set out to become a champion of the freedom of the press, of the right to privacy, or of freedom from arrest under so-called general warrants (in the writing of which, a prosecutor would name a crime but not the alleged criminals, leaving that detail to the judgment of the arresting officer). Nor did the catalyst for these achievements, Wilkes's enemy, John Stuart, 3rd Earl of Bute, set out to make Wilkes the leading English radical he became. It was by incurring Wilkes's hatred that Bute inadvertently raised John Wilkes, MP for Aylesbury, "a private gentleman . . . of inferior, but independent condition," into the Jack Wilkes who commanded the London mob and became the first member of the House of Commons to move that the franchise be extended to every adult male Briton.[17]

It was likewise by happenstance that Bute arrived at a position in life from which he could be hated, not only by Wilkes but also by wide swaths of the politically aware English population. Born to nobility and acquiring great wealth through marriage, Bute moved to London shortly after the Jacobite rising in 1745. There he made friends with Frederick, Prince of Wales, the son of George II, and with Frederick's wife, Princess Augusta. After the prince's untimely death in 1751, Augusta turned to Bute for guidance and friendship. Presently, she appointed him tutor to her son, the future king George III, who came to regard his Scottish mentor as "my dearest friend."

Little love was lost between the English and the Scots, the former identifying the latter with the tyranny and Catholicism of James II and the bloody, failed insurrection of James's grandson, Bonnie Prince Charlie. The future king, at least, was above such prejudice, and Bute, although he held no formal office, became the young royal's chief adviser. And when George succeeded his grandfather, George II, to the throne in 1760, Bute accumulated a string of official titles, including, in 1761, secretary of state for the Northern Department, precursor to the Foreign Office. Beyond that, Bute exercised outsize influence on the sovereign through friendly, private channels—that is, he became a "favorite."

If, as Thomas Babington Macaulay held, "favorites have always been odious in this country," Bute, on account of his Scots birth, was doubly odious. Nor did it improve his public appeal that he, a Stuart, was a close relation of the defeated Young Pretender, then ensconced in the Papal State of Rome and still not disabused of his dreams of reclaiming the English throne.[18]

Bute's high-speed rise in British politics didn't stop until he reached the ministerial summit as first lord of the Treasury—effectively, prime minister—on May 27, 1762. Wilkes greeted the new premier with the first edition of his weekly newspaper, *The North Briton*.

The title was a play on a common synonym for Scotsman as well as on the name of an existing pro-government paper, *The Briton*, a dull and dutiful propaganda sheet produced by the novelist Tobias Smollett.[19] Under Wilkes's editorship, *The North Briton* took aim at the Bute ministry "with an acrimony, a spirit, and a licentiousness unheard of before even in this country," in the words of Horace Walpole, diarist, parliamentarian, aesthete, and son of the former prime minister. In his first twenty days in office, Bute absorbed more abuse than Walpole's father had "after twenty years."[20]

Wilkes charged the administration with cutting short Pitt's successful war-making to grant the defeated French terms of peace that they hadn't earned on the battlefield. It was Bute, as we have seen, who engaged Henry Fox to speed the treaty through the House of Commons, bribing or punishing recalcitrant members as that practiced nose-counter judged necessary.

Neither did Bute enhance his popularity by championing a new tax on cider to help defray the cost of the Seven Years' War. Englishmen no more relished royal excisemen tromping through their orchards and barging into their homes than American colonists did the king's revenue agents plaguing them with stamps. The cider bill became law in 1763, but protest and rioting led the Commons to weigh its repeal. "The poor man's walls of mud and covering of thatch [are] his castle," famously said William Pitt in a speech against the tax, "where though the rains might enter, the king could not."[21]

Lord Bute presently wondered if he hadn't risen a political rung too high. Among the wealthiest men in the kingdom, he needed no employment. A renowned amateur botanist, a patron of science and the arts, a generous donor to Scotland's colleges and universities, and the father of five sons and six daughters, all by his beloved wife, Mary Wortley Montagu, he was unaccustomed to public obloquy.

Yet stonings, assassination threats, hisses, and humiliation were his thanks for serving his royal pupil. In the gifted propagandistic hands of Wilkes and his *North Briton* collaborator, the poet Charles Churchill, Bute appeared not as the peacemaker he knew himself to be but as the agent of a secret alliance between France and Scotland and—still more scurrilously—the adulterous lover of George III's mother, the symbol of their supposed affair being a jackboot draped with a petticoat. Sick and tired, Bute tendered his resignation on April 8, 1763.

The king next called George Grenville, fifty, a career politician with acknowledged expertise in fiscal affairs, to form a government. Though prolix, peevish, and in financial matters, pedantic and tiresome, Grenville was at least no Scotsman, and *The North Briton* momentarily fell silent. But it blazed forth on April 23 with its forty-fifth number in response to the king's speech that marked the close of the parliamentary session.

The speech was the king's only one that he read aloud to the Houses of Parliament. For the most part, the words he spoke were those of his ministers, and Wilkes, after larding His Majesty with insincere courtly praise, attacked ministerial self-congratulation over the peace treaty and cider tax. As for Bute, the editor charged, the only place to which he had retired was the shadows, where he would continue to advance the Stuarts' un-English agenda of "the absolute, independent, unlimited power of the crown."

Wilkes did not dispute the prerogative of the crown but insisted that the people, too, had their rights, "and I hope, the fine words of Dryden will be engraven on our hearts. 'Freedom is the English Subjects prerogative.'"

As for the sovereign himself, the editor wished "as much as any man in the kingdom to see the honor of the crown maintained in a manner truly becoming royalty. I lament to see it sunk even to prostitution."[22]

George III was among *The North Briton*'s two thousand or so readers,[23] and he resolved to make number 45 the final edition. His legal advisers, combing the previous forty-four numbers, had found no satisfactory grounds for legal action against the publicly unacknowledged editor and his printers. Number 45, they were quite sure, had strayed from licentiousness to sedition, and they moved to prefer charges against the guilty parties.

Troubles now rained down on the man who devoutly regretted that he had chosen to print even a dozen copies of his "Essay on Woman." The ministry caused the scandalous text to be read aloud to a packed House of Lords on November 15, 1763, the solemnity of the occasion being marred by the character of the reader, Lord Sandwich, a rake and whoremonger every bit as notorious as Wilkes.

Next door, on the same day, the House of Commons resolved that number 45 was indeed a seditious libel and moved for the common hangman publicly to burn it. In the debate, the member for Hastings, Samuel Martin, whom *The North Briton* had also roughly treated,* rose to return the favor, impugning Wilkes's personal courage.

On November 16, Martin and Wilkes fought a duel in Hyde Park. Wilkes, shot in the abdomen at a distance of six paces, survived thanks to the buttons on his clothing, which deflected the ball to his groin. Christmas found him in France, a fugitive from English justice (for the House had decided that parliamentary privilege afforded no protection against

---

* "The most treacherous, base, selfish, mean, abject, low-lived and dirty fellow that ever *wriggled* himself into a secretaryship," *The North Briton* had branded Martin, who, as secretary of the Treasury during the campaign to push across the Treaty of Paris, reportedly manned the Treasury cash window to distribute Henry Fox's bribes. Cash, *John Wilkes*, 153, 92.

seditious libel) and still aching from his open and infected wound. Even so, he had enjoyed a measure of vindication. On December 3, a Wilksite crowd overwhelmed the hangman who was attempting to burn number 45. On the sixth, Lord Chief Justice Charles Pratt in the Court of Common Pleas struck down the legality of general warrants in their application to the search of private property. And the members of the Beefsteak Club, appalled by the two-facedness of their president, Lord Sandwich, in prosecuting their fellow member Wilkes, expelled that hypocrite from the club.

The cry of "Wilkes and Liberty" meanwhile resounded on both sides of the Channel. In Paris, the famous exile basked in the company of the open-minded Frenchmen, Voltaire included, who admired his politics and marveled at his gallantry.* A nineteen-year-old Italian dancer named Gertrude Corradini gladdened his nights and caused him not to repent of their affair even after she made off with such few valuables as he possessed. Altogether, Wilkes assured a French correspondent, he was "never so happy" as in exile.[24]

It would be good if that were so, because Wilkes could not return to England except to go to prison. He was expelled from Parliament and convicted, in absentia, of libel. On November 1, 1764, following five unanswered summonses, he was declared an "outlaw," thus stripped of his rights and protections under British law by the Court of the King's Bench.

The coming of the Rockingham ministry in the summer of 1765 filled Wilkes with hope. The marquess himself, along with two of his senior colleagues, the Duke of Grafton and General Henry Conway, had been friendly enough in the past.[25] They would at least entertain his demands for relief in his hour of need. Heavily in debt, Wilkes needed money as much as or more than legal vindication. A remunerative ambassadorship, perhaps to Constantinople,[26] would be acceptable, he let it be known, along with a royal pardon, a lump sum payment to compensate him for his troubles, in and out of exile, and a reasonable pension.[27] Lauchlin Macleane, who had led the toasts at the stemware-smashing bacchanal in December

---

* "You set me in flames with your courage, and you charm me with your wit," said Voltaire. Cash, *John Wilkes*, 189–90.

1765 to celebrate Burke's election to Parliament, pressed Wilkes's case with the new government.

"Burke and Wilkes" was one of the toasts of that unforgettable party, but Burke, on sober reflection (and perhaps in obedience to Rockingham), kept Wilkes at a discreet distance. To his brother, Richard, who was preparing to visit Wilkes in France as a ministerial go-between, Burke observed that, though the motives of the former government were political, the indisputable charge against the exiled firebrand was that of blasphemy, "for which it would be rather awkward to desire his pardon."

"If Wilkes has the least Knowledge of the Nature of popularity and the smallest degree of attention to his own Interest," Burke closed, "he will wait the convenience of his friends who do not forget him. But this [is] to be insinuated more or less, or not at all according to your discretion."[28]

Discretion was never to be Wilkes's strong suit, and the exile sneaked back to London in May 1766, to argue his case in person, hiding himself at the home of a Mr. Stewart, a friend of Burke's.[29] Negotiations, some of them with Burke himself, spanned the next three weeks. With the Rockingham side declining to budge from a previously proffered payment of £1,000 a year, to be disbursed privately—an offer that Wilkes had spurned as "clandestine, eleemosynary, and precarious"—the disappointed fugitive returned to France.

Grenville's ministry ended once the king could no longer bear his first minister. No policy differences caused the breach. The problem lay rather with Grenville who, like some insolent Boston Son of Liberty, would forget himself and presume to dictate policy to the young king. "When he has wearied me for two hours," George complained, "he looks at his watch, to see if he may not tire me for an hour more."[30]

Rockingham, thirty-five years old, was personally unabrasive, clean-living (a fact that always counted with George III), and very rich; his ancestral lands in Yorkshire, Northamptonshire, and Ireland brought him £34,000 a year.[31] In 1745, at the age of fifteen, he had run away from the family estate at Wentworth to help the Duke of Cumberland fend off the Jacobite uprising of that year and give chase to the fleeing Young Pretender; it was a patriotic act of disobedience that made his parents pop their buttons. The intrepid youth grew up into a Whig grandee of no great ambition who had the good judgment to attempt few speeches in the House of Lords, where he took his seat in 1751. But he was an enlightened farmer, a knowing appraiser of ancient Roman coins, and an accomplished man of the turf who made friends and kept them, Edmund Burke not least.

What Rockingham was not was a professional politician, like Grenville, or a national hero, like Pitt, or the king's uncle, like the Duke of Cumberland. It was indeed at Cumberland's behest that George III invited Rockingham to form a new government, whose miscellaneous personnel, including Cumberland himself, comprised that inherently unstable political body, a coalition. At the start, it was not at all clear who was the first minister, as the cabinet meetings were held under Cumberland's roof. Only when the duke, who was morbidly obese, dropped dead on October 31, 1765, at the age of forty-four, was the leadership question finally settled.

THE HOUSE OF COMMONS TO WHICH BURKE WAS ELECTED FOR THE FIRST time in December 1765 could hardly have contained the 558 members who could, if they wished, have sat in it. The chamber was a former royal chapel measuring fifty-eight feet by thirty-three. To a later German visitor, the place resembled the choir of a Lutheran church in Prussia, except, presumably, for the sight of the odd MP "lying stretched out on the one of the benches." The members, not removing their coats or spurs, looked as if they had just arrived or were making ready to leave.[32] They spoke "with but little gravity," and the poor speakers had to shout to be heard above the racket of their impatient listeners. But the benches fell silent for the best speakers, men like the elder Pitt who, disdaining prepared remarks, never lacked for the right word.[33] Even so, Burke, who was almost instantly sorted among the rhetorical masters, had to strain to make himself heard, including to members and visitors (if allowed) who arrayed themselves in second-story galleries on three sides of the House.[34]

The new parliamentary session began with near unanimous agreement that the Americans needed a reminder of their properly subordinate place in the empire. Certainly, they were freeborn Englishmen, but as Burke

noted, "without subordination, it would not be one Empire. Without freedom, it would not be the British Empire."[35]

These sentiments provided the kernel of the Declaratory Act, which,
modeled on the 1719 Dependency of Ireland Act, stipulated that Parliament
"had, hath, of Right ought to have full power and Authority to make Laws
and Statutes of sufficient force and validity to bind the Colonys and People
of America Subjects of the Crown of Great Britain in all cases whatsoever." The resolution passed the House overwhelmingly, with only the Pitt
faction balking at the all-encompassing word *whatsoever.* The truth, they
held, is that Parliament had no constitutional right to lay a direct tax on
the king's American subjects.[36]

Burke had already made his first plunge into parliamentary debate. On
January 17 a colleague asked him to present a petition from the Manchester
manufacturers for relief from the Stamp Act. "I know not what struck me,"
as Burke reported to his friend O'Hara, "but I took a sudden resolution
to say something about it, though I had got it but that moment, and had
scarcely time to read it, short as it was; I did say something; what it was, I
know not upon my honour; I felt like a man drunk."

At length, Grenville himself answered Burke, who, "now heated," stood
to reply, only to be cut short by a fellow member of the Rockingham party,
Sir George Saville, who had caught the speaker's eye. "However," Burke's
account proceeds, "I had now grown a little stouter, though still giddy, and
affected with a swimming in my head; So that I ventured up again on the
motion, and spoke some minutes, poorly, but not quite so ill as before. All
I hoped was to plunge in, and get off the first horrors; I had no hopes of
making a figure."

In those modest hopes, the new member surely failed, on the authority
of no less a critic than David Garrick, the first actor of the day, who raved
about the newcomer's "Virgin Eloquence."[37]

Burke spoke extemporaneously, but informing those impromptu
remarks were hours of research into the commercial, legal, and financial
structure of the British Empire. Will Burke watched him in awe. He marveled that it was as if his friend had personally stood to gain 20 percent
from the commerce of the empire as a whole, just for himself.[38]

The work* took a heavy toll on his health[39] but won him reviews even more glowing than Garrick's. The eminent William Pitt,† the sparkling and witty Charles Townshend,‡ the bluestocking Mrs. Montagu,§ and the Great Cham himself, Samuel Johnson, soaked him in praise. "[He] gained more reputation than perhaps any man at his [first] appearance ever gained before," declared the lexicographer.[40] Burke, said a future fellow MP, with reference to the long, drawn-out American situation, "was the only man who could keep up the attention of the House on a Subject already threadbare."[41]

In keeping with the prohibition against the reporting of parliamentary speeches, no transcript of Burke's remarks exists, but scraps of evidence convey the thrust of his ideas and the stream of his words. Like Rockingham but unlike Pitt, Burke did not deny that Parliament could, by right, impose taxes for the purpose of raising revenue. What he did dispute, again in company with Rockingham, was the wisdom of exercising that right in a self-defeating cause: "There is in every Country a difference between the Ideal," reads one of the notes he made to prepare himself to speak; "and the practical constitution—They will be confounded by Pedants, they will be distinguished by men of sense; they may not follow from the rules of metaphysical reasoning but they must be the rules of Government."[42]

Not the least of the rules of government was the necessity of winning elections, and Burke urged the House to heed the protests of their con-

---

* The American question, which dominated parliamentary proceedings from February till April 1766, and of whose details Burke was an acknowledged authority, produced "one of the most exhaustive investigations carried out by the eighteenth-century House of Commons," according to the editors of Burke's *Writings and Speeches*. If British statecraft failed at this critical juncture, it was not through lack of the members' application, least of all the indefatigable Burke's. Lock, *Edmund Burke*, 1:223.

† Burke "had delivered his sentiments thr'o the Medium of a Much better understanding than he [Pitt] was ever endowed with, and with a Degree of precision which he believed was never before heard in that house." C., 1:243.

‡ "Tho he had all along formed the highest Idea of [Burke's] abilities, he owned that on that occasion he went beyond his utmost conception." C., 1:243.

§ "Mr. Burke spoke divinely, yes divinely, don't misunderstand me, and report he spoke as well as mortal man could do, I tell you he spoke better." C., 1:242.

stituents over the economic damage that Grenville's tax had dealt them. "Nothing can hurt a popular assembly so much," reads a phrase from a later note, "as the being unconnected with its constituents," the very people, he added, borrowing from the Book of Acts (17:28), "in whom we live, move and have our being."[43]

"Some say," as Burke told the House, "commerce ought to be neglected till dignity is established," that is, the dignity of the government that would presently have to retreat in the face of colonial protest. "It is wrong, because our dignity is derived from our commerce."[44]

The Rockinghams carried the resolution to repeal the Stamp Act by a vote of 275–167. The king gave the measure his assent on March 18, 1766, the same day as he signed the Declaratory Act.

News of the vote to repeal spread joy in the colonies. Bostonians and New Yorkers celebrated with fireworks and heavy drinking, the residents of Williamsburg, the colonial capital of Virginia, with a "ball and elegant entertainment."[45] The Protestant churches resounded with sermons.[46]

In their delight, the Americans overlooked the Declaratory Act, which reminded the colonists that the repeal of the Stamp Act was a decision taken to mollify British shipping and manufacturing interests, not to redefine the relationship between themselves and their imperial masters. (If that were so, Grenville demanded, the government ought to enforce the law, not run away from it.) Indeed, the Declaratory Act preceded the repeal legislation, and it, unlike the repeal, passed the Commons almost by acclamation.

The administration of the Marquess of Rockingham ended on July 30, 1766, only one year and twenty days after it began. As no great issue of public policy sped the Rockinghams to power, so none hastened their exit. The administration suffered from internal instability as well as the king's wandering eye. George III wanted a new face, in this case William Pitt's, or rather that of the 1st Earl of Chatham, as George III had raised Pitt to the peerage as part of the ministerial reshuffle. As for Rockingham, he proved as mild-mannered and generous at the end as he had been at the beginning, encouraging his followers to remain in their ministerial offices, if Lord Chatham would keep them.

An individual whom Chatham would not hire was Edmund Burke, whom a Rockingham colleague, Henry Seymour Conway, had commended to the new prime minister ("the readiest man upon all points perhaps in the whole House") as a candidate for a position on the Board of Trade. Chatham could not disagree about Burke's abilities but bridled at his economic ideas, which "can never be mine."[47] To Chatham, foreign trade existed to serve the interests of the state. Burke, who had fought unsuccessfully in Parliament to repeal the British prohibition against the export of soap from Ireland, advocated, if not free trade, then a less rigid form of mercantilism.[48]

In the immediate wake of the change of administration, Burke occupied himself by cataloguing the former government's achievements in a pamphlet entitled "Short Account of a Late Short Administration."

Besides the repeal of the Stamp Act and the corresponding declaration of the "Constitutional Superiority of Great Britain" over her obstinate and insolent (even if fiscally wronged) American colonies, the Rockinghams had led the Commons in denouncing the high-handed tactics by which the crown had prosecuted and harassed John Wilkes. They had taken steps to lower or remove cumbersome duties and regulations. They had repealed the cider tax, had "sold no Offices. They obtained no Reversions or Pensions, either coming in or going out, for themselves, their Families, or their Dependants."

"The Removal of that Administration from Power," he concluded, making the best of life in opposition,

> is not to them premature; since they were in Office long enough to accomplish many Plans of public Utility; and by their Perseverance and Resolution, rendered the Way smooth and easy to their Successors; having left their King and their Country in a much better Condition than they found them.[49]

ALMOST A YEAR HAD PASSED SINCE BURKE'S ELECTION TO PARLIAMENT. He was savoring the success he had made and enjoying the work for which he seemed to have an almost superhuman capacity. Late in 1766 he rose to speak on dangers to the national credit. Sir Matthew Fetherstonhaugh, a well-to-do landowner and member for Portsmouth, listened with admiration and bemusement. " 'But perhaps,' " he remembered Burke as saying,

"this house is not the place where our reasons can be of any avail: the *great person* who is to determine on this question may be a being far above our view; one so immeasurably high, that the greatest abilities (pointing to Mr Townshend), or the most amiable dispositions that are to be found in this house (pointing to Mr Conway), may not gain access to him; a being before whom 'thrones, dominations, princedoms, virtues, powers (waving his hand all this time over the treasury bench, which he sat behind), all veil their faces with their wings:' but though our arguments may not reach him, probably our prayers may!" He then apostrophized into a solemn prayer to the Great Minister above, that rules and governs over all, to have mercy upon us, and not to destroy the work of his own hands; to have mercy on the public credit, of which he had made so free and large a use. "Doom not to perdition that vast public debt, a mass seventy millions of which thou hast employed in rearing a pedestal for thy own statue."

At this point, Augustus Hervey, a naval officer and member for Saltash, called Burke to order, "to the regret of many."

Burke replied: "I have often suffered under persecution of order, but did not expect its lash while at my prayers."[50]

CHAPTER 5

Lord Rockingham's brain and tongue

A few thousand people who thought that the world was made for them, and that all outside their own fraternity were unworthy of notice or criticism, bestowed upon each other an amount of attention quite inconceivable to us who count our equals by millions.

—SIR GEORGE OTTO TREVELYAN, *THE EARLY HISTORY OF CHARLES JAMES FOX*, 1880

I f, on March 9, 1769, not one butterfly fluttered in the ample midsection of Charles Fox as he strode into the House of Commons, it was because that chamber was almost a second home to him. The sight of benches lined with members twice his age was hardly intimidating—he had been watching parliamentary debates since he was fourteen. Nor did the knowledge that his seat was his father's gift, and that at nineteen, he had technically been too young to claim it, seem to humble him. On the contrary, witnesses remarked on the supreme self-confidence of the new member from the rotten* borough of Midhurst.

A visitor in the strangers' gallery, spotting something extraordinary in the newcomer's swarthy face, confident bearing, and dramatic slash of eyebrow, fished around for something to draw on. Finding no paper—the rules of the House prohibited notetaking in the gallery—the onlooker sacrificed a swatch of his own shirt on which to sketch the striking figure of the youngest member of the House of Commons.[1]

---

* The borough sent two representatives to Parliament but was home to only one voter; as of 1794, at least, it counted no houses.

Only by the calendar could the brash MP be counted a political novice. Charles's father, Henry Fox, now Lord Holland, formerly the leader of the Commons and the henchman of Lord Bute, had filled his son's ear with information for the practical politician. He had told him about the futility of opposition, the sanctity of the constitution, and the evanescence of gratitude. And as Holland was a great collector of enemies, young Charles had learned whom to hate. The list encompassed the leaders of most of the Whig factions, including the Duke of Bedford; Lord Chatham, the Great Commoner; and Lord Shelburne. Neither did those grandees love Holland, memories of the wholesale proscriptions of 1762 still burning bright in their memory.

In Holland's telling, the independence of Parliament was the great desideratum. The king presented one kind of threat to that independence, the aristocracy another, the common people (though they hardly mattered) a third, and the press a fourth. And as political philosophy held small interest for Holland, neither did it much engage Charles. Factions, personalities, loyalties, honors, offices, emoluments, and most of all, hatreds were rather the basis of Foxite politics as Charles began his career.

Properly speaking, the Foxes were neither Tory nor Whig. They shared neither the archetypal Tory's reverence toward church and king, nor the pure-bred Whig's deference to the great aristocratic families who had governed the country almost uninterruptedly since William and Mary assumed the throne that James II had hurriedly vacated in 1688. Holland regarded himself as a career ministerialist, a servant of the king's government, whatever that government might be. But if one associates "Tory" with toploftiness, a deeply imbued sense of entitlement to wealth and power and social position, along with a systematic disregard for the multitudes not so endowed, Holland and his favorite son indeed conformed to the Tory type.

So thoroughly and uncritically did Charles absorb these lessons that, for all intents and purposes, the novice member was the parliamentary representative not of the rotten borough of Midhurst (whose vendable vote his father had bought) but of Lord Holland himself. The 1768 elections were a Fox family event. As Midhurst returned two members to Parliament, Holland's brother, Lord Ilchester, scooped up the other seat for his twenty-one-year-old son and heir, Lord Stavordale. Charles's elder brother, Stephen, known within the family as Ste, made his own parliamentary debut with a victory (not, in his case, bought and paid for) in the borough of Salisbury, where his grandfather and namesake, the self-made financier and courtier, had gone to school.[2]

The Rockingham government had come and gone by the time the third generation of Foxes arrived in Westminster. The successor administration, nominally headed by the gout-stricken Pitt but actually in the unsteady hands of the Great Commoner's protégé, Augustus Henry Fitzroy, 3rd Duke of Grafton, was tottering over the recurrent controversy surrounding John Wilkes and the gathering crisis in America.

Still officially outlawed, Wilkes had returned to England to resolve his legal troubles and, defiantly, to stand election for Parliament. To Grafton's dismay and the exile's delight, the voters of Middlesex chose Wilkes as one of their two representatives in the House of Commons in the general election of March 1768.

Grafton wanted no part of Wilkes and still less of Wilkes's adoring masses. The prime minister would take such steps as needed to thwart the former fugitive, Grafton assured George III, while avoiding, to the best of his ability, the appearance of punishing the Middlesex voters—of "finding fault only with the People for their Joy too riotously testified at the late Election."[3]

It was as a duly elected member of the House of Commons, therefore, that Wilkes, on April 27, surrendered to authorities to face the charges against him stemming from the publication of *North Briton* number 45 and "Essay on Woman." Convicted in 1764, he was now belatedly sentenced to two years' imprisonment. Wilkes watched the unfolding of the next phase of his political career from the window of his well-appointed cell at the King's Bench Prison, in Southwark, South London.

On May 10 massive crowds gathered at nearby St. George's Fields to demand their hero's release. British troops read the protesters the Riot Act and opened fire on the many who refused to disperse. Making political hay of the five resulting fatalities, Wilkes denounced the ministry for intentionally provoking the "St. George's Fields Massacre," as the radical press styled the killings. Grafton, who had resisted calls for the outlaw's expulsion from Parliament, now demanded it—as did the large Commons majority that voted Wilkes out of their chamber on February 3, 1769.

In a February 16 by-election to fill Wilkes's vacant seat, the Middlesex electors defiantly returned him to office. They would do the same in March and April, although on the third time around, the ministry would produce an opponent almost as doughty as Wilkes himself.

On March 8, Edmund Burke rose from his seat in the Commons. His brogue had long since become a familiar sound to his fellow MPs, but they were accustomed to hearing it at the end of debates, not at the beginning. The novelty of introducing a parliamentary resolution was "a weight upon my Mind," Burke confessed to the House. The nagging sense of a duty to speak had plagued him for months while the fear of failing had tied his tongue. Steeled to the imperative of duty, he now moved that Parliament investigate the conduct of the civil and military authorities in the May 1768 killings at St. George's Fields.

Burke assured the House that he had no intention of interfering with the courts. Neither did he support "a Lax and effeminate execution of Justice," nor the withholding from government of any of its just powers, "judicial or executive, civil or even Military." No Wilksite radical was the right-hand man, and, increasingly, the brains and the tongue, of the Marquess of Rockingham.

"Order I know must be preserved at any rate or at any price," Burke went on. "If the Voice of the Magistrate will not do it; The Staff of the Constable must do it; If the Staff fails we must have recourse to the Sword of the Soldier. If nothing but blood can purchase peace, it must be purchased with blood. Peace is the great End in *all* Governments; Liberty is an End only in the Best. I am far[,] I have ever been far[,] from entertaining any extreme or immoderate thoughts upon that subject."

As to his ideas on liberty, Burke proceeded, they "have been always very much tempered . . . pitched a key lower than I think is common, because I am afraid of myself." In all circumstances, he was, he said, by principle and constitutional makeup, a hater of both "violence and *innovation*."[4]

The Wilksite mob was hardly blameless—"in the Insolence of their

Triumph" they were "extremely outrageous." What Burke wished to condemn was the growing practice of incorporating the Army into the civil government, not reserving the troops as a final resort, after the sheriffs and petty constables and high constables had failed to keep the peace, but of mobilizing that blunt weapon as a first resort: "If you take away the Civil Execution of justice[,] you maim and mangle the whole constitutional Polity of England."

The question was put and the House divided to vote. Burke's motion failed in a landslide, 245–39.[5]

The Grafton ministry, having twice overridden the will of the Middlesex freeholders, now staged a third election, for April 13, featuring the novelty of a live opponent in the person of Henry Lawes Luttrell, army officer and eldest son of an Irish earl who had entered Parliament in 1768 for the Cornish borough of Bossiney.* Luttrell, a product of Westminster School and Christ Church, Oxford, was happy to give up his safe seat for the privilege of contesting with Wilkes, to whose excoriation he had devoted his maiden speech in the House. Though he lost, four to one, to his bête noire in the Middlesex polling, he won in Parliament two days later, as the House of Commons voted, 197–143, to uphold the resolution "that Henry Lawes Luttrell Esq. ought to have been returned a member for Middlesex to serve in this present Parliament for the county of Middlesex."[6]

In his loathing of Wilkes and disdain for the ballot box, Luttrell found fast friends in the anti-Wilksite Foxes. Holland House became a Luttrell campaign stronghold, and Ste seconded Luttrell's nomination in a speech to the Middlesex electors.[7] The parliamentary reversal of the popular vote, though it seated Luttrell, did not endear the winner to his enraged constituents. The artificial, if plucky, new member for Middlesex was hissed in theaters, accosted on the street, and attacked in the newspapers.[8] Neither did Wilkes's unseating burnish the popularity of the Fox sons.

Ste had blurted it out on the floor of the House that Wilkes owed his

* A pocket borough, a tiny seaside village with perhaps twenty cottage-size houses, Bossiney nonetheless returned two representatives to the House of Commons until the 1832 Reform Act scrubbed it from the electoral rolls.

Middlesex victories to "the scum of the earth."[9] The words came ill from the mouth of the grandson of Sir Stephen Fox, who, some remembered, had begun his storied financial career as a royal page boy. Self-appointed representatives of Fox's "scum" later accosted Stephen, in the company of Charles, on a London street, and threatened to "rip out his fat guts and let out the unaccounted millions,"[10] the final two words alluding to the fortune that, according to an unwarranted claim of the Lord Mayor of London, Henry Fox had stolen from His Majesty's Treasury.

THE MIDDLESEX FREEHOLDERS, HAVING LOST THEIR CASE IN THE COMmons, turned next to the king. Their quarrel was not with His Majesty, their petition read, but with "certain evil-minded persons, who attempt to infuse into your royal mind." Such insinuating counselors were busily replacing British liberty with executive tyranny. Issuing general warrants, denying trial by jury, harassing printers, contriving libel actions, overriding the will of the electorate, inciting military executions, and suppressing the freedom of debate in Parliament itself, they were destroying the constitution as they alienated America.

The petitioners named no minister in the Grafton government but lamented that the "irreligion and immorality, so eminently discountenanced by your majesty's royal example, encouraged by administration both by example and precept." Could the Londoners have had in mind the notorious affair of the unhappily married prime minister, the Duke of Grafton himself, with the courtesan Nancy Parsons? In April 1768 the pair had flaunted their liaison at the opera in the very presence of Queen Charlotte.[11]

Unwilling to "interrupt your royal repose," the petitioners would ordinarily have sought redress through their parliamentary representatives. But they had no representative, they reminded the king, at least none whom they had constitutionally chosen. In this regard, they cried, they were no better than slaves.[12]

WAS LIEUTENANT-COLONEL LUTTRELL, OR WAS HE NOT, FINALLY AND lawfully and irrevocably seated? The legal complexities of the question made necessary a new hearing, on May 8, 1769. Here was a matter much larger than Middlesex and Luttrell, greater, even, than the fate of the people's own Jack Wilkes. The government's contention—supported by, among others, Dr. Johnson in a pamphlet entitled *The False Alarm*—was that the House of Commons, as the arbiter of its own rules and of the fitness of its own members, was certainly within its rights to expel a representative it judged to be infamous.

Alexander Wedderburn and Burke took up the argument for Wilkes and the petitioners. Charles Fox, as undaunted by his tender age as he was by the gravitas of his opponents, rose to take the pro-Commons, anti-Wilkes side. Though his words were unrecorded, the reviews of his remarks were glowing. "He spoke with great spirit, in very parliamentary language, and entered very deeply into the question on constitutional principles," said one.[13]

Lord Holland, recipient of similar admiring reports, seemed proudest of the fact that Charles had not read from notes, let alone a text, but spoke "all off-hand, all argumentative, in reply to Mr. Burke and Mr. Wedderburn. . . . I hear it spoke of by everybody as a most extraordinary thing, and I am, you see, not a little pleased with it. My son Ste spoke too, and (as they say he always does) very short and to the purpose. They neither of them aim for oratory, make apologies, or speak of themselves, but go directly to the purpose . . . ; but I am told that Charles can never make a better speech than the one he did on Monday."[14]

It was no small thing to talk down the formidable Burke, who had sealed his own colloquial fame by besting Dr. Johnson years earlier in dinner table conversation about India.[15] Burke had been aware of Charles since 1763 or 1764, when the new MP was still a schoolboy. Marking what might have been their first meeting, the fourteen- or fifteen-year-old Fox appraised the author of *The Sublime and Beautiful* as "one of the most agreeable men I have known."[16] In any case, the ministry's side prevailed, and Luttrell and Wilkes remained, respectively, in the House of Commons and jail.

It was, however, Burke's defense of Wilkes that earned its speaker international recognition. When the Boston Sons of Liberty sat down to an open-air dinner in Dorchester on August 14, 1769, they raised their glasses, first to the king, "Queen and Royal family," and then, at length, to Wilkes and the "illustrious Patriots in Ireland"; "the free and independent electors of the county of Middlesex in Great Britain"; Catherine Macaulay, the freethinking English author; "Paoli Pascal, the brave Corsican" (Corsica having recently fallen victim to a French invasion); William Beckford, the Whiggish Lord Mayor of London; the Marquess of Rockingham—and the Wilksite friend of America, "Mr. Bourke."[17]

IN THE AUTUMN OF 1769, CHARLES, HIS YOUNGER BROTHER HENRY, AND their parents decamped to Paris, where Charles, in the words of his biographical descendant, Earl Russell, "made himself remarked for his losses at play." Madame du Deffand, the hostess and *salonnière*, was one of those who shook her head in wonder at how easily gold coins slipped through the young man's fingers.[18] Further acquaintance with Fox did not lessen her disapproving amazement, either of him or of his boon companion, Richard FitzPatrick. "Where they get the money, I do not understand," Deffand—then in her late seventies but, as the long-ago mistress of the Regent of France, well versed in the ways of wealth and power—wrote to her friend Horace Walpole.

> I should never have believed it, if I had not seen for myself that there could be such madness. . . .
>
> No doubt [Fox] has plenty of spirit, and above all great talents. But I am not sure that he is right in the head. . . . He seems to live in a sort of intoxication. . . . I declare it horrifies me; his future seems to me frightful. . . . At twenty-four to have lost everything, to owe more than one could ever pay, and not even to care about it: nothing is more extraordinary. . . . It is such a pity: he has so much intelligence, goodness, and truthfulness, but that does not prevent him being detestable.[19]

Charles returned to London, and to business, on the eve of the opening of the 1770 parliamentary session. He gambled all night at the Star and Garter Tavern in Pall Mall, hard by the Houses of Parliament, and presented his rumpled, sleepless form to the Commons on January 9, but he spoke there with "much applauded fire."[20]

On January 25 he was on his feet again in the House to join the debate over the perennial Middlesex question. Petitions and remonstrances against the Grafton ministry's conduct toward Wilkes were descending on Parliament and the crown; before long, 38,000 freeholders accounting for between a quarter and a third of the "county," or country, voters in England and Wales, affixed their signatures to documents demanding relief from the Commons' electoral high-handedness. In the cities, 17,000 petitioning Englishmen and Welshmen represented about 20 percent of the urban vote. True, for the most part, the "the soberest & most weighty part of the nation" refrained from joining the "patriotic" movement, as Wilkes's cause was known; though, as the ministerialist John Robinson put it, in their impressive raw numbers, the protests "affect the vulgar & may rouse a spirit which wd better be quieted."[21]

Neither was Rockingham so keen on raising "a spirit" among the aggrieved multitudes. It was thanks to Burke's firm and respectful advocacy* that the Rockinghams came to encourage petitioners beyond Middlesex, and to orchestrate petitions to the crown, as the Middlesex freeholders had done, rather than only to the House of Commons. For Burke, the fundamental problem was "the whole scheme of weak, divided and dependent administrations," a type that encompassed Rockinghams' firefly incumbency as well the foreshortened Grafton ministry.

Grafton—who once defused a diplomatic crisis with the clever ruse of dispatching a hot-headed royal naval officer halfway around the world to allow that officer's warlike provocation to be constructively forgotten by an aggrieved French court (in which diversion the prime minister had a friendly accomplice in the French ambassador)—had a great capacity for friendship and little inclination to rancor. Of Grafton, Fox said that he

---

* "It was only Edmund Burke's persistence, supported by [William] Dowdeswell," the Rockinghams' leader on the floor of the House, "that overcame the objections of the other Rockinghamite leaders to the course of petitioning the Crown for a redress of grievances." Rudé, Wilkes and Liberty, 107.

would act with him "with more pleasure, in any possible situation, than with any one I have ever been acquainted with." When Wilkes first went to jail, Grafton paid him a visit, not to lend political support but to hear the prisoner's side of the story.[22]

Now, as prime minister, Grafton deplored the "rage of popular clamor" and speculated that the instigators of the petition drives, presumably including the energetic Burke, could expose themselves to criminal prosecution on account of allegations "injurious to Parliament, and dangerous to the Constitution."[23] William de Grey, member for Newport, Cornwall, a government man and former solicitor-general, said that it was shocking to him that such "base-born people" as the "mechanics and booksellers" of Westminster should have the temerity "to address the Throne, whose gates they ought not to enter."

The Lord Mayor of London, William Beckford, to whom the Sons of Liberty had lifted a toast, reminded the House that "the 40 [shilling] free-holder* has as good a right as a large property-owner to send a man to Parliament. I never measure the patriotism of a man by the number of his acres. I have known the greatest rascals in the Kingdom in laced coats."[24]

The January 25 debate featured Wedderburn, once more taking Wilkes's side, laying it down with a scholar's authority that no judicial precedent existed to support the ministry's position. "Young Charles Fox, of age but the day before, started up and entirely confuted Wedderburne," Walpole reported of the jurist's unexpected antagonist, "producing a case decided in the courts below but the last year, and exactly similar to that of Wilkes. The Court, he said, had no precedent, but had gone by analogy. The House roared with applause."[25]

GRAFTON'S GOVERNMENT, WEAKENED BY MINISTERIAL DEFECTIONS
and by its leader's own preference for hunting and racing over the business

---

* Ownership of property that yielded, or could yield, forty shillings, or two pounds, a year, was the minimum to qualify a man for the vote under a law dating from 1429 in the reign of Henry VI.

of state,* was hanging by a thread when the reluctant prime minister submitted his resignation on January 29, 1770. Succeeding him was the wry
and amiable Frederick, Lord North, a choice that exactly suited Charles
Fox's mother. "I hope," wrote Lady Holland from Nice, where she and
Lord Holland were vacationing, "Lord North has courage and resolution.
Charles being connected with him pleases me mightily. I have formed a
very high opinion of his lordship, and my Charles will, I dare say, inspire
him with courage."[26]

Charles's retentive memory, deep store of knowledge, spontaneous wit,
and fast-paced, "impetuous eloquence" would have been a formidable
weapon on the opposition side of the House.[27] That North fully realized as
much was obvious in the prime minister's almost immediate conferral on
the young member from Midhurst an appointment as a junior lord of the
Admiralty. Some began to speak of the "phenomenon of the age."[28]

Still, the patriotic clamor continued, with the livery of the City of London moving to the head of the line of petitioners.[29] The previous July seven
city emissaries appeared at a levy to hand a remonstrance to the king, as
was their right. Receiving the unwanted document, His Majesty handed
it to a lord-in-waiting and "instantly" turned to resume conversation with
the Danish minister, Baron Dieden.[30] As George III may or may not have
discovered in his own reading, the petitioners recited the by-now-familiar
grievances associated with the Wilkes prosecution, for instance, the issue
of general warrants, the seizing of persons and private papers, and the
trampling of the right to trial by jury. They anticipated a contention of
Burke's that the king's corrupt advisers had "brought into disrepute the
civil magistracy, by the appointment of persons who are, in many respects,
unqualified for that important trust, and have thereby purposefully furnished a pretence for calling in the aid of a military power."

And the City of Londoners added this: "By a scandalous misapplication
and embezzlement of the public treasure, and a shameful prostitution of

---

* "We read of a Cabinet meeting specially summoned by the Prime Minister and then not
attended by him, in consequence of some engrossing interest at [the racecourse at] Newmarket." Fitzroy, *Autobiography*, xxxiv.

public honors and employments; procuring deficiencies of the civil list to be made good without examination; and, instead of punishing, conferring honors on a pay-master, the public defaulter of unaccounted millions"— that is, Lord Holland.

The debate on the floor was over a motion to censure the petitioners for attempting to withdraw "His Majesty's Subjects from their Obedience to the Laws of the Realm." Stephen Fox spoke in favor and Burke, immediately following Charles's brother, argued, in a politically nuanced way, against.

Before long, Burke would publish his *Thoughts on the Cause of the Present Discontents*, the first of his great political tracts. In the House of Commons on March 19, he furnished a preview of that masterwork in remarks that Henry Cavendish, one of the earliest parliamentary reporters, captured on the wing.

Burke counseled against hard measures toward the angry, perhaps impudent, authors of the remonstrance, who had gone so far as to declare that "the present house of commons do not represent the people." "In a legal, and technical sense of reasoning," Cavendish records Burke as saying,

> The house of Commons is the only representative of the people. Sir, this is technically true, let the conduct of that House of Commons be what it will. I am bold to say, legally, and technically speaking, they are the representatives of the people. But the people of the city of London, who are not so well instructed as we are in the principles of law, proceed by a sort of rough, vulgar common sense upon this question—to make parliament the only Representatives of the people, they think there should be some agreement with the people: they think there should be some attention to their interests. We know, that this house is just as much the representatives of the people, as if they had the greatest connexion with their opinions: but we know, because we are enlarged in our opinions, but they are confined, we know, sir, in our opinions, we know from Lord Coke, from whom you have learnt, and whom you might teach, that every man's reason is not the reason of the law.

It was the part of wisdom, then, not to antagonize the petitioners by condemning them—"There is no reason for taking a violent step for plunging yourselves into new difficulties."

It was in the tradition of the Fox family not to oppose the government, whoever led it, but to serve it and, of course, to profit by it. Burke, who remarked that, on any given question, he was likely to be found in the minority, was born for the opposition in which he would spend all but a scattered few months of his career, and he did not waste the opportunity to remind the House of the grievances in the London petition.

Under the Grafton ministry, between 1768 and 1769, English exports to the thirteen colonies had fallen by £698,000, or 31 percent. The petitioners, said Burke, see in America "a state of rebellion, or next to rebellion," yet the ministry had taken no action. "They feel the loss of their trade, they feel the loss of national dignity, they feel the discontents of the Colonies."

They lament, too, the government's submission to the French conquest of Corsica and the decline in the market price of British perpetual sovereign bonds, the 3 percent consols, to slightly over 84, from just shy of 90 in 1769. It was a distressed price, a "war price," though Britain was at peace.

"They see," Burke went on ("the house was rather noisy," Cavendish reported), "I am making a detail of the affairs of this country, that makes the people think the House of Commons is not their representative."

The authors of the remonstrance had complained about "the secret unremitting influence of the worst of counsellors," and Burke repeated the charge. He spoke of "a dark, secret influence which deranges, and makes perpetual changes in Administration, disabling them from doing any good, but not from doing anything bad: and this house takes no notice of it."

Governments came and went, some of them, like Rockingham's, in the blink of an eye. Seven prime ministers had held office since 1757, and all but one, the Duke of Newcastle, were still alive. "Each had his day. The parliament supported it." Now came North, "whom God long preserve, for whom this house has the greatest respect."

Burke denied any intent to cast blame but only to explain the vehemence of the petitioners from the City of London:

When they see so many marks of dissatisfaction in government: when they see Ireland, which I wonder by the bye I forgot to mention; when they had seen Ireland in a state of very great distraction, the parliament hastily prorogued, no appearance of a Session for two, for four years: when the people see the situation of the City of London, of America, of things at home, and in Ireland, they believe there is misconduct in Government. Fancying the House of Commons take no notice of it, they think, they are not their representatives. They think so grossly, vulgarly, not legally, and technically speaking.[31]

Burke himself admitted to a weakness for "vehemence and asperity" in parliamentary debate. But there was a kind of rapture, too, in his rhetorical invention, quite as spontaneous as Fox's but even richer in allusion and metaphor. "All kinds of figures of speech crowded upon him," James Boswell observed. "He was like a man in an orchard where boughs loaded with fruit hung around him, and he pulled apples as fast as he pleased and pelted the Ministry."[32] It was a mark of Burke's rise in the world that the ministerialists and their agents were beginning to pelt him back.

Even before the publication of *Thoughts on the Cause of the Present Discontents* in April 1770, Burke was under heavy suspicion of writing the brilliant, cruel, lacerating, and deeply informed political essays whose author signed himself "Junius." Whoever he was, Junius had little use for the king and the purest contempt for the king's prime minister. "Sullen and severe without religion, profligate without gaiety, you may live like Charles II, without being an amiable companion, and for aught I know may die as his father did, without the reputation of a martyr."* So wrote Junius of the Duke of Grafton. The mystery man, with his unmatched malice and almost too polished prose, became the talk of the town.[33]

---

* In 1788 a spiritually transformed Grafton issued a pamphlet urging "the Clergy, Nobility and Gentry" of England to renounce their "irreligion and profaneness" so as to set an example for the rest of society. "The common people must be brought to see, in their superiors, a more general attachment to religion, and to the service of the Church, before you can expect any alteration to take place in their morals. The very mention of such an idea subjects me, I am aware, to the derision of many." Fitzroy, *Hints &c. Submitted*, 5–10.

The antagonists of the Rockingham party would not have wasted their invective on a political nullity, and there was no doubt whom Sir William Bagot, Tory MP for Staffordshire, had in mind when, at the end of March 1770, he said that "the business of Parliament might, very well, and quietly, and perhaps to better purpose, be conducted without so much learning and so much oratory as the House abounded with at present." Bagot resumed the offensive a few days later with the well-traveled smear that Burke was "a Black Jesuit, educated at St *Omer's*, fit to be secretary to an inquisition for burning heretics."[34] For the next twenty years, hostile caricaturists would follow Bagot's lead by depicting the Church of England communicant as a soutane-and-biretta-outfitted Jesuit sitting down to a dinner of potatoes and whiskey.

As Burke was worth attacking, so was he worth protecting, and Lord John Cavendish, a son of the 3rd Duke of Devonshire, mounted such a stout defense that Bagot suddenly recalled how much he admired Burke's *Sublime and Beautiful*—really, the book was "beyond description." Swatting away that proffered hand of friendship, Burke took up the topic of English social class in a changing world. He himself was a member of a new breed, which he designated *Novus homo*.

The new man was just the one to enunciate the political creed of the Rockingham party, which Burke did to the applause both of his contemporaries and of readers unborn. He wrote for the Rockingham leadership as much as he did for the public, as the aristocrats were little given to abstract political thinking. The party indeed had no ideology and no grand program. It was, in a sense, its virtues: high-mindedness, nobility of spirit, adherence to the constitution. Let others lower themselves in the scramble for office and emoluments. Rockingham's party was above such things (or, perhaps, as some might have imagined, too rich to need to compete for them). *Thoughts on the Cause of the Present Discontents* was Burke's thirty-thousand-word explanation of what the Rockinghams were about.

That something was wrong with Great Britain was, to Burke, a point too obvious to belabor. The government was indolent, except where it was despotic. "Rank, and office, and title" no longer commanded the respect they once had. The colonies were "slackened in their affection and loosened from their obedience." Everything indeed was confused and off-kilter—in parties, in Parliament, even in families.

The people were not to blame, Burke wrote. Not that they were always in the right. In fact, they were "frequently and outrageously" in the wrong. However, "I do say that in all disputes between them and their rulers the presumption is at least upon a par in favor of the people."

What was wrong, Burke went on, was rather the spread of the insidious power of the "King's friends." It undermined Parliament. It subverted the strength of formerly independent political parties and factions: "A cabal of the closet [i.e., the king's inner sanctum] and back-stairs was substituted in the place of a national Administration."[35]

Burke rejected the twin fears of government by the mob (the third house of Parliament, said the wits) or by the sleepy peers in the House of Lords. The clear and present danger stemmed from "the sinister designs of wicked men, who have engrossed the Royal power."[36]

Unlike Junius, Burke attacked no individuals, but he did name Lord Bute, under whose direction Charles Fox's father had scattered the Whig officeholders of 1762 to the four winds and by whose impetus the "Court Cabal" came into being.[37]

Then as now, the unqualified friends of the concept of party or faction were few and mute. Bute spoke for many when, in the House of Lords in 1766, he declared that "all faction and party ought as much as possible to be discouraged; and that the present Ministry [the Marquess of Rockingham's] ought to enlarge their bottom from different sides."[38] Or, as Chatham had earlier put it, "Not men, but measures."

No, Burke insisted, men must govern, men connected by friendship, principle, common interest, long association. In such a party, "the most inconsiderable man, by adding to the weight of the whole, has his value, and his use; out of it, the greatest talents are wholly unserviceable to the public." Isolated individuals artfully installed in makeshift ministries for the very purpose of failing were no match for the king's friends: "When bad men combine, the good must associate; else they will fall, one by one, an unpitied sacrifice in a contemptible struggle."

"If," Burke concluded,

the reader believes that there really exists such a Faction as I have described; a Faction ruling by the private inclinations of a Court, against the general sense of the people; and that this Faction, whilst it pursues a scheme for undermining all the foundations of our free-dom, weakens (for the present at least) all the powers of executory Government, rendering us abroad contemptible, and at home dis-tracted; he will believe also, that nothing but a firm combination of public men against this body, and that, too, supported by the hearty concurrence of the people at large, can possibly get the better of it.[39]

George Onslow, MP for Guildford, once a loyal follower of the Marquess of Rockingham, had voted for the repeal of the Stamp Act and against the expulsion of John Wilkes. But now, in February and March 1771, a con-verted pro-government man, he was leading the Commons in the condem-nation of the newspaper publishers who had willfully violated the ancient strictures against the reporting of parliamentary debates. How would the likes of the *Political Register* skirt the rule against notetaking in the vis-itors' gallery? Why, they would station Augustine Wall, equipped with nothing more than an astonishing memory, to listen and report, usually with passable accuracy.[40]

When a pair of officials of the City of London set free a number of the publishers and printers who had been taken into custody for reporting on the proceedings of the House of Commons, George III lent his weight to Onslow's cause. To the prime minister, Lord North, His Majesty demanded that the two defiant officeholders, Lord Mayor Brass Crosby and Alderman Richard Oliver, be committed to the Tower, lest the authority of the House be "totally annihilated."[41]

The question was one for the Commons to decide, and the formida-ble John Dunning, a defender of Wilkes whose learning and eloquence earned him £300* per court appearance, argued for the freedom of the

---

* Samuel Johnson's government pension brought him exactly that amount once a year.

press. One of his contentions was that the voice of the House was not necessarily the voice of the people, and it was this strand of his argument that Charles Fox, rising to speak on behalf of the North government, chose to attack.

As usual, Fox spoke fast, one word chasing another yet each word placed where a painstaking author, reading over his draft at leisure, would have wanted it. No, Fox allowed, Parliament was not the people. It was something better.

The constitution had appointed the House "the only revealers of the national mind, the only judges of what ought to be the sentiments of the kingdom," and, beyond that, "an assembly of the first property in the state." Whatever duty the members owed to their constituents, they owed a higher one to justice. "We are chosen the delegates of the British electors for salutary not for pernicious purposes; to guard, not to invade the constitution: to keep the privileges of the very freemen we represent, as much within their proper limits, as to control any unwarrantable exertion of the royal authority."

Democracy was no part of the English constitution, Fox went on. To maintain the constitution in its present form was the duty that the members were sworn to uphold. They were "neither to encroach upon the legal jurisdiction of the peers, nor the just prerogatives of the sovereign," but as a necessary part of the constitution, "to maintain the privileges of parliament."

"Perhaps the Honorable and Learned Gentleman," Fox continued, addressing Dunning,

> will tell me, that nothing but the "soul of absurdity" could suspect the people of a design against their own happiness. Sir, I do not suspect the people of any such design, but I suspect their capacity to judge of their true happiness. I know they are generally credulous, and generally uninformed; captivated by appearances, while they neglect the most important essentials, and always ridiculously ready to believe, that those men who have the greatest reason from their extensive property, to be anxious for the public

safety, are always concerting measures for the oppression of their own posterity.

Like his father before him, Charles Fox wished the rabble to know how little he cared for their opinions, knowledge, and judgment. "If," said Fox,

we are driven from the direct line of justice, by the threats of a mob, our existence is useless in the community. The minority within doors, need only assault us by their myrmidons without, to gain their ends upon every occasion. Blows will then carry what their arguments cannot effect, and the people will be their own agents, though they elect us to represent them in parliament. What must the consequence be? Universal anarchy, Sir.

He concluded: "Therefore as we are chosen to defend order, I am for sending those magistrates to the Tower who have attempted to destroy it; I stand up for the constitution, not for the people; if the people attempt to invade the constitution, they are the enemies to the nation."[42]

The government carried the motion, and Crosby and Oliver went to the Tower, in Oliver's case to the cell, or rather "apartment," that Wilkes had comfortably occupied. A year earlier Dunning had spoken so long and so well in support of the London petitioners that the municipal authorities presented him with a golden box, inside of which was a certificate granting him the Freedom of the City of London.

The people had heard Fox and his brother, too, and so had the "rabble." By one account, the junior lord of the Admiralty Charles goaded them from the window of a coffeehouse in Palace Yard. "This youth," according to the unfriendly *London Evening Post*, "for above half an hour, was . . . shaking his fist at the people, and provoking them by all the reproachful words and menacing gestures that he could invent." And as Fox was egging on the crowd, so was his friend George Selwyn, gambler and wit and himself a member of Parliament,* pounding on Fox's back to spur him on.

"These are our Senators," the *Evening Post*'s correspondent lamented; "these are the men whom our gracious King supports, and for whose sake he exposes his person to something much more serious than scorn and contempt. I am truly sorry to see him so shamefully ill-advised."[43]

* Albeit one who never once spoke a word in the House on any occasion in forty-four years.

CHAPTER 6

An unmanageable creature of the state

I am arrived at the pinnacle of all that I covet, by affirming
the Company shall, in spite of all the envy, malice, faction and
resentment, acknowledge they are become the most opulent
company in the world.

—ROBERT CLIVE, 1725–74, FIRST BRITISH GOVERNOR OF THE BENGAL

PRESIDENCY OF THE EAST INDIA COMPANY

Ralph Verney, born in 1714, second son of a Buckinghamshire land-owner, was twenty-three years old when his elder brother's death left him heir to the family title and estates. His marriage, in 1740, to Mary Herring, daughter of a director of the Bank of England, added a wedding dowry of more than £40,000 to the Verneys' already substantial means.

The death of Verney's father, in 1752, unlocked the family gold, and Ralph, now the 2nd Earl Verney in the Irish province of Leinster, set about spending it. He cast his eye on Claydon House, the Verneys' Buckinghamshire family seat. It was stately enough, to be sure, but a distant runner-up in scope and magnificence to Stowe House, the neighboring palace of the political Grenvilles. Verney envisioned a new wing to his two-story, seven-bay residence, complete with a domed rotunda and a grand ballroom, and he put the design in motion. For the here and now, he commissioned Luke Lightfoot, woodcarver extraordinaire, to create pedimented door cases, wall niches, ceiling ornamentation, and inlaid ivory and marquetry for the grand staircase leading to the first floor. Gardens, trees, books, and pictures would complete the visible evidence of the countywide balance of power tilting in favor of the Verneys.

The new earl entered Parliament in 1753 as member for the family-controlled borough of Wendover. An alumnus of Christ's College, Cambridge, he was elected a fellow of the Royal Society in 1758. "A man of great plainness" was a tribute he received in death, but it was not so in life. "Lavish in his personal expenses, and fond of show," a county history records,

> he was one of the last of the [Irish] nobility who, to the splendour of
> a gorgeous equipage, attached musicians constantly attendant upon
> him, not only on state occasions but in his journeys and visits: a brace
> of tall negroes with silver French horns behind his coach and six,
> perpetually making a noise.[1]

The music lover sat mostly silent in the House of Commons, but he spent loyally, and easily within his £10,000 per annum income, in support of the government, and more broadly, as he put it, of "the business of the Crown." And when, in 1762, the successor administration of Lord Bute presented its plan for the Peace of Paris to the House of Commons, Verney got on his feet to second the motion. Lord Holland had asked William Burke to prod the reluctant orator to make the effort, and William found the right words.

It happened that Lord Holland and Verney each counted William Burke as his protégé. The relationship with Holland was cut-and-dried: William was supplicant, debtor, and acolyte. Matters were more complex with Verney. Though fourteen years older than William and William's unquestioned superior in society, politics, and wealth, Verney at times seemed almost to be under the younger man's spell. "He has as great a sway with Lord Verney, as I ever knew one man to have with another," attested Lord Holland in November 1763, in the wake of the signing of the peace to which Verney lent his voice.[2]

When the Rockinghams came briefly to power, in July 1765, it was William Burke, not Edmund, who joined the government as undersecretary of state to General Henry Seymour Conway. It was a signal honor for a man who was known, if at all, as an author, with Edmund Burke, of *An Account of the European Settlements in America* (1757), as a minor colonial functionary in the West Indies, and as the self-interested advocate of the theory that sugar-rich Guadeloupe (in which William had quietly accumulated some real estate during his year of colonial service) was a richer jewel in the imperial diadem than all of frozen Canada.

The elevation of William was pleasing to Verney, reflecting, as it did, some measure of respect, however oblique, on himself. Rockingham removed all doubts about Verney's political standing when, four months later, he named the earl a privy councilor. Verney, who had never held ministerial office, was properly grateful, and he never strayed far from the Rockingham fold.

As a member of the government, even a subministerial undersecretary, William needed a seat in Parliament, and Verney stood ready to supply one. Since the earl had exchanged his family borough for the Welsh constituency of Carmarthen, Wendover was in his gift, and he offered it to William. (No mere trinket, as such rotten boroughs commanded prices in the thousands of pounds.) Declining it, William persuaded Verney that Edmund, his talented kinsman, would be a worthier recipient. Verney agreed but did not stop trying to advance William's career. In 1766 he eased his friend into a seat in the East Wiltshire constituency of Great Bedwyn.

All this cost money. Verney had his £10,000 a year, and the Burkes had recently come into funds of their own: £3,000 on the death of William's father in 1764, and £6,000 on the death of Edmund's older brother, Garrett, in 1765. In 1766, Lord Holland lent the Burkes, collectively, £500, as Edmund, William, and Edmund's younger brother, Richard, formed a single financial unit. Before long, the Burkes were counting their unrealized profits from Verney-financed speculation in the shares of the East India Company.

FOUNDED ON NEW YEAR'S EVE 1600, THE GOVERNOR AND COMPANY OF Merchants of London Trading into the East-Indies, as its baptismal name resounds, was a commercial enterprise and private nation-state combined. The largest business enterprise in the world, it exchanged Britain's gold and silver for India's spices, silks, muslins, saltpeter, opium, and tea. A quasi-sovereign power, it deployed an army and navy, entered into treaties, and made war. And if it did not consistently earn a high return for its English shareholders, it was the Bank of England itself for its enterprising employees, or "servants," whose lucrative side businesses absorbed as much of their time and attention as the operations of the company that employed them.

The company's affairs would preoccupy Edmund Burke at intervals throughout his parliamentary career, alternately as supporter, critic, and prosecutor. Misconceived speculation in the shares of the East India Company would bankrupt the lesser Burkes, William and Richard, and therefore—as the kinsmen shared a common purse—would impoverish Edmund. Charles James Fox, too, would play his part in the fortunes of the corporation whose financial travails soon contributed to the provocations that brought about the American Revolution.

By the grant of Queen Elizabeth I, the East India Company enjoyed the exclusive right to conduct English trade east of the Cape of Good Hope and west of the Straits of Magellan. As a near monopoly, the company was as well-hated and well-envied as any modern-day technology giant. Some of its critics resented the wealth that a lucky few servants trundled home; others, the simple fact of the company's government-conferred exclusivity; and still others, including Adam Smith, the "strange absurdity" of a joint stock company exercising sovereign power over millions of people half a world away from its corporate boardroom.* Meanwhile, William Beckford, radical voice of the City of London (and slave owner), rose in Parliament to denounce an "unconstitutional monopoly" that generated a "revenue of two millions [a year] in India, acquired God knows how, by unjust wars with the natives. That their servants come home with immense fortunes obtained by rapine and oppression, yet the Proprietors received no increase of dividend."³

Geography alone made the company unwieldy, if not impossible, to manage. Directives from India House on Leadenhall Street in London were six to ten months on the water before reaching Fort William, the company stronghold in Calcutta, on the northeastern coast of the subcontinent. Thus a year or more would elapse before a letter in response to a communication reached London on a return voyage, by which time

* Smith, *Wealth of Nations*, 602.

commodity prices, wars, consumer tastes, the company's financial position, or other critical business variables were likely to have rendered irrelevant one or both ends of the seagoing correspondence.

In ignorance did India House manage, and in ignorance did the buyers
and sellers of East India securities invest. The company briefed the proprietors on the general state of the business at least four times a year but
issued nothing resembling what a modern investor would recognize as
intelligible financial statements. It was the dividend payout, and the expectations for future disbursements, that provided the main objective under-
pinning of the stock price.*

There was no law against trading on what is today known as material
nonpublic information. It might well violate the canons of taste, which
Lord Holland frequently did to the cost of his reputation and that of his
sons, but the tasteless offender faced no risk of prosecution under the law.
In any case, with regard to the East India Company, there was precious little current material information, public or nonpublic, to go on.

While the charter of 1600 spared the company from British competition in India, it could not keep the French or the Dutch away. Nor could
it protect the company from the vicissitudes of Indian politics, from the
demands of Britain's own revenue-hungry House of Commons, from its
dividend-seeking proprietors, or from the ever-present temptation of its
distant employees to feather their own nests.†

It is debatable, in fact, whether such monopolistic privilege as the crown
conferred helped or hindered the company and its owners, creditors, and
customers. Without British competitors, the monopolists seemed to forget who their customers were. Unfocused on pleasing others, the direc-

* Surveying the eighteenth-century London stock market, contemporary scholars found
one exception to the general tendency of share prices to rise and fall in accordance with
corporate earnings: "It is only in the case of the East India Company that share prices have
no statistically significant relation to profitability." Mirowski, "Rise (and Retreat)," 575.

† Among the committees by which the directors attempted to govern their distant enterprise were those on "Private Trade" and on the "Prevention of Private Trade." That they
coexisted suggested management's ambiguity toward their servants' divided loyalties.
Bowen, *Revenue and Reform*, 35.

tors, executives, employees, and stockholders rather worked to enrich themselves, whether in overpaying for shipping services (as some of the shipowning directors were wont to do) or demanding and receiving an imprudently high dividend (as the proprietors recurrently did).

ROBERT CLIVE HAD COME TO INDIA AS AN EIGHTEEN-YEAR-OLD CLERK, or "writer," in 1744. It had taken him fifteen alternately storm-tossed and becalmed months to reach the place that he immediately wished he had never laid eyes on. Friendless, discouraged, and heavily in debt, the future hero of the Battle of Plassey would have ended his career before it started except for the twin misfirings of the pistol with which he intended to kill himself. His life spared, he resolved to succeed and duly advanced from secretarial drudgery to more demanding work in the accountant's office. He availed himself of the company library and presently found his métier as a commissioned ensign in the East India Company military service. (He had always been a scrapper.)

Plucky and resourceful, Clive distinguished himself in small-unit actions against the French who, like the British, were maneuvering to gain a commercial and military foothold in Bengal. Major Stringer Lawrence, Clive's superior, called his underling, now Lieutenant Clive, a "born soldier."

As lucky with money as he was in battle, the soldier was presently earning commissions on the supplies he procured as commissary for the company's troops. The now Captain Clive and his new bride, the seventeen-year-old Margaret Maskelyne, embarked for England in March 1753, "two days after Clive had arranged for all of his estate in India to be invested in diamonds."[4]

It was not unusual for the company's servants to return home with pocketsful of money; Clive himself, not yet thirty, was worth £40,000. Nor was it unheard of for these nabobs to turn on their heels and go right back to India, as Clive and Margaret did in 1755. It was on this tour of duty, Clive's second of three, that the company secured control of the province of Bengal. For the capture of that prize, the directors and stockholders of the East India Company had Clive to thank. He was, as he didn't mind reminding India House, the victor of the Battle of Plassey, on June 23, 1757.

In truth, the victory near the Plassey mango groves owed as much to treachery as it did to firepower. A company force of 3,000, led by Clive, faced 50,000 Bengalis, their elephants "all covered with scarlet embroidery," their "drawn swords glittering in the sun," their "heavy cannon drawn by vast trains of oxen."[5] Fortunately for Clive, a senior figure in the opposing Bengali force, Mir Jafar, was true to his treacherous word: he betrayed his side as soon as the fighting started. It was Jafar's duplicity, combined with Clive's seducing words (and to be sure, cool head under fire) that won the day. Now, in conformity with the terms of his perfidy, Jafar became, at least in name, the Nawab of Bengal. He paid the company an immediate cash settlement of £2.5 million along with the promise of future revenue. He expelled French traders from Bengal and presented Clive with gifts worth £234,000 along with a *jagir*, a swath of real estate that produced, for Clive, an annual income of £27,000.

The victor, his eye on a comfortable future in England, made further personal investments in diamonds and negotiated the purchase of bills to be drawn on the Dutch East India Company in the grand total of £230,000. When he returned to Great Britain in 1760, he was worth £300,000. Lord Chatham hailed him as a "heaven-born general."[6] To the East India directors, Clive summed up his achievements in these few words: "this great revolution, so happily brought about, seems complete in every respect."[7]

Clive went back to India for a third and final time in May 1765 to effect a revolution in revenue. Within three months of his arrival, he inveigled a concession that, so he said, would raise the company to its greatest glory and highest prosperity. This was nothing less than the right to collect and retain the tax receipts of the so-called Mughal provinces of Bengal, Bihar, and Orissa. The privilege was an office, a "Diwani."

The territory thus acquired was an area larger than France and Spain combined. It boasted a population of 20 million and an army of fifty thousand. It would generate vast riches for remittance to Britain, so everyone agreed.[8]

"Every object, every sanguine wish is upon the point of being completely fulfilled," exulted Clive to his friend Robert Orme, "and I am arrived at the pinnacle of all that I covet, by affirming the company shall, in spite of all the envy, malice, faction and resentment, acknowledge they are become the most opulent company in the world."[9]

A commentator on the Indian side of the transaction correctly saw the matter in a different light. "The English have now acquired dominion over the three subahs [provinces] and have appointed their own district officers, they make assessments and collections of revenue, administer justice, appoint and dismiss collectors and perform other functions of governance," concluded Ghulam Husain Salim Zaydpuri, a clear-eyed contemporary Muslim historian. "The sway and authority of the English prevails . . . and their soldiers are quartering themselves everywhere in the dominions of the Nawab, ostensibly as his servants, but acquiring influence over all affairs. Heaven knows what will be the eventual upshot of this state of things."[10]

To secure these lucrative privileges, Clive pledged to the emperor, Shah Alam II, an annual cash payment and the protection of the company's armed forces. Terms were solemnized in the Treaty of Allahabad, which was "done and finished in less time than would usually have been taken up for the sale of a jack-ass," as another historian, Ghulam Hussain Khan, described it. The date was August 12, 1765.[11]

Clive, who would devote the next two years to checking his employees' tendency toward "Rapacity and Luxury" (though sparing himself his own prohibitions against personal speculation on the company clock), now sat down to the pleasant work of reporting home on his triumphs. To the officers and directors at Leadenhall Street, he advised that the Diwani would yield an annual revenue of £1,650,900. Less circumspect with private correspondents, he reckoned the value of the new arrangements at as much as £4 million a year.[12] In any case, he said, the company would no longer need to send silver and gold to India to pay for the products it shipped to England; Indian tax revenues themselves would pay for the silks and muslins and tea that filled the company warehouses.

What Clive did not foresee was the risk of collections running smaller, and the costs of military action trending higher, than he had projected. Bedazzled by the imagined future, he predicted a doubling in the price of the company's shares within three years.[13] In September 1765, he instructed his agents in London: "I must request that you will invest all the money that you may have of mine in India stock for I am convinced something very advantageous must proceed from the present flourishing condition of the East India Company. You will therefore, if you can, purchase stock with the gold sent you by this ship, either in Holland or England."[14]

And six months later, with more urgency: "Whatever Money I may have in the public Funds, or anywhere else, and as much as can be borrowed in my name, I desire may be, without loss of a minute, invested in East India Stock."[15]

NEWS OF THE COMPANY'S DIWANI, WHICH REACHED LONDON ON APRIL 19, 1766, did not catch everyone unawares. Clive's lawyers, who had received their ciphered[16] instructions some weeks earlier, were hard at work to secure the cash and credit with which to begin buying. (Clive had overestimated the liquid resources at his disposal in London.) The lawyers' inquiries for financial accommodation necessarily kicked up dust and set rumors racing. Nor did Clive's agents scruple to tip their friends, Lord Holland among them,[17] to the good thing to which they were privy. The company's share price, which, before the news got out, traded at £165, moved higher.

Lord Holland, as usual flush with public funds, invested heavily in East India shares. Clive's agents, too, their principal's credit secured, bought aggressively. By the end of May, the absent mogul had accumulated a position worth £129,630. Holland managed to invest nearly twice as much.[18]

To validate the rising share price and set up expectations for a continued advance, the ardent bulls pressed the company's directors to raise the dividend, which had long been fixed at 6 percent, to 8 percent. The chairman of the board, or court, of directors, George Dudley, wisely resisted.

Expecting that very nice bump-up in revenue was one thing, actually procuring it was another, and moving those anticipated, possibly very large sums safely to London, where they might be paid out to the stockholders, was something altogether different. As to the latter point, the company, as Dudley judged, could find itself "in great affluence abroad and bankrupt at home." He appealed to Clive to export as much marketable Indian merchandise as possible while drawing on London for funds as little as possible. Loading the company's homebound ships with gold and silver would strip bare of circulating coin the very Indian economy on which the company's prosperity depended.[19]

Besides, observed the cautious men at East India House, the speculators were not the only ones counting the company's promised windfall. Parliament, hungry for revenue in the wake of the Seven Years' War, wanted its share. The company must be taxed, George III contended: it was "the only safe method of extracting this Country out of its lamentable situation owing to the load of Debt it labours under."[20] All in all, who could say how much of Clive's Diwani would finally be disbursable? At the June meeting of the Court of Proprietors, the stockholders who demanded a boost in the dividend left empty-handed.

They did not intend to be disappointed at the next quarterly meeting, in September, and some began to campaign to force a vote for a rise to 10 percent, up four full percentage points. William Burke, Lord Verney, and Lauchlin Macleane belonged to this speculative vanguard.

The three, in company with many others—whose number would ultimately include Richard Burke, Edmund's brother, and the translator Samuel Dyer—were embarked in a project they called the "great Scheme," a kind of stock market syndicate, or pool operation. It would operate in London and Amsterdam for the single purpose of lifting the price of the shares of the East India Company. And—a marker of the participants' certitude and rashness—it would operate with futures contracts and with borrowed money.

Macleane, whom we last encountered leading drunken toasts to John Wilkes at the party to celebrate Edmund Burke's election to Parliament at Christmastime 1765, was the principal mover in the initiative, and Verney its main source of cash. William Burke, contributing moral support but no cash, was Verney's partner, sharing half the assets of their joint account and an unlimited liability for their joint debts,[21] though, as Verney would later realize (if he didn't already know it), William had no money, only the highly contingent promise of money in the form of the unrealized gains in his and Verney's trading account. As to that, all seemed well for now: the company share price, which had climbed to £186 in mid-June, was pushing toward £200.[22] To ensure a satisfactory result in the looming dividend referendum, William and like-minded investors agitated to win over voting shareholders.

A contested eighteenth-century East India shareholder vote bore little resemblance to a twenty-first-century proxy contest. The company's bylaws allowed one vote, and one vote only, to every registered investor holding at least £500 worth of stock. However, the designing rich men who had built substantial positions in the company's shares had no intention of yielding their influence to a one-man, one-vote democracy. To evade it, they deconstructed their large holdings into £500 units, thereby multiplying that one vote in a workaround called "splitting."

The investors would lend their shares to trusted nominees, one qualifying £500 share per nominee—for instance, to the butler, the footman, a cousin, and so on. The nominees, their names solemnly entered in the corporate register, would vote as instructed and return their certificates after the meeting. In 1766 there was nothing new about this universally decried, openly practiced evasion. The difference now was the larger scale of the splitting operations. Lord Holland, standing four square behind the push for a 10 percent dividend, contributed his block of shares to be split for that cause. On September 26, 1766, against the directors' opposition, the men of the great scheme succeeded.

Whatever the purpose of the one-holder, one-vote rule, it failed to end factionalism, promote harmony, or forestall rancor within the directorate and proprietorship. The company was riven between the adherents and opponents of a higher dividend, between submission and resistance to the government's demands for a share of the company's profits, and between the friends and enemies of Robert Clive. At least Laurence Sulivan, Clive's former friend turned embittered rival for control of the East India board, could agree with Clive on the dividend question. Each favored a raise, though Sulivan was said to have entertained well-considered doubts about the wisdom of so great a drain of corporate cash.[23]

Shortly after the stockholders voted in support of the 10 percent dividend, William Burke wrote to Charles O'Hara with news of the Burkes' good fortune. The kinsmen were sitting on a trading profit in East India shares of "at least" £12,000, William reported, a windfall he was happy to credit to Verney's remarkable generosity:

> It would be idle to use words to express what we owe to this Mans disinterested unaffected worth and goodness to us. The season too is so critical, that surely we may think it providential, and without any superstitious vanity too, if the thought of it, reminds us to endeavour to grow better Men as we grow richer. It is our good fortune you see to have this advantage without even the Imputation of Stock jobbing, or the term of Bull or Bear being applicable to us.[24]

Verney was all those fine things, but the Burkes, William's protestations to the contrary notwithstanding, were most definitely bullish; they expected—and indeed had worked on behalf of—a higher share price. Both William and Richard, Edmund's brother, had stood (or in Richard's case, presently would stand) as the holder-of-convenience in a voting splitting campaign.[25]

As to "stock jobbing," a general term of opprobrium for financial speculation, it too was apt. Margined, or leveraged, speculators, such as the members of the pool in which the Burkes were operating, face heightened risk. In a rising market, all is well; the extra shares acquired with the proceeds of borrowing magnify one's gains. In a falling market, the same debt enlarges one's losses. Vulnerable as they were, however, Verney, Macleane, William Burke, et al. had no intention of cashing out their gains. With the hope imbued by rising prices, they had every confidence that the best was yet to come.

SEPARATELY, BY THE FIRST HALF OF 1767, BOTH CLIVE AND LORD HOLland sold about half of their East India shares. They were voluntary sales, not forced liquidations. What led them to take a profit—simple prudence, a need for cash, a suspicion that the market had gotten ahead of itself—is beyond knowing.

While the stock price continued to rise into 1769, the company would not, in fact, deliver the earnings that Clive had foreseen in the giddy first flush of the acquisition of the Diwani. Net income would begin a long downtrend in 1767,[26] and by 1772 the East India Company would have one foot in the grave of bankruptcy.

As Holland and Clive were stepping away, William Burke and Lord Verney were holding fast to shares valued at £55,000. Given that William's cash contribution was probably little or nothing, Verney indeed seemed to answer William's description of a man of "disinterested unaffected worth and goodness to us."*[27]

In May 1767 the successful share-splitters of September 1766 redoubled their efforts to secure another boost in the dividend, to 12½ percent from 10 percent. The high-dividend agitators, including Verney, Macleane, and William Burke, succeeded, once more over the opposition of the directors, but at the cost of provoking a government that was eager to claim its own share of the Diwani spoils. Bills came before Parliament to roll back the dividend and shield the company from the "Clan of temporary Stockjobbing Proprietors" that would murder that golden goose for the sake of one sumptuous omelet.[28]

EDMUND BURKE, THOUGH AN AUTHORITY ON FOREIGN TRADE, AN ORIGinal thinker about public finance, and a correspondent and friend of Adam Smith, had only the vaguest idea of his own financial position. He spent freely, in a good-natured, open-handed way, rarely asking where the money came from. (Not from Parliament, certainly, as the MPs were unpaid, and little enough from his labors on the *Annual Register.*)

Jane Burke managed every household detail, from paying bills to retrieving scattered parliamentary papers to fending off unpaid creditors. Edmund's grown son, Richard, assisted in juggling the kinsmen's books and in the allied business of withholding worrisome details from his father, whose thoughts and concerns were everywhere but on the family ledger. It is not quite true that the elder Burke had mastered the "art of living on

---

* "It is hard to believe," writes the historian Lucy Sutherland, "that had they sold out in the next few years, Verney would have handed over to William half of this big capital sum, but even if the arrangements meant no more than that William enjoyed one half of the dividends (over £1,400 per annum) and had a right to one half of any capital gains, it was a princely gift." Sutherland and Woods, "Speculations," 337.

nothing a year." The art he had mastered was rather the one of borrowing and not repaying, though rare was the creditor who seemed to expect repayment or who protested the absence of it.

Burke must have known about William's speculations. What William told Charles O'Hara in the above-quoted letter, he would surely not have withheld from his kinsman and housemate. It is as certain as conjecture can be that Edmund Burke, while likely ignorant about the financial details, shared in the sense of well-being that an unrealized gain affords the person who could possess that profit simply by uttering the word *sell*.

Anthony Chamier, a retired stockbroker and founding member, in 1764, of the Literary Club, with Edmund Burke, Dr. Johnson, and Sir Joshua Reynolds, among other eminences, was bearish on the East India Company. He seems to have heard the Burkes talking it up to Sir Joshua. In any case, he advised the portraitist to stay away. Chamier, who went on to occupy positions of trust in the government of Lord North, told the memoirist and politician John Nicholls that, for his troubles in touting off Reynolds from what likely would have proven a heavy loss, the Burkes never forgave him.[*29]

---

* The translator and critic Samuel Dyer, the first elected member of the Literary Club and a close friend of Edmund Burke, inherited £8,000 on the death of his mother and brother, which he duly lost in East India investments. Immediately upon Dyer's death, in September 1772, according to Edmund Burke's biographer, Peter Burke, William hurried to Dyer's rooms in Castle Street, London, "and there seized and destroyed a large quantity of manuscript. [Sir Joshua] Reynolds happening to come in, found the room covered with the papers, cut up into the minutest fragments, there being no fire in the grate. Reynolds expressed some surprise, and Mr. William Burke hurriedly explained that 'the papers were of great importance to himself, and none to any body else.'" Another published version of the story identifies Richard Burke as the scissors-wielding visitor. Some authors speculate that the papers concerned the anonymous incendiary essayist "Junius"; in the long-running parlor game of guessing Junius's identity, Edmund Burke's name came up frequently but, according to the consensus of modern scholarly opinion, inaccurately. Other authors, more plausibly, propose that Dyer's papers concerned failed East India speculations, but all are guessing. One item of documentary evidence does connect Dyer to the Burkes and the great scheme. Verney's papers contain an entry that commingles the debts supposedly owed by Edmund Burke with the much smaller sums supposedly due from Dyer. Evidently, Dyer invested his money without consulting his fellow clubman Chamier. Dille, "Dyer, Samuel"; Burke, *Public and Domestic Life*; Wecter, "Burke and Kinsmen," 3.

The speculation, the excitement, the fat new dividend, the oft-invoked comparisons of the arc of the East India share price to the catastrophic South Sea Bubble of 1720, and—finally—the government's desire for a new source of revenue combined to lead Parliament to take up legislation to regulate and tax the East India Company in 1767. It was a rare stockholder-statesman who could bring himself to support such a policy thrust, and William Burke, member of Parliament for Verney's pocket borough of Great Bedwyn, was not that disinterested party. Nor was his partner, moneylender and member for Carmarthen, Lord Verney.[30]

The bill would return the dividend to 10 percent and tax the company the annual sum of £400,000. The opposition blanched at this intrusion into the affairs of a duly chartered corporation and wondered where it would lead. Why, if Parliament was going to set itself up as a regulator of dividends, the financial condition of an investor-owned company would soon become common knowledge. Many shuddered at the prospect of this breach of confidentiality, a commentator in *Gentleman's Magazine* remarking that it was "not difficult to foresee the ruinous consequences."[31]

Edmund Burke joined the debate in the House of Commons at the end of May. In keeping with his general defense of private property, he opposed government intervention. Hewing to his notes, he would have warned that the legislation would introduce a "Revolution" in the whole "Policy of this Country with regard to its Laws its Commerce and its Credit. You are," he jotted to himself,

> going to restrict by a positive arbitrary Regulation the enjoyment of the profits which should be made in Commerce. I suppose there is nothing like this to be found in the Code of Laws in any Civilised Country upon Earth—you are going to cancel the great line which distinguishes free Government.

In response to the claim that a 12½ percent East India Company dividend presented a risk to England's public credit, Burke had a retort at the ready: "Upon what calculation can you shew, that ten per Cent can be divided without detriment to publick Credit; and yet that 2½ more, is so likely to *subvert* it, that you will *subvert* your Laws to save it."[32]

Over Burke's reasoned objections and the defection of two leading members of the Chatham government, the dividend bill passed, 152–86. However, in the time-honored way of a strong bull market, investors met bad news with a shrug, and the East India share price continued its rise.

ON MAY 1, 1768, BURKE ANNOUNCED TO HIS BOYHOOD FRIEND, RICHARD Shackleton, that he was on the way to becoming a country squire:

> I have made a push with all I could collect of my own, and the aid of my friends to cast a little root in this Country. I have purchased an house, with an Estate of about 600 acres of Land in Buckingham-shire, 24 Miles from London; where I now am; It is a place exceed-ingly pleasant; and I propose, God willing, to become a farmer in good earnest.[33]

The cost was £20,000, and just as Burke would later put it, the place was "rather superb for us."[34] It had been a little superb for the seller, too, one William Lloyd, who was as "improvident and debt-ridden" as the Burkes themselves.[35] Everything had to go, including paintings and statuary. The £20,000 price included £2,800 for the art collection.

Burke borrowed the purchase price. He raised £10,000 through a mort-gage broker and £4,000 from Admiral Sir Charles Saunders, a fellow mem-ber of the Rockingham party. Signs point to the self-destructively generous Lord Verney as the source of the remaining £6,000 and to William as the intermediary. Neither Edmund, the ultimate recipient of the funds, nor William, who borrowed them, formally acknowledged a debt to Verney, and neither did the unbusinesslike Verney record a loan to the Burkes. The East India share price was still rising, and the joint William Burke–Lord Verney trading account showed large unrealized gains.[36]

The Burke biographer F. P. Lock describes the main floor of Burke's new estate:

Visitors were received in the large central hall, which was "set round with busts of marble or porphyry." To the left of the entrance was the library, on the right the main stairs and the housekeeper's apartment. Ahead, a door led to the formal drawing-room, which overlooked the garden. . . . To the left of the drawing-room was the breakfast-parlour (where tea and coffee were served after dinner).[37]

Of a morning, seated amid newspapers in the breakfast room, the elder Richard Burke would needle his distinguished brother by reading aloud the published versions of his speeches embellished with "startling interpolations."[38]

"Beaconsfield," or "Gregories," as the estate was alternatively known, was no bargain. Not counting the art collection, Burke had paid £17,200, or 34.4 times the farm's projected annual revenue; 29 times revenue was closer to the prevailing valuation.[39] Then as now, location counted, and Beaconsfield was relatively handy to London. Nor did it diminish the value of the property that the poet Edmund Waller, one of Burke's favorites, had once owned it or that Buckinghamshire was Verney's county.

By custom and in law, land was the sine qua non of the serious statesman. The Property Qualification Act of 1711 made obligatory a certain minimum holding of landed property for members of Parliament. And while the law was easily circumvented, a politician's acres were his badge of social and professional inclusion. An appraising observer had commented, not long after Burke's parliamentary debut, on the "power of his eloquence, his comprehensive knowledge in all our exterior and internal politics and commercial interests." He had astonished everyone. All the newcomer wanted was "that sort of dignity annexed to rank, and property in England, to make him the most considerable man in the Lower House."[40]

But dignity could not pay the mortgage expenses, taxes, repair bills, and operational costs that can so easily surprise and overwhelm the novice homeowner. At a mortgage rate of 4½ percent (about one percentage point over the long-dated British sovereign bond yield), Burke would owe his creditors £630 a year, or £130 more than the £500 that, Burke estimated, the farm produced in annual revenue. Mortgages were nonamortizing; one paid only the interest. The principal was callable, usually at six months' notice. In short, Beaconsfield, for all its charm, was a financial millstone that Burke carried only with the help of intermittent borrowing, usually from friends who loved him more than their money, which, once borrowed by him, they were never to see again.*

IN 1766, THERE HAD BEEN SOME THOUGHT AT INDIA HOUSE THAT THE Diwani would prove the "salvation of the Company." Facts to the contrary trickled in slowly but by early 1769, Clive's successor as governor of Bengal, Harry Verelst, was advising London that "the advantages of your late acquisitions have been exaggerated beyond all bounds."[41]

Clive had committed to defend the Mughal provinces; in the five years ending 1770–71, the cost to do so almost doubled, to £1,093,006. The surge in civil expenses over the same half decade outstripped even the military ones, reaching £2.1 million from £725,198. The necessity of expense control, down to the details of building a new church ("simplicity should be preferred to rich and expensive ornament"), became the running theme of Leadenhall Street's communiqués to its distant Indian servants.[42]

Not even the company's fast-growing volumes of imports were an unalloyed benefit, as they met with no reciprocal growth in British demand for the Indian merchandise. Shipments of tea and silk, especially, filled the company's imposing London warehouses to overflowing. Between 1763 and 1772, inventories tripled as sales growth sputtered. Indeed, the company unsuccessfully struggled to recover even the pace of revenue growth it had recorded before the Seven Years' War.[43]

Late in February 1769, Parliament returned to the East India business that it had taken up in 1767. The bill that came before the House of Commons directed the company to step up its exports of British products to India (a nudge to redirect the management away from conquest and back to commerce) and to continue to pay £400,000 a year into His Majesty's

---

* Such friendly creditors included Rockingham, David Garrick, Sir Charles Saunders, Sir Joshua Reynolds, Dr. Richard Brocklesby, Lord Holland, and Lord John Cavendish. Wecter, "Burke and Kinsmen," 26, 45–46.

depleted Treasury. The government would raise no objection to a return of the dividend to the 12½ percent rate that Verney and William Burke had worked to effect in 1767 if the General Court voted to raise it.[44]

Almost a quarter of the members of the sitting 1768 House of Commons owned the company's shares, including Verney, William Burke, and Macleane.* Edmund Burke, both as a sleeping partner in the great scheme and a member of the political opposition, was thoroughly aligned with the company's defenders. So when Burke rose to denounce the ministry's bill to continue to strip £400,000 a year from the enterprise on which his family circle was betting their all (and then some), he was following the Rockingham party line and his own convictions.

He spoke late in the debate, following Lord Clive, on February 27, 1769. The author of the Diwani demanded that the directors must henceforth answer to Parliament, no longer to the stockholders, and he warned that a war in Bengal could deflate the elevated East India share price.[45] If so, the City of London might shudder, as the capitalization of the company had reached £11 million.[46]

Burke replied to Clive with courtly praise: "The orient sun never laid more glorious expectations before us." He beckoned the House not to shirk its imperial duty: "If we make war shall we not conquer? If we conquer, shall we not keep? You are plunged into Empire in the east. You have formed a great body of power, you must abide by the consequence. Europe will envy, the East will envy: I hope we shall remain an envied People."

Burke begged to differ with Clive's idea of surrendering the governance of the company to Parliament. It was under private control that the East India enterprise had become "a great, a glorious Company." As he had done two years earlier, Burke rejected the government's right to tax the corporate earnings: "It is a ransom."

There admittedly remained the risk of a bear market. "With regard to

---

* "Some 23 per cent of all the members of the 1768 Parliament owned Company stock at one time or another between 1764 and 1774, and there were, on average, 118 sitting Members holding stock at any given time between 1768 and 1774." However, according to Bowen, "There is no evidence . . . of stockholding MPs voting, speaking, or acting as a *bloc*." Bowen, *Revenue and Reform*, 31–33.

the fall of the stock," said Burke, "whenever there shall be a war it will fall. Let us know our evils, that we should not be afraid of what is to come. The calculation will be [made] upon the probability of this chance: the consequence that ought to be drawn is, profit from your prosperity, and bear like men your adversity."[47]

Adversity was the furthest thought from Macleane's mind. His goal was to round up votes to elect Laurence Sulivan and Henry Vansittart to the East India Company Court of Directors at the April meeting (and in May, while they were at it, to reinstate that 12½ percent dividend). Once installed, Sulivan, a former company chairman, and Vansittart, a onetime governor of Bengal, would take charge, marginalize Clive, and restore the old prosperity.

It was Macleane's idea to conduct his search in Amsterdam, where futures trading was legal (London prohibited it) and where some of the participants in the great scheme lived. To entice the Dutch holders of split-table shares to lend those securities, Macleane promised to return the stock in July 1769 at an assigned value of £280 a share, up almost 8 percent from the then-quoted price.

Macleane led a syndicate of twenty-three investors in this effort, a group that included William Burke and Edmund's brother Richard, as well as Shelburne and Verney. Sulivan and Vansittart stood as financial guarantors. And when the votes were counted in April (1,459, the most ever), the two emerged victorious.[48]

However, celebrations were cut short by the arrival, on May 23, of the East India ship *Valentine* bearing unwelcome news of an outbreak of fighting in southern India and of a potential French move against company assets in Bengal. Neither report was well documented, and both, of course, were dated. Still, the share price buckled from £273 to £230 within a month. The decline proved devastating to the Macleane group. The financier Isaac Barre opined to Shelburne that there had been nothing like it "since the South Sea year so great a crush in stock matters."[49] But the damage was localized within the community of East India Company bulls. Nor would such a moderate pullback likely have ruined unmargined investors who had not encumbered themselves with a promise to deliver stock on a future date at £280; the *Valentine*'s arrival rendered that price exorbitant.

IT CAN'T BE SAID OF EDMUND BURKE THAT HE ALLOWED WILLIAM'S (AND now Richard's) speculations to distract him from politics or from his new love of farming. London was already abuzz with rumors about the Burkes' exposure to the falling East India share price when the least financially aware of the three Burkes wrote to Charles O'Hara, on May 31, to declare that he, Edmund, had never been in better health, "nor on the whole more easy in Mind," than he was at that very moment.

"My own endeavours have been of so little service to me in my Life," he wrote, "I am so much the Creature of Providence, in every good Event that has befallen me, that I have grown into perfect resignation in every thing, but the Virtue of that Temper." He added that Will and Dick had just gone off to town: "they Love you as I do, and I think it a particular addition to our felicity in our mutual friendship that you have no objection to our association but are kind enough to be willing to fall in, and make one among so odd a set of people."[50]

The next day, Edmund and Richard addressed a follow-up letter to O'Hara who, it now became clear, had joined the Burkes in their leveraged flyer; Richard estimated his loss at £250 "or thereabouts."

"My dear friend," Edmund wrote,

I cannot be easy from the Letter which I wrote to you a day or two ago, and the flattering impression it must naturally have left upon your mind. I wrote indeed in much security, and in the greatest Tranquility of heart that can be conceived; not at all apprehending the ruin of our Situation in the light, I now see and feel it but too distinctly. I am heartily sorry you should have any share in the loss. If you proposed to come here, as I flatter myself you did, for any pleasure you proposed in our Company, this motive can subsist no longer. If your own affairs make a visit to London necessary, we are so circumstanced, that the sight of a friend will be a real cordial. It is all that is now left. You may easily guess the cause. Adieu.

Both Edmund and Richard enjoined O'Hara to say nothing about the losses, but Grenville's private secretary was already spreading the news of the failure of the stock brokerage firm in which the affairs of Macleane, Vernon, and the Burkes were entangled. "Lauchlin Macleane I hear is absolutely ruined," reported Charles Lloyd; "Ld. Shelburne is very deep. Lord Verney has paid 27 thousand on one bargain. The Burkes are likely to be great sufferers."[51]

In fact, Shelburne, Macleane's inattentive financial backer, wound up losing £40,000, Macleane at least £90,000. William Burke and Richard Burke lost everything and spent the rest of their lives trying to get rich again but never succeeding.

Edmund Burke bore his share of the family financial damage and a subsequent cost as well. Elevated to the Court of Directors thanks to the vote-splitting contest to which William Burke and Richard Burke lent their support, Laurence Sulivan was in a position three years later to support a protégé for the vacant position of governor of the province of Bengal. The name of the new reforming governor was Warren Hastings.

CHAPTER 7

Member for Holland House

Beautiful passages from Virgil, Horace, Tacitus, Juvenal, and
Cicero seemed always to present themselves to his memory without an effort. When speaking in Parliament, he knew how to avail
himself of their assistance or to convert them to his purpose with
a promptitude and facility that it is difficult to imagine. Burke
himself was not his superior on this point.

—SIR NATHANIEL WILLIAM WRAXALL ON CHARLES FOX, IN WRAXALL,

HISTORICAL AND POSTHUMOUS MEMOIRS, 2:22

" I am in the last degree of distress for money," Burke confessed in May
1770.[1] Fox, though he seemed to feel not in the least distressed, was
himself perennially short of funds. To supply their respective wants—
Fox to pay his gambling debts, Burke to complete his long, drawn-out
purchase of Beaconsfield—the needy orators hitched their wagons to the
wandering star of Richard Burke.

Edmund's brother was the collector of customs at the Caribbean island
of Grenada. Bringing to bear the knowledge and prerogatives of his colonial office, Richard resolved to invest in the heavily forested volcanic earth
of nearby St. Vincent. The transaction would be his "great affair" and the
financial redemption of himself and his kinsmen.

Richard was not then present at the scene of his anticipated real estate
coup. Nor had he spent much time in the West Indies. Fearful of his health
and loathing the climate, he had done most of his customs collecting from
England. But health took a back seat to necessity after the 1769 collapse of
the Burkes' East India project.

Richard had been absent from his Grenada post since 1765, and he did
not return willingly or happily. His colonial service superiors, who ques-

tioned his competence and honesty and suspected him of malingering, rather commanded him to report for duty. With the help of a loan from Lord Verney,[2] Richard booked passage to the West Indies late in the spring of 1770. "He goes into a bad Climate among worthless and disagreeable people," Edmund grumbled to his old friend Shackleton; "but I hope the goodness of Providence in his favour is not yet exhausted."[3]

Once arrived in Grenada in October,[4] the collector set about putting his plan in motion, though from whom and with what he could buy, and on what authority his counterparty could sell, remained open questions.

The British Crown, owner by conquest during the Seven Years' War of most of the property on St. Vincent, was prepared to sell tracts to the public for the king's profit. To secure an uncontested title meant paying a full price. It was the safe way to proceed but not the way to which Richard Burke was naturally drawn.

The contending camps of nonwhite residents comprised the "red Caribs" (the indigenous people, or Indians), and the "black Caribs" (slaves or former slaves). The reds were open to selling, while the blacks were unwilling to sell, unless at the point of a gun. Which side owned which land was sometimes a hotly contested question. French property holders and speculators, operating outside the pale of British authority, were willing to buy land from the Caribs, though with unclear title to what they had purchased.

Any who attempted to speculate in this manner did so at their personal hazard. It was only the veto of the British governor of Grenada, Robert Melvill, that stayed enactment of a law that would have subjected a convicted unauthorized dealer in crown lands to the death penalty.[5]

An unsigned "Letetr from St. Vincent's" in the London *Public Advertiser* of March 20, 1771, alleged unsavory practices in financial dealings with the natives. "A Number of Adventurers, with a few Dollars in their Pockets," said the dispatch, "are come from Granada, and making some of the poor Indians drunk, have, for a few Dollars, bought from 500 to 1000 Acres a Piece. They brought with them Conveyances ready drawn, to which they have got the Negroes to put their Marks; and these are the Titles which these Adventurers expect that Government will confirm to them."[6]

Richard did, in fact, wind up buying twelve hundred acres of mainly forested land on the northwestern coast of the island, most of it unsuitable for cultivation,[7] and he had indeed arrived there from Grenada with a Verney-provided bankroll. However, the parties from whom he bought were red, not black, and the nature of the deeds or conveyances with which he concluded his transaction is unknown. To Richard's credit, his counterparties went unplied with alcohol, though his purchase did drive a new wedge between the reds and the blacks and failed to pass muster alike with his colonial superiors and the crown.[8]

"Government disputes it for the present," Edmund Burke briefed Shackleton on Richard's "considerable" purchase in July 1771; "but if he prevails, as I trust he will, his establishment will be considerable; and he will be under no necessity of making a long stay in that remote and disagreeable part of the world."[9]

British authorities nullified the purchase not long after Richard concluded it. He was undaunted. Argument, political influence, and if need be, litigation would overturn it. The attempt to undo the ruling proved long and unavailing, though not for lack of Richard's effort, nor of that of his brother and their well-placed friends. In the West Indies, Richard demanded that he, and he alone, should succeed to the control of the governmental finances of Grenada and St. Vincent (and not just Grenada's customs receipts), thereby displacing the colonial treasurer with whom he had been feuding. It was an ultimatum in character with the man who described himself to the Irish painter James Barry as "of all mankind, the laziest, idlest, and most indolent in every thing but a dispute."[10] A lawsuit that Richard filed to dislodge the treasurer from his place succeeded only in gumming the financial machinery of the colonial government during the protracted length of the litigation.[11] In England, the Burkes, presently in company with Fox, would press their claims on British officials all the way up the ministerial chain of command to the first minister, Lord North, and through North to the king himself.

Richard found little to like in squalid, sweltering, and vermin-infested St. George's, the newly slapped-together capital of Grenada. Nor were the

MEMBER FOR HOLLAND HOUSE

island merchants from whom he exacted the king's taxes happy to see him there (though, the easygoing Richard protested, he levied his 4½ percent tax "with a gentle and accommodating hand").[12] The collector yearned for home but could not leave until London approved his request for a furlough.

It was none other than David Garrick, a friend of all the Burkes, who put in a well-placed word for Richard. Garrick seems also to have button-holed a friend at the Treasury to reopen the decision to abate the cancelation of Richard's investment. In any case, an interim judgment reversed that abatement, and the Burkes, temporarily, could indulge their hopes. But hard on the happy decision came a new ruling that canceled Richard's purchase all over again.

It was at this discouraging juncture, in December 1772, that another shaft of sunlight peeked through the stationary cloudbank of the Burkes' finances. Charles Fox, at the age of twenty-three, now prepared to take his place as a lord of the Treasury—and presently, as a partner in Richard's great affair.

THE TREASURY APPOINTMENT WAS FOX'S SECOND MINISTERIAL POST-ing. He had resigned from the Admiralty, where he sat as a junior lord (one of seven), in February 1772.

Politically, Fox was still his father's son, no friend of John Wilkes, as we have seen, still less of "the people." Speaking against the seating of Wilkes in the House of Commons, the twenty-year-old Fox had declared that the contest was between the House "and the lowest scum of the people." To this, the forty-year-old Burke had nimbly replied, "Low as I am, and hum-ble as the gentleman opposite may think me, when I am pleading the cause of the people, I fear the laugh of no man."[13]

In Parliament, Fox sat on the government side of the House with Lord North, where he discharged his principal duty of defending the policies of the ministry against opposition attack, including Burke's heavy salvos.

Lord North, himself a quick and ready debater, a sparkling wit, and a master parliamentarian, counted himself lucky to have the prodigy on the ministerial bench. When Fox spoke, according to his most comprehending biographer, he was always on the offensive, truculent, aggressive, dangerous; he could turn in a moment from juvenile insolence to what seemed like passionate sincerity; from heaping raucous abuse on Burke (with whom as likely as not he had just dined), he would suddenly drop to a level of deep-throated emotion as he explained by a succession of brazen paradoxes that the liberties for which their ancestors had died in the field (and of his own, he might have added, on the scaffold) depended on the arrest of some pettifogging pamphleteer. He spoke so fast that the amazing perversity of his argument escaped undetected; what remains of them is a monument of ingenuity and insolence, coming from a young man of twenty-one, and addressed to an assembly of retired military men and squires.[14]

Almost invariably, Fox's staccato paradoxes served the interest of the government that employed him, for Lord Holland had warned against the futility of opposition. So it was expected, in February 1772, when petitioning clergy of the Church of England appealed to the House of Commons for relief from the obligation to subscribe to the Thirty-nine Articles of Religion, that Fox would join Lord North in refusing to hear their arguments.

The Thirty-nine Articles, to this day, encompass the canon of belief of the Church of England and the Anglican Church in North America, from the doctrine of God to the principles of sin and salvation, to scripture and creeds and sacraments. Was it not enough, the dissenting clergy asked, that they subscribe to the Bible in general without specifically signing on to, for instance, the third Article of Religion, which holds that "as Christ died for us, and was buried, so also it is believed, that he went down into Hell"?

Like his sovereign and, for that matter, Edmund Burke, North held the church and its dogma to be theologically and constitutionally essential to the British state. Never was "the test" so important as it was at that moment, George III wrote to North, given "a general disinclination to every restraint," a disinclination notable among Presbyterians as a sect and in Charles Fox as an individual.[15]

In Parliament, Fox was a frequent speaker. Outside Parliament—at his clubs, at Newmarket—he was a habitual gambler and a knowledgeable horse player. Women and drinking, too, filled his leisure hours, as church-going did not. So his rising to address a point of religious belief might have attracted curious attention. His opening expression of sympathy for the petitioners would have surely interested North.

Fox said he would gladly receive the petition if, by rejecting it, his vote were misconstrued as a rejection of the dissenters' ideals. For them, he had sympathy. Yet he quickly added, "He must be against receiving it, as a reception would be a kind of engagement to proceed."

Having threaded that rhetorical needle, Fox veered off to register his personal, legislatively irrelevant disapproval of the rule that bound every Oxford undergraduate to affirm his belief in the Thirty-nine Articles, no matter that he understood not even one of them.[16]

Reports of Fox's remarks on the floor of the House sat ill with the king. "I think," he told North, "Mr. C. Fox would have acted more becomingly towards you and himself if he had absented himself from the House, for his conduct cannot be attributed to conscience, but to his aversion to all restraints."[17]

Burke too opposed the motion to receive the petition, but he argued on the ground of a Christian believer and on the point that the clergy of the state's church, as a condition of their accepting a public salary, were bound to affirm the doctrine of the church they served.

The mere fact of the existence of a petition, he said, refuted the peti-tioners' complaint that their right to hold a private opinion had been abridged. A priest's conscience was his own. It was rather his public teaching that the church had a right and duty to regulate. Nor was it enough, as some of the petitioners proposed, for the clergy to subscribe to a general belief in the Bible as an alternative to the creed of the Church of England.

The Bible, Burke continued, was "one of the most miscellaneous books in the world."[18] It comprised a "collection of an infinite variety—Cosmogony, Theology, History, Legislation, Prophecy, Psalmody, Ethicks, Controversy," the very opposite of a summary of doctrine "in which a man could not mistake his way."[19]

Which biblical books would the petitioners be prepared to subscribe to, and which would they not?

> Will they exclude the book of Esdras, which has by some been rep-
> robated? Will they admit the Song of Songs as one of the privileged
> books. . . . The same questions may be put with the respect to the
> epistles: as some of them have been deemed Apocryphal. If they will
> not retain any or all of these, what will they retain as undoubted
> repositories of the divine word? If we begin to shake foundations, all
> these captious questions will necessarily be agitated.

Besides, British society had an indisputable call on the individual, even in matters of religious doctrine. "Every man," Burke added, "must make a sacrifice of something to society; and allow that society, of two evils, to chuse the least, to impose upon a few individuals perhaps a disagreeable restraint, rather than introduce disorder and confusion into the whole body politic."[20]

Burke and Fox and 215 others voted to refuse the petition against the 71 who voted to accept it.*

But Burke, having opposed the measure to exempt the Church of England's clergy from the obligation to attest to the Thirty-nine Articles, stood four-square with the movers of a bill to allow Presbyterian and other dissenting Protestant clergy to forgo that requirement. Here Burke argued from the simple ground of fair play: "The Dissenters do not desire to partake of the emoluments of the Church. Their sole aim is to procure liberty of conscience."[21]

---

* The debate amused Edward Gibbon, who sat down at his club, Boodles, on St. James's Street, to extend mock congratulations to his friend and editor, John Holroyd, "on the late victory of our dear mamma, the Church of England. She had last Thursday 71 rebellious sons, who pretended to set aside her will on account of insanity: but 217 worthy champions, headed by Lord North, Burke, Hans Stanley, Charles Fox &c. though they allowed the thirty-nine clauses of her testament were absurd and unreasonable, supported the validity of it with infinite humor." Burke, at least, was not among these cynical Christians. Fox, *Speeches*, 1:15.

Opponents of this Toleration Bill (which handily won the approval of the House of Commons only to be defeated in the Lords) had argued that its passage would endanger the state. It would do no such thing, Burke countered in words that might have amused Lord North had the prime minister been present in the House of Commons to hear them. It was impossible that the bill threatened the stability of Great Britain, because if it did, said Burke, senior members of the government—"whose business is to watch over the welfare of the community, and have given this house such weighty reasons for believing that they never slumber nor sleep, but constantly attend the helm"—would hardly have absented themselves from this momentous debate.[22]

The nearsighted North, though rarely absent from his post while the House was in session,[23] was not invariably awake,[24] and Burke's ribbing of the prime minister touched on that point of vulnerability.

There was one issue of public policy, at least, on which Fox would stake his honor, place, and reputation. This was a proposal to deny members of the royal family (in particular, the descendants of George II) the right to marry without the monarch's consent. King George, who would wield the matrimonial veto, had indignantly watched his brothers marry beneath their royal station, the Duke of Cumberland to the green-eyed Mrs. Anne Horton, in 1771, and the Duke of Gloucester to Lady Waldegrave ("beauty itself!" marveled Horace Walpole),[25] in 1766, but which fact was only disclosed to the king in 1772. The king banned both couples from court.

"The right of approving all marriages in the Royal Family had ever belonged to the Kings of this realm as a matter of public concern," declared George III in the message he sent to Parliament proposing legislation to "guard the descendants of George the Second, from marrying without the approbation of His Majesty."[26] It was the only time but one in his reign that George personally introduced a piece of legislation.[27] Let "every nerve be strained to carry the Bill," the king commanded Lord North.[28]

Fox did not wait for the arrival of the royal communiqué, dated

February 20, 1772, to reach the House before announcing a most astounding decision. He was resigning his position at the Admiralty in protest. But, wondered even the friends of this enfant terrible, protest of what?

In protest, to start with, of the evident royal slap at the legitimacy of the Fox family; if the king's Royal Marriages Act had been law in 1744, Fox's own parents could likely not have married. It will be recalled that parents of the future Lady Holland, the Duke and Duchess of Richmond, opposed her marriage to the untitled young Henry Fox. Not surprisingly, then, in 1753, Lord Holland had mounted intense and politically costly opposition to an act to bar (as one of its objectives) romantic young aristocrats from marrying below their rank. Lord Hardwicke, the lord chancellor who moved the eponymous Hardwicke Marriage Act, never forgave Holland for his highly personalized obstruction.[29]

By no means was Charles Fox alone in taking umbrage at the king's Marriages Bill. Edmund Burke and the Rockingham Whigs as a unit opposed it. Let fecundity take its course, and the king could one day rule over the love lives of many thousands of subjects, their argument went.[30] "It seemed to me," said Burke, "bad as a regulation and worse as a precedent."[31]

It wounded Fox that North had failed to invite him to a meeting of commoners to discuss the Marriages Bill. It was a snub, indeed, that all too closely fit the pattern of North's neglect of the overall interests of the Fox family. Lady Holland found the prime minister's conduct "most unpardonable."[32]

A catalogue of Charles Fox's grievances, which shortly appeared in the pages of a London newspaper, featured the prime minister's recanting on his promise to appoint William O'Brien to a well-paying colonial post. O'Brien, an impoverished actor, had eloped to America with Susan Strangways, a first cousin of Fox's with whom the fifteen-year-old Charles had been desperately in love.

A second grievance had it that North, in immediate need of Charles's advice on matters of state, would roust his Admiralty lord out of bed at three in the morning for consultations at Downing Street. This, at least, was a clear fiction. Everyone knew that the last place to find Fox in the wee hours was in his own bed.*

In debate over the Marriages Bill, Fox was at pains to distinguish his opposition to the legislation from his allegedly friendly feelings toward North. Even so, said Fox, the bill was "big with Mischief."[33]

"Though I had never been in the House of Commons since I had quitted Parliament," Horace Walpole reports on the scene on the floor,

> the fame of Charles Fox raised my curiosity, and I went this day to hear him. He made his motion for leave to bring in a bill to correct the old [Hardwicke] Marriage Bill. . . .
>
> [Edmund] Burke made a long and fine oration against the motion. . . . Two-thirds of this oration resembled the beginning of a book on speculative doctrines, and yet argument was not the forte of it. Charles Fox, who had been running around the house talking to different persons and scarce listening to Burke, rose with amazing spirit and memory, answered both Lord North and Burke, ridiculed the arguments of the former and confuted those of the latter . . . , his words flowed rapidly; but he had nothing of Burke's variety of language or correctness, nor his method, yet his arguments were far more shrewd. He was many years younger.
>
> Burke was indefatigable, learned, and versed in every branch of eloquence; Fox was dissolute, dissipated, idle beyond measure. He was that very morning returned from Newmarket, where he had lost some thousand pounds the preceding day; he had stopped at Hocherel, where he found company, had sat up all night drinking, and had not been in bed when he came to move his bill, which he had not even drawn up. This was genius, almost inspiration.[34]

---

* "It is certain," according to the same journalistic source, "that Lord Holland had settled an additional £2,000 per annum on Mr. Charles Fox, as an equivalent for the place which his regard to his dignity obliged him to throw up." Or more than the equivalent; the Admiralty post in fact paid £1,000 per annum. The implied appeal for an extra thousand pounds from Lord Holland also has an autobiographical ring to it. *The Craftsman; or Say's Weekly Journal* (London), February 29, 1772.

FOX, AT LEAST, HAD NO NEED OF THE COUNSEL TO "LIVE PLEASANT" that Burke dispensed to an anxious acquaintance. Enjoyment came naturally to him and to the lucky people who found themselves in his company. Relieved of his unexacting duties at the Admiralty, flush with his creditors' money, Fox exactly conformed to Burke's precept. He seemed as incapable of anxiety as he was of thrift, sleep, marriage, or diligence. He took pleasure in the House of Commons, in the intellectual company of women and men alike, in books, cricket, shooting, Shakespeare (whose poetry he could liberally quote from memory),[35] drinking, and of course, gambling. He loved racing and, in partnership with Lord Foley, kept a stable of as many as thirty horses. Accounted a good handicapper, he was reputed to lose less at the track than he did at Almack's or Brooks's, where his calamitous record with dice and faro tested even his father's net worth.

Fox had not merely opposed the king's Marriages Act but drafted a bill of his own to repeal its Hardwicke predecessor. Fox's speech to move his motion was a triumph, but when the day came to present his bill for parliamentary consideration, the statesman was nowhere to be seen. Breezing into the House, Fox discovered that his handiwork had just been tossed out, undebated. It seems that he was delayed at the track.

"I have passed two evenings with him at Almack's," Fox's friend, George Selwyn, attested; "and never was anybody so agreeable, and the more so from his having no pretensions to it."[36] At Almack's, Horace Walpole reports, there generally was "ten thousand pounds in specie on the table." The young bucks started play "by pulling off their embroidered clothes" or turning them inside out, "for luck." They donned "pieces of leather, such as are worn by footmen when they clean the knives, to save their laced ruffles; and to guard their eyes from the light, and to prevent tumbling their hair, wore high-crowned hats with broad brims, and adorned with flowers and ribbons."[37]

But the talismans brought no luck. One story had it that Charles and his brother, Ste, combined to lose £32,000 in only three consecutive nights of play. Another, in Gibbon's telling, had Charles losing £11,000 at the game of hazard over the course of twenty-two straight hours.[38]

Light verse mocking Charles's reverses made the rounds of London society:

If he touches a card, if he rattles a box,
Away fly the guineas of this Mr Fox . . .
No man can play deeper than this Mr Fox,
And he always must lose, for the strongest of locks
Cannot keep any money for this Mr. Fox.[39]

Drawing up a list of things that everyone wanted to know, Walpole included the mystery of calculating longitude, the nature of the philosopher's stone, "the certificate of the Duchess of Kingston's first marriage,* the missing books of Livy, 'and all that Charles Fox had lost.'"[40]

Fox seemed impervious. He might lose his friends' respect but never their love. He was "born to be loved," said Burke (at a much later date when Burke no longer loved him). "His judgments are never wrong," wrote Lord Carlisle, one of Fox's closest Eton friends, to Selwyn; "his decision is formed quicker than any man's I ever conversed with; and he never seems to mistake but in his own affairs. . . . I sometimes am determined never to think about Charles's affairs or his conduct about them; for they are like religion; the more one thinks, the more one is puzzled."[41]

But Carlisle, who had guaranteed £16,000 worth of Charles's debts, could not easily put his friend's affairs out of mind.[42] Carlisle's own gambling debts and his money gone to mistresses forced the young nobleman to retire to Castle Howard, the family's palatial North Yorkshire seat, there to "wait for his rents."[43] Writing to Carlisle, Selwyn bristled at Lord Holland for his seeming indifference to Charles's plight and that of Charles's creditors. "Charles you say has not wrote to you," Selwyn addressed Carlisle. "There is no accounting for that or for him but by one

---

* Elizabeth Chudleigh, Duchess of Kingston, conspired with her first husband, Augustus John Hervey, to deny their secret marriage in 1744, for the purpose of allowing Hervey's and her respective second marriages to go forward, hers in 1769. Corley, "Chudleigh, Elizabeth."

circumstance, and that is, that the gratification of the present moment is the God of his Idolatry."*[44]

It's true that Fox lived happily in the moment while abusing the generosity of his monied friends. They had guaranteed a grand total of £92,000 of his and his brother's debts. Charles and Ste incurred these obligations by selling annuities on their lives. The contracts entitled their investors, or annuitants, to receive a fixed annual sum during the brothers' lifetimes. Thus the annuitants wagered not only on the Foxes' longevity but also on their creditworthiness. It was no tribute to Lord Carlisle's financial astuteness that he committed himself to stump up as much as £16,000 should the compulsive gamblers fail to perform.[45]

When, in 1772 and 1773, bank runs and collapsing share prices left Charles and Ste even less solvent than usual, Carlisle and his fellow guarantors were called upon to pay what the brothers could not. At this juncture, the dying Lord Holland dispatched his old Paymaster's Office henchman, John Powell, to buy up the annuities, thereby canceling the brothers' debts. In the performance of this duty, Powell made such insulting, aggressive, and unreasonable demands on Carlisle and the other annuitants and guarantors that the nobleman was reduced to taking his case to Lady Holland. His appeal to the Foxes' family honor falling flat, Carlisle resigned himself to the unpleasant possibility of paying a great deal of money that he did not possess.† It did not sweeten his disposition in the midst of these trials that Charles had lost £900 in a billiards game.[46]

Asked how, given the chaos and squalor of his finances, Fox could sleep at night, the insouciant debtor retorted, in so many words, How could his creditors sleep at night?[47] Yet Carlisle never broke with Charles, and

* Among Holland's innumerable faults was his careless generosity to the friends and acquaintances who approached him for money. Selwyn's name turned up on a list of his debtors, as did those of Edmund Burke and William Burke. Fox-Strangways, *Fox, First Lord Holland*, 2:357.

† Contrary to the Fox family's telling of this unedifying story, Carlisle indeed wound up paying an annuity that Charles Fox would not or could not, while "the threat of being required to advance the full sum hung over his head for many years." Duncan, "Frederick Howard," 9.

Charles, when he returned to government in the second Rockingham ministry, procured a remunerative post for the otherwise unemployable nobleman. It was no easy thing to hold a grudge against Charles Fox.

Reports of Charles's financial misadventures plunged Lord Holland deeper into the depression that age, disappointment, disease, and years of accumulated political grudges had brought on him. He had traded reputation for money, but Ste and Charles were making fast work of his money. "Never let Charles know how excessively he afflicts me," he cautioned Ste in 1772.[48]

Still, he would no more reprove his sons now that they were grown men than he did when they were boys. Lady Holland had no such qualms. She freely expressed the rage she felt at the sons whose recklessness she blamed for their father's decline. "How painful this idea must be to you," she reproached Ste. "Charles does not yet feel it, but he will severely one day; so he ought. And indeed, Ste, fondly as I once loved you both, I do not scruple distressing you by telling you how much you are in the wrong; indeed, you ought to feel it, and let it be deeply imprinted on your mind."[49]

FOX, THOUGH NO OBVIOUS CANDIDATE FOR A POSITION OF TRUST IN PUBlic finance, was nonetheless appointed a lord of the Treasury on December 28, 1772. He was at the same time a money partner of Richard and Edmund Burke in their great land affair.[50]

Perhaps the new Treasury lord had carried with him his reputation for indolence at the Admiralty, where he attended just thirty meetings out of a possible 390.[51] In any case, by August 1773, Edmund Burke was gratified to see Fox pressing Richard's case with the Treasury "with more activity than was usual with him."[52] Fox had his good reason to press, for, as Edmund put it, the lands in question were those "purchased by Mr. Fox and Mr. [Richard] Burke."[53]

Richard, too, believed he could see signs of progress after a constructive meeting with John Robinson, a trusted aide to Lord North. The first minister's notorious indecision and laziness had endowed Robinson with considerable executive power.[54]

Edmund Burke, in looking back over Richard's life, claimed that he found in his brother "an Integrity that no temptation could corrupt."[55] Certainly, in Edmund's eyes, Richard could do no wrong, and he laid his brother's troubles at the feet of the official who organized the sale of crown lands on such ceded islands as St. Vincent. This obstructionist, Sir William Young,[56] was indeed a wily and formidable foe, who himself speculated in St. Vincent lands and returned home with a deficit in his official accounts of more than £150,000.

Conspirators against Richard, so Edmund contended, had pushed through a treaty that unjustly turned Richard's property over to the black Caribs. Indeed, Edmund alleged, Sir William and his co-conspirators had fomented the 1769–73 Carib War between the British and the natives for the very purpose of denying Richard his just claims—of this, he assured Rockingham in September 1773, "there is no Doubt."[57]

Nor is that unproven contention the most puzzling element of the great affair. Still more curious is a scheme that Lord North proposed for a roundabout settlement of Richard's claim. He would, suggested North, make a grant of the Richard Burke–Charles Fox land to General Robert Monckton, whose capture of Martinique during the Seven Years' War had earned him a large claim to parliamentary preferment.

Now then, North explained, Monckton would sell his lands to Richard and Fox at a concessionary price. The general would get his reward, perhaps £10,000, and Richard and Fox would at last possess some property to call their own.

The men of the great affair, while they recoiled at North's proposed underhanded method, approved of his objective, and they put forward an alternative approach, one "clear open, simple, and to be avowed to the world."[58] North liked his scheme,* however, and began to pursue it, but without first securing Monckton's pledge to sell his property, some four

* The land grant idea was North's, so Burke informed Rockingham in September 1773, but it might have originated with George III. In June the king had suggested to North that Parliament take the lead in awarding Monckton with property to which he himself rightly held some claim. The king advised North that while he was ready to lend Monckton "any reasonable assistance," he was not then in a position to make the worthy general "a royal present as you suggest." George III and North, *Correspondence*, 1:139.

thousand acres, at the intended below-market price. Presently, the general succeeded in finding an arm's-length buyer to pay a full £30,000 price.[59]

"So crude, so unguarded, so boyish" was North's bungled execution of his own plan, as Burke complained to Rockingham in September 1773, "that to this minute I stand amazed how a man but two days acquainted with mankind or their Business could have acted as he did."[60]

Burke drafted arguments against the treaty for Lord North to read (Fox gathered up the documents at Beaconsfield for presentation to the first minister) and composed a memorial, summarizing Richard's position, for the eyes of the attorney-general, Lord Thurlow. Instructions appended to this second document, dated November 17[, 1773], read: "let Ch. Fox have it [the memorial] with a Note desiring him to shew it this day to Thurloe. it will be better than an hundred discourses—as the points are more compacted—Now—Now we must press—for we draw to a good or evil conclusion—I shall be here before dinner at half after 3 I hope."[61]

There was no good conclusion, either for the great affair or for its original mover. The Treasury refused to accept the argument that the Red Caribs legitimately sold or that Richard could have legitimately bought; the partners lost their final appeal in 1775.[62]

Like his nemesis, Sir William Young, Richard returned home with a deficit in the public funds he had collected, though of an order of magnitude smaller than Sir William's. Richard was suspended from his customs post in 1775 by the inspector-general of Barbados, John Felton, and charged with, among other infractions, a failure to keep "the Monies received by you for Duties in the Kings Chest under the Joint Locks of the Comptroller agreeably to the express Instructions for the purpose, but have appropriated the same from time to time for your own use." The missing sums totaled £2,185. 7s. 10d.[63]

The proceedings dragged on for years, with the crown, in 1778, restoring Richard to his customs post ("mistakes may be twisted into transgressions," he had protested),[64] reminding him to pay his arrears and then—following another report from the inspector-general—revising up the balance owed to more than £9,500 from the original £2,185. 7s. 10d. Declining to pay, Richard, in 1779, again became an ex-commissioner of customs. As late as 1784, we find him once more seeking relief from any obligation to pay, passing blame to others, including his successor as customs collector, John Menzies, whom he accused of stealing his slaves; Richard had kept eleven of them.[65]

Customs officers, hated and feared by the merchants they taxed, inadequately supported in London, had no easy time of it. "Richard Burke's standards seem to have been those of the service as a whole," judges the historian P. J. Marshall. "There is no reason to believe that he was an especially scandalous officer."[66] He was rather a hapless one.

EDMUND BURKE AND CHARLES FOX WOULD TOIL TOGETHER IN THE eight-year impeachment of Warren Hastings, but in the negotiation over the company's financial salvation and managerial control, the two championed opposing causes. Fox assailed Clive for his alleged crimes against India—"the origin of all plunder, and the source of all robbery,"[67] while Burke, in defending Clive and the chartered rights of the company against the encroachment of ministry and crown, held forth with what a parliamentary observer described as "a vehemence uncommon amongst our modern Orators."[68]

For once, Fox lined up with the popular side of a public issue. In the new narrative, Clive was a "monster in assassination, usurpation and extortion."[69] His ill-gotten wealth, according to this indictment (leveled in the newspapers and in a pair of revelatory new books),* had come out of the hide of the Bengali people, millions of whom had perished in the great famine of 1769–70. Here, the charge continued, was a disaster that the company had caused or, at least, failed to prevent and did scandalously little to remediate.

Neither did the threatened suspension of the East India dividend, first divulged in September 1772, quiet what Burke called the "phrenzy of the people." A stockholder might condemn Clive or deplore the famine,

* Ferishta, *History of Hindostan*; Bolts, *Considerations on India Affairs*; Sutherland, *East India Company*, 221.

but the mooted loss of his payout* evoked a qualitatively different rage.[70] Meanwhile a select parliamentary committee to investigate the company's conduct, headed by General John Burgoyne, the future loser of the Battle of Saratoga, was known to be preparing charges against Clive and other ranking company servants.

Burke, on behalf of himself and the rest of the Rockingham party, conceded nothing to the public rage against Clive. He was the victim of a grab for power by North and the king. What Clive's accusers wanted wasn't justice but the vast patronage that political control of the company would shower on them.

The Rockinghams did get their way with Clive, at least. So persuasive was the accused in his own defense—"leave me my honor, take away my fortune!"—that the House wound up voting him its thanks rather than its condemnation.[71] But on the substantive matter of government control—or as Burke styled it, stockholder disenfranchisement—the Rockinghams were decided losers. North's East India Regulating Bill, of June 1773, cleared the Commons by a vote of 131–21.[72] No more was the company its own sovereign power.

Fox, in victory, singled out Burke as "the only one who had carried any degree of consistency in his opposition."[73] Perhaps, too, Lord Holland's son recognized in Burke's aspersions on the British electorate the doctrine he learned at his father's knee.

He would not blame the company for the problems before them, Burke told the Commons in April:

> It was the people, who were grown so indifferent to the welfare of their country on the one hand, and so grossly corrupt on the other, that there was no proposal, how destructive soever to the liberties of the kingdom, which a ministry could make, but what the people would readily comply with. They were [Mr. Burke said] a most servile

---

* Shareholders eventually accepted the offered 6 percent dividend, down from 12½ to which it had been raised in March 1771.

degenerate herd, destitute of capacity to distinguish, or virtue to relish, what was good.[74]

Fox's enlistment in the great affair gave promise of an adult desire to earn, or at least obtain, an independent income. The junior lord of the Treasury talked about becoming a professional handicapper,[75] marrying a rich heiress,[76] or making himself over into a fee-producing lawyer. As to the latter trial balloon, Fox's friends knew better.*

Those friends loved him anyway. In 1772 a backbench parliamentarian named John Crawford nervously rose to his feet to make the speech he had carefully, and unwisely, written out. His overprepared effort was "ill-timed, ill-received, ill-delivered, languid, plaintive, and everything as bad as possible," as Crawford confessed to Stephen Fox. "Add to all this that it was very long; because, being pompously begun, I did not know how the devil to get out of it. The only thing I said, which was sensible or to the purpose, was misrepresented by Burke."

It was Charles Fox who sprang to the rescue. "He explained and defended what I had said with spirit, warmth, and great kindness to me. I am really more pleased at receiving a proof of kindness from Charles, whom I admire and love more and more every day, than I am hurt at not succeeding in a thing in which I had no right to succeed."[77]

Yet this forensic knight errant retained much of the Eton schoolboy. He repaid North for the honor of naming him a lord of the Treasury by compiling an attendance record at Treasury meetings of 50 percent over the course of a fifteen-month tenure.[78]

The lords met to decide matters as varied as the financial position of the East India Company, the diminished quality of the British coinage, American tax collections, and outlays for national defense. Lord North, the first lord of the Treasury, found this business important enough to command

---

* The betting book at Brooks's records a wager: "Mr. Burgoyne betts Charles Fox 50 guineas that four members of the club are married or dead before Charles Fox is called to the bar." The general would have collected. Trevelyan, *Early History of Fox*, 463.

his presence at virtually every meeting. The other three junior lords were almost as faithful.[79]

Fox's participation improved markedly from the spring of 1773, when the East India Company's money troubles came to dominate the Treasury proceedings. Caught in the wash of the 1772 British banking crisis, management sent emissaries to the Treasury to plead forbearance on customs duties due to the crown.

Financial trouble bore down on Lord Holland as he lay dying. It went without saying that the family honor required the discharge of Charles's and Stephen's gambling debts, the full magnitude of which their father was yet unaware. Whatever those obligations proved to be, the credit collapse had reduced the value of the assets with which to meet them, including the shares of the East India Company.

Late in November 1773, Holland issued instructions to John Powell at the Paymaster's Office (who continued to look after his money) to sell his long-dated annuities, stocks, estates, and other assets sufficient to discharge the debts of Charles Fox, "not exceeding the sum of one hundred thousand pounds." Powell was likewise to make whole Charles's friends who had been loyal enough, and rash enough, to stand Charles guarantor.

Exactly how much the brothers cost their father is unrecorded, but an informed guess places the sum not far from £240,000.[80] The Burgoyne Committee's revelation that Clive had received £234,000 in legally dubious payments after the Battle of Plassey had sufficed to shock the British public, but the full cost of Holland's subsidy of his sons' bad habits did not emerge in the father's lifetime.

Charles Fox reverted to his policy of nonattendance at Treasury meetings late in 1773. He skipped the meetings of December 22 and January 20, 1774, the subject of which was the status of Lord Holland's outstanding accounts from his time as paymaster general of the forces.[81] Fox took his leave from the Treasury with the receipt of a note of one sentence in February: "Sir, —His Majesty has thought proper to order a new Commission of Treasury to be made out, in which I do not see your name—North."[82]

Holland died on July 1, 1774; Lady Caroline, twenty-three days later. Stephen, never well and now morbidly obese, died in December the same year.

On the authority of the *Oxford Dictionary of National Biography*, Holland's "most significant bequest, that of his enmities, went to his favorite son, Charles James Fox, through whom Holland continued to take revenge from beyond the grave."[83] Even so, not long after his father's death, Charles Fox exhibited a remarkable change in political personality. Presently joining the opposition led by the Marquess of Rockingham and Edmund Burke, he was on his way to becoming a man of the people.

CHAPTER 8

The reluctant prime minister

"See that great, heavy, booby-seeming changeling!" the chancellor
remarked to a companion. "You may believe me when I assure
you as a fact, that, if anything should happen to me, he would
succeed me in my place, and very shortly after come to be First
Commissioner of the Treasury."

—CHANCELLOR OF THE EXCHEQUER CHARLES TOWNSHEND, IN 1767,

POINTING OUT LORD NORTH TO A COMPANION AND VENTURING A

PROPHECY ABOUT THE FUTURE PRIME MINISTER

Frederick (Lord) North was born in 1732 into a world of certitudes. He knew that he would succeed his father, Lord Guilford, in the peerage to which Guilford had been raised in 1729 (and by which title North's father, the third Lord Guilford, will be known in these pages). He knew that an ancestor had founded Trinity College, Oxford, which he would attend. And he knew that after his studies at Trinity, he would enter the House of Commons, along with many another eldest aristocratic son. And because the borough of Banbury, with its eighteen voters, belonged to his family, he could be sure that it would elect him to Parliament for as long he chose to stand. (Indeed, he was only once opposed.)

At Eton College, which he entered at the age of ten, in 1742, North made up in talent what he lacked in application, "often careless and absent but . . . in general, at the head of his form." To North's father, the lower master of Eton, Thomas Dampier, filed this report: "I am pleased to see in many instances how both the masters and boys love him, and that he really, by his behavior, deserves it from both, which is not often the case."[1]

North shone at Oxford as he had at Eton. He went up to Trinity College in 1749, at the age of seventeen. In 1750 his tutor, the Reverend James

Merrick, addressed his charge directly: "It is an unspeakable satisfaction to me that you have by God's blessing been made sensible of the importance of religion before your entrance to public life. Your improvement in piety, at this season of your life, will be the best preparation for every future scene of it."[2]

Late in life North went blind,* and it was to the old prime minister that the playwright Richard Cumberland paid tribute. "When all but his illuminated mind was dark around him," his epitaph began.[3] North's mind had been lit by the odes of Horace and other classical texts and by modern French literature and bookish conversation. "No famous Englishman ever lived who had a more ardent and disinterested love of books," said Sir George Otto Trevelyan of Charles James Fox.[4] Not far behind Fox in bibliophilic ardor were North and Burke.

In 1751 North, in company with his stepbrother and Oxford classmate William Legge, 2nd Earl of Dartmouth, set off on their Grand Tour. It is hard to imagine a pair of Englishmen less likely than the studious North and the pietistic Dartmouth (whose political adversaries would later mock him as the "Psalm Singer") to blaze the wild-oats-sowing trail later trod by Charles Fox and his relays of boon companions to the Continent's alternative educational hot spots.

In the solemn and learned company of a Mr. Golding (specifically vetted by Mr. Dampier of Eton for his sobriety, political reliability, and awkward bearing), North and Dartmouth called at The Hague (where they kissed the hand of the princess royal), Leipzig (where they studied for nine months

---

* As did King George III. The physical resemblance of Frederick Lord North to his future sovereign, George III, was sufficiently striking to support speculation that the two were half-brothers.

Gossips recalled that the future prime minister took the name of his godfather, Frederick, Prince of Wales, and that Frederick was the biological father of the future king, born in 1738, six years after North.

Guilford, North's father, was a gentleman of the bedchamber of the prince's, in which capacity he served the prince as companion and dresser. The prince, a bounder and a libertine, was not above cracking jokes about the brotherly similarities between his godson and his biological son, but no known scandal ever attached to Lady Montagu, North's mother, only child of the first marriage of George, Earl of Halifax. She died in 1734, in her mid-twenties, after the birth of her second child, also named Lucy, who lived for less than two weeks.

under the historian and constitutional scholar Dr. Johann Jakob Mascov), and Hanover (where they met the British Whig politician and patronage broker the Duke of Newcastle). They visited Berlin, where many balls gave rise to much late sleeping, and Vienna, Rome, and Paris. Reports reached home that North shone on the dance floor, over which, many years later, his youngest daughter, Charlotte, expressed surprise: "I . . . who remember him only with a corpulent heavy figure, the movements of which were rendered more awkward and were impeded by his extreme nearsightedness before he became totally blind. In his youth, however, his figure was slight and slim; his face was always plain, but agreeable, owing to its habitual expression of cheerfulness and good humour; though it gave no indication of the brightness of his understanding."[5]

Upon the return of North and Dartmouth to England in 1754, Dartmouth took his place in the House of Lords, North in the House of Commons. ("Lord" was a courtesy title accorded to the eldest son of an earl; by law, Frederick North was a commoner.) In 1756 North married Anne Speke, age sixteen, whose looks, charm, and dowry impressed few but the smitten bridegroom. He remained enchanted during the thirty-six years of marriage that their children accounted a model of mutual love and devotion.

The story of North's early political career is the rise to prominence in public finance of a man who couldn't make his private ends meet. Named a junior lord of the Treasury in 1759, North remained at his post for six years, impressing a succession of chancellors of the exchequer with his knowledge of the government's taxing and spending machinery.

North's not inconsiderable Treasury income of £1,400 a year failed to balance his domestic accounts, so it is all the more notable that he voted to enact the controversial Cider Tax of 1763. To the squires of Somersetshire, including his neighbor Sir William Pynsent, a relation of North's mother-in-law, the tax was an abomination and North's vote a betrayal. The personal cost of that decision dawned only following Sir William's death in 1765, as North uncomplainingly remarked to his father: "Our neighbor Sir Wm Pynsent has left all his estate to Mr. Pitt. It is reported, & from pretty good authority, that he left it all to me but alter'd his will in consequence of the Cider Tax."[6] Then again, North's costly vote can be seen not so much as an act of selfless courage as an expression of a political philosophy innate and immovable. As he supported the tax, so did he oppose John Wilkes and so would he defend the Thirty-nine Articles of the Church of England and condemn the American radicals. By and by he would reflect that not once in his career had he supported a popular measure.

That North was destined for big things was early apparent to George III who, in March 1767, pressed the Duke of Grafton to install him as chancellor of the exchequer in place of the insubordinate Charles Townshend. North, then grazing in the lush pastures of the paymaster general of the land forces, had no interest in relinquishing the emoluments of that office or in offending the incumbent chancellor. But Townshend's unexpected death in 1767, at the age of forty-two, forced a change in plans. North, at the age of thirty-five, became the government's new chief financial officer.

The new chancellor at once turned to plugging the revenue holes that the Rockinghams' repeal of the Cider Tax (among other reductions to the Treasury's revenue) had left and that Townshend had been unable to fill with a proposed land tax. The forever cash-flow-negative East India Company demanded North's attention as did the rising discontents of the professedly overtaxed and underrepresented American colonists. Ever inclined to please his sovereign, North lined up with George III in resisting American demands. "I think no line can be drawn," said he; "you must possess the whole of your authority, or no part of it."[7]

In February 1768 the new chancellor presented his first budget to the House of Commons. "I believe Lord North did well," reported a witness to the speech, George Selwyn, "for he had his hands full of papers, a great deal of arithmetic at his command, with a true Budget face."[8] North, as chancellor, would repeat this annual performance fifteen years in a row.

In October 1768, North took on the additional job of leader of the House of Commons. It fell to the leader to organize the timetable of government business, defend the government in debate (and reciprocally bear the attacks of the government's opponents), announce the king's assent to legislation when that imprimatur was obtained, and deliver the sovereign's messages to the House. Apart from the speaker of the House, nobody spoke more frequently than the leader or was expected to know or remember more than he. It wasn't just for the low timbre and deliberate cadence of his speeches that North earned the sobriquet "Boreas," after the Greek god of the north wind. Loquacity was a job requirement.

To his father, on December 1, 1769, North said that he wanted no more of it. It had been a beautiful late autumn day, and he yearned not to be doing what he was charged with doing and, in fact, had never wanted to do. "I always hated my part, but this aversion increases daily," the son told his father. "It is very hard, that when a man has no favour to ask but his own dismission, he is not able to attain it in two years, I can not bear to lead this life any longer."[9]

There would be much more of this from North over the years. In the meantime, without relinquishing the post of chancellor or surrendering the leadership of the House, he acquired a third title—none other than prime minister. The date was January 28, 1770.

Why a man whose shoulders sagged under his first two jobs would acquiesce in a third is partly attributable to North's conception of the nature and function of the parliamentary chief executive. He denied that the English constitution made room for one, and he refused to hear the words *prime minister* spoken in his home. A first minister among equals, he regarded himself, that and nothing more. "Not that he said this by way of evasion," as he was later quoted as telling the House of Commons, "he meant to evade nothing but the charge of presumption of his being Prime Minister, a presumption he had never assumed and which therefore he ought not to be charged with."[10]

Though humble and overburdened, North was not without ambition. He worked to earn the respect of his father, and Guilford basked in his son's success as much as Holland did in Charles Fox's. Nor did the diffident politician refuse when George III, in a sign of high royal favor, presented him with the Order of the Garter, after which North, seated in the Commons, answered to the title, "the Noble Lord in the Blue Ribbon." He was the first commoner to be so honored since Sir Robert Walpole in 1726.

Besides, North, a father of five with appearances to keep up, needed the money. He required, as well, such continuing tangible favors of royal preferment as loans and sinecures. Real wealth came late in life to his father, and Guilford saw no reason to share it with his elder son. So North buckled down to the work that he continued to insist would be better performed by others.

Certainly, Britain could have found a better wartime leader than North, and many another politician would have better attended to the official correspondence that North habitually left unread. Yet it was the amiable, wry, nonconfrontational, philosophically unimaginative, and frequently indolent North who led a government that lasted for twelve years. In the first ten years of the reign of George III, beginning in 1760, a half-dozen ministries had risen and fallen.

Not many weeks had passed in his dozen-year tenure before North demonstrated the gifts that explain his improbable political longevity. One of these was his prowess in running debate. No more than Fox was North given to hours-long disquisitions like the ones in which Burke excelled. The younger Pitt appraised North's speaking style as "cheerful, elegant and sportive." To these a critic might have added "concise."

George Grenville, the former Whig prime minister whose short-lived government had preceded the year-long Rockingham ministry in the mid-1760s, got to his feet in late February 1770 to demand that the House of Commons take a good hard look at the funds it appropriated to the sovereign and his royal household. North, correctly hearing an imputation of financial wrongdoing from an ambitious member of the opposition, extemporized his reply:

> It is exceedingly pleasant to find gentlemen, who have themselves benefited by the munificence of the Crown, and who are themselves hourly pocketing the public money, making so strict an examination into the disbursements of the Civil List, and weeping so tenderly over the oppression of their poor country. However, as I would at all times rather reason than rail, and as I am desirous of leaving the liberal field of invective wholly open to the enemies of administration, I shall proceed at once to the reasons which induce me to oppose the present motion.[11]

"Even those who opposed the minister involuntarily loved the man," testified a political contemporary of North, the memoirist Sir Nathaniel Wraxall.[12] North was as imperturbable as he was witty, and he scored some of his best points by not rising to the bait of his tormenters. He had been prime minister for only a week when he dropped a self-effacing remark on how little his new ministerial colleagues and he yet knew one another. Burke seized the opening and proceeded to compare the new government to a house of whores. "They remind me," he said,

> of certain ladies, who do not think it necessary to know their gentlemen, provided they are well paid. The noble lord [North] tells us, his new office fell upon him: it is an escheat. I wish him joy of it. Thus the lady might say, I fell down; he fell upon me. The office fell upon the noble lord in the same manner. He is willing to go up-stairs or down-stairs, backwards or forwards. If the lady's name is known, her lodgings known, there is no objection to friends or enemies; none to strangers, to Spaniards, French or Dutch: it is 'Si Signor, oui Monsieur, yaw Mynheer!' In passing a joke, or in serious earnest, I will say, that the man who will act with persons he does not know, until he can hold out no longer, of all principles, acts upon the most dangerous; though it is now held out as dignity and duty.[13]

This was manifestly unfair to North, who was neither unusually venal nor unprincipled. The first of the precepts by which he lived was a resistance to change. Whether in politics, religion, or colonial relations, North liked things just the way they were and long had been.

Thus, he preferred the old, submissive Irish Parliament to the one that, in 1769, shockingly rejected an order from London concerning a new item of financial legislation. Having made their point, the dissidents agreed to fall into line, but the unmollified crown-appointed Lord Lieutenant of Ireland, George Townshend, sent the Irish lawmakers packing for the rest of the legislative session.

By the same token, North preferred the generation of American colonists who withheld their criticism of the Houses of Parliament. To North, as to his sovereign, the colonists resembled children* who should speak when spoken to and, even then, only within the bounds of propriety. North had voted for the 1765 Stamp Act and against its 1766 repeal. He had concurred with the overwhelming majority who supported the 1766 Declaratory Act, by which Parliament reminded its obstreperous charges that though it might, in its wisdom, choose to rescind some taxes, it retained the right to lay others. And he had voted for the 1767 Revenue Act, the second of the five Townshend Acts, which set duties on paper, glass, paint, lead, and tea—so-called external taxes, to which the American Whigs had given at least their tacit assent, as distinct from such internal levies as the hated stamp tax. But no proper American patriot was prepared to accept the language of the preamble to the Revenue Act, which stipulated that proceeds of the new tariffs would pay the salaries of colonial governors and judges, officials who were previously beholden to their often-hostile colonial paymasters.†

What Townshend wanted, he told the House of Commons, was a "stable administration . . . by whom America might be taught obedience."¹⁴ North wanted nothing less.

DISOBEDIENCE WAS RATHER THE PREVAILING STATE OF THINGS IN BOS-ton, Philadelphia, New York, Virginia, and other American towns and colonies. Nor did rebellious Americans confine their protest to remonstrances humbly addressed to His Majesty King George III. To protest the 1765 Stamp Act, a Boston mob spent a night dismantling the mansion of the chief justice and lieutenant governor of Massachusetts, Thomas Hutchinson.

* "I shall always consider that this country, as the parent, ought to be tender and just; and that the colonies, as the children, ought to be dutiful." Thus wrote so fast a friend to America as the Marquess of Rockingham, in a letter to the speaker of the Massachusetts Assembly, in May 1767. Thomas, *Townshend Duties Crisis*, 1.

† Customs commissioners reported to the British Treasury Board in April 1767 on the plight of customs officers in America: "The oppression the officers of this Revenue labor under in America . . . have lately grown to such an enormous height that it has become impossible for them to do their duty." Forster, *Uncontrolled Chancellor*, 125.

Taking his accustomed place in court the next day, Hutchinson apologized for his appearance (his robes, along with the rest of the contents of his house, were gone or flung into the mud) and said he had nothing more to fear: "They can only take away my life, which is but little value when deprived of all its comforts, all that is dear to me, and nothing surrounding me but the most piercing distress."[15]

Enactment of the Townshend duties in 1767 interrupted the peace that had briefly followed repeal of the Stamp Act. In February 1768 the Massachusetts House of Representatives addressed a circular letter to the legislative assemblies of the other twelve colonies urging a united front against Parliament-levied taxes, whether external or internal.

Lord Hillsborough, newly installed secretary of state for the American colonies, bridled at the news and fired off his own circular letter directing the crown-appointed American governors to quash this "open opposition and denial of the authority of Parliament."

Hillsborough was a wealthy collector of Irish rents and English honors: as to the latter, he ultimately garnered a barony, two viscountcies, two earldoms, and a marquessate, "making him, by this reckoning, the equal of Wellington and twice as honored as Nelson." In politics he was among the staunchest of the King's Friends. Jobholder, sinecurist, and yes-man par excellence, he was a political associate, and relation through marriage, of Lord Holland.

His character "is conceit, wrongheadedness, obstinacy, and passion," attested Benjamin Franklin of the new colonial overseer,[16] though even Hillsborough could see that the Townshend taxes yielded more in trouble than in revenue. If, so Hillsborough's letter to the governors went on, "there should appear in the Assembly of your Province a disposition to receive or give any countenance to this seditious Paper [the Massachusetts circular letter], it will be your duty to prevent any proceeding upon it by an immediate Prorogation or dissolution."

But the American post proved faster than the king's ships, and eight colonies had signed on to the Massachusetts project before Hillsborough's letters reached America. Obedient to the secretary of state's command, governors in at least seven colonies gave noncompliant legislatures their walking papers. Yet new elections only brought the return to office of the troublemakers of whom His Majesty's government wished to see the back of. American voters and their Whiggish representatives were playing out the all-too-familiar British script of the electors of Middlesex and John Wilkes.[17] For his insistence that Parliament must enforce its right to tax the American colonists, the historically obscure Hillsborough earned his place among the great inadvertent English founders of America, alongside Lord North and King George III himself.

The British seizure in June of John Hancock's sloop *Liberty* in consequence of the patriotic merchant's nonpayment of import duties on a cargo of Madeira wine set up a wave of protest in Boston. A riot duly followed, in which some sixty-seven British officials—"Commissioners, their familys, Clerks, Tide waiters &c."—fled their homes and offices for the safety of His Majesty's ship *Romney*, moored in Boston Harbor. George III would soon despair that Massachusetts was "a Colony in which the exercise of all civil power and authority was suspended by the most daring Acts of force and violence."[18]

"A nation of freemen, a polite and commercial people," was the verdict of the jurist William Blackstone on the character of the English people of the late 1760s, but not even so gentle a race as the British could turn its cheek to the accumulated insults of Adams and Otis and their radical brethren. General Thomas Gage, commander of British forces in North America, advised a show of force. "Quash this Spirit at a Blow," he urged William Barrington, the secretary at war in London, "without too much regard to the Expense, and it will prove economy in the End. Such Resolute and determined Conduct, will Astonish the rest of the Provinces, and damp the Spirit of Insurrection, that may lurk amongst them, and prevents its appearance."[19] On Hillsborough's orders, by the end of November, four British regiments, of five hundred men each, had landed in Boston, "Drums beating, Fifes playing, and Colours flying."[20]

Contrary to the warlike threats of the Sons of Liberty, the deployed British encountered no American musket fire, but British merchants soon felt the sting of the colonial boycott that Sam Adams had instigated early in 1768.[21] For Adams, who yearned for the return of Puritan simplicity in a

Boston that had alarmingly warmed to luxury, the nonimportation agreement served the double purpose of bearding the British and restoring a measure of the self-denying spirit of Cotton Mather.[22]

To the crown officials in Boston, the rhetoric of the American legislators was only a little less alarming than the menaces of Adams's Mohawks, who serenaded them late into the night with drums, horns, and Indian howls. In the summer of 1768, James Otis, a leading patriot lawyer whose on-again, off-again political radicalism made him enemies on all points of the ideological compass, issued "the most violent insolent abusive treasonable Declaration that perhaps was ever delivered." Otis denounced Lord Hillsborough's prose (of which the colonists had lately read all too much) as the "performance of a schoolboy," though what could one expect from a great British noble who attended Oxford and Cambridge for the sole purpose of "Whoring, Smoking and Drinking."[23]

More radical on this occasion than Sam Adams himself, Otis denounced the members of Parliament as "a parcel of Button-makers, Pin-makers, Horse Jockeys, Gamesters, Pensioners, Pimps and Whore Masters." Lest there be any doubt about where Otis stood on the Townshend Acts and the nature of British government, he demanded that Parliament rescind its every tax and recalled with fondness the republican interregnum of Oliver Cromwell and the regicide of Charles I.

If Sam Adams looked forward to the final cutting of ties with Great Britain, he was too wise a politician to say so. Not even in the heat of 1768 did he make bold to deny Parliament's authority over the American colonies. Reading the letters and petitions that issued from the Massachusetts General Court to British officials that year (including one from Adams to Rockingham), one would have supposed that the Sons of Liberty, like John Dickinson, the influential Whig who signed himself "A Farmer," revered the mother country along with its king and parliament. Adams, who reverenced no king and no parliament, refused to risk his cause by running too far ahead of public opinion.[24]

As a practical matter, the heavier the weight of British taxation and the more irksome the occupying Redcoats, the happier a politician was Sam

Adams—"the worse, the better" was his approach to Anglo-colonial relations. Conciliation and compromise he regarded as threats as great to his revolutionary program as the British lion itself.

Thus, Lord Hillsborough did Adams no favors in 1769 by disclosing a ministerial plan to remove all the Townshend duties except for the tax on tea and to refrain from future taxation except for the purposes of regulating trade. By this time, merchants on both sides of the Atlantic had had their fill of economic warfare. The Americans, perhaps, were more fed up than the British, since the local Tories had been busily publicizing the many instances in which professed American patriots secretly bought up British goods for profitable clandestine resale. Now the radical factions of the leading American towns and cities turned on one another, the New Yorkers goading the Bostonians with especial vehemence over the Tory-surfaced discovery that the Bible-thumping "Saints" had imported five thousand packs of English playing cards while Sam Adams prated on about the evils of English luxuries.[25]

"The pride of the Bostonians is lowered," exulted General Gage in February 1770, as the boycott was visibly dying. "After a fair struggle between Patriotism and Interest, the latter seems to have gained a compleat Victory."[26]

IN BOSTON, ON THE NIGHT OF MARCH 5, 1770, A SQUAD OF NINE BRITISH soldiers faced off against a jeering crowd* of Sam Adams's Mohawks. The civilians, finding the trouble they had come looking for, pelted the troops with curses, clubs, and oyster shells. One Redcoat, knocked off his feet, rose and fired his musket into the crowd. More muskets rattled, and five Americans fell, three dead and two mortally wounded in what the patriots were quick to mark as the "Boston Massacre."

In London, on the same day, Lord North opened debate in the House of Commons on a motion to repeal Townshend's 1767 Revenue Act. In

---

* Those martyrs to liberty, as Sam Adams eulogized the victims, were rather "a motley rabble of saucy boys, negroes and mulattoes, Irish teagues and outlandish jack tars," according to his cousin, John Adams, who successfully defended the British soldiers against murder charges in subsequent trials. Miller, *Sam Adams,* 179.

removing this thorn from the Americans' side, however, the ministry chose to leave one bristle under the colonial skin: the tea tax.

Debate opened with a reading of a petition by the Merchants and Traders of the City of London who dealt in North America. Their business, they pleaded, was in "an alarming state of suspension."

On the other side of the Atlantic, Hutchinson despaired of the silence from London that met his every appeal for orders and advice. While the cadence of transatlantic correspondence was out of the hands of His Majesty's government—General Sir Henry Clinton, British commander in chief in America, would later tap his foot for as long as seven months awaiting a London dispatch*—Hutchinson had a different problem: London ignored him.

In the House of Commons on March 5, Lord North did not get far in his opening remarks before condemning the "illegal" American boycott. "When the Stamp Tax was first proposed," said the prime minister, "I saw nothing unjust, nothing uncommercial, nothing unreasonable in it— nothing but what Great Britain might fairly demand of her colonies. America took flame; America united against it. . . . A change of ministers took place [in which the Rockinghams assumed power]; and with it a change of measures. The act was repealed; and by what we now see, it produced a fallacious kind of calm."

"Perhaps," North went on, speaking words that Hutchinson could have written for him,

> It would have been better to have let things subside into their old channel, without meddling with American taxes; to have rested there; to have hoped that the pretentions of America would not have been renewed. We repealed the act when America was in a flame; we laid on a new tax when America was calm. It is easy to say what sort of opinion such conduct must have given the Americans of the wisdom and authority of this country.

---

* Of sixty-three letters tracked between May 1778 and February 1781, six reached Clinton in fewer than six weeks, forty in up to three months, and seventeen in as many as seven months. Whiteley, *Lord North*, 163–64.

True to Hillsborough's trial balloon, North moved to repeal every Townshend duty but the one on tea. At three pence a pound, the tea duty had lifted the price of a pound of tea sold in Boston to three shillings versus two shillings four pence in London. But gone were the taxes on glass, paper, paints, and lead.

North lamented the ingratitude of the American colonists, who refused to vouchsafe a word of thanks for "the many kind acts" with which Parliament had favored them. "On the contrary, we are treated as hard taskmasters, because we will not give up an undoubted right of the legislature." Nor would Great Britain ever yield to threats.

On the bright side, North added, radical American agitators were finding it necessary to threaten loyalist merchants with tar and feathers.[27] It was a welcome sign that the nonimportation agreement was coming unstuck.

The "spirit of insurrection" among American colonists was indeed inconstant. When unprovoked, they tended to revert to feelings of goodwill toward the mother country. The opening weeks of 1770 were one such peaceful interlude, though that fact was not immediately apparent in Westminster. British merchants could not yet know that the nonimportation agreement was indeed becoming a dead letter.

News of the Boston Massacre did not officially come before the House of Commons until April 25. Burke wagged his finger at the government for its neglect of American affairs and likened its bungling in Boston to the ministerial persecution of John Wilkes. He promised that he would soon "open a more ample view of the government of America for three years past" and, as a foretaste of that promised speech, added, "Speculative, loose plans of government are the most dangerous things possible."[28]

The Edmund Burke whom the Sons of Liberty had toasted in 1769 was no supporter of the Boston mob or even a friend of John Wilkes. It was the seating of Wilkes in Parliament, in obedience to the oft-expressed preference of the voters of Middlesex, that he favored—"the cause, not the person," imprudent and unprincipled as he judged that person to be.[29] Burke had indeed used the occasion of his first speech in the House of Commons to demand the repeal of the Stamp Act, but he joined with his Rockingham colleagues to assert parliamentary power "to bind the Colonys and People of America Subjects of the Crown of Great Britain in all cases whatsoever."[30]

The right "to bind" and the advisability of exercising that right, however, were separate and distinct. In every country, Burke reminded the House, there is a "difference between the Ideal; and the practical constitution— They will be confounded by Pedants, they will be distinguishd by men of sense; they may not follow from the rules of metaphysical reasoning but they must be the rules of Government."[31]

Conciliation and practicality were therefore Burke's watchwords. To a ministerial proposal to admit American members into the Houses of Parliament, Burke pointed to the wide Atlantic; the idea of Yankee MPs shuttling between London and the east coast of North America was "against the order of Providence."[32] To a bid by the Duke of Bedford to resurrect a statute from the time of Henry VIII for the purpose of prosecuting treasonous conduct in America, Burke retorted that "the stores of Henry VIII" were "more dangerous than the arms of Boston." And to a series of resolutions proposed by Lord Hillsborough to denounce the criminal behavior of the Massachusetts Whigs, Burke retorted with a string of arguments that he prefaced with the kind of badinage that leavened the long parliamentary sessions.

> I suppose the gentlemen on the other side have calculated this matter with their usual arithmetic; though they have a minority of speakers, they have a majority of votes. There is an economy of argument on the other side: what I thought was prudence I now find to be beggary; like the man who kept his coat buttoned up, not to keep out the cold, but to hide the want of a waistcoat. [Many members called out question! question!][33]

Yet, as much as Hillsborough and North themselves, Burke stood on the principle of the political subordination of America to the mother country. "We have a great empire to rule," he told the House, "composed of a vast mass of heterogeneous governments, all more or less free and popular in their forms, all to be kept in peace, and kept out of conspiracy, with one another, all to be held in subordination to this country."[34]

Nor would the Sons of Liberty likely have cheered remarks that Burke dropped in 1769 concerning the Townshend duties. Because Parliament was yet in no position to repeal them, the wisest course was not to discuss them.

> Why go on with the parade of parliamentary debates, which is poison, gall, and bitterness to the Americans? The more eloquence we display, the further we deviate from wisdom. What is done must be done silently, and in the [king's] closet.

To which Burke added, "I would be to the Americans personally a friend; to their power an eternal enemy."[35]

THE GREAT QUESTION OF AMERICA EVENTUALLY BROUGHT OUT THE best in Edmund Burke, as it presently would in Charles Fox, and completed the sealing of the friendship that had begun to ripen with the misplaced hopes of a quick killing in St. Vincent real estate. In Fox, the American conflict hastened his evolution from Holland-like Toryism to opposition leadership. In Burke, it revealed a depth of wisdom and an acuity of foresight that won him trouble while he lived, and fame thereafter.

The American war, and the long prelude to war, inspired in Burke three of his great state orations: "Speech on American Taxation," 1774; "Speech on Conciliation with America," 1775; and "Letter to the Sheriffs of Bristol," 1777. They confirmed his standing as the brains and voice of the Rockingham Whigs and formed the foundation of his claim to forensic immortality. His "Speech on American Resolutions," which sounds the themes to which he returned throughout the American crisis, can be read as the overture to his three masterworks.

Not until April 10, 1778, did Burke acknowledge the inevitability of American independence,[36] and he showed no great enthusiasm for it after the United States was born. What he told the House of Commons in 1770 was that America could not be governed from Britain.

Burke was, of course, a politician, and his "Resolutions" served a partisan political interest. His rising to speak in the House of Commons on May 9 was part of a coordinated party effort to discredit the North government; the Duke of Richmond was preparing to deliver a nearly identical message to the House of Lords.

True to the spirit of parliamentary opposition, Burke steered clear of understatement. British policy toward America was no mere miscalculation, but the product of "such Madness, inconsistency, folly Negligence as has no parallel in any time."

Having dealt with the question in general, he next turned to the American policy particulars. All was settled in 1766, he said, which happened to be the year the Rockingham ministry left office. Succeeding governments, tiring of "the Tranquility we enjoyed," taxed, goaded, and provoked the colonists in the cause of defending British sovereignty.

Lord Hillsborough, with his 1768 threat to dissolve any colonial assembly that adopted the Massachusetts line toward taxation by Parliament, crystallized the government's errors toward America. "There was a general suspension of Government throughout the Continent," Burke declared, not exaggerating much, as Hillsborough prorogued at least seven colonial assemblies, including (much to the propagandistic benefit of the Sons of Liberty) the Massachusetts one.[37]

Not surprisingly, disorder was concentrated in Boston, the seat of unruly American democracy, where "any thing with the appearance of a man" was allowed to vote. (Typically unenforced was the Massachusetts ordinance restricting the franchise to voters who paid a property tax.)[38] "Their legal assemblies being dissolved," said Burke, "irregular meetings were called together, and every thing was running fast to the last degree of violence on our Side, and every Species of fury on theirs."[39]

It was to forestall the venting of that fury that British troops disembarked from their transports as if for a hostile landing. That Sam Adams organized his nonimportation agreement under the nose of the British occupying force was enough to show that the militarization of British policy was "a striking Effect of the Imbecillity of Force."[40]

As usual with opposition initiatives, Burke's resolutions condemning the government's conduct were doomed to parliamentary failure, and each was negatived.

The ministry's approach to America continued to hew to the line laid down in the king's speech of November 8, 1768, to wit: A "steady Persever-ance" in "supporting the Constitution, and inducing a due Obedience to the Authority of the Legislature."[41]

AMERICA WAS AN INTERMITTENT PARLIAMENTARY CONCERN. IT NEVER drew a crowd the way the Wilkes controversy did, and now it attracted almost no one. Between 1771 and 1773 the House of Commons debated exactly one American measure. (It concerned the legality of courts-martial in the colonies.) It received no American remonstrance and enacted, or negatived, no America-themed resolution.

For Burke, politics in general had gone into eclipse. The North minis-try's commanding majority made opposition worse than futile. To oppose for the sake of obstruction held no charm for him or for the Rockinghams. Happily, there were turnips—and peas, carrots, wheat, hay, and the other crops and cover crops that Burke cultivated at Beaconsfield.

He farmed not only for the love of it but also for profit. In his south Buckinghamshire neighborhood, the great Whig statesman was accounted "the most successful" farmer, and "without any unusual expense."[42]

Burke was a methodical, observant, and systematic farmer. A stu-dent of the noted agriculturalist Arthur Young, he was a tinkerer and an empiricist. In 1769–70, he planted an acre's worth of carrots to fatten a pair of bacon hogs. The hogs ate the carrots but failed to put on weight until they switched to barley meal. The orator-farmer was not downcast, he assured Young: "He is but a poor Husbandman who is discouraged by one years ill success where he acts upon good authority, or pursues a rational principle."[43]

Politics and farming resembled one another in more ways than one. "I do think I know pretty much well what to do," Burke told his friend and helpmeet Charles O'Hara on the narrow question of wheat, clover, and the 1771 spring crops; "but to make an effectual farmer something else is req-uisite besides skill and diligence. Of this I can assure you."[44] It didn't rain and didn't rain, and then suddenly it poured. Luck played its part at Westminster and Beaconsfield alike.

If Burke's politics were prescriptive, his farming was experimental. He tested different techniques of plowing and field drainage and, like John Adams of Massachusetts, was a close student of manure. He found a money crop in carrots, and he fed cabbages to his cows (with more than satisfactory results in the quality of the resulting butter). He embraced the thinking about crop rotation, originated in Belgium and popularized by "Turnip" Townshend, 2nd Viscount Townshend, in the early decades of the eighteenth century but not yet widely practiced in Burke's corner of Buckinghamshire. Crop rotation was the big idea. To maintain the fertility of his fields, the progressive farmer would grow wheat, turnips, barley, and clover in a four-year sequence. No need to let the ground lie fallow. Sheep might browse in the clover, fertilizing the earth as they munched. Burke enthusiastically practiced and proselytized for the "Norfolk four-course system."

As for farm labor, Burke believed, there should be no economizing. You got what you paid for. "All profit of Lands is derived from Manure and Labour," he advised O'Hara; "and neither of them, much less both of them, can be had but at a dear Rate. I should not even consider the cheapness of Labour in any particular part as a very great advantage. It is something without doubt."[45]

By hitching a brace of oxen to his plow in addition to, or in lieu of, horses, Burke found that he could plow as much as an acre a day; his twenty-first-century mechanized descendants might do sixty times as much.

"The soil here is gravelly and bears a beautiful verdure," James Boswell marveled during his visit in 1783; "and the ground is formed into swells and hollows as if in a Mould by an exquisite Artist."[46]

In September 1771, Burke was building a windmill. "I think it will pay its charges," he told O'Hara:

These occupations, if they do not totally banish my Mind, they suspend many Cares, sorrows, and anxieties. They are my dearest pleasures; they would be so in a State of the greatest prosperity; and they have something soothing to a mind that is sore, and sick from many Griefs. I do not know how, but they bring one nearer, and by a gradual slope down to our Natural repose; and our Grave is thus gently prepared for us, like one of the trenches into which we throw our grain in the hope of resurrection. All the rest is vanity.

There are different kind of vanities, Burke continued, some better—"more sprightly"—than others. Politics was among the worst. "Most assuredly," he told O'Hara, "that if the thing were to do again I never should meddle with them. Either the thing itself is something wrong; or the time is unfavourable; or I am not made for the thing, or for the time."[47]

The General Assembly of the Province of New York would not have credited that self-appraisal. The New Yorkers had been reading about the Ciceronian orator who had faced down the Grafton ministry in the cause of John Wilkes and who had declared, in his "celebrated speech" of January 9, 1770 (according to a New York newspaper account), that "the Americans are contending only for an inalienable right; the right of taxing themselves, which is inseparable from every country that boasts the least degree of freedom. When they crossed the Atlantic, they did not give up the rights of Englishmen."[48]

In any case, the death of New York's English agent created an opening that the legislature invited Burke to fill. He was on the job in May 1771.

A colonial agent, as a representative of the people, was appointed by the legislature. To Hillsborough, "the people" deserved no say in a matter that was properly the concern of their betters, namely governor and king, and he tried to subject the selection process to a royal veto; Burke successfully spurned the argument.

The legislature enjoyed no such autonomy. No bill enacted by a colonial assembly became law without the assent of Britain's Board of Trade, and it fell to Burke to monitor the sometimes mazy legislative vetting process. He was a year on the job when John Cruger, Jr., speaker of the New York Assembly, asked his assistance in speeding approval of a pair of bills in which he had a particular interest, one to discourage private lotteries, the other to combat distemper. Burke predicted that the "royal allowance" would shortly be forthcoming. One year later the lords commissioners rejected both.

Nevertheless, Burke proved a diligent and enterprising colonial agent. He investigated claims by French investors who sought royal confirmation of titles to tracts of land in the Lake Champlain region of New York. He advocated for the Assembly in controversies over the New York–Quebec border, on one occasion earning a letter of commendation, and a raise in pay, for his "attention to the interests of the Colony in regard to the territorial rights, and to the private property of the Grantees under New York against the Canadian claims."

His position paid £500 a year, one-third of which he was in "urgent need" of as recently as May 1770. However, Burke told Delancey in August 1772, "If I accept the salary, which I am informed, is not the most considerable advantage of employment, *and which you know is a small object to me*, it is solely lest, I should hurt the delicacy of any gentleman who might succeed to the office, by putting him under the difficulties in accepting that emolument which another had declined" (emphasis added).

The assemblymen were left to reconcile that lofty expression of disdain for money with Burke's request, in a postscript, for £80 a year with which to pay the salary of his clerk.[49]

In May 1775, before the Revolutionary War cut short his American career, Burke performed the awkward service of presenting to the House of Commons a "Remonstrance" from the New York Assembly that attacked the very Declaratory Act that the Rockinghams had written and passed into law. Honorably, if at times unenthusiastically, he did his duty.

THE LENGTHY ROLL CALL OF INADVERTENT FOUNDERS OF THE UNITED States would be incomplete without the corporate presence of the East India Company. It was to support the company's wobbly finances that the North ministry pushed through the Tea Act of 1773. And it was the Tea Act that provided the company with financial relief sufficient to sell its Bohea blend in America at prices even lower than those on offer from the patriotic smugglers. The act afforded such relief while fatefully retaining the Townshend tea duties; to repeal them, North contended, would convey the lack of British resolve that never failed to embolden the American radicals. Besides the bargain-loving Yankees would hardly spurn the company's cheap tea on the pretext of a piddling tax.

On the night of December 16, 1773, scores of Mohawk Indians, curiously resembling Yankees, clambered aboard three of the company's vessels moored in Boston Harbor, hoisted chests of tea from their holds, and dumped the contents into the frigid waters of Boston Harbor.

News of the Boston Tea Party (and similar demonstrations in New York and Philadelphia) at first stirred small reaction in England—"Any Remarkable Highway Robbery at Hounslow Heath would make more conversation than all the disturbances of America," Burke reported to Rockingham. However, if "slow to anger" was the ministry's policy, the government was not for that reason quick to forgive.[50]

Three punitive measures, the so-called Intolerable Acts, presently issued from the House of Commons, each passed with heavy majorities and meager opposition. Charles Fox now joined Burke in condemning the measures of the government whose door Lord North had only recently shown him.

The Port Bill* closed Boston to seaborne civilian trade at least until the inhabitants of that nest of sedition had compensated the East India Company for its losses. Nor was Great Britain bound to reopen the port immediately following such restitution. "It will remain in the breast of the king not to restore the port until peace and obedience shall be observed in the port of Boston," said Lord North.

---

* Following the Boston Port Bill came the Administration of Justice Act, which shielded royal officials accused of a capital crime committed while protecting established authority from the justice of local American juries; and the Massachusetts Government Act, which shifted political control of the province from elected officials to the crown-appointed governor. The Quebec Act, also of 1774 vintage, while not customarily counted among the Intolerable Acts, scored higher, on the colonists' odious scale than did the ones just named. Introduced into Parliament by Lord Dartmouth, North's stepbrother, who had succeeded Hillsborough as secretary of state for the colonies, it extended the boundaries of Quebec south to the Ohio River and west to the Mississippi and gave countenance in that province to the Catholic Church and the French civil law. American Whigs could hardly top the denunciations of Isaac Barré, who called the act a "monstrous production of tyranny, injustice and arbitrary power." Miller, *Origins of American Revolution,* 376.

Fox, always attentive to the rights and dignity of the House of Commons, objected that because the town had picked a fight with Parliament, it was for Parliament to decide when the quarrel was over. It was none of the crown's business, "not that, said he (in a kind of sneer), there is any reason to distrust his Majesty's ministers."

Not even Isaac Barré, dogged opponent of the North government and loyal friend of America (where he had fought in the Seven Years' War and from which he returned home with a bullet in his cheek), denied that the Boston Mohawks deserved to be punished for a patently illegal act. Nor did Burke condone the alleged crimes. Instead, he asked why the accused parties were not on hand to defend themselves and why the British forces in Boston had not prevented the disturbances in the first place. He predicted that the consequences of blocking up this or that American port would be "dreadful, and I am afraid destructive; you will draw a foreign force upon you, perhaps at a time when you little expect it; I will not say where that will end."

To which Burke added,

I abhor the measure of taxation where it is only for a quarrel, and not for a revenue; a measure that is teazing and irritating without any good effect; but a revision of this question will one day or another come, wherein I hope to give my opinion. But this is the day, then, that you wish to go to war with all America, in order to conciliate that country to this; and to say that America shall be obedient to all the laws of this country.[51]

A month later, on April 19, in support of an opposition motion to repeal the tea tax, Burke delivered his promised "Speech on American Taxation." He spoke for two hours. ("Go on, go on!" someone cried when, halfway through, he wondered aloud if he was not tiring the House.) It was less a speech about public revenue than an essay on government.

Inasmuch as a self-respecting member never read from a text in the House of Commons, it was an essay extemporized, not written. As Burke spoke, Sir Henry Cavendish, a member for the pocket borough of Lostwithiel, took down his words in shorthand. So proficient was Cavendish, and so fluent was Burke, that the shorthand text was almost ready for the press. "The most excellent speech that has perhaps ever been uttered in a public assembly," the *London Evening Post* accounted the result, a judgment that, if it stretched a point in the service of political fidelity (for the *Post* reviled the North government), did not necessarily break it.[52]

Burke proffered no policy to resolve the American dilemma but reviewed the steps by which Britain had blundered into it. That Britain was the blunderer, Burke had no doubt, with the exception of the enlightened thirteen months of the Rockingham ministry, during which the stamp tax was repealed and peace settled over the colonies.

Yet in the beauty and power of its language, and in the essential correctness of its judgments, Burke's oration surpassed politics. He spoke with courage, too, particularly about America, which he identified not as a child but as a singularity. "Nothing in the history of mankind is like their progress," he told the squires and ministers and colonels who had not yet stopped comparing the colonies to a pack of troublesome adolescents. To Burke, the colonies rather resembled "antient nations grown to perfection," and it beggared belief that they had sprung from "the bleak and barren shore of a desolate wilderness three thousand miles from all civilized intercourse."[53]

It was England itself that had nurtured them, said Burke. It endowed them with capital, a constitution, and a form of self-government, even if it likewise saddled them with "monopoly." By monopoly, Burke meant the Navigation Acts, of which the earliest was a production of the Rump Parliament led by Oliver Cromwell in the mid-seventeenth century. The laws restricted seaborne colonial trade to British ships and colonial consumption of finished, imported goods to British manufactures, in exchange for which America sent raw materials—in short, said Burke, an arrangement of "commercial servitude and civil liberty."

The crisis-inducing trouble was the heaping of new taxes on the existing regime of coerced trade.

> You cannot have both by the same authority. To join together the
> restraints of an universal internal and external monopoly, with an

universal internal and external taxation, is an unnatural union; perfect uncompensated slavery.

George Grenville, whose short-lived government passed the Stamp Act into law in 1765, was a lawyer who, like many of his profession, "thought better of the wisdom and power of legislation" than it deserved. "He conceived," Burke continued,

> and many conceived along with him, that the flourishing trade of this country was greatly owing to law and institution, and not quite so much to liberty; for but too many are apt to believe regulation to be commerce, and taxes to be revenue.

It was about this time, in the wake of the Seven Years' War, that the river of American trade deepened and widened. It overflowed its banks, said Burke,

> and spread out upon some places where it was indeed improper, upon others where it was only irregular. It is the nature of all greatness not to be exact; and great trade will always be attended with considerable abuses. The contraband will always in some measure keep pace with the fair trade. It should stand as a fundamental maxim, that no vulgar precaution ought to be employed in the cure of evils, which are closely connected with the cause of our prosperity.[54]

When he got to the story of the Townshend duties, Burke lingered long and sympathetically over their eponym. Charles Townshend, he said, "was the delight and ornament of this house, and the charm of every private society which he honoured with his presence." He had his faults, of course, including "perhaps an immoderate passion for Fame; a passion which is the instinct of all great souls. He worshipped that goddess wheresoever she appeared; but he paid his particular devotions to her in her favourite habitation, in her chosen temple, the House of Commons."

The collective character of the House, said Burke, included an

abhorrence of vice, most particularly the vice of obstinacy. A vain persistence in an opinion that would better be abandoned did special harm "in
the changeful state of political affairs." Yet it happens, "very unfortunately,
that almost the whole line of the great and masculine virtues, constancy,
gravity, magnanimity, fortitude, fidelity, and firmness, are closely allied to
this disagreeable quality, of which you have so just an abhorrence; and in
their excess, all these virtues very easily fall into it."

Townshend, who sought popularity as much as he did fame, went to the
opposite extreme of obstinacy. "To please universally was the object of his
life," said Burke of the author of the fateful law; "but to tax and to please,
no more than to love and to be wise, is not given to men."

So the Townshend Acts, like the Stamp Act, were duly repealed, and
"what woeful variety of schemes" have followed:

> what enforcing, and what repealing; what bullying, and what submit-
> ting; what doing, and undoing; what straining, and what relaxing; what
> assemblies dissolved for not obeying, and called again without obedi-
> ence; what troops sent out to quell resistance, and on meeting that resis-
> tance, recalled; what shiftings, and changes, and jumblings of all kinds
> of men at home, which left no possibility of order, consistency, vigour,
> or even so much as a decent unity of colour in any one public measure.[55]

It is not quite true that Burke had no suggestion for resolving the American dilemma. "Seek peace and ensue it," he said, after the psalmist; "leave
America, if she has taxable matter in her, to tax herself." He declined to
parse the question of rights: "I do not enter into these metaphysical distinctions; I hate the very sound of them. Leave the Americans as they
antiently stood, and these distinctions, born of our unhappy contest, will
die with them."

And he said this: "When you drive him hard, the boar will surely turn
on the hunters."

And this: "Tyranny is a poor provider. It knows neither how to accumu-
late, nor how to extract."

Yet Burke went on to defend the Rockinghams' Declaratory Act with its assertion of colonial subordination to British legislative authority. What he failed to do, in the debate that followed his speech, was satisfy Lord North that the repeal of the tea tax would not incite new demands from the insatiable Massachusetts radicals.

Said North: "Convince your colonies that you are able, and not afraid to controul them, and depend on it, obedience will be the result of your deliberation; let us conduct ourselves with firmness and resolution throughout the whole of these measures, and there is not the least doubt but peace and quietude will be restored."

Charles Fox, taking Burke's side, observed that a tax can be laid to regulate commerce, raise a revenue, and/or assert a political right. The tea tax answered the third purpose only, "done with a view to irritate and declare war there, which, if you persist in, I am clearly of the opinion, you will effect, or force into open rebellion."

Rockingham himself had taken pains to organize a strong showing by the opposition, but the motion to repeal the tea tax fell by a lopsided vote of 182–49.[56] Burke's words, as they so often did, resounded loudest with posterity.

It was probably too late, in any case. In America, elections were in the works to select delegates to the First Continental Congress. Seated in September, at Carpenters' Hall, Philadelphia, the delegates voted to suspend all commercial contact with the mother country and to swear off "every species of extravagance and dissipation, especially all horse-racing, and all kinds of gaming, cock-fighting, exhibitions of shews, plays, and other expensive diversions and entertainments."[57] A false report that General Gage had Boston under attack rousted thousands of armed men out of their Philadelphia homes to march in the common defense. While the warlike spirit was on them, the hotheads cursed "the King and Lord North, general Gage, the bishops and their cursed curates and the church of England."[58]

It is unlikely that they cheered Edmund Burke.

CHAPTER 9

Wearing Washington's colors

> Above all, I hope it will be a point of honor among us all to sup-
> port the American pretensions in adversity as much as we did in
> their prosperity, and that we shall never desert those who acted
> *unsuccessfully* upon Whig principles.
>
> —CHARLES FOX ON RECEIPT OF NEWS OF THE AMERICAN DEFEAT
>
> AT THE BATTLE OF LONG ISLAND, OCTOBER 1776

Wil128Dowdeswell was a sturdy, honest, and hardworking
presence in the councils of the Rockingham Whigs. He led
the party on the floor of the House of Commons and advised
its chief in private. He was chancellor of the exchequer during the 1765–66
Rockingham ministry, though not the marquess's first or even second
choice for that demanding post. So suited was Dowdeswell "to the drudgery of the office," Horace Walpole was moved to sneer, "that he was fit for
nothing else."

Yet it was Burke, Britain's most poetic politician, who wrote to tell Rockingham, in 1773, that "we cannot find a leader whom a man of honor and
judgment would so soon choose to follow."[1] The trusty Dowdeswell was
that man.

In voting to support the seating of John Wilkes, to repeal the Stamp Act,
to pass the Declaratory Act, and to placate the American colonies without
relinquishing (and without unnecessarily discussing) Parliament's right to
tax them, Dowdeswell hewed to the Rockingham line. Like Burke, he condemned what he took to be the crown's secret and corrupting influence on
Parliament. In Parliament, he spoke frequently, often in support of Burke.

Opposition was no way to get rich, as Lord Holland had so often reminded his sons and as Dowdeswell, a father of thirteen, could personally attest. Unwell and borne down by years of political frustration, he wrote to Rockingham in 1774 about the "impossibility of doing good in opposition and the despair of being able to do it if we were again called into Administration."[2]

On hand for Burke's "Speech on American Taxation," Dowdeswell heard the great orator put words in the mouth of Lord North for the pleasure of refuting them. Probably, said Burke, "the noble Lord" would answer his arguments with the insinuation that the opposition acted from no higher motive than a hope to change places with the king's well-paid jobholders.

"Let him enjoy this happy and original idea," Burke continued.

> If I deprived him of it, I should take away most of his wit, and all of his argument. But I had rather bear the brunt of his wit, and indeed blows much heavier, than stand answerable to God for embracing such a system that tends to the destruction of some of the very best and fairest of his works. But I know the map of England, as well as the noble Lord, or as any other person; and I know that the way I take is not the road to preferment. My excellent and honorable friend under me on the floor [Dowdeswell], has trod that road with great toil for upwards of twenty years together. He is not yet arrived at the noble Lord's destination. However, the tracks of my worthy friend are those I have ever wished to follow; because I know they lead to honour. Long may we tred the same road together.[3]

Unassuming though he was, Dowdeswell could not have missed the flattering allusion to himself and, indirectly, to his failing health. Under medical advice to avoid the English winter, he sought refuge across the Channel, at Nice; in February, he died there, at the age of fifty-three. "Of all the men I ever knew he was the best to act with in publick, and to live with in private," wrote Burke to Dowdeswell's widow.[4] Before long, Fox could answer that description.

In 1774 Burke enjoyed new political success to complement his spreading rhetorical fame. Lord Verney, whose wealth had brought him to Parliament, could no longer afford to make his protégé the customary gift of his pocket borough of Wendover. Rockingham had already supplied an alternative when an inquiry arrived from Bristol. Would Burke care to fight for the opportunity to represent Britain's second-largest commercial center? He accepted the challenge, declined Rockingham's family constituency, the borough of Malton, and mounted the Bristol hustings. "To reconcile British superiority with American liberty shall be my great object, as far as my little faculties extend," he told the electors. He promised to defend liberty—a "liberty connected with order," as he hastened to add—and commerce, which "has ever been a very particular and a very favourite object of my study."[5] To Burke's mind, they were the two principal sources of British greatness.

Burke secured 2,707 votes, enough to win one of Bristol's two seats. Henry Cruger, the more popular of the two victors with 3,565 votes, was an American by birth (a nephew, in fact, of the speaker of the New York Assembly); his family pursued trading interests on both sides of the Atlantic and boasted strong connections in New York politics. Following the election, Cruger promised the Bristol voters to be their servant. Burke took the opportunity of Cruger's pledge to promise the opposite: "You chuse a Member, indeed, but when you have chosen him, he is not Member of Bristol, but he is a Member of *Parliament*."[6] Burke would vote his conscience, not necessarily that of his constituents.

It was not so much their consciences as their bank accounts that drove the merchants of Bristol and London to complain to Parliament about the dwindling state of Anglo-American trade. "A total stop is now put to the export trade with the greatest and most important part of North America," pleaded the petitioners to the House of Commons in January 1775; "the public revenue is threatened with a large and fatal diminution, the petitioners with grievous distress and thousands of industrial artificers and manufacturers with utter ruin."

Rather than air these entreaties in open debate, North chose to bury them in committee—"buried in oblivion," as Burke quipped, "though not in sure and certain hopes of a joyful resurrection." Going on in this lighthearted vein, Burke had the House in stitches, but he presently reversed course to hold up visions of a bloody civil war, of "slaughtered innocents," ruinous taxes, economic stagnation, and—for the ministerial authors of the calamity—"condign punishment," a not-so-subtle threat to impeach the prime minister.[7]

Fox, coming to Burke's support, promised to make North answer for "the mischiefs occasioned by his negligence, his inconsistency, and his incapacity: he said this not from resentment but from a conviction of the destructive proceedings of a bad minister."

IN THE COMMONS, NORTH CUSTOMARILY WORE FULL COURT DRESS, complete with sword and, of course, blue sash, the ribbon attesting to his membership in the Order of the Garter. The swarthy Fox habitually dressed down, rarely shaved or bathed.

North now addressed himself to Fox, "who found so many causes of censure and who disclaimed all resentments." Was there not a time, North wondered, when Fox "approved of at least some part of his conduct?"

Only North knew the meaning of the suggestive phrase "some part." Did it allude to Fox's appointment, at the tenderest of ages, to positions of trust in the Admiralty and Treasury; to the prime minister's well-intended if unsuccessful assistance in the St. Vincent's land affair; or to something else entirely? Whatever it was, Fox flew into an unparliamentary rage. Certain it was, he said, that his private resentments had no bearing on his public conduct, else "I might have long since justly charged the noble lord, with the most unexampled treachery and falsehood."

The speaker called Fox to order, the House "grew clamorous," and Fox sat down—before quickly jumping to his feet. Again and again he sat down and stood up, "and on rising each time repeated the same words; but at length, assuring the House he would abstain from every thing personal, he was permitted to proceed."[8]

Words spoken on the floor of the House of Commons rarely drew blood. Partly this was owing to the essential philosophical alignment of the Tories and Whigs. "Church and King" was the Tory motto, but the Whigs, too (or most of them), were royalists and Christians, even if dissenters from the

Church of England composed the "main effective part of Whig strength."[9] And whatever their differences over the Thirty-nine Articles, few members of the House of Commons would have quibbled with a word of the king's adulatory description of the "beauty, excellence and perfection of the British Constitution."[10]

In times of peace, political differences were largely tactical, not ideological, with offices and emoluments being more frequently contested than right and wrong. Of course, a skilled debater could turn the molehill of a turnpike bill into a philosophical mountain, and hyperbole was the stock in trade of Burke and Fox.

As witty as he was imperturbable, North was a dangerous adversary on the floor of the House. In a debate over the legality of Britain's employing foreign troops in America, Burke had ridiculed the legal arguments of North's solicitor-general, Alexander Wedderburn, who, he charged, had "ransacked history, statutes and journals" to support the unconstitutional policy of employing Hessians to fight the ministry's war.

"Let us," said Burke,

strip off all this learned foliage from his argument; let us unswathe this Egyptian corpse, and strip it of its salt, gum and mummy, and see what sort of a dry skeleton is underneath—nothing but a single point of law! The gentleman asserts that nothing but a Bill can declare the consent of parliament, not an address, not a resolution of the House . . . so that we find a bill is nothing, an address is nothing, a resolution is nothing, nay I fear our liberty is nothing, and that, ere long, our rights, freedoms and spirit, nay the House itself, will vanish into a previous question.

North, in reply, said he

desired to know whence the proofs and authorities of a point of law could be better drawn than from history, statutes, and journals; he did not think it was from wit, or flowers of eloquence, that they should be deduced. He admired the hon. Gentleman's method of proving a resolution to be, nothing; an address, nothing; a Bill, nothing; and by the same mode of reasoning he was inclined, he said, to conclude, that a long witty speech was—nothing.

RECONCILIATION OF THE COLONIES WITH THE MOTHER COUNTRY WAS the hope not only of the British Whigs but also of the ministry and, as John Adams had come to believe, of most Americans as well. It was the heart's desire not only of such colonial peacemakers as John Dickinson, the "Pennsylvania Farmer," but also of William and Richard Howe, senior commanders, respectively, of the king's land and naval forces in North America. North himself, though he vacillated between warmaking and peacemaking, not infrequently yearned for reconciliation, and he proposed a series of steps to achieve that end in February 1775.

The North plan offered any colony or province that wished to tax itself with the opportunity to collect those funds, though the amount of tax would still be Parliament's to decide. By this means, North trusted, the entire contentious issue of taxation would disappear. The colonists would grasp the hand of fellowship as readily as they accepted their subordination to Parliament and the king. And if they rejected it, said North, "their blood must be upon their own hearts."[*][11]

Charles Fox tendered sarcastic congratulations to the prime minister for his belated embrace of peace. "It is now seen what the effects are which a firm and a spirited opposition will produce," he said, beginning to sound like a recruit to the Rockingham corps.

The North scheme, Burke protested, was more oppressive than the one it sought to replace. It would leave the colonies no other choice but to

contribute to a service which they cannot know, in a proportion which they cannot guess, on a standard which they are so far from

---

[*] Duly enacted, the proffered scheme of self-taxation found one taker only in North America: the loyal province of Nova Scotia. W&S, 3:161–62n1.

being able to ascertain, that parliament which is to hold it, has not
ventured to hint what it is they expect.[12]

IN MARCH 1775, THE MONTH BEFORE THE BATTLES OF LEXINGTON AND
Concord, Burke presented the Commons with an alternative peace plan,
which he styled "Speech on Conciliation with America." It was an address
remarkable both for the liberality of its ideas and the beauty of its language.
As he had in "Taxation," Burke urged the House to regard American prosperity not as a threat but as a blessing. Prosperity on the American side of
the Atlantic would redound, through trade, on the British.

Burke began speaking at three-thirty in the afternoon and sat down
between two and a half and three hours later, "during which time the
attention of the House was riveted to him," as the parliamentary record
generously reported.[13] North's plan was fashioned from complexities and
contingencies. Burke's derived from the single idea of peace:

> Not Peace through the medium of War; not Peace to be hunted
> through the labyrinth of intricate and endless negociations; not
> Peace to arise out of universal discord, fomented, from principle, in
> all parts of the Empire; not Peace to depend on the Juridical Deter-
> mination of perplexing questions; or the precise marking the shad-
> owy boundaries of a complex Government. It is simple Peace; sought
> in its natural course, and its ordinary haunts. It is Peace sought in
> the spirit of Peace; and laid in Principles purely pacific. I propose,
> by removing the Ground of the difference, and by restoring the *for-
> mer unsuspecting confidence of the Colonies in the Mother Country,*
> to give permanent satisfaction to your people; and (far from a scheme
> of ruling by discord) to reconcile them to each other in the same act,
> and by the bond of the very same interest, which reconciles them to
> British Government.

The phrase "former unsuspecting confidence" was an American coinage. Burke seized on it, urging steps to restore that reflexive trust. For him-

self, he would repeal the Intolerable Acts and remove every tax intended to raise an American revenue, while retaining the seventeenth-century Navigation Acts that reserved for the mother country exclusive rights in shipping and the colonial export trade.

Burke's position on the Navigation Acts accorded with that of the delegates to the First Continental Congress. The American representatives "cheerfully" agreed to submit to Parliament's restrictions "for the purpose of securing the commercial advantages of the whole empire to the mother country, and the commercial benefits of its respective members."[14]

Besides, the laws were more formidable in the statute books than they were on the docks of Boston, Philadelphia, or New York. Lax enforcement was all to Burke's taste, and he coined a durable phrase, "salutary neglect," to describe it.

Simplicity and magnanimity were the themes of his speech, but Burke had not forgotten the Declaratory Act, and the status he sought for the colonies was one of "a profitable and subordinate connexion with us." In that sense, Burke was closer to North than to the Adams cousins of Boston.

Again, Burke regarded America with frank astonishment. Reviewing the growth in its population and exports, he marveled that Britain's "trade with America alone is now within less than £500,000 of being equal to what this great commercial nation, England, carried at the beginning of this century with the whole world!"[15]

Neither the Dutch nor the French nor the English had matched the daring and enterprise of the New England whaling fleet or the prodigies of the American farmer. "When I contemplate these things," said Burke,

> when I know that the Colonies in general owe little or nothing to any care of ours, and that they are not squeezed into this happy form by the constraints of a watchful and suspicious government, but that through a wise and salutary neglect, a generous nature has been suffered to take her own way to perfection: when I reflect upon these efforts, when I see how profitable they have been to us, I feel all the

pride of power sink, and all presumption in the wisdom of human contrivances melt, and die away within me. My rigor relents. I pardon something to the spirit of Liberty.

Burke had no use for the spirit of suppression.

America, Gentlemen say, is a noble object. It is an object well worth fighting for. Certainly it is, if fighting a people be the best way of gaining them.

Besides, force is a temporary expedient.

It may subdue for a moment; but it does not remove the necessity of subduing again: and a nation is not governed, which is perpetually to be conquered.

And if you do not succeed in battle,

you are without resource; for, conciliation failing, force remains; but force failing, no further hope of reconciliation is left. Power and authority are sometimes bought by kindness; but they can never be begged as alms, by an impoverished and defeated violence.

To those who protested that America would react to the removal of English taxes by demanding new concessions, Burke posed a question: was it really prudent "to form a rule for punishing people, not on their own acts, but on your conjectures?"[16]

Burke seasoned his text with aptly chosen data on imports and exports and with phrases he recalled from the Old and New Testaments, Juvenal, Horace, Virgil, Aristotle, Milton, and Shakespeare. Often, in aptness and cadence, his own words shone as bright as the classical ones he quoted. Thus, for instance, "All government, indeed every human benefit and enjoyment, every virtue, and every prudent act, is founded on compromise and barter. We balance inconveniences; we give and take; we remit some rights, that we may enjoy others; and we chuse rather to be happy citizens, than subtle disputants."[17]

"An Englishman is the unfittest person on earth, to argue another Englishman into slavery."[18]

Force was the essence of the business model of the Anglo-American slave trade; argument hardly figured in it. To the proposition of the British governor of Virginia, Lord Dunmore, that Virginia's enslaved people be freed in exchange for their pledge to support the loyalist cause, Burke temporized. But condemn the slave trade he did, and in that condemnation he alluded to Dunmore's refusal to outlaw it, when the Virginia House of Burgesses presented him with a bill to do just that and which the Articles of Association of the Continental Congress, in a resolution dated October 20, 1774, did actually attempt to do. "An offer of freedom from England," Burke remarked, "would come rather oddly, shipped to them in an African vessel, which is refused entry into the ports of Virginia or Carolina, with a cargo of three hundred Angola negroes."[19]

Burke's plan met the rejection to which the opposition's slight numbers in the House of Commons doomed it, but it won the admiration of his thoughtful contemporaries. Anticipating posterity,* the wholly partial critic Lord Rockingham told Burke that "the manner and the matter were equally perfect." Charles Fox, who would lose Burke's friendship by quoting a passage from "Conciliation" back to its author on the floor of the House at the opening of the French Revolution, now rose to second his friend "with the greatest ability and spirit."[20]

IF NOT FINALLY A SUCCESSFUL IDEA, CONCILIATION PROVED A HARDY one, on both sides of the Atlantic. Its advocates pursued it after shots rang out at Lexington and Concord on April 19, 1775. It survived the British frontal assault on the entrenched American positions at the top of Breed's Hill in the Massachusetts town of Charlestown, on the morning of June 17, 1775, and lived in the breast of General William Howe, the losing general in that battle (which took its name from Bunker Hill, the neighboring ele-

---

* "The Speech on Conciliation" was once a staple of history instruction in American secondary schools. The historian William F. Byrne tells the story of encountering "an elderly woman who promptly recited to [me] a passage from the Speech on Conciliation with America, memorized as part of an American high school curriculum in the 1930s."

vation whose ultimate capture gave Howe his Pyrrhic victory) and in that
of his brother, Admiral Richard Howe, commander of British naval forces
in America.

In one of the final American attempts to fend off war and thereby independence from Britain, the Second Continental Congress issued an appeal
to George III three weeks after Bunker Hill. Later styled the Olive Branch
Petition, it begged His Majesty's "royal magnanimity and benevolence" in
putting the "most favorable construction" on the petitioners' prayer that
"the former harmony between [Great Britain] and these colonies may be
restored." The petitioners would forbear from describing the "irksome
variety of artifices" with which the king's ministers had afflicted them but
rather would seek the repeal of the offending statutes to the end of effecting a "happy and permanent reconciliation."[21] With varying degrees of sincerity, every congressman put his name to it.

There were reasons to doubt American candor. Preceding the Olive
Branch Petition on the congressional docket was a vote to authorize the
American invasion of Canada and a "Declaration of the Causes and Necessity of Taking Up Arms." The king, though he declined to receive the
petition, nonetheless answered it with an August proclamation "for Suppressing Rebellion and Sedition" in North America, outrages carried out
by "divers wicked and desperate Persons."

The pages of the London Gazette, the government's newspaper of
record, presently filled with addresses and petitions taking the ministry's
side. The tea merchants and slave-ship owners of London and Bristol might
bewail the prospect of war with their American customers, but hundreds
of Manchester signatories urged George III to knock the Yankees' heads
together. "Whatever Check our manufactures may receive by a necessary War," their petition read, "we shall chearfully submit to a temporary
Inconvenience rather than continue subject to lawless Depredations from
a deluded and unhappy People."[22]

The Rockinghams opposed the ministry for the highest of motives. The
marquess himself, along with such colleagues as the Dukes of Portland
and Richmond, was too rich to care about the emoluments of office. In any

case, there seemed not the slightest chance of displacing the North ministry, which could expect to outvote the opposition on an ordinary motion
by a margin of two or three to one.

At least, in this first summer of the American war, the anti-ministerialists
could marshal the newly enlisted tongue of Charles Fox. Not yet formally
aligned with the Rockinghams, Fox had broken free of the government,
and he complemented Burke's gift of oratory with genius in debate. "With
Burke for artillery and Fox for cavalry," as Fox's biographer observes, "the
Whig army had no reason to despair."[23]

It was rather the British Army, and the government whose orders it
obeyed, that the opposition despaired of. In November 1775, Fox moved
for an accounting of military expense in North America. No doubt, he told
the Commons, the figures would show an outlay exceeding "any one of the
Duke of Marlborough's campaigns, while in the midst of repeated victories, he was immortalizing the British name," and that conjecture was as
far as Fox's inquiry was allowed to carry. His motion was negatived without a division.[24]

Fox, though still a professed believer in the subordination of America to
Parliament, made no bones about his loyalties in the contest with America. He spoke of "my illustrious friend, General Washington,"[25] and wore
Washington's colors, buff and blue, in the House of Commons. If the boys
at Brooks's were amused, so too, in different way, was a cartoonist on the
London *Westminster Magazine*, who, in 1776, drew Fox as a bemused witness to an attack on Britannia by a tomahawk-wielding Indian that the
artist had tagged America.[26]

In February 1776, Fox introduced a motion to inquire "into causes of
the Ill Success of the British Arms in North America." While it was true
that the king's forces had hurled back the American assault on Canada,
General Howe had abandoned Boston and sailed off to Nova Scotia with
his ten thousand men. British officers had deprecated the colonial troops
as tyros and poltroons. Yet these military nullities had held their own
with the professional British Army. North, in response to Fox, recalled an
opposition speaker in the early portion of the debate who had charged his

government with "wickedness, ignorance, and neglect." The prime minister "was certain he was mistaken in the first, and the two others remained
to be proved."

There was indeed no inquiry, but British arms, the following summer, chased George Washington's little army off Long Island and might
have destroyed it except for General Howe's ill-timed caution at Brooklyn
Heights. Hardly was the ink dry on the Declaration of Independence* when
American militiamen fled the British amphibious landing at Kip's Bay, on
the East River shore of Manhattan island, in such pelting haste as to cause
General Washington to take the name of the Lord in vain and to threaten
the cowards with his sword and cocked pistol.

If Valley Forge marked the psychological bottom of the American cause,
the Battle of Long Island might have scraped military low ebb. It was a
summer of ill omens. At Oxford University, six weeks before the victorious British assault on New York, two of the best-hated men in Massachusetts, Thomas Hutchinson and Peter Oliver, the former governor and former
chief justice of Massachusetts and long since exiles to the mother country,
received the degree of Doctor, in Jure Civili, Honoris Causa, in recognition
of their distinguished service to the British Empire. The date was July 4, 1776.

"The Panic may seize whom it will," wrote John Adams on receipt of
the news of the disasters at Long Island and New York, "it shall not seize
me."[27] Charles James Fox was no less resolute when the news found him
at the Newmarket track on October 13. Reaching for pen and paper, he
urged Lord Rockingham to resist the call from his fellow Whig magnates

---

* The only known comment on the Declaration of Independence by either Burke or Fox
was Fox's, in an August 17, 1776, note to Burke: "the declaration of independency seems
to be an event which we ought not surely to pass over in silence." C., 3:291. John Wilkes
read it and defended it in Parliament against a fellow Whig's claim that Thomas Jefferson's
masterpiece was "exceedingly rude and ill-written." Precisely, countered Wilkes: "That,
Sir, is the very reason why I approve of it most as a composition, as well as a wise political
measure, for the people are to decide this great controversy. If they are captivated by it,
the end is attained. The polished periods, the harmonious, happy expressions, with all
the grace, ease and elegance of a beautiful diction, captivate the people of America very
little; but manly, nervous sense they relish even in the most awkward and uncouth dress
of language." PH, 18:1404–5.

to stay away from Parliament in protest of the ministry's war policies: "A secession at present would be considered as a running away from the conquerors, and we should be thought to give up a cause which we think no longer tenable." What was wanted was rather a ringing affirmation of the opposition's ideas and objectives.

In 1768, North had declared to the Commons that he would never consider repealing the Townshend duties "until he saw America prostrate at his feet."[28] Seeming to recall North's uncharacteristically bellicose language, Fox closed his letter to Rockingham: "If America should be at our feet (which God forbid!), we ought to give them as good terms (at least) as those offered in Burke's propositions."[29]

Fox next wrote Burke to confess what he had chosen not to tell Rockingham. "I do not know that I was ever so deeply affected with any public event either in history or in life," he began. London was exulting over its victory, "excessively." It wasn't the battle so much that deflated him, Fox went on (for the issue was by no means decided), but "the sad figure that *Men* make against *Soldiers*."[30]

In the summer of 1776, the indistinct timeline of the friendship of Burke and Fox marked a clear point of union, both personal and political. On the telling of Fox's cousin, Lady Sarah Lennox, Fox "left off all his fine acquaintances last year and lived quite with Mr. Burke." "Very Steady in his opposition," she continued, Fox the gambler had given up cards and confined his betting to the track.[31] The alliance of the two greatest parliamentary speakers of the age was sealed.

It was a time, too, when Fox, age twenty-seven, began to overtake Burke, forty-seven, as unofficial leader of the anti-North forces on the floor of the House. Burke was well aware of it. He even seemed able to identify the date and circumstances of Fox's ascendancy. It happened on October 31, 1776, the opening day of the autumn session of Parliament, when to Fox had fallen the honor of moving an amendment to the Commons' address of thanks to George III for his ceremonial opening speech.

The address that Fox would move to amend (though not so much to amend as rip up and replace) expressed the Commons' "detestation and abhorrence" of the American rebellion, the Commoners' joy over the success of the king's forces in Canada and New York, and their satisfaction "that your Majesty continues to receive assurances of amity from the several courts of Europe."[32]

That the opposition continued to show its face in the House owed something to Fox, who had successfully argued against a proposed boycott of St. Stephen's Chapel and the ministry that ruled inside it. Now he rose to "exhort his Majesty to make the only proper use of his Victory," and to substitute, for the king's speech, the arguments that Edmund Burke had devised.

"The Americans had done no more than the English had done against James II," Fox began, in a reference to the king whom the Whigs had sent packing in 1688. He rejected the ministry's triumphalist coloring of the Battle of Long Island (a victory of discipline over liberty—was the noble lord in the blue ribbon really proud of it?) and scoffed that Spain and France would stand peaceably by when His Majesty's forces were chasing George Washington through the American wilderness. If, as North asserted, said Fox, "we were in the dilemma of conquering, or abandoning America; if we are reduced to that, I am for abandoning America."

"I never knew Charles Fox better," Burke marveled to a Bristol political friend, Richard Champion, "or indeed any one, on any occasion. His speech was a noble performance."[33] The notable feature of what followed was not that the motion was defeated by the customary lopsided vote (232–83) but that, after Fox sat down, no one on the government side of the aisle, including the solicitor-general, Alexander Wedderburn, stood up to reply.

Burke marked Wedderburn's silence, and the passage of a few days did not soften the rage he now directed at the ministers sitting opposite, the solicitor-general to start with. "Rejoiced I am, Sir," Burke began,

> that the learned gentleman has regained, if not his talent, at least his voice; that as he would not, or could not reply the other night, to my hon. friend, charmed as he must have been with the powerful reasoning of that eloquent speech, he had the grace to remain silent.

Burke compared Wedderburn to "Milton's devil, prostrate 'on the oblivious pool,' confounded and astounded, though called upon by the whole

Satanic host." If Wedderburn was mute, he was not powerless, as "the learned gentleman has now called to his assistance, the bayonets of 12,000 Hessians."

"It was well said, on another occasion," Burke went on, "that your speech demands an army!—and I may say, that the learned gentleman demands blood; reasoning he says is vain;—the sword must convince America." There was nothing personal in this, Burke assured the House.

Samuel Johnson qualified his almost boundless admiration for Burke with the complaint that, in Parliament, he spoke "too frequently* and too familiarly."[34] James Boswell, after listening spellbound to Burke one day, concluded that the great orator enthralled the House of Commons but did not seem to persuade it. The Duke of Richmond, who happened to be Fox's uncle, once heard Burke admit this very incapacity. Earnestly and vehemently though he made his arguments, Burke told the nobleman, he could not bring his audience around to his way of thinking. To this, Richmond replied that it was Burke's very vehemence that led some (though not, he was quick to add, himself) to suspect that some undisclosed private interest was the engine of his eloquence.[35]

Burke, perhaps recalling the duke's words as he tore into Wedderburn and the entire North government, now declared a personal interest. He had been the colonial agent for—the parliamentary representative of—New York. The ministry, he charged,

> has burnt the noble city of New York; . . . has planted the bayonet in the bosoms of my principals;—in the bosom of the city; where alone your wretched government once boasted the only friends she could number in America.[36]

The phrase "my principals" left no doubt that the member from Bristol was beholden to another constituency besides the one that elected him; he had indeed represented New York since 1771. And now he reminded the House

---

* Between 1774 and 1780, he addressed the House almost four hundred times, out-talking any other member of his party. From 1774 to 1776, only Lord North spoke more; from 1776 to 1780, Burke placed a respectable third, behind only North and the voluble Fox. W&S, 3:1–2.

that the ministry had refused to accept the Assembly's remonstrance because the New Yorkers had dared to question Parliament's powers over them.

All this was bad enough, said Burke in his grand finale, but the king had chosen to drag God into it. A royal proclamation had set aside December 13 as a day of public fasting and humiliation. There would be prayers to heaven "to vouchsafe a Special Blessing on our Arms. Both by Sea and Land."[37]

Jesus had said, "My peace I give you," Burke continued, "but we are, on this fast, to have war only in our hearts and mouths; war against our brethren. Till our churches are purified from this abominable service, I shall consider them, not as the temples of the Almighty, but the synagogues of Satan."[38]

BURKE AND FOX SHARED MANY THINGS: A DEVOTION TO JUSTICE, ESPE-cially for the downtrodden; forensic genius; a love of literature and the ancient languages; membership in Samuel Johnson's Literary Club; an abhorrence of the American war and, more broadly, of the North government; jealousy of the encroaching power of the crown over Parliament; and a chronic shortage of ready money.

They were unlike in many other ways. One was a happily married family man, the other, a defiantly dissolute bachelor;* the one, an Irish émigré, the other, a descendant (down an illegitimate line) of Charles II. They were farmer and horse player; home-rooted Briton and Francophile man of the world; devout member of the Church of England and no churchman at all.

---

* One morning the late-rising Fox greeted a pair of visitors, including a dissenting minister, who had called at his home to talk politics. "His complexion was of the dirtiest colour and tinged with a yellowish hue," one of the guests recorded; "his hair was exceedingly black, uncombed, and clotted with the pomatures and small remnants of powder of the day before; his beard was unshaved, and together with his bushy eyebrows increased the natural darkness of his skin; his nightgown was old and dirty; the collar of his shirt was open and discovered a broad chest covered with hair; the knees of his breeches were unbuttoned; his stockings were ungartered and hung low upon his legs; his slippers were down at his heels; his hands were dirty; his voice was hoarse like that of a hackney coachman who is much exposed to the night air. Yet under all these various disadvantages his countenance was mild and pleasing." Brooke, "Fox, Hon. Charles James."

George III shared little enough with either one, but the king, like them, felt the constraints of earthly wealth. To be sure, the king felt that pinch less frequently, and on an altogether different scale, than either unpaid member of Parliament, but not even the sovereign's resources were limitless. Since the start of his reign in 1760, George III had had to make do with an annual revenue of £800,000.

However, the king had not made do but chronically exceeded his allotted sum. He spent to meet the expenses of the civil government and the royal household—the salaries of the ministers and other public officeholders, as well as the holders of pensions and sinecures and the king's domestic staff, not excluding the master of the Jewel Office, cofferer of the household, master of the buckhounds, and so on.[39]

The Civil List, as the royal allowance was known, was a tender topic. Under the constitution, the Commons held the taxing and spending power, but the king was a fiscal island unto himself. Since, by law and custom, he was above reproach, the opposition referred its financial complaints to his advisers and ministers. Nor did those critics squander the opportunity to blast the king's men when the sovereign issued his occasional awkward request for funds with which to meet a royal overdraft.

In some respects, George's financial hygiene was not much better than Charles Fox's. Each spent (or gambled) without the constraint of a budget, confident that his debts would be paid, in one case by the Commons, in the other by the indulgent Lord Holland. Neither cultivated the homely art of record-keeping. The sovereign issued no regular financial reports but presented himself to the Commons when his debts became unmanageable. He had done so in 1769 and was back again in 1777.

Between those years, the Civil List had accumulated a deficit of more than £600,000. Naturally, said Lord North in presenting the tab to the House, the king's loyal and faithful Commons would pay it. Moreover, they would grant the sovereign a bump-up in annual revenue, from £800,000 to £900,000, to provide "for the better support of his household and of the honor and dignity of the crown."

The opposition was powerless to vote down the payments, though not to protest the "corrupt influence" of the crown. The "wanton profusion of ministers" and the "shameless prodigality" of the crown were the outward signs of a Parliament that, with the taxpayers' own money, the king had bought and paid for.

It was bad enough that the king overspent. Nothing short of insulting was the absence of credible records with which to justify a new requisition of money. Particularly vexing, said Fox, was the claimed outlay by the Board of Works of £513,000 since 1769 on palace, park, garden, and house—and other things, too, that it was unwilling or unable to recall. "Why trouble the House with such an account at all," he demanded, "unless to add mockery to contempt, and blend insult with derision?"[40]

Even so, the North government did its duty, and the speaker of the House of Commons, Sir Fletcher Norton, presented the money bill to the king for his royal assent in a full-dress ceremony at the House of Lords on May 7, 1777.

Norton was a tough, tactless, and irascible lawyer who owed his election as speaker, in 1770, to Lord North. Seven years later, as dyspeptic and coarse as ever, he had abandoned his strict ministerial loyalty in favor of an occasional nod to the opposition.

For the occasion, the king was crowned and seated on his throne, bedecked with regal ornaments, attended by the lords (each in his robe) and by his officers of state. "By this Bill, Sir," Norton began, referring to "An Act for the Better Support of his Majesty's Household, and of the Honour and Dignity of the Crown of Great Britain,"

> and the respectful circumstances which preceded and accompanied it, your Commons have given the fullest and clearest proof of their zeal and affection for your Majesty. For, in a time of public distress, full of difficulty and danger, their constituents labouring under burthens almost too heavy to be borne, your faithful Commons postponed all other business.

To be sure, the times were anything but flourishing. However, the king's friends were quick to object, it was not the speaker's place to attempt to enlighten them on that sensitive point. "And, with as much dispatch as the nature of their proceedings would admit," Norton continued, the Commons have not only granted to your Majesty a large present supply, but also a very great additional revenue;—great beyond example; great beyond your Majesty's highest need.

"Need"?* It hardly fell to a commoner, even a speaker of the House of Commons, to presume to tell His Majesty what he needed and what he didn't. Norton closed with what, to governmental or royalist ears, might have sounded like a homily on household management: "But all this, Sir, they have done, in a well-grounded confidence, that you will apply wisely, what they have granted liberally."[41]

Back at the House of Commons, the arch-ministerialist Richard Rigby accused Norton of speaking not for the members but for himself, and of insulting the king in the bargain. The vehemence of his condemnation disquieted the Treasury bench, on which sat North and his chief ministers—as it well might have done. John Dunning, one of the Commons' foremost legal minds, required only a few words to describe the risks of disavowing the speaker's remarks to the king (as Rigby, for one, was prepared to do): "The dignity of the House was gone, if the Chair was permitted to be degraded."[42] As for the country, declared Governor Johnstone, a strong opposition voice against the American war, it was in "truly dreadful" condition, and Norton had done well to remind the king of the "generous efforts of parliament to relieve him in such a season, as the most powerful recommendation in future to frugality in the expenditure, and economy in the management of the bounty they were conferring on him." It was plain that the government side of the House, pushed by Rigby, had overreached.

In leading the speaker's defense, Fox moved a motion that Burke had drafted but was too hoarse himself to move. Speaker Norton, it said, had expressed, "with just and proper energy," the zeal of the House in support of the "honour and dignity of the Crown" in the current, trying circumstances.[43]

And when, at length, the joint Burke-Fox motion came up for a vote, it was carried without a division, "almost unanimously." Burke fairly hugged

---

* Norton insisted he said "expense," but notetaking witnesses took down "need."

himself. To a Bristol political friend, he wrote on May 9: "I do not remember a more extraordinary day in Parliament."[44]

Lord North was as downcast as the opposition was uplifted, the king observed, and he assigned John Robinson, a confidant of North's and the king's alike, to find out what was the matter. Robinson, string-puller, nose-counter, and political administrator par excellence, reported that the source of North's troubles was financial. The prime minister had debts of £10,000, while his annual private income brought him less than £2,500.

The king instantly wrote to North with an offer of help. Certainly, he was in a position to help now that his own finances, thanks to the settlement of the Civil List, were "perfectly at ease."

"I therefore must insist," he went on,

> you will now state to me whether 12, or £15,000 will not set Your affairs in order; if it will, nay, if £20,000 is necessary I am resolved you shall have no other person concerned in freeing them but myself; knowing now my determination it is Easy for You to Make a proper Arrangement, and at proper times to take by degrees that Sum. You know me very ill if you do not think that of all the letters I have ever wrote to you this one gives me the most pleasure, and I want no other return but Your being convinced that I love You as well as a Man of Worth as I esteem you as a Minister.[45]

Gratefully accepting, North drew £16,000 over the next five years from the secret service account, a clandestine subsegment of the Civil List that Robinson discreetly oversaw.

That the crown wielded its "corrupt influence" over the House of Commons was an article of faith in opposition ranks, and knowledge of the secret compact between king and prime minister would have done nothing to dispel it. However, George III already had North's loyalty—there was no sense in paying for it again. More likely it was North's fortitude that the king wished, if not to buy, then to buttress.

Did North consider himself bought? Six weeks later, he admitted to Edward Thurlow, the attorney-general, "I certainly always have wished and so still wish, to quit my present situation, & will take the first fair & honourable opportunity of doing it, but I am under such obligations to the king that I can never leave his service, while he desires me to remain in it."[46]

FOX SPENT PLEASANT DAYS IN SEPTEMBER 1777 IN CHATSWORTH, THE 81,000-square-foot palatial country home of William Cavendish, 5th Duke of Devonshire. The enchanting young duchess, Georgiana, was much taken with Fox who, with his companion, John Townshend, quoted Shakespeare to each other and to her at the most remarkable length. "I have always thought," wrote Georgiana to her mother, "that the great merit of C. Fox is his amazing quickness in seizing any subject—he seems to have the particular talent of knowing more about what he is saying with less pains than anybody else—his conversation is like a brilliant player of billiards, the strokes follow one another, piff paff."[47] She called him "the Eyebrow."

The company at Chatsworth was indeed "very pleasant and very amiable," though the ruling opinion held that the opposition should wait for events to direct their strategy; no planning, no effort, was necessary. Altogether, said Fox, the aristocrats were "as unfit to storm a citadel as they would be proper for the defence of it."

In a lengthy and warm reply ("My dear Charles"), Burke commiserated with Fox about the highborn Whigs. Their indolence was a consequence of their happy personal circumstances—"honest disinterested intentions, plentiful fortunes, assured rank and quiet homes." Burke meant no disparagement; these were the characteristics of "those whom we most love and trust."

War had robbed English politics of its good sense, almost of its coherence. "In Liverpool they are literally almost ruined by this American War; but they love it as they suffer from it. The Tories prospered by it. The Clergy are astonishingly warm in it—and what the Tories are when embodied, united with their natural head the Crown, and animated by their Clergy, no man knows better than yourself."

The older man, forty-eight, would not presume to counsel the younger one, twenty-eight, he said, but Burke could hardly help himself. "Lay your foundations deep in public opinion," he urged Fox. Do not be in such a hurry. Avoid excessive ardor. As to Fox joining the Rockingham party, what a fine thing that would be. He could serve the party better "than any man I know," even if Burke would never so advise him.[48]

Burke's genius, unlike Fox's, was the uncharismatic kind. His written words, so beautiful on the page, lost something of their force when he spoke them in Parliament. His Irish accent was as thick as if he had "never quitted the Banks of the Shannon," and his unwelcoming, bespectacled face was "full of Intellect but destitute of Softness, and which rarely relaxed into a smile, did not invite approach or conciliation."

These are the recollections of Nathaniel Wraxall, who entered the House of Commons in 1780 as a follower of Lord Germain and an ally of Lord North. Though one makes allowances for the memoirist's political loyalties, Wraxall paints a realistic picture of the Burke that many saw, of the

> mixture of Petulancy, Impatience and at times of Intractability, which greatly obscured the Lustre of his Talents. His very Features, and the undulating Motions of his Head while under the Influence of Anger or Passion, were eloquently expressive of this Irritability, which on some Occasions seemed approach towards the Alienation of Mind.

A very different politician was Fox, Wraxall observes, whose smile was "irresistible" and "whose very Errors or Defects produced Admirers and Imitators."[49] To know Fox was to love him and, in general, to forgive him everything, even his prodigious debts.

There were dissenters. The king despised Fox, and Lord George Germain could not have been overly fond of him.* Nor did Fox's wearing of George Washington's colors in the House of Commons endear him to every English patriot.

---

* In February 1779 news of the acquittal of a Whig admiral, Viscount Keppel, of the capital charges that a Tory admiral, Hugh Palliser, had brought against him touched off riotous celebrations in London. Fox, Keppel's second cousin and zealous supporter (in which cause Burke and Rockingham joined), took it upon himself to direct a London mob on a mission of window-breaking, including at the residences of Lord Germain, Admiral Palliser, and the Navy minister, Lord Sandwich. Naturally, when the disorders became a topic of discussion in the House of Commons, Fox urged that the perpetrators be pardoned.

THE HARD WORDS SPOKEN IN PARLIAMENT DIDN'T INVARIABLY BOUNCE off thick political skin but sometimes touched the tender nerves of personal honor. Such instances brought with them the risk of an invitation to continue the discussion with dueling pistols.

It happened to Burke on the evening of December 3, 1777, when Solicitor-General Wedderburn rose to defend himself against Burke's imputation that the celebrated lawyer had compromised his legal judgment to curry political favor with Lord North. Tempers in the House were already frayed, with the opposition hounding the North government over the news of Burgoyne's surrender to American forces at the Battle of Saratoga.

By accident, as Wedderburn was on his feet, Burke filled a momentary silence in the House with his laughter—or as Wedderburn styled it, "one of his loud hysterical laughs." If, the solicitor-general continued, "that gentleman did not know manners, *he as an individual* would teach them to him; that he had not the good will of that gentleman and did not wish for it; but he was ambitious of having *even his respect*, and would force it from him."[50]

Burke rushed from the House to draft a note informing Wedderburn that he would gladly receive his instruction in good deportment if the solicitor-general would be so good as to name the place, date, and time. Fox and others caught up with Burke before the improbable, nearsighted duelist could sign his challenge. A cooler Burke, with Fox standing by, produced a less incendiary message, to which Wedderburn replied with the conciliatory assurance that he had intended no menace. "My dear Burke," wrote Rockingham as the clock struck midnight, "My heart is at ease."[51]

On November 25, 1779, Fox's words provoked more than the threat of violence. The provocation began with the announcement by William Adam, a Scottish lawyer and former independent member of Parliament, that a government so rich in talent as the North ministry, and one so deep in the confidence of the nation and the king, deserved, and would henceforth receive, his full support.

Fox, in the course of heaping ridicule on the new ministerialist, branded him as a "Beast of Nature," a "Pest of Society," and a "Libeller of Mankind."[52] At least those epithets, attributed to Fox, turned up in the newspapers, and

Adam demanded that Fox disavow them. Fox refused—after all, he had not said them—and the two men, each with his second, agreed to meet at eight in the morning at Hyde Park on November 29, 1779.

They faced each other with pistols at a distance of fifteen paces. Adam called on Fox to fire. "Sir," Fox answered, "I have no quarrel with you." So Adam fired, his shot catching Fox in the midsection; Fox returned fire and missed. Was Adam satisfied? a second asked, to which the challenger answered: "Will Mr. Fox declare he meant no personal attack on my character?" Fox, replying that this was no place for apologies, bade his opponent carry on, which Adam did, firing and missing. Fox discharged his second pistol into the sky.

The affair thus concluded, Fox was prepared to admit, as he had not been under threat, that he had intended no personal affront. "Sir," said Adam, "you have behaved like a man of honor." For Fox, it was a perfect duel. He had acquired a gallant flesh wound and, in Adam, a new friend. As to the former, he was able to quip that Adam must have been using government gunpowder, so weak was the charge.[53]

They loved Fox all the more at Brooks's and New Market for his casual courage. It was of a piece with the story that Topham Beauclerk told about an evening he spent with Fox at the faro tables. What little money Fox possessed he lost that evening, and Beauclerk worried that his friend might give in to despair. Checking in on him the next morning, he discovered Fox serenely reading Herodotus. Beauclerk was a man about town, a member of Dr. Johnson's literary set, and a prodigious collector of books; still, he found the scene incongruous. "What would you have me do?" Fox answered him. "I have lost my last shilling!"[54]

The Duchess of Devonshire, who well knew the Fox magic, was among the sixty ladies who thronged the lobby of the House of Commons on February 2, 1778, to hear Fox move a motion to prohibit the government from sending more regular British troops out of the kingdom to America.

The ladies, including the wife of the speaker of the House, Lady Norton, pushed past the doorkeepers to take their seats in the gallery. An uncounted number of male visitors, or as the House denoted all nonmembers, "strangers," likewise jostled their way into St. Stephen's Chapel.

A stranger was admitted on the sufferance of the members of Parliament. If even a single member objected, the speaker was bound to order the sergeant to clear the gallery. In this instance, a member did object, and the galleries were duly cleared, first of men only, later of the ladies, too (after the objection that state secrets were no more secure with female strangers than with male ones).

Fox rose, made a joke about the welcome reduction in the size of his audience, and moved his motion for an inquiry into the "present alarming State of the Nation." He reviewed the long train of ministerial incompetence that had provoked a distant, futile war while robbing the home islands of their defenses. The minimum peacetime military establishment was reckoned to be 17,000, not counting the forces stationed in Ireland, Gibraltar, and Minorca. As Fox spoke, the number of troops in Great Britain did not exceed 15,000. France was preparing for war, as the City of London, on the evidence of falling British security prices, had clearly taken note. "It would be madness to part with any more of our army," charged Fox, before moving the following: "That an humble Address be presented to his majesty, that he will be graciously pleased to give orders, that no more of the Old Corps [i.e., the regular British Army] be sent out of the kingdom."

Fox spoke plainly and briefly and resumed his seat in a silent House. No minister, not even North, attempted a reply. There was no debate. "In this singular situation," the parliamentary record states, "the question was called for, and the [House] divided: For Mr. Fox's motion, 165; Against it, 259."[55] The vote exaggerated the political strength of the government that North so reluctantly led.

CHAPTER 10

Mercy for the slaves
and sodomists

It was commonly observed, he spoke too often in parliament; but
nobody would say he did not speak well.

—SAMUEL JOHNSON ON BURKE, 1770, IN BOSWELL, *LIFE OF JOHNSON*

In the scintillating London of literature and politics, there lived a tavern
keeper named John Green and a coal heaver named John Grainger. On
April 20, 1768, a crowd of seething men, Grainger included, massed
outside Green's place of business, the Roundabout Tavern, near the Thames
at Shadwell. They would destroy it and kill him, if they could.

What provoked Green's assailants was, in the first place, a wage dispute, and in the second, the perennial enmity of English Protestant labor-
ers toward their Irish Catholic brethren. Green, negotiating on behalf of
some London coal barge operators, had hired free-market Irish workers at
a lower wage than the organized English ones demanded.

The doughty Green, defying the mob, barricaded the house, collected
his armaments—a brace of pistols, a faulty musket, a blunderbuss—and
deployed his meager forces. Besides himself, they numbered two or three,
including a sixty-year-old sailor who had been drinking at the bar.

Outside, the raging coal heavers, some shouting "Wilkes and liberty!", others threatening to have Green's "heart and liver," threw rocks
and procured firearms. A gun battle began at midnight and banged on
till morning. Green, stationing himself by the windows at the top of the

house, killed two of the attacking party. The Roundabout was pocked with 260 bullet holes. Green was unscathed.

No watchman, volunteer constable, or magistrate had appeared at the scene to investigate, let alone help. Except for Henry Fielding's compact corps of "Bow Street Runners," London had no proper police force to respond—such awaited the coming of Sir Robert Peel and his "Bobbies" in 1829. In the light of day, Green sought out the authorities and confessed to his killings. "Mr. Green," a Justice Hodgson declared in committing him to Newgate Prison pending trial, "you are one of the bravest fellows who ever was."

Seven coal heavers, Grainger among them, were arrested, convicted, and sentenced to death for "feloniously, wilfully and maliciously" shooting at Green; perhaps six of the seven were Irish Catholic.[1] They were hanged in the gallows that were knocked together, especially for the occasion, near the site of the siege. Some fifty thousand spectators, guarded by six hundred British troops, attended the executions.[2] The crowds dispersed peacefully. Horace Walpole, writing to a friend, expressed the hope that "our mobs are subsided."[3]

MANY SUSPECTED THAT EDMUND BURKE, THOUGH A MEMBER OF THE Church of England, was secretly a Roman Catholic. Was he not Irish, and had he not, in 1778, worked to repeal the anachronistic "disability" laws that barred the Catholics of Ireland, England, and Scotland from landowning, voting, holding political office, performing military service, entering the legal and academic professions, and much more? Such strictures, many dating from the Glorious Revolution of 1688, were enforced only intermittently, but their obsolescence made them no less repugnant to liberal minds. Burke subscribed to the view of the jurist Sir William Blackstone that "it ought not to be left in the Breast of every merciless Bigot to drag down the vengeance of these occasional Laws upon inoffensive though mistaken Subjects, in opposition to the lenient inclination of the civil magistrate, and to the destruction of every principle of toleration and religious Liberty."[4]

Burke omitted no sect from his support of religious tolerance. He wished Methodists, Presbyterians, Catholics, and "Pagans" the free exercise of their consciences. In this respect, he resembled Fox, though Burke, unlike his good friend, devoutly believed in the risen Christ and in the life of the world to come. He regarded these doctrines as basic to the universal Christian faith—"the whole Christian Church, East and West" as he put it to Dr. John Erskine, a leading Church of Scotland theologian, in 1779.

And "If," Burke went on,

> on Account of such sentiments, people call me a Roman Catholick,* it will give me not the smallest degree of disturbance. They do me too much honour, who aggregate me as a Member to any one of those respectable Societies which compose the body of Christianity. Wherever they choose to place me, I am sure to be found in extraordinary good Company.[5]

The North government duly enacted the Papist Act of 1778 for England and Ireland, but in the face of anti-Catholic rioting in Edinburgh and Glasgow, it withdrew companion relief legislation for Scotland in 1779. The uncompensated victims of that violence petitioned the House of Commons for financial compensation, and Burke spoke for ninety minutes on their behalf.

The local magistrates, said the member for Bristol, had not only failed to protect their Catholic constituents but equally had failed to bring the guilty parties to justice. That was bad enough, but the unrepentant riot makers, organizing themselves as "The Committee for the Protestant Interest" and meeting under the roof of St. Giles, the principal Calvinist church of Edinburgh, had had the effrontery to publish a pamphlet exhorting their fellow Christians to proscribe their Catholic neighbors, neither to lend to them nor to borrow from them nor to say hello as they passed them on the street. A universal cold shoulder might drive them out of Scotland forever.

---

* In the same rhetorical vein, Burke told the House in 1777 that he took no umbrage at being called an American. "If warm affection, towards those over whom I can claim any share of authority, be a crime, I am guilty of this charge," he said, before quickly adding that nobody was more "zealous" than he for the "supremacy of Parliament and the rights of this imperial Crown." W&S, 3:313.

Burke had read "copious" extracts from the pamphlet to his fellow members, during which, a newspaper reported,

> Lord North had fallen into a sound Sleep, which the House did not perceive till these Words happened to drop from Mr. Burke in Support of an Argument; without adverting to the noble Lord's Situation— "Government is not dead; it only sleepeth." The Peals of Laughter upon this Occasion were universal, and the Minister Opening his Eyes was informed of the Occasion by his next Neighbour, and then he joined in the Mirth. Mr. Burke pleasantly remarked, now that the House was in a good Humour, and Government awake, which he had long doubted of, he hoped it would be the proper Time to call them to the Exercise of Humanity.[6]

The House, however, did not humor Burke, and Lord North carried his point that the victims of the Edinburgh and Glasgow outrages would be indemnified, if at all, by local officials, not by the House of Commons.

"I RISQUE ODIUM IF I SUCCEED, AND CONTEMPT IF I FAIL," SAID BURKE IN February 1780, in the preface to his speech at the House of Commons on eliminating useless public offices and sinecures. "I know," he told the House, "that all parsimony is of a quality approaching to unkindness; and that (on some person or other) every reform must operate as a sort of punishment." He approached his quite essential mission "with a tremor that shakes me to the inmost fibre of my frame."[7]

Burke needn't have worried about pulling the rug out from under the overfed supernumeraries. Nor was it his intention. To abolish wasteful spending was only the means to the end of checking the king's unconstitutional influence. This control the king bought with the pensions and sinecures he too freely distributed. By reasserting its power over the public purse, the House of Commons would strike a blow for the purity of the constitution and the independence of Parliament.

"The whole of our grievances," Burke had contended a few months earlier, was traceable to "the fatal and overgrown influence of the crown; and that influence itself to our enormous prodigality." He had indeed claimed as much ten years earlier in his *Thoughts on the Cause of the Present Discontents.*[8] It was fundamental Rockingham party doctrine.

The essential thing, Burke daringly began his prescription for fiscal improvement, was to emulate Britain's inveterate enemy. Under Jacques Necker, finance minister to King Louis XVI, France was conducting a "regular, methodical system" of public finance. Britain, unreformed, had accumulated £14 million in debt in the past year alone. "For God's sake," Burke urged the House, "let not this be the only fashion of France that we refuse to copy."[9]

With economic reform, Burke had picked the popular side of a public issue. Some forty petitions to curb public spending and end "government by cousinhood and connection"[10] were making their way to Parliament. Grounds for grievance abounded. To credit the York petitioners, trade, manufacturing, and land rents were plunging as taxes and the national debt relentlessly rose.

Ireland was in a state of near revolt, while Spain and France, allied against Britain in the interminable American war, menaced the home islands from the lightly defended English Channel. Let not a new tax be laid, prayed the "Gentlemen, Clergy and Freeholders" of York, until the House of Commons abolished "unmerited pensions," every sinecure, and "all exorbitant emoluments."

Some of the king's disgruntled subjects, invoking the hallowed name of John Locke, dared to form independent committees, to which "the power of the people is to be delegated," bypassing Parliament altogether in the cause of restoring "the liberties of the people to their ancient purity."[11] Lord Rockingham and Charles Fox, acknowledged friends of the people though they were, deserved no place in this democratic movement, according to one of its founders, the Reverend Christopher Wyvill. Better, said he, that it operated outside the walls of a corrupted Parliament.

Nonetheless, within those walls Fox championed Burke's plan for economy, efficiency, and honesty in government. Nothing, in his view and Burke's, could be less competent and more corrupt than the government of Lord North. As viewed from the twenty-first century, the North ministry was not especially venal, but at the time its failures in war and fiscal management were plain. On June 16, 1779, the day the government acknowledged a breach with Spain that would shortly add that Bourbon power to the ranks of Britain's warring enemies, Burke tongue-lashed the ministry for its "monstrous ignorance." Calling him to order, the speaker asked if he had some motion to make.

"Oh, Sir," Burke shot back, "I could give the House a motion: The Impeachment of the minister [pointing to Lord North] might be deemed a very proper one!"[12] Climbing down from this parliamentary precipice, Burke allowed his motion to be withdrawn, but later that year he drafted extensive articles of impeachment against North and his senior ministers. These, too, came to naught, lying dormant among his papers.

In anticipation of Burke's "Speech on Economical Reform," visitors and members alike thronged St. Stephen's Chapel to hear what proved a highly unusual oration on fiscal policy. Not many such speeches have matched Burke's in length, a full three hours and twenty minutes, and perhaps fewer in the ratio of epigrams, classical allusions, and metaphor to fiscal facts and figures. And if, from time to time, the audience grew impatient with the details of plans for selling off the king's forests, abolishing the Board of Trade, or laying an ax to the offices of the Green Cloth, grooms of the stole, lords of the bedchamber, and masters of the horse, Burke rewarded them with some glittering new rhetorical turn.

He spoke to introduce five separate bills, each concerned with a particular area of proposed economy. More important, even, than the £200,000 or £300,000 a year in savings that such reforms could achieve (out of a total budget of £19.7 million), he declared, was the nation's deliverance from the "secret corruption" of the crown. At least fifty members of Parliament, currently in the pocket of king and ministry, would be set free and uncorrupted, regret it though those well-compensated members might.

Burke said that he intended to economize "by principle," not by detail. One such principle concerned the Paymaster's Office, on which Lord Holland and his family had feasted for generations and on which Burke himself would soon nibble.

That all subordinate treasuries [he said], as the nurseries of mismanagement, and as naturally drawing to themselves as much money as
they can, ought to be dissolved. They have a tendency to perplex and
distract the public accounts, and to excite a suspicion of government,
even beyond the extent of their abuse.[13]

Burke cast no aspersions on Lord Holland nor even on the current paymaster, Richard Rigby, whom he despised. If the profits of the Paymaster's Office
were offensively large, said Burke, they were nonetheless legally obtained. To
render them less offensive, he proposed that the government's cash balances
earn interest for the government rather than for the paymaster, while safely
on deposit at the Bank of England. This proposed reform, presently adopted,
took effect just in time to deny Burke, who succeeded Rigby at the Paymaster's Office in 1782, the paymaster's customary bags of gold.

What Burke, age fifty-one, did not propose to abolish were the crown-
conferred pensions for long-serving statesmen. "There is a time," said he,
"when the weather-beaten vessels of the state, ought to come into harbour.*
They must at length have a retreat from the malice of rivals, from the perfidy of political friends, and the inconstancy of the people."[14]

TURNING TO THE CIVIL LIST, BURKE PROPOSED A SET OF INCENTIVES TO
improve the quality of management. As it was, the Commons bailed out the
overspending king. Under Burke's plan, overspending would be matched
by a compensating program of underspending even if, in consequence of
that retrenchment, someone must go unpaid. Judges, ambassadors, royal
tradesmen, royal nephews, sinecurists, and the prime minister, who drew
their pay from the Civil List, would be at risk.

Burke proposed, perhaps a bit mischievously, a rank order of seniority for salaried claimants. Judges would stand first in line for payment—
"It is the public justice that holds the community together," he declared.

---

* That time, in fact, arrived for Burke in 1794, when he gratefully accepted an annual pension of £2,500. However, it would have taken even more prescience than Burke possessed to
foresee that the king and he would have mended their differences in common cause against
the then-unimagined French Revolution.

Foreign ministers would come second, and tradesmen third. The crown's workaday staff would come fourth, the royal family fifth, higher-paid staff sixth, the ordinary pension list seventh, and the offices of honor around the king eighth.

The salaries and pensions of the prime minister, the chancellor of the exchequer, and the other high commissioners of the Treasury would be paid with the residue. If no funds remained, the disappointed ministers would have to do without; they could lay no claim on next year's budget. "This plan, I really flatter myself," said Burke, "is laid, not in official formality, nor in airy speculation, but in real life, and in human nature, in what 'comes home (as Bacon says) to the business and bosoms of men.'"[15]

A twenty-first-century financial theorist would recognize in Burke's scheme the germ of the idea of the alignment of interests between the individual executive and the organization he serves. Or as Burke himself expressed the spirit of the thing: "Interest, the great guide of commerce, is not a blind one. It is very well able to find its own way; and its necessities are its best laws."

Burke was a friend to Adam Smith's ideas as well as to the Scottish philosopher himself, so his reforming eye naturally fell on Britain's Board of Trade. Because, as Burke put it, "commerce . . . flourishes most when it is left to itself," a trade bureaucracy would hardly be missed if it no longer existed. For other reasons, too, the Burkes wished it ill. It was the Board of Trade that had rejected Richard's contestable claims to real estate on St. Vincent.*

Burke likewise proposed to abolish the sinecures attached to the Royal Mint and Artillery, and he pushed for the extinction of the independent Welsh judiciary. While England made do with twelve judges, Wales—"about the tenth part of England in size and population; and certainly not a hundredth part in opulence"—somehow needed eight.[16]

Burke ridiculed the many royal palaces that time and the "resistless tide

* Other tangles between family and board may explain Burke's animus. Klinge, "Burke, Economical Reform."

of manners" had rendered obsolete. It was absurd to preserve nothing about them except the burden they laid on the public finances, he told the House.

> Our palaces are vast inhospitable halls. There are bleak winds, there, "Boreas, and Eurus, and Caurus, and Argestes loud," howling through the vacant lobbies, and clattering the doors of deserted guardrooms, appal the imagination, and conjure up the grim spectres of departed tyrants—the Saxon, the Norman, and the Dane, the stern Edwards and fierce Henrys—who stalk from desolation to desolation through the dreary vacuity, and melancholy succession of chill and comfortless chambers. When this tumult subsides, a dead, and still more frightful silence would reign in this desert, if every now and then the tacking of hammers did not announce, that those constant attendants upon all courts, in all ages, Jobbs,* were still alive; for whose sake alone it is, that any trace of ancient grandeur is suffered to remain.

"These palaces," Burke continued, "are a true emblem of some governments; the inhabitants are decayed, but the governors and magistrates still flourish. They put me in mind of *Old Sarum*, where the representatives, more in number than the constituents, only serve to inform us, that this was once a place of trade, and sounding with the 'busy hum of men,' though now you can only trace the streets by the colour of the corn; and its sole manufacture is in members of parliament."[17]

"I have very little to recommend me for this or any [other] task," Burke told the House in the stock self-deprecating vocabulary of eighteenth-century British statesmanship. North, however, declared that Burke's speech was not only one of the finest he had ever heard but also such "as no gentleman in that House but the hon. member, he believed, was equal to, although he had the happiness to know, that there were many who had very brilliant parts."†

---

* We would say "boondoggle." Johnson's dictionary, spelling *job* with one *b*, defines it as a "low mean lucrative busy affair." "Job, n.s.," Johnson, *Dictionary*.

† Magnanimous praise indeed from a man who, eight months earlier, had been the object of Burke's impeachment outburst.

The only member to register dissent was the eccentric Lord George Gordon, third son of a Scottish duke and a former navy officer who, becalmed in naval rank and denouncing the American war, resigned his commission and entered Parliament, where he presently sought repeal of the Catholic relief law, formally titled the Papist Act of 1778.

"The whole business," said Gordon of Burke's fiscal plan, "was a juggle between the worthy member from Bristol and the noble lord in the blue ribbon." Insisting that the House divide over this contention, Gordon discovered that he was the lone yea vote, a party of one.

What Lord North admired was Burke's eloquence, not his politics, and weeks passed before he allowed a debate over the substance of the economic reform legislation. When all was said and done, only the abolition of the Board of Trade commanded a parliamentary majority. Burke, though he did not publicly acknowledge his personal distaste for that inconsequential agency, shone in the debate over eliminating it.

On March 13, William Eden, a member of Parliament, diplomat, and a Board of Trade commissioner, tried to win the board a stay of execution by informing the House that it had, since its inception, 108 years before, published 2,300 folio volumes of reports and records. Was Burke unaware that John Locke and Joseph Addison, both former Board of Trade sinecurists, had contributed their genius to parts of those hefty works?

Reading Cicero in translation was something that Burke could not abide, he once remarked to a friend; similarly, reading Burke in paraphrase in the parliamentary record perhaps only hints at the listening pleasure that Eden unintentionally provoked.

No, Burke said, he would not read those volumes, but should his bill, or rather the single clause of that bill pertaining to the Board of Trade, be put to death, the 2,300 works would survive as a monument to it.

"After having indulged himself for some time," the *Parliamentary History* records,

in a succession of images full of wit and abounding in ridicule, in which the dull, senseless, sluggish contents of 2,300 volumes in folio, large enough to fill the room he was now speaking in, were contrasted with the transcendent talents, solid knowledge and exalted characters of those great and wise men who were called in as witnesses, to stamp authority upon folly, to give currency to dulness, and induce the committee to believe that what was laborious was useful. He grew more serious, and said, as a board of trade he detested that which his clause tended to abolish, because he regarded it as useless, idle, and expensive; considered as an academy of Belles Lettres, into which it was now converted, he was willing to bow his head in reverence to the great and shining talents of its several members.[18]

One such member was Eden himself, author of "Four Letters to the Earl of Carlisle." Carlisle, too, was a commissioner and a poet besides. Charles Fox's creditor and former boon companion, he had served as Eden's fellow commissioner on a 1778 mission to end the American Revolution. Edward Gibbon, a third commissioner, fondly recalled the £750 a year he had earned at the Board of Trade for not much work at all. So provided for, he wrote his history.*

To these "professors," Burke continued, "he owed all possible deference, and from that deference it was that he wished to rescue them from the ignominy of being degraded to a board of trade."[19]

PERHAPS THE MOST CEREBRAL OF BURKE'S MANY ADMIRERS WAS SIR WILliam Jones, a London-born philologist, orientalist, and lawyer. Son of a dis-

---

* Gibbon's appointment to the Board of Trade in 1779 inspired an anonymous satirist to take up his pen:

> King George, in a fright
> Lest Gibbon should write
> The hist'ry of England's disgrace,
> Thought no way so sure
> His pen to secure
> As to give the historian a place.

Could the author have been Charles Fox? The politician and memoirist Sir Nathaniel Wraxall believed so, even if others, including Fox's nephew, the third Lord Holland, disputed it. "I know, however," Wraxall records, "that some years afterwards, when his effects in St. James's Street were seized for debt, and his books were sold, a set of Gibbon's *Decline and Fall of the Roman Empire*, in the first leaf of which work Fox had with his own hand inserted the stanzas in question, produced a very considerable sum, under the belief or conviction that he was their author." Wraxall, *Historical Memoirs*, 2:24.

tinguished mathematician, young William attended Harrow School, where his proficiency in Greek earned him the sobriquet "the Great Scholar." At Oxford, Jones translated *Arabian Nights* from English back into the original Arabic; by and by, with publication of his *Grammar of the Persian Language* in 1771, the Great Scholar became "Oriental Jones." Arabic, Hebrew, and Persian were among the twenty-eight languages in his repertoire. In 1774 Jones acknowledged the influence of Burke's *Sublime and Beautiful* on his own newly published *Poeseos Asiaticæ Comentariorum*, a much-admired work on Eastern poetry. This was a year after Jones's election to the Literary Club.

If Jones did not hear Burke's "Speech on Economical Reform," he read it, not once but twice. He thought about what he had read and about its author, too, and he conveyed those musings in a letter to Lord Althorp.

Actually, Jones corrected himself, he had not merely read but had "devoured" it with "rapture." It "had given me such delight," he said,

> that I wished immediately to impart the pleasure which I received, to you, who had so well prepared me for it. High as my expectations had been raised by your praises, they were, I assure you, by no means disappointed. It is a noble composition, and the most extraordinary example I ever knew of retentive memory, strong reason and gay imagination: some passages are no less just and solid than others are brilliant and sparkling.

Because Jones's Whiggish politics differed from Burke's, quibbles and demurrers followed. "But—," he continued,

> (this unhappy exceptive particle too often intervenes, in some cases from envy, in others from ill-nature; in this, as you will easily believe, from my love of truth) the speech has blemishes; like the sun, it has great fire, spreads light, and makes flowers blossom, but it has spots. The style has neither purity, simplicity, nor grace; and the metaphors are poured out with such profusion that the mind instead of being satisfied, is only dazzled. The epigrams, which close almost every

paragraph, are excellent as epigrams but ill-paced in a speech on the
most important interests of a nation on the brink of ruin.[20]

Granted, wrote Jones, humor is essential to holding the interest of
an audience during a long oration: "but would the oration have been
near so long if some of the nosegays of rhetorick had been removed?"
A twenty-first-century reader, unaccustomed to hours-long oratory,
might imagine a brilliant violinist performing some beloved con-
certo. At the cadenza, the soloist begins to improvise—it is his or her
opportunity to parade a few minutes of hard-won virtuosity. But three
minutes turns into a quarter-hour of showy self-indulgence. The audience begins to slip away, and even the string section of the accompanying orchestra eyes the door.

Jones had been called to the bar in 1774 at Middle Temple. He would later
distinguish himself in India on the Bengal supreme court, but for now he
rode the Welsh circuit. He rejected Burke's proposal to abolish the Welsh
courts, which must shunt those litigants onto the English courts. Such a
plan would especially disadvantage poor litigants: "How many industrious
tenants will then be greater slaves than they are even now to the tyrannical
agents and stewards of indolent gentlemen?"[21]

TO THE NOBLE CAUSES OF CATHOLIC EMANCIPATION (NEVER A VOTE-
getter in eighteenth-century Britain), relief for imprisoned debtors, and justice for the murderers of a pair of pilloried sodomites, Burke brought moral
courage and eloquent words along with, at times, a lofty indifference to the
opinions of his Bristol constituents. "They are," he said of the electorate in
general, "naturally proud, tyrannical, and ignorant; bad scholars and worse
Masters."[22] He did not make an exception for the voters who sent him to
Parliament.

Unlike Charles Fox, who craved and earned his constituents' affection, Burke treated popularity as a by-product of the successful pursuit
of the people's interests, of which he, not they, was the best judge. Certainly, the merchants of Bristol were little inclined to share his conviction that defaulting debtors ought not to be locked away in jail or, after

they had attested to a good-faith effort to discharge their obligations, be freed to make a fresh start in life. Within that bustling commercial city, sentiment ran strong that leniency toward bankrupts meant the ruination of credit.

Arrest for unpaid debts entered the English penal code in the thirteenth-century reign of Edward I, and in one essential the law remained much as King Edward had left it. The debtor pledged his freedom—his "body"—as the security for his loan. If insolvent and friendless, he remained behind bars until his creditor released him, or as happened from time to time, most recently in 1776, Parliament emptied the prisons of their debtors by "acts of grace." Or if not of grace, then of necessity, when the population of insolvent debtors overwhelmed the space in which to house them.

In February 1780, Lord Beauchamp brought forward a bill to advance the liberalizing spirit of the 1776 amnesty in the case of insolvent debtors owing more than £100. The idea was to remove from "merciless or revengeful" creditors the awful power to incarcerate a debtor indefinitely. Under the legislation, judges would decide if a debtor, having surrendered his all-in satisfaction of his creditor's claims, should be held or released. Opponents of the measure had scoffed that there were probably no more than fifty such hapless prisoners to be found in the London jails of Westminster and Southwark. Well, replied Beauchamp, let these critics "ask themselves whether the liberty of fifty Englishmen, so circumstanced, was not an object worthy [of] their attention?"

Burke dutifully presented a petition from Bristol opposing the Beauchamp measure—but speaking for himself, he said he supported the bill. Indeed, he wished that it had gone further by adding a clause to allow "honest debtors" to escape the lifetime incubus of a single financial mistake.*

The Beauchamp reform was no more popular with Westminster's

---

* Later, in explaining his position to the disapproving merchants of Bristol, Burke observed that imprisonment for life turns a civil judgment into a criminal one and so operates "to scourge misfortune or indiscretion with a punishment which the law does not inflict on the greatest crimes." W&S, 3:635–36.

merchants than it was with Bristol's. Why change the ancient law now? a lawyer retained by Westminster demanded of the House. Did it spring from some dubious conviction that "people now living [had] grown wiser than their ancestors?"

Charles Fox, who was planning to seek a Westminster parliamentary seat next election, presented a petition on behalf of his prospective constituents. For himself, Fox told the House, he "defended the principle of the Bill, and said it was equally liberal, humane and laudable."

Fox's precarious finances were an open secret, as were Burke's recurrent money troubles, in company with those of his brother, Richard, and his cousin, William. Perhaps Lord George Gordon, recently elected member for Ludgershall, Wiltshire, had these biographical details in mind when he rose to oppose the bill immediately after Fox had spoken in support of it.

Lord Gordon declared that most of the members were in no position to hold a disinterested opinion on bankruptcy. The House of Commons, he said, was largely filled with debtors, many of whom had "not even a table, a chair, or a three-legged stool to sit down upon, that they could call their own."

Unmistakably alluding to Burke, Gordon conceded that "the hon. gentleman had great eloquence, but though he might admire the wreath of flowers that grew out of the fertile bog of his understanding, he [Gordon] was not to be deceived."[23] Lord Beauchamp's bill was buried in committee.*

IN FEBRUARY 1780, THEODOSIUS READ, A PLASTERER, AND WILLIAM Smith, a hackney coachman, were caught breaking the sodomy laws at a coffeehouse at St. George's Field. Arrested and charged, they were tried, found guilty ("by a very respectable jury"), and sentenced to six months in jail and to an hour in the pillory.[24]

In that device of public humiliation, the prisoner stood, half-crouched or on tiptoes (depending on his height), defenseless, his arms and head

---

* Imprisonment for debt in Britain was abolished in 1869.

locked in their respective cutouts, facing whomever might show up to taunt or pelt him.

If the spectators were sympathetic—as were Daniel Defoe's in 1703*— they might gently toss flowers. If hostile, they would heave mud, manure, rotten eggs, the carcasses of small animals, or rocks.

Bright and early on April 10, 1780, some twenty thousand Londoners thronged St. Margaret's Hill to pass judgment on Read and Smith. Presently, a rock came whistling at Smith's head; it caught him behind the right ear and killed him. His body was laid on the floor of the pillory, as the mob refocused its attention on his companion. At the end of sixty minutes, Read too lay bleeding.

Capital punishment was unexceptional in eighteenth-century England. At the Tyburn gallows, public executions took place eight times a year, with the crowds sometimes treated to as many as twenty simultaneous hangings. The menu of judicial punishments in the Georgian age encompassed whipping, exile, branding with a hot iron, and—in cases of high treason—hanging, followed by disemboweling and quartering. But the newspaper account of the ordeal of Smith and Read deeply moved Burke, and he so informed the House of Commons the next day.

Writers of the criminal laws, he reminded his fellow members, must "take care wisely and nicely to proportion the punishment so that it should not exceed the extent of the crime." The purpose of punishment was to protect the innocent by preventing crime, not to "oppress and torment" the guilty.

The king had taken a coronation oath to "temper justice with mercy," yet the circumstances of this case placed His Majesty in violation of that sworn pledge. "The pillory," said Burke, "had always struck him as a punishment of shame rather than of personal severity. In the present instance

---

* The future author of *Robinson Crusoe*, convicted of seditious libel for his satirical pamphlet *The Shortest Way with the Dissenters*, was sentenced to three hour-long confinements in the pillory. His friends used the occasion to sell copies of the offending publication, as well as a new Defoe production, *Hymn to the Pillory*, to admiring spectators. Cavendish, "Daniel Defoe Put in the Pillory," *History Today* 53, July 2003, https://www.historytoday.com/archive/daniel-defoe-put-pillory.

it had been rendered an instrument of death, and that of the worst kind, a death of torment."

Burke wanted the members to know how much he reviled "sodomy," a crime that could "scarcely be mentioned, much less defended or extenuated." Yet nothing he could say against the crime would spare him the smirking libels of his enemies for the humane defense of the alleged sodomists.[25]

The libels duly appeared in consecutive issues of the *London Morning Post*, April 13 and 14. "Unmanly" was the verdict of the reliably Tory newspaper on Burke's humanity. Behold, the paper said, "this man [Burke] condemning in the highest terms, the just indignation of the people, because it was levelled at a *sodomite!*"*

If no other man stepped forward to bring in legislation to outlaw the pillory, Burke told the House of Commons, he would himself.†

Three weeks after the death of William Smith, Burke again rose to plead the cause of mercy. A pair of seamen on a British privateer had mutinied against a captain who, in defiance of the law, had attacked neutral shipping while illegally flying an American flag. The captain of this benighted vessel, the *Eagle*, was a pirate, Burke protested, and the mutineers, John Williams and James Stoneham, certainly did not deserve the death sentence that the Court of Admiralty had pronounced on them. "Mercy," said Burke,

was not dependent, at least it ought not to be dependent, on the mere caprice of any man; it was absolute part of the law of the land, and was

---

* Burke filed an affidavit in the King's Bench, dated May 31, 1780, against the author of the paragraphs for "defaming, Calumnating and injuring this Deponent" and inciting "the People to Commit Murder in the Cases therein mentioned." Burke said that he had removed himself from the proceedings, turning everything over to his lawyers, so that he "might not be actuated by passion." The offending author, William Finney, was sentenced to three months in prison. C., 4: 350–51.

† No such bill has been found. The undersheriff of Surrey was acquitted on charges of dereliction of duty that resulted in the prisoner's death. W&S, 3:586.

as much to be attended to as justice; nay, justice itself called as loudly as human compassion could for mercy.

Moving to stay the execution of the prisoners pending a new inquiry, Burke had to fight for the House's attention since, as the speaker observed, his remarks were not pertinent to the business then at hand. But North spoke up, promising to lend assistance, and Williams and Stoneham got off with their lives. They were pardoned on condition of their agreeing to serve in the Royal Navy.[26]

ON ONE DELICATE ISSUE, AT LEAST, BURKE WAS UNWILLING TO PROVOKE his Bristol constituents. He had condemned the slave trade in passing remarks in the House of Commons in 1777 during debate over the Africa Company. There was nothing of the great set piece in either of these declarations but rather a matter-of-fact expression of repugnance. No one heard his plan for a comprehensive "Negro Code" in April 1780 because, like his draft of articles of impeachment against North and his cabinet, it remained in a drawer.

The opening lines of his code are morally uncompromising and, just as Burke judged, not calculated to win him votes in a seaport community whose members included the owners of victuallers to and investors in slave ships.

> Whereas [he wrote to himself] it is expedient and conformable to the principles of true religion and morality, and to the Rules of sound policy, to put an end to all traffic in the persons of Men, and to the detention of their said persons in a State of Slavery . . .

However, odious though it may be, the slave trade was established in practice and law. One could not ignore the interests of the merchants who, breaking no laws, had built their lives and businesses around it. Thus, let the odious trade be halted "as soon as the thing can be effected without producing great inconveniences in the sudden Change of practices of such long standing, and during the continuance of the said practices, it is desirable and expedient, by proper regulations, to lessen the inconveniences and evils attendant on the said Traffic, and state of Servitude, until both shall be gradually done away."[27]

Burke and Fox saw eye to eye on economic reform, but they parted company on parliamentary reform. Concerning the frequency of elections, qualifications for the franchise, the equity and existence of the so-called rotten boroughs, and other matters of electoral contention, Burke was unmovable. As England's glorious unwritten constitution could not be improved, so it should not be changed. Once upon a time, Fox was as unyielding as he, but Lord Holland's son was throwing off his family prejudices for a host of new ones.

Alderman John Sawbridge, a radical member for London, had moved a motion to shorten the maximum life of a sitting Parliament every year since 1771. It was his hobbyhorse. Seven years, the limit in place, dated from the Septennial Act of 1715 at the start of the reign of George I. Long-lived, stable Parliaments would save money and constitute a bulwark against the exiled, lurking Stuarts, the Whigs who enacted that bill contended. It would likewise, incidentally, entrench the position of the Whig majority. Sawbridge argued for a compression to one year.

Perhaps the furthest thing from the minds of the authors of the Septennial Act was that King George's descendants would come to pose as great a threat to the liberty of England as the tyrannical James II ever did. Yet such, the descendants of those Whigs contended, was the state of things in 1780. On April 6, John Dunning persuaded the House of Commons to pass his instantly famous resolution, "The influence of the crown has increased, is increasing and ought to be diminished."[28]

A month later, when the House took up Sawbridge's annual motion, the new Fox blessed it. Year-long parliaments would shorten the king's political reach, he contended. If one of his constituents were to ask him how it was that the unpopular and ineffective North administration—"the most unprincipled prostitute tools that ever disgraced this country," as Sawbridge styled it in 1775—could so long cling to office, Fox said that he would reply, "The first cause was the influence of the crown, the second, the influence of the crown, and the third, the influence of the crown."

Fox ridiculed objections that annual, or even triennial, elections would impoverish all but the richest independent candidates, thereby advantaging the ministry's picked (and subsidized) favorites. Burke, speaking against the Sawbridge motion, argued the opposite.

It was a curious debate, protégé versus mentor, because each shared the Dunning worldview, which was indeed the Rockingham creed. Where they divided was over the nature of the people who vote.

While governing in the interest of the people is a "great and glorious Object of Government," Burke declared, a popular election itself is a "mighty Evil. . . . The voters are corruptible. They are men; it is saying nothing worse of them. Many of them are but ill informed in their minds, many feeble in their Circumstances; and easily overreachd; and easily seduced."[29]

"Continual Elections" destroyed Rome, said Burke, though with nothing more to debauch the voters than "faction, bribery, bread and stage Plays." It would be worse in Britain, which had liquor.

Triennial elections would mean "Triennial Corruption, Triennial Drunkenness, triennial Idleness, triennial fury." More frequent elections would create the demand for more public offices and more public spending. County boroughs would relinquish agriculture to "grow politicians."

The prior general election had cost the nation £1.5 million, the individual, independent candidate in that contest about £3,000. (Subsidized ministerial candidates of course paid less.) Yes, Burke acknowledged, in theory election day was the day of judgment for the members of Parliament as they accounted for their words and deeds before the jury of their constituents. In life and experience, however, it was a day of ruinous expense, a burden that fell heaviest on the backbench country gentlemen. Indeed, said the land-poor owner of Beaconsfield, landed fortunes were often encumbered "with debts, with portions, with jointures and tied up in the hands of the possessor by the Limitations of settlement. It is material, it is in my opinion a casting consideration in all the Questions concerning Election. Let no one think the charges of Elections a trivial matter."[30]

Sawbridge's motion went down to defeat, 182–90, with Lord North and the terrible Richard Rigby, who in 1770 had opposed an initiative against election bribery, joining Burke on the winning side. Burke's speech exposed him to heavy abuse outside the House of Commons but won him "infinite honour" inside it.*

CHARLES LENNOX—THE 3RD DUKE OF RICHMOND, FORTY-FIVE YEARS old, a brother-in-law of Lord Holland and an uncle of Charles Fox—had heard about Burke's speech. It interested him because he intended to make the opposite arguments in a speech he was preparing to deliver to the House of Lords. Would Burke, then, the duke wrote him, please forward a summary of his principal points? He did not omit the purpose to which he intended to put the requested information.

Richmond, proprietor of the magnificent West Sussex estate called Goodwood, heir to the income from a tax† on coal shipped from Newcastle, was married, in 1757, to the winsome Lady Mary Bruce. "The perfectest match in the world," Horace Walpole called it: "youth, beauty, riches, alliances, and all the blood of all the kings."

Richmond cultivated interests in military affairs (he had seen active service in the army), painting, sculpture, scientific agriculture, building, racing, and foxhunting. He judged that £7,000 was not too much to pay to build a heated kennel for his dogs. Turning to politics, he aligned himself with the Rockingham interests. "I think he will become a considerable man," said Burke, hearing him speak.

In the Lords, Richmond was a frequent speaker, a mover of motions, and a stepper on toes. He protested the North government's American policies and indeed its every other policy. The ministerialists disliked and dreaded him. Many people did. "If there were two dukes of Richmond in this country," said Charles Jenkinson, North's secretary of war, "I would not live in it."[31]

Richmond's message disturbed and offended Burke, who was feeling overwhelmed by work even before the duke added another unwelcome assignment to his burdens. Perhaps, Burke replied, his grace would care to

---

* Lord John Cavendish to Lady Spencer, C., 4:237.

† It yielded a shilling per chaldron, or slightly less than three tons. Richmond's income from all sources ran to £19,000 a year.

review *Thoughts on the Cause of the Present Discontents*, in which Burke had presented arguments against triennial Parliaments that Richmond, at the time of its publication ten years earlier, had lavishly praised. "I little expected that your Grace should choose to go out of your way to destroy these little works which I had endeavor'd to cast up about my reputation," Burke wrote, "and to expose quite naked to the odium of his Constituents, and perhaps of a great part of the Country, a person whose chief ambition is to be distinguished by your friendship."

ON THE MORNING OF JUNE 2, 1780, TENS OF THOUSANDS OF PEOPLE assembled at St. George's Fields to await the signal from Lord George Gordon, head of the Protestant Association, to march on the Houses of Parliament. The people pinned blue cockades to their hats, a symbol of allegiance to Gordon and the Protestant Association and of antipathy to Catholics and their pope. At eleven o'clock they stepped off, walking silently, except for the cheers they raised while passing Protestant churches, John Wilkes's house, and (especially) the Admiralty building. They walked in blazing heat behind banners lettered with the words "No Popery" and a petition demanding repeal of the 1778 Papist Act. Once arrived at their destination on Parliament Street, Lord Gordon dumped the enormous parchment roll onto the floor of the House of Commons. The signatures, and the marks in lieu of signatures, numbered 120,000.

The protest gained numbers en route. Men, women, and boys of all ages and conditions joined the line of march, not every recruit knowing exactly where they were going or why. The main body totaled some sixty thousand by the time it reached Westminster. Their sheer numbers emboldened the protesters and hangers-on. The near absence of constables near the Houses of Parliament reciprocally frightened the politicians. It would come to light that Lord North had forgotten to issue the order to mobilize such scant civil authority as the capital city possessed to manage Gordon's well-advertised human inundation.

Before long the respectable elements of the Protestant corps began to disperse. The menacing and mischief-making remainder, numbering fourteen thousand or so, pounded on the parliamentary doors and tried to force their way inside. Repulsed, they turned their anger on individual peers and members of Parliament, or on their carriages. Burke, who had championed Catholic relief in the House and primed Rockingham to help it move through the Lords, entered St. Stephen's through a gauntlet of curses. North's hat was plucked from his head, the thief cutting it to pieces and selling the souvenirs for a shilling apiece.[32]

Many peers, shocked by the scene they viewed from their coach windows, ordered their drivers to turn around. The few who persisted arrived at the Palace of Westminster breathless and rumpled. Some were cut or bruised. Others were sprinkled with the white powder that the mob's rough handling had shaken from their wigs. Taking their seats, in a chamber resplendent with tapestries depicting England's victory over the Spanish Armada in 1588, the noblemen formed a discouragingly sparse audience for the address that the Duke of Richmond had hoped would change the course of British constitutional history.

The duke, a favorite with the mob for his espousal of democratic causes, met with no trouble outdoors. Once launched on his speech, he assured the House that he, like they, believed in a hierarchical society, a system "ordained by Providence for the highest purposes." Even so, each grown man must have his vote and the life of a Parliament must be shortened. Reform was not merely desirable. It had become necessary.

Richmond caught someone out of the corner of his eye. It was Lord Montfort, who was not seated but standing and speaking. Richmond, visibly angered by the interruption, appealed to the woolsack for order, but Montfort persisted.

[He] begged the noble duke's pardon, and assured his grace, that he had not the least intention of giving him any offense; but, as a peer, he thought it his duty to rise and acquaint their lordships of the perilous situation one of their own members stood in at that instant, he meant Lord Boston, whom the mob had dragged out of his coach and were most cruelly mal-treating. He hoped the noble duke would thank him for the interruption he had given him, for probably the life of the noble lord would be endangered, if not speedily assisted.[33]

"This immediately excited the attention of their lordships," the record continues, as the remnant of peers, gathered in small groups, weighed next steps. It was suggested that the members themselves might lend a hand to Boston. However, Richmond interjected, if they did sortie together, "as a House," William Murray—1st Earl of Mansfield, chief justice of the King's Bench of Great Britain, "the learned lord on the woolsack"—must lead the procession, and the bearer of the speaker's mace should precede Mansfield. The jurist, seventy-six years old, said he would certainly comply, "if their lordships thought it proper." It proved unnecessary, however, as Boston suddenly appeared in the chamber, "his hair all disshevelled, and his clothes almost covered with powder."

The disturbances of Friday, June 2, seemed to have run their course by Saturday afternoon. But they flared up on Saturday evening and raged for the next six days. By the time they finally flickered, the rule of law had yielded, first to mob rule and second to de facto martial law.

Prisons were emptied, the Bank of England repeatedly attacked, and a giant Catholic-owned distillery was set ablaze. Catholic churches and schools were sacked or demolished (including, to the government's embarrassment, the chapels of the Sardinian and Bavarian ambassadors), and the houses of prominent political figures were emptied of their contents and torched. On Wednesday night, June 7, spectators on London Bridge could count thirty-six separate fires. Except for the absence of a breeze, many fewer but larger fires might have raged.

Protestant advocates of religious toleration fared little better than the Catholics for whom they spoke. Lord Mansfield, one of those liberal spirits, lost his Bloomsbury house, including its magnificent library, to some drunken prisoners from Newgate, though the escapees found no use for the rope they had brought with which to hang the absent judge. The Grosvenor Square home of the Marquess of Rockingham, garrisoned by two hundred troops and some leading Whig politicians, including Charles Fox,[34] escaped destruction. So did Burke's house on Charles Street, St. James's Square, thanks to the timely arrival of sixteen soldiers, acting on orders of the North government.

Burke, having seconded the Catholic relief bill, well knew the danger he was in but dismissed the troops the next morning. He removed his papers* and books to safety and ventured out into the streets, sword at his side, where he was overheard to address a gaggle of would-be tormenters: "If you want me, here I am, but never expect I shall vote for a repeal of the Act I supported." To which one of them replied, "He's a gentleman, make way for him."[35]

The supineness and indolence of the municipal authorities was the scandal of the city and the court. In the ordinary case of riot, the magistrates might appeal for help from the army, but the English constitution, whether or not it prohibited such intervention (as some legal lights contended), certainly did not prescribe it. Thus, many a small mobbing ended not with a reading of the Riot Act but with the unforced decision of the window-breaking, fire-starting, sometimes skull-fracturing participants to call it a night.

It was King George III, acting on advice from Attorney-General Wedderburn, who gave the order allowing the troops to shoot—lacking such a legal opinion, the soldiers and militiamen had previously hung back from the violence, in spectator fashion, to the glee and contempt of the mob. The balance of power now tipped in the authorities' favor. John Wilkes, whose long experience in civil disorder had generally placed him on the rioters' side of the barricades, now joined the militiamen in defending the Bank of England. "Fired five or six times at the rioters at the end of the Bank," he jotted in his diary. "Killed two rioters directly opposite to the Great Gate of the Bank; several others in Pig Street and Cheapside."[36]

It was all very well to extinguish the fires, bury the dead (estimated at between three hundred and seven hundred people), bring the guilty to jus-

---

* In 1782 he was still having trouble locating the papers that he had hurriedly carried away. C., 4:434.

tice, and put one of the great cities of Europe back together again, but how could such an outrage have happened?

Not the least of the blows that England had absorbed in that terrible week, the Rockingham Whigs and their friends agreed, was the precedent of military force deployed against British subjects. Burke upbraided the ministry for "establishing a military on the ruins of a civil government." Walking to the House, he said, he had watched the soldiers standing guard on London's once-peaceful streets. It called his mind to Paris, Berlin, or St. Petersburg more than "the capital of a government limited by law." Agreeing with his friend, Fox said he would "much rather be governed by a mob than a standing army."[37]

THE DUKE OF RICHMOND, PICKING UP WHERE HE HAD LEFT OFF ON the first day of the riots, again brought forward his plan to abolish the rotten boroughs and establish universal male suffrage. Producing a bill from his pocket, he devoted ninety minutes to describing its details. When he finished, Lord Stormont rose to say that because the English constitution was perfection itself (Richmond's and Stormont's mutual friend, the great Montesquieu, had said as much), surely nothing good could come from changing it. Richmond's bill was tossed without a division.

Burke, too, turned his attention to the marginalized and powerless. Four hundred and fifty men, women, and children had been arrested in the rioting, and after lightning-fast trials, sixty-two had been sentenced to death. To Lord Chancellor Edward Thurlow, Burke addressed an appeal for mercy. He did not argue against capital punishment per se, only against indiscriminate, wholesale executions. The maximum number should be six, Burke judged. They should be hanged on the same day at dispersed points of the city. As for the other prisoners, they should be sent to jail, to the prison ships—"hulks"—anchored on the Thames, or enlisted in the navy. "The sense of Justice in Men," wrote Burke, "is overloaded and fatigued with a long series of executions, or with such a carnage at once as rather resembles a Massacre than a sober execution of the Laws. The Laws thus lose their Terror in the minds of the Wicked, and their reverence in the minds of the Virtuous."[38]

Besides, said Burke, bigotry—the underlying crime of the riots—is one of which the nation itself was guilty. It was a poison that had been circulated "from our Pulpits, and from our presses, from the heads of the Church of England, and the heads of the Dissenters. By degrees these publications have driven all religions from our own Minds, and filled them with nothing but a hatred of the religion of other people, and of course with a hatred of their persons, and so, from a natural progression, has led them to the natural destruction of their Goods and houses and to attempts upon their Lives.

"Toleration," Burke observed, "is a new virtue in any Country. It is a late ripe fruit in the best Climates."[39]

Lord George Gordon himself had never raised a hand against persons or property during the weeklong riot. He was appalled by the death and destruction for which he was, as he himself seemed to acknowledge, in some measure culpable. "For God's sake," he had cried out to his followers at one point, "go home and be quiet, make no riot and noise."[40]

But someone had set the fires, caused hundreds of deaths, humiliated Great Britain in the eyes of the world, and set an example for anarchy in a kingdom that had become rather too quick to riot. The government decided that Gordon was that man. A pair of king's messengers bore him away from his home in Welbeck Street. He was indicted for high treason "to compass or imagine the death of the king" and/or "to levy war against him in his realm." He was clapped in the Tower of London to await trial. After many postponements, the date was fixed for February 5, 1781; the chief justice of the King's Bench, Lord Mansfield himself, presided.

The trial began at nine in the morning. The jury delivered its verdict, after a half-hour's deliberations, at five-fifteen the next morning. The septuagenarian judge, the opposing counsel, the jurors, and the defendant—all had somehow retained consciousness through more than twenty hours of argument and deliberation.

Gordon's brilliant lead lawyer, Thomas Erskine, made many ingenious arguments* and destroyed the credibility of a principal government witness. He acknowledged that Gordon might have been guilty of a lack of foresight, but that was not the charge against him. "Gentlemen," he addressed the jury, "we are not trying whether he might or ought to have foreseen mischief, but whether he wickedly or traitorously preconceived or designed it."[41]

As persuasive as he had been, Erskine was unprepared for the verdict—he had warned Gordon not to get his hopes up—and he fainted at the words "Not guilty."

Mrs. Montagu, *salonnière*, critic, and social reformer, spoke for many in London society when she called the verdict a blessing. The enormity of the riots had cleared the political air, she said, "and I hope in a great degree cured the epidemical democratick madness. The word petition now obtains nowhere, the word association cannot assemble a dozen people. We are coming to our right senses."[42]

---

* Erskine, in his wee-hours closing argument, allowed himself to speak the vehement phrase "by God," as in "I say, by God, that man is a ruffian who shall, after this, presume to build such honest, artless conduct as evidence of guilt." *The Edinburgh Review*, in 1810, counted that blasphemy as something unique: "It is, indeed, as far as we know, the only instance of its kind in the history of modern eloquence."

CHAPTER 11

"O God! It is all over!"

Though acting together to a common point as members of the
House of Commons, and embarked in the same cause, their intimacy seemed always to commence and to cease at the entrance of
the lobby.

—SIR HENRY WRAXALL ON THE FRIENDSHIP OF EDMUND BURKE AND

CHARLES FOX, IN WRAXALL, *HISTORICAL AND POSTHUMOUS MEMOIRS*, 2:37

G eneral elections were festival days in eighteenth-century England.
Whatever else a candidate might deliver, the voters expected ale
and food. If necessary, a politician might debate the issues, knock
on doors, or advertise in the newspapers, but it was usually unnecessary. In
the 1780 general election, fewer than one-third of the 271 constituencies in
England and Wales were actually contested.[1] For the rest, the contending
parties arrived at a negotiated settlement. In the so-called close, or rotten, boroughs—like Lord North's Banbury, Burke's Wendover, and Fox's
Midhurst—parliamentary seats were handed down like heirlooms or
bought and sold like dry goods.

By law, the lifespan of a Parliament could extend no more than seven
years, but the sovereign, on the advice of his ministers, could order a parliamentary dissolution, with a general election to follow, whenever the
time seemed right. In the summer of 1780, George III and Lord North
agreed that the time had come. In the Gordon Riots, the king had acted
when others quailed. Besides, the shock of that uprising had chilled the
public's interest in political experimentation. News of the British capture
of Charleston, South Carolina—complete with two thousand American

Continentals, including three generals, along with three hundred cannons, two frigates (with their batteries intact), and a bounty of military stores*— provided a rare break from the usual bleak run of British war news.

The news from Charleston reached a riot-torn London on June 15; secret deliberations about a snap election started soon thereafter. The cabinet kicked the decision over to North, who consulted his election manager, John Robinson. On the eve of the decision to dissolve the sitting Parliament, a visitor to Downing Street asked North for his prognosis. "I really cannot say more than this," the prime minister dryly replied, "that the doctors are now met in consultation on the case in the other room, and you know that the result on such occasions is generally death."

To forestall such a possibility, the king and his prime minister mobilized resources. They spent £62,000 in all, and not a little of that to deny the opposition the prestige of a victory in Westminster and Bristol. Finding a deficiency in the king's privy purse, North signed his name to a £30,000 loan from the royal banker, Henry Drummond. He did so on the understanding—or, as the king would later insist, misunderstanding—that the crown would repay the debt.[2] This failure to communicate would help to facilitate the improbable and short-lived Fox-North coalition government of 1783–84.

The 1780 election was a defining event for Burke and Fox alike. Winning Westminster, the largest and most hotly contested borough, Fox became the de facto leader of the opposition and the "man of the people"—not exactly a democrat but leaning in that direction. Withdrawing from Bristol without a fight, Burke stood revealed as less a politician than as a transcendent orator and political philosopher who happened to hold a seat in the House of Commons.

If North never supported "a single popular measure," Fox, after his victory at Westminster, would hardly support any other kind. Burke, though never earning the people's adulation, would nonetheless take up the people's causes. The weaker and more vulnerable the person or people he championed, the greater his ardor in the cause.

---

* A defeat worse than the British had suffered at Saratoga and "the most serious reverse, until Bataan, ever suffered by the United States army." Miller, *Triumph of Freedom*, 517.

Once Burke remarked to James Boswell how glad he was to live in London, far away from his constituents in Bristol. Living among the voters, he would have to be on his best behavior. Boswell wondered what on earth the workaholic parliamentarian, loyal husband, and member of the Church of England was talking about. The same words would better have fallen from Fox, who rarely got to bed before five a.m. or left it before two p.m. When Burke and Fox walked out of St. Stephen's Chapel together at the end of a long parliamentary session, it was Fox who headed to Brooks's, Burke who made a beeline to wife and home. Now and then the political friends would rub elbows at a sitting of the Literary Club, or at Beaconsfield, when Fox dropped in to visit. Where they were least likely to meet was at the racetrack, by a faro table, or in a courtesan's anteroom, Fox's preferred haunts.

Burke carried not living among his constituents to the extreme of hardly visiting them. He had dropped into Bristol in 1775, a year after he was elected, and again in 1776. He had not returned until August 1780, leaving scarcely enough time before the polling began to say hello, let alone to raise an election committee to counter the organizations mobilized by his enterprising rivals.[3]

Burke's 1774 election was a Bristol rarity. The voters elected two Whigs— Henry Cruger was the other—an unusual occurrence in a two-member constituency that customarily split the ticket between Whig and Tory. Burke was doubtful that another two-Whig result was possible in 1780, especially after Cruger's side declined an offer from Burke's side to abandon the race for the consideration of £2,000. Burke retained his doubts about his own chances even after one of the two Tory hopefuls, the fiftyish Richard Combe, dropped dead on the eve of the voting.

By his public support of Catholic emancipation, mercy for imprisoned debtors, and free trade with Ireland, as well as by his known opposition to the slave trade, Burke had alienated certain Bristol interests. Even so, he reckoned that he commanded the strong support of the city's leading merchants.[4]

How large a pool those respectable beings formed out of the five thousand or so Bristol electors was one imponderable. Money was another. Discussing it with his campaign managers, Burke pledged to contribute £1,000 that he didn't happen to have. (There was no time to think, he later admitted, he had just blurted it out.)[5]

A defiant newspaper advertisement, dated September 1, reaffirmed Burke's commitment, contrary to the rumors that he was weighing withdrawal. Even so, only two days later, Burke was telling the Duke of Portland how sick he was of politics and how eagerly he would be done with it, except that the news of his leaving Parliament would "kill" William Burke. En route to India, once more to repair his finances, cousin Will was counting on the reflected prestige of Edmund's presence in Parliament* to open important doors.[6]

On September 6, Burke delivered a long, confident apologia for his parliamentary service at the Bristol Guildhall. As to his four-year absence from his friends and supporters, the incumbent reminded the voters of the hundred-odd miles between Bristol and London: "I could hardly serve you as I have done, and court you, too." He invited them to recall that his devotion to their private interests had seemed to transform him at times from a parliamentarian to a ship broker. "If some lesser matters have slipped through my fingers,"† he said, "it was because I filled my hands too full; and in my eagerness to serve you, took in more than my hands could grasp."[7]

At the close of this address, Mayor John Bull moved a resolution thanking Burke for his "humane attention to the circumstances of even the lowest ranks of the community." Accompanied by "a large body of most respectable gentlemen," the candidate proceeded to the Exchange to announce his commitment to the race.[8]

But the badly paved Bristol streets had left him footsore, and he labored under a heavy cold. Cruger, too, was sick, and Combe had just died. The odds against him were "desperate," Burke judged. After a day of

---

* On September 28, William addressed an almost hysterical appeal to Portland to lend Edmund £500 for the purpose of lifting a mortgage on Beaconsfield, the proceeds of which had been earmarked for William's own urgent financial needs. "For God sake dear duke of Portland," William pressed, "find the means of standing in the Gap." It would prove a temporary problem, he assured the nobleman, thanks to the vistas that were opening up to him in India. India, where desperate debtors went to become solvent, proved no cure for William. C., 4:292.

† Perhaps the inveterate punster was alluding here to the occasions, in 1775 and 1777, when he disappointed the Bristol soap makers.

campaigning—too much food, too many forced smiles—he had run out of energy, "jollity," even puns.[9]

Writing to Rockingham, the reluctant candidate confessed that, as a rule, the cost of failure counted more heavily with him than did the gratification of success. As to the fine art of pressing the flesh, he would leave it to others: "Oh which of my sins have made me live in Elections!"[10]

Discouraging early returns decided the issue. "I decline the Election," Burke began his September 9 withdrawal speech. By and by, he alluded to the departed Combe, "The worthy Gentleman, who has been snatched from us at the moment of the Election, and in the middle of the contest, whilst his desires were as warm, and his hopes as eager as ours, has feelingly told us, what Shadows we are, and what Shadows we pursue."

Portland was there to hear him. "My Lord," he reported to Rockingham, "it was a most moving Scene . . . which struck every Spectator with Awe— The solemnity of a suffering People, bewailing the Loss of their best friend."[11]

The Bristol election produced another partisan sweep, this time for the Tories, as Cruger, too, was defeated. Burke lingered awhile at the scene of his rejection. A spectator now, "I felt a serenity which I never before experienced," he told Lady Rockingham.[12]

FOX, WHO REMAINED IN THE THICK OF THE FIGHT AT WESTMINSTER, wrote to ask Burke for electioneering help. After a word of condolence on the Bristol outcome, he addressed his friend as he would a father confessor. The London crowds were pressing him hard on "popery," Fox said, and he wasn't sure what to do about it. In response to a voter who had asked him whether he supported repeal of the Papist Act, Fox replied no. At this, the voter turned on his heel and announced that he wouldn't vote at all.

Fox was one of three candidates running for two Westminster seats. Admiral George Rodney, the prohibitive favorite, hero of the January 1780 relief of Gibraltar, was at sea. The contest at the hustings therefore boiled down to Fox versus the government's candidate, the colorless Thomas Pelham-Clinton, Earl of Lincoln. On September 15, the polling stood as follows:

O GOD! IT IS ALL OVER!

Rodney,   4,476

Fox,   4,059

Lincoln,   3,315[13]

The American war slogged on, the times were hard, and the issues of electoral and economic reform still hung in the air, yet it was the supposed menace of the Church of Rome that dogged Fox's campaign. To meet it, the candidate issued a broadside:

> *To the worthy and independent Electors of the City and Liberties of Westminster.*
>
> *Gentlemen,*
>
> *The malicious and groundless reports, which have been spread, make it necessary for me to assure you, that notwithstanding all that has been said, I have never supported, nor ever will support, any measure which can by any means be prejudicial to the Protestant Religion, or in any way tend to establish Popery in this Kingdom.*
>
> *I am, Gentlemen, your faithful*
>
> *And obliged humble servant,*
> *Charles James Fox*
> *St. James's Street, Sept. 14, 1780.*[14]

"I have," Fox wrote to Burke, "dwelt upon this rather long because if any were to think that I had given up in the smallest degree the great cause of Toleration for the sake of a point of my own I should be the most miserable man in the world. Amidst all the Acclamations which are at this moment dinning in my ear, and for which you know I have as much taste as any man."[15]

Fox, previously the member for Malmesbury, had never before fought an election, and he found the experience exhilarating. The none-too-impartial *Public Advertiser* newspaper described him "rush[ing] forward like a Hero" to the rostrum and contrasting "the Thunder of his Eloquence against the Imbecility of his Opponent," Lord Lincoln.[16]

However, when the opportunity arose to defend the most basic civil rights of the English Roman Catholics, the hero's heart failed him.* "Pray judge me severely," Fox invited Burke, "and say whether I have done wrong. They wanted me to leave out the words *have supported* but I told them all fairly that if I were sure that the Success of my Election depended upon it, I would not do it."

Fox's letter closed: "Since I began my letter I have laid my hand upon one of my handbills and inclose it to you, tho' God knows it is not worth the groat you will pay for it, Adieu yours ever most affectionately."[17]

Nothing suggests that Burke took exception to Fox's evasion of the fundamental question of the Catholics' right to live and worship free of legal persecution. Just returned from Bristol, he rather dropped everything to campaign for his friend in Westminster, adding his support to that of the likes of John Wilkes, Richard Brinsley Sheridan, and the Duchess of Devonshire. Fox, talking himself hoarse, secured 4,878 votes, behind Rodney's 5,298 but well ahead of Lincoln's 4,157. After the votes were in, Fox partisans sat their favorite down on a chair, hoisted him onto their shoulders, and paraded him around his new constituency. Admiral George Young, standing in for the absent Rodney, was similarly chaired and borne aloft, but only the landlubber seemed to enjoy his ride: "Mr. Fox laugh'd at all danger—and 'so may the gift of smiling never depart from him.'"

"THE PART I TOOK IN HIS CANVASS WAS FATIGUING ENOUGH," BURKE informed Lady Rockingham. "The Triumph was more so; as we rejoiced, much more honestly than temperately, for two days together." The many toasts that followed a celebratory dinner at the Bedford Arms in Covent Garden included one to the former member for Bristol. The revelers wished him a new set of constituents, this one worthy of him.

---

* On June 20, with the embers of the Gordon Riots scarcely cold, Fox spoke against a measure to repeal the 1778 Catholic Relief Act. It was not a controversial view. North, Burke, and Wilkes all spoke on the same side, and the motion was agreed to. Fox, *Speeches*, 1:277.

For the first time since 1765, Burke was without a constituency. The general election had left the balance of power within the House of Commons undisturbed. It had, however, evicted John Sawbridge, the exponent of electoral reform, and Burke, the champion of economic reform. Maybe this was an omen, Burke reflected: Would it not be absurd if he were to return to Parliament as the member from someone's rotten borough and— from that little "postern or sallyport"—attempt to move the caliber of legislation he had done while representing the kingdom's second city?[18]

Weeks passed without a sign from Lord Rockingham. If Burke was going to return to Parliament, it would have to be by someone's gift. The Duke of Portland might see his way clear to finding him a seat, but the most logical donor was the nobleman who could suddenly seem to find neither his tongue nor his pen.

"I trust," Rockingham wrote to Portland on September 22, "that Mr. Burke can not think that I am *unfeeling* about his situation."[19] It would be strange if Burke did not. Still unemployed on November 1, he told a friend that he would willingly stand again for Parliament if, once inside it, he could hope to achieve something. "But if I were to follow my own wishes, I sincerely assure you I never would put my foot within the door of St. Stephen's Chappel."

Rockingham did finally bestir himself, and on December 7, 1780, Burke enjoyed a foregone victory at a by-election in the marquess's personal constituency of Malton. How honored he was, Burke assured his Malton colleague, William Weddell, to be joining him soon in the House of Commons. Weddell was Rockingham's brother-in-law.

Burke's worry that his demotion to a gifted obscure parliamentary seat from a contested, prestigious one would exact a toll on his political standing proved overblown. The new member for Malton was, and would long remain, the brains and spirit of the marquess's segment of the Whig opposition. That he would also become his party's millstone was a problem that had its roots not in Burke's loss of Bristol but in his passionate, sometimes inconveniently expressive conscience.

ON FEBRUARY 3, 1781, A MIGHTY BRITISH NAVAL SQUADRON, CONSISTING of fourteen ships of the line, a number of frigates, and some three thousand assault troops, bore down on the tiny Dutch island of St. Eustatius. Situated in the northern Leeward Islands, southeast of the Virgin Islands, St. Eustatius presented the British invasion force with a picture of lush vegetation climbing the slopes of a long-dormant volcano, tidy rowhouses recalling the Amsterdam streetscape and war matériel seeming almost to burst from dockside warehouses. Guarding this treasure was a garrison consisting of fifty-five or sixty soldiers, including invalids, and a cannon or two. The Dutch governor, Johannes de Graaff, required no deliberation before signaling an affirmative answer to the British demand to surrender.

Admiral Sir George Rodney, Fox's newly elected fellow MP for Westminster, was the British commander to whom de Graaff surrendered—unconditionally, just as Rodney insisted. The admiral, in joint command with Major-General John Vaughan, proceeded indiscriminately to seize people and merchandise. He stripped the islanders of financial records, money, and personal possessions.

Some of these people were Americans to whom Governor de Graaff had already endeared himself. On November 16, 1776, the Dutch governor had returned the salute of the visiting American man of war *Andria Doria*. Auspiciously, in so doing, de Graaff had registered the first official foreign acknowledgment of the independence of the United States. Rodney was evidently familiar with this historical detail. "My Happiness is having been the Instrument of my Country in bringing this Nest of Villains to condign Punishment," the admiral wrote of the spirited and cosmopolitan people of St. Eustatius. "They deserve scourging and they shall be scourged."[20]

British nationals as well as Frenchmen, Dutchmen, and Jews of indeterminate nationality were also resident on the island. St. Eustatius was a free port, lightly taxed and regulated, and it accordingly flourished, not least in the trade of what His Majesty's Government defined as contraband. Undeniably, the island was a key logistical cog in the miniature American war machine. It was to extinguish such trade that Great Britain declared war on the United Provinces of the Netherlands on December 20, 1780.

Burke did not dispute the crown's prerogative to wage war and make peace. What he rose to question in the House of Commons in May 1781 was the cruelty, wantonness, and impolicy of Rodney's scourging. He remarked on the deadly hurricane that had torn through the region in October 1780. It seemed, said Burke, "the particular visitation of Heaven, as if the Deity had meant thereby to check the fury of mankind against each other, and reconcile them by the sense of their common necessities."

If the Dutch commander gave up in reliance on Rodney's mercy and clemency toward "the dominion, the territory, the public property, and every thing that belonged to the united states [of the Netherlands]," Burke observed, he made a grave mistake. Rapacity was Rodney's style, and the Jews felt it most.

The conquerors ordered the heads of the Jewish households to prepare for deportation; they would leave the island in twenty-four hours. Their wives and children would stay behind; the men could take neither money nor any other kind of property, and where they were going was none of their business. The Jews were stripped, searched (their captors not forgetting to slit open the linings of their clothes), and held under guard. Thirty were borne off to St. Kitt's. The rest, following three days' imprisonment, were released to return to their families "that they might be melancholy spectators of the sale of their own property."

The brutality meted out to the stateless Jews was especially repugnant, Burke told the House.

> If Dutchmen are injured and attacked, the Dutch have a nation, a government, and armies to redress and revenge their cause. If Britons are injured, Britons have armies and laws, the laws of nations (or at least they once had the laws of nations) to fly to for protection and justice. But the Jews have no such power, and no such friend to depend on. Humanity then must be their protector and ally.

Rodney did not contest the brutal facts. The "Smugglers, Adventurers, Betrayers of their Country and Rebels to their King," he wrote, "had no Right to expect a Capitulation, or to be treated as respectable People. . . . No Terms whatever were allowed them; their Persons were Prisoners of War; all their Property was forfeited."[21]

Fox rose to support Burke, even at the expense of his fellow member

for Westminster. Indeed, he went beyond support to identify and commend the mainspring of Burke's politics. "The conduct of the admiral
and general on the capture of St. Eustatius was," said Fox, "so exceedingly impolitic and dangerous that it was no wonder that his hon. friend,
whose liberal mind was always active in protecting his fellow-creatures,
and in exalting the character of man by the correction of the vices that
degrade, while they outrage humanity, should have called the attention
of the House to this subject."[22]

In December 1781 a resolution that the House organize itself into a
Committee of the Whole House to examine the confiscation of "Goods
and Merchandize found in the Island of *Saint Eustatius*" went down to
defeat, 163–89. On paper, Rodney was a rich man, for the law allowed him
a one-sixteenth share in the recovery of enemy property, which, in the case
of St. Eustatius, was valued at as much as £3 million. But French warships
intercepted the convoy in which it was making its way to Britain, and all
but a fraction of Rodney's hypothetical riches vanished into the holds of
the enemy vessels. As for the remainder, the admiral spent years in the
losing cause of defending himself in British courts against the aggrieved
property-holders of St. Eustatius; in the end, he paid out more in damages
than he kept in plunder.

Rodney fared better at sea than on land. His victory over the French in the
Battle of the Saintes in April 1782 earned him the freedom of many English
cities, a barony, a £2,000-a-year pension, and the lavish praise of Charles Fox
and Edmund Burke, Rodney's former accusers who, in the unfamiliar role
of officials in the government that succeeded North's, rose stoutly to praise
the admiral they had previously condemned. "If there was a bald spot on the
head of a Rodney," said Burke, "he had no objection to cover it with laurels."*

---

* Burke's private opinion was more nuanced. "After all," he wrote to the Duke of Portland
in May 1782, "one must admire the ways of Providence which has hung all these Trophies on
such a Post, as we know this Rodney to be, a perfect fool, a compleat Rascal, and (as many
think) a Poltroon into the Bargain, has done us a more brilliant, and all circumstances
considered, a more effectual Service, than the best, wisest, and bravest commanders have
ever performed to this Country. But we ought to drink the draft with thankfulness, without
considering whether the Cup that holds it be of Gold or of Clay." C., 4:456

IN FEBRUARY 1781, AS RODNEY WAS RAVISHING ST. EUSTATIUS, AN IMPOV-
erished twenty-six-year-old poet addressed a desperate cry for help to
Edmund Burke. George Crabbe, who had arrived in London the previous
April with £3 in his pocket, was a village-trained apprentice in the arts of
surgery and pill-making. Failing in medicine, he came to London to seek
his fortune in literature. His verse proving unsalable, he sought help from
Lord North (whom his father vaguely knew), from Lord Shelburne, and
from Lord Chancellor Thurlow. At least Thurlow sent him away with a civil
explanation: his lordship had no time to read poetry. Neither, objectively,
did Burke, but he opened the letter that Crabbe left at his Charles Street
door and began to read. "I am one of those outcasts on the World who are
without a Friend without Employment and without Bread," it said. "My
existence is a Pain to me . . . and I have only to hope a speedy end to a Life
so unpromisingly begun."²³

Crabbe paced up and down Westminster Bridge all night before knock-
ing on Burke's door in the morning. It opened to "one of the first Englishmen, and in the capacity and energy of his mind, one of the greatest human
beings," as Crabbe later put it.²⁴ Burke read his poetry, helped him to revise
it, gave him money, and introduced him to his friends. He commended
Crabbe's subsequently much-praised *The Library* to James Dodsley, the
bookseller, who published it. After Crabbe announced his intention to
enter the clergy, Burke helped him to secure an appointment as domestic
chaplain to the Duke of Rutland.

Crabbe offered Burke the dedication to several of his early publications, including *The Newspaper*, a diatribe in verse about corrupted journalism, but the intended honoree, "probably from modesty, declined
anything of this kind," the poet's son, also George and also a man of
letters, would recall.

A German visitor to the House of Commons in 1782, Charles P. Moritz,
described Edmund Burke, "a well-made, tall, upright man," as looking
"elderly and broken."²⁵ The statesman did not seem so broken either to
Crabbe or to Humand Rao, a Brahmin from the Maratha Confederacy in
central India who visited Beaconsfield in the summer of 1781. Burke had

a long-standing interest in Indian affairs and, of course, in the East India Company. A member of the Select Committee on India, he was perhaps the best-informed politician on Indian affairs of any who had never visited the subcontinent. His reverence for the Hindu religion and for "the black primates" of India mystified William Burke and, no doubt, many another Englishman. Rao was in England on diplomatic business.

Mary Shackleton, daughter of Burke's boyhood friend, Richard, got a report of Rao's visit from Burke himself. "Tho' he had a servant he prepared his own dinner," she recounted his version,

> using I think neither animal food nor wine, eating off the ground stripped from his waist up, and throwing away his dinner if any one came within a certain distance from him. It seems being in company with Sir Joshua Reynolds, Ed. Burke and some other men, he was so pleased with the expression on their countenances, tho' he could not understand their conversation, that he desired his interpreter to inform them that in his country there was a beast called the Rhinoceros, which sustained her young by her look, and to this he compared himself being fed by their looks.[26]

ON SEPTEMBER 3, 1780, OFF NEWFOUNDLAND, THE CREW OF A ROYAL Navy vessel observed someone on the American brig *Mercury* throwing objects overboard. That someone turned out to be Henry Laurens, former president of the Continental Congress and, now, American envoy to the Netherlands; the objects were Laurens's not-quite-unsinkable state papers. Fishing the documents out of the water, the British discovered that Laurens was bound for Holland to raise money and conclude a treaty of friendship and commerce with the Dutch government. The soggy parchment did double duty of providing the pretext for Britain to declare war on the Netherlands and to clap Laurens in the Tower of London on suspicion of high treason. And there the American diplomat remained.

Burke had championed the cause of many prisoners, including John Trumbull, a former Continental Army officer who had come to England in

1780 to study painting but wound up in a cell in Bridewell Prison for seven months on charges that his army service was a treasonous act. Burke led a successful effort to bail him out.

Shortly thereafter—it was August 1781—Burke took up Laurens's cause as a means to securing the safety of General John Burgoyne. Taken prisoner at the Battle of Saratoga, Burgoyne was sent home to England under parole but was presently recalled by his American captors. Burke, who had taken refuge in the general's London house during the Gordon Riots, now took up another humane cause, the exchange of one star wartime captive for another.

To set the diplomatic wheels turning, Burke appealed to Benjamin Franklin; the two had known each other as colonial agents before the Revolution, Burke for New York, Franklin for Massachusetts, Pennsylvania, New Jersey, and Georgia. "I apply to you," Burke addressed the U.S. minister plenipotentiary in France, "not to the Ambassador of America, but to Dr. Franklin the Philosopher; my friend, and the lover of the Species."[27]

Franklin the philosopher was more than ready to help. He was indeed in possession of a congressional resolution authorizing the exchange, which he forwarded to Burke (Franklin having no official communication with the king's ministers). "Since the foolish Part of Mankind will make Wars from time to time with each other," he added, "not having Sense enough to settle their Differences, it certainly becomes the wiser Part, who cannot otherwise prevent those Wars, to alleviate as much as possible the Calamities attending them."[28]

Having secured the permission of Laurens and Burgoyne to work on their behalf with the British government, Burke pressed for Laurens's release from the Tower. He had never met the American, but "from the very beginning I have been much affected by his Condition."[29]

WHEN BURKE AND FOX DISAGREED, WHICH WAS RARELY, THEY WERE able to contend without rancor. Perhaps their most instructive point of disagreement was over the Clandestine Marriages Act, which became law only over the anathemas that Henry Fox had hurled at it during and long after its successful passage through Parliament in 1753. This was the law against so-called runaway marriages, such as the 1744 elopement of Henry, Charles's father, then thirty-eight years old, and the daughter of the 2nd Duke of Richmond, Lady Caroline Lennox, twenty-one. The son of the self-made, universally admired Sir Stephen Fox, financer of Charles II, did not care to regard himself as a parvenu.

No sooner, then, did Lord Beauchamp introduce a "Bill to Remedy Certain Inconveniencies in the Marriage Act," in May 1781, than Charles Fox upped the ante by proposing to wipe that legislative eyesore from the statute books. Beauchamp objected to a letter of the law that held that no marriage was valid if the bans, or announcements of intent to marry, were published in a church or chapel that had not been standing in the year of the act, 1753. The victims of this arbitrary legalism, said Beauchamp, were the innocent children of couples who had inadvertently violated it. In the eyes of the law, the issue of such negligent parents were disinherited bastards.

Charles Fox was not the only member of the House to press for repeal of the Royal Marriages Act, but he outdid all others in the eloquence and fervor of his arguments. The particular point on which Burke and he crossed swords was the age at which young lovers might legally tie the knot. The law, and Burke, said twenty-one; younger couples required the permission of parents or guardians. Fox wanted no statutory minimum.

Like the elder Fox, who unfailingly took his son's side in childhood disciplinary tribunals at Holland House, Charles lined up with the young. Marriage, a natural right, was not to be abridged by legislation, he told the House: neither on account of, say, the tender age of the bride, nor because of the social class of the groom.

> The season of youth was the season of passion, when the heart possessed all its feeling and sensibility, untainted by the mercenary considerations which afterwards our commerce with, and knowledge of, the world were likely to inspire. . . . It was passion and not reason that was the best capable of providing for our happiness in wedlock.

Fox, who was thirty-two years old, was conducting a torrid affair at about this time with the beautiful actress Mary "Perdita" Robinson. "Philosophers might argue as they pleased for the prevalence of reason," he continued in this vein, "it was, however, a fact, which neither moralists nor philosophers could deny, that nature had planted passion in the heart of man for the wisest purposes, both of religion and life."

Some had objected that impetuous marriage of the very young pro-duced only children and poverty. Fox did not deny the risk, but it was the way of the world: "Such was the provision of nature, that when persons entered into the state of wedlock they were doomed to suffer its hardships or to enjoy its pleasures. It was a consequence which the legislature of this country could not by its authority prevent. As well might they attempt by power or by art to overcome all of the other dispensations of nature."

A statutory age of marital consent, said Fox, was akin to a Catholic order of celibacy. It affronted both the Protestant faith of Great Britain and the liberty-loving dogma of Whiggism.

Fox's speech on the Marriages Act was counted among his best and most persuasive. In the season of youth, "which this Marriage Act labours and intends to blast," said the bachelor,

> a young man, a farmer, or an artisan, becomes enamoured of a female,
> possessing, like himself, all the honest and warm affections of the
> heart. They have youth, they have virtue, they have tenderness, they
> have love—but they have not fortune. Prudence, with her cold train of
> associates, points out a variety of obstacles to their union, but passion
> surmounts them all, and the couple are wedded. What are the conse-
> quences? [H]appy to themselves and favourable to their country. Their
> love is the sweetener of domestic life. Their prospect of arising family
> becomes an incentive to industry. Their natural cares and their toils
> are softened by the extacy of affording protection and nourishment
> to their children. The husband feels the inticement in so powerful a
> degree, that he sees and knows the benefit of his application. Every
> hour that he works brings new accommodations to his young family.

Now, Fox proceeded, consider the lot of the same young lovers under the strictures of the Marriages Act. Passion will continue to have its way, but—marriage being out of the question—"enjoyment satiates the man and ruins the woman; she becomes pregnant." Her lover flees to avoid the expense of raising the child he never intended to father "or remains the corrupter and disgrace of his neighbourhood."[30]

Burke supported the Marriages Act, and his arguments, like Fox's in the opposite cause, disclosed as much about the temperament of the speaker as they did about the speaker's politics. Ardor was a poor substitute for judgment, said Burke as he urged the House to have "mercy on the youth of both sexes; protect them from their ignorance and inexperience; protect one part of life by the wisdom of another; protect them by the wisdom of laws."

Burke bent over backward to remind his vehement adversary how much he admired and respected him and how deeply it hurt him to have to disagree. Said he in reference to Fox, "To suffer the grave animadversion and censorial rebuke of the honourable gentleman, who made the Motion; of him, whose good nature and good sense the House look upon with a particular partiality; whose approbation would have been one of the highest objects of my ambition; this hurts me."

To Fox, as to his outraged father before him, the true object of the Marriages Act was to protect the aristocracy from the likes of the man who became Lord Holland. Burke chose to speak to that point, because he himself was sometimes accused—or so he had been told—of "being a man of aristocratick principles." He denied it.

> If by aristocracy they mean the Peers, I have no vulgar admiration, nor any vulgar antipathy towards them. I hold their order in cold and decent respect. I hold them to be an absolute necessity in the Constitution, but I think they are only good when kept within their proper bounds.

If it ever came to a showdown, he pledged, "I would take my fate with the poor, and low, and feeble."[31] Reciprocally, Burke assured the House that he would join the high and mighty in battle against the malicious many, should things ever come to that.

Thanks, it was said, to the power of Fox's oratory, the legislation to repeal the Marriages Act passed the Commons by a vote of 90–27. Heavily amended in committee, the bill failed in the Lords.

THE INTERMINABLE AMERICAN WAR DID, IN FACT, END. ODDLY ENOUGH, the British met defeat in Virginia, the state where Tarleton's raiders had chased Governor Thomas Jefferson out of his office and back to his plantation Poplar Forest; where the "Arch-Traitor and Parricide [Benedict] Arnold" had run riot; where the state exchequer was empty and the state credit exhausted; and where General von Steuben, famed drillmaster of Valley Forge, despairing of the wretched Virginia militia he now commanded, allowed himself to regret that he had ever left Prussia to contribute to the defense of a country "where Caesar and Hannibal would have lost their reputations, and where every farmer is a general, but where nobody wishes to be a soldier."[32]

What redeemed Virginia, on October 18, 1781, was the presence of the French fleet and some eight thousand French regulars by the port of Yorktown. Trapped by the encircling allied forces, General Cornwallis surrendered the heart of what remained of British arms in North America.

News of the disaster inconveniently reached London on Sunday, November 25, 1781, just two days before the opening of Parliament. Up the chain of ministerial command spread the word, from the secretary of state for the colonies, Lord George Germain, to the secretary of state for the Northern Department, Lord Stormont, to Lord Chancellor Thurlow. Better, the three ministers decided, if they trooped as a body to Downing Street to tell North. Duly apprised, the prime minister opened his arms "as he would have taken a ball in his breast" and cried, "O God! It is all over!"[33]

It was not quite over, however, either for the North ministry or King George. The new session of Parliament would open on November 27 with the king's ceremonial speech from the throne. The address was already drafted, but something must be said about the 7,500 British troops who were now in the custody of General Washington. The updated text did not exactly say that the war would continue. Then again, it suggested no change in strategic direction, either, but rather recalled the king's unstinting efforts to "restore to my deluded subjects in America that happy and prosperous condition which they formerly derived from a due obedience to the laws" and His Majesty's continued "firm confidence in the protection of Divine Providence."[34] It did not sound as if George was giving up.

The words that the king read aloud from his throne in the House of Lords (where both peers and commons had gathered to listen) were not necessarily his. Conventionally, the king's ministers wrote them. The address completed, the king withdrew to allow each house to frame its reply and move amendments. In the Commons, the opposition chose Charles Fox as its spokesman.

A pair of North partisans, preceding Fox, tendered the king the customary Address of Thanks. The first of these apologists, Charles George Perceval, all but blamed Yorktown and the preceding defeats on the disloyal members of the opposition who had "incited America to resistance."[35] To win the war, Parliament must close ranks and speak with one patriotic voice.

Perceval, age twenty-five, had served one year in Parliament. Fox, who had thirteen years under his belt, proceeded to instruct the fledgling member in all he had missed. For himself, said Fox, he had watched the steady development of a system of governmental indolence, incompetence, and subversion. He had witnessed the ministers'

> progressive madness, impolicy, or treachery; and he was now confounded at their presuming to look the Commons' House of parliament in the face, much more to sit and hear such an address to the throne [i.e., Perceval's thanks to the throne] moved for at such a juncture. That they should dare bring down such a speech after what they have done, was to him a subject of astonishment, nay, a subject of horror. It shewed that they were divested of all modesty, as well as principle, and they had formed the dreadful resolution of going on to the last act of the tragedy, and completing the ruin which they had so successfully begun.

Fox wished Perceval to know that, if the opposition had had its way, there would have been no war. "They had opposed it in all its progress; they had warned, supplicated, and threatened; they had predicted every event, and in no one instance had they failed in predicting the fatal consequences that had ensued from their obstinacy or from their treason."

"Their conduct," Fox charged the twelve-year-old ministry, "was unprecedented in any age or in any history; it beggared the records of nations: for in all the annals of kingdoms ruined by weakness or by treachery, there was not an instance so glaring as the present, of a country ruined by a set of men, without the confidence, the love, or the opinion of the people, and who yet remained secure amidst the storms of public disaster." So there would be no unanimity in the House of Commons.

Perhaps North lifted an eyebrow when he heard Fox disavow any personal ambition for high office on the ground that the prime minister and his colleagues, by their very misconduct, had rendered those places contemptible to "men who loved their honor." It would have been a little unclear when Fox had adopted those compunctions. He had, between March 1778 and July 1780, "been involved in no fewer than six conversations on the possibility of resuming his political connection with North"—which he would indeed do, to widespread shock and some amusement, in 1783.[36]

At the end of a very long speech, Fox challenged the House to vote its conscience. He called on the members to conduct themselves as delegates of the people, not as "creatures of the ministry." They must answer the question, "Did they really believe that we could ever conquer America?" The truthful response would leave the North administration with the tiniest of minorities, Fox said, speculating that North himself, "in his soul," might himself vote nay.[37]

North would indeed vote nay. "Great Britain will suffer more in the end than her enemies," he had told the king on March 25, 1778, "not . . . by defeats, but by an enormous expense, which will ruin her, and will not in any degree be repaid by the most brilliant victories."[38] Even so, the prime minister denied that the war was about anything other than Parliament's constitutional right to tax and govern British colonies. Fox, he noted, had threatened him with "impeachment and scaffolds," but that would not deter him "from the preservation of the rights and legislative authority of parliament."

Burke rose next and "with great warmth," according to the parliamentary reporter, "reprobated the language of the noble lord." What particularly inflamed Burke was the prime minister's invocation of parliamentary "right" as a cause of hostilities. "Good God! Mr. Speaker," Burke thundered,

> are we yet to be told of the rights for which we went to war? Of excellent rights! Oh, valuable rights! . . . That have cost Britain thirteen provinces, four islands, a hundred thousand men and more than seventy millions of money. Oh, wonderful rights! That have lost to Great Britain her empire on the ocean, her boasted, grand, and substantial superiority, which made the world bend before her! Oh, inestimable rights! That have taken from us our rank among nations, our importance abroad, and our happiness at home; that have taken from us our trade, our manufacturers, and our commerce; that have reduced us from the most flourishing empire in the world to one of the most compact, unenviable powers on the face of the globe! Oh, wonderful rights! that are likely to take from us all that remains!

Because the ministry could tax America, it had decided that it must tax America, let the risks and consequences be what they may. "This was their language," said Burke. "Oh, miserable and infatuated men!"

Burke imagined the prime minister surveying the beasts of the field. Behold the most excellent wool on the back of a wolf, the noble lord would have mused: "A wolf is an animal that has wool; all animals that have wool are to be shorn, and therefore I will shear the wolf." Reasoning in just this way, said Burke, North concluded, "The Americans have money; we want it, we will have it."

In describing the futile marching and countermarching of British forces in America, Burke spoke the phrase "excrementitious evacuation," like that of the human body. He threatened North with impeachment and likened Britain to a dead animal, while the "vermin which fed on it still had an existence." Borrowing a line from Alexander Pope, he compared the war to a wounded snake, which "drags its slow length along," and he warned the House against hugging that serpent to its breast, lest it "sting us even to the last agony of dissolution."[39]

At length, the twenty-two-year-old William Pitt, son of the great Earl of Chatham, rose to heap his indignation on that of Fox and Burke. Pitt was a newcomer to the House of Commons, but nobody could have intuited that fact by listening to his perfectly orated, highly controlled attack. Pitt, who, like Burke and Fox, entered the House as the occupant of an uncontested seat presented by a well-connected mentor, allied himself with the opposition wing led by his father's disciple, the Earl of Shelburne. His first speech, in February 1781, into which he was goaded by calls from the opposition benches, was a triumph, in the bipartisan opinion of Burke, Fox, and North. John Debrett, bookseller and publisher of parliamentary records, recalled the voice that uttered those words as "rich and striking. . . . His manner [as] easy and elegant; his language [as] beautiful and luxuriant."[40]

Now, in the debate over the king's speech, Pitt asked why the ministry had clung to its war, and he answered his own question, "The real truth was, it was an appendage of the First Lord of the Treasury too dear to be parted with: it was the grand pillar, built on the ruins of the constitution, by which he held his situation; the great means of extending that baleful influence of the crown on which alone he placed all his security!"

"The moment Mr. Pitt sat down," according to *Parliamentary History*, "a buz of applause pervaded the House, and it was some little time before the Lord Advocate of Scotland [Henry Dundas], who rose immediately, could obtain a hearing."

Burke showed none of Pitt's icy composure in rising a second time to describe the butchery that, as he imagined, awaited British loyalists at the hands of the American victors. As he spoke, his "whole frame was violently agitated." Later, in a reflective mood, he invited the House to ponder a singular set of facts. Because Earl Cornwallis was constable of the Tower of London, Henry Laurens was his prisoner. And because Laurens's son,

Colonel John Laurens, had accepted Cornwallis's surrender at Yorktown, "Earl Cornwallis was prisoner to the son of his own prisoner."*

"This was a circumstance," Burke continued, "that would incline a man the least addicted to superstition, to think that there was a special Providence in this affair, brought about for the purpose of humbling the proud, and teaching to all the vicissitudes of human fortune, the duties of tenderness and humility."[41]

A week later, on December 3, Burke requested North's cooperation to complete the proposed Laurens-for-Burgoyne exchange. Time was of the essence in light of Laurens's failing health, said Burke who, hearing nothing from the prime minister whose impeachment he had threatened, renewed his appeal on December 15. On December 17 he asked the House of Commons for permission to bring in a bill to regulate the exchange of all prisoners of war.

Burke was on his feet—"on his legs," was the contemporary expression— for ninety minutes. He described the gratuitous cruelties that the British jailers had visited on their distinguished American inmate. He compared the Tower to the French Bastille, judging the latter the more humane. He approvingly quoted the passage in Franklin's letter in which the American philosopher had ruminated on the propensity of the "foolish part of mankind" to wage wars.

A Tory member, Lord Newhaven, objected to the reading in Parliament of the letter of "an open and avowed rebel" and declared that the offending lector should be "sent to keep company with Mr. Laurens in the Tower." That lector, Burke, replied that he wasn't rich enough to afford the amenities available for purchase by well-to-do inmates—"such a prison was better adapted to the rank and fortune of the noble Lord." However, "if he (Mr. Burke) could enjoy the company of such men as Mr. Laurens and Dr. Franklin, he should not at all regret being shut up from the company of the

---

* Young Laurens—twice wounded in battle, a onetime aide-de-camp of George Washington and, while seconded to Europe on a diplomatic assignment, an assistant to Benjamin Franklin—had captured an enemy redoubt at Yorktown. He negotiated the terms of the British surrender in company with the Viscount de Noailles. Laurens was killed at the skirmish of Combahee River, South Carolina, on August 27, 1782.

noble Lord."[42] The motion to give leave to Burke to introduce his bill was passed unopposed.

At last, on December 31, none other than Lord Mansfield granted Laurens bail, and fifteen months after he entered the Tower, the captive was allowed to walk out of it, with the understanding that he would continue the work of effecting a suitable exchange. On January 5, 1782, Laurens was a visitor at Beaconsfield. "He is an exceedingly agreeable and honourable man," his host reported to Franklin. In the exchange of prisoners that was finally secured, America received Laurens and Britain, Cornwallis.[43]

North, too, was a captive, but there could be no parole and no exchange except by the king's assent or by a vote of censure in the House of Commons. Over the course of his twelve-year ministry, North had frequently offered his resignation; George would never hear of it, nor would he now. Neither, yet, would the Commons withdraw its confidence in North's government.

North, whose great gift was equanimity, could be seen in early 1782 playing his customary game of whist at White's, a Tory version of Brooks's. He continued to entertain at home with dinners and open houses.[44] Living in this long-familiar, amiable fashion, he was not necessarily putting on a brave face. Famously indecisive, North was ambivalent about his office, but no small part of his vacillating soul yearned to be done with it. Now a united opposition—the Rockinghams and Shelburnes, the Foxes and Burkes, and the Barrés and Pitts—ached to rid him of it.

On January 24, Fox moved for an inquiry into the "Causes of the Want of Success of the British Navy." North stoutly defended his first lord of the Admiralty, Lord Sandwich, but the motion was defeated by a margin of only nineteen votes—in the first vote of the new Parliament in November 1780, the government had mustered a majority of eighty-two.

On February 22, General Henry Conway—age sixty-one, a retired army officer, long-serving member of Parliament, and leader of the House of Commons in the Rockingham ministry of 1765–68—proposed a motion, addressed to the king, to stop the American war. The intrepid Conway, who had fought the French at Fontenoy and the Jacobites at Culloden but who had opposed the American war from the start, lost his bid by a single vote. He returned five days later to move a halt to "offensive war" in America, and this time won, thanks to the defection of tax- and war-weary independent MPs, by a vote of 234–215. This proved the administration's only defeat in the House of Commons; an opposition motion of no confidence, on March 15, fell short by nine votes (though the government had expected a deficit of twenty or thirty).[45]

In that part of his mind that retained any interest in office, North had hoped to survive long enough to negotiate the peace. It was not to be. The opposition was determined to expel him, and it was preparing to move such a motion on March 20. North, in that part of his mind that wanted nothing to do with high office, had been ready to resign almost since the day he started.

Resignation was one thing, but a vote of censure and removal by his fellow members of Parliament was a prospect not to be borne, and he drafted his final letter of resignation to the king on March 18. "Your Majesty is well apprized that, in this country, the Prince on the Throne, cannot, with prudence, oppose the deliberate resolution of the House of Commons," it said. King William III and George II had each yielded more than once to the will of the legislature. "The concessions they made were never deemed dishonourable, but were considered as marks of their wisdom, and of their parental affection for their people."

Not even this ringing document, which historians appraise as a major British state paper, could persuade George to cut him loose, and North followed up on March 19 with a warning about the next day's parliamentary showdown: "It is generally imagined that we shall be beat tomorrow; if it should happen, I must quit my place immediately, and shall remain in the Journals for ever stigmatized upon record of a Vote of Parliament for my removal, which I believe has seldom, if ever, happened to a minister before." Would not the king save North "from disgrace"?

"Remember, my Lord, that it is you who desert me, not I you," said the king, as minister and sovereign parted company following a ninety-minute meeting at St. James's Palace prior to the opening of the March 20 session of the House of Commons.[46] The buzzing House awaited North's arrival, the opposition determined to fire him before he could resign, while North,

Burke sat for Joshua Reynolds in 1774. Joshua Reynolds, *Edmund Burke, 1729–1797 Statesman, Orator, and Author,* oil on canvas, 1774, National Galleries, Scotland. *(ARTGEN / Alamy Stock Photo)*

Charles James Fox sat for Anton Hickel in 1794. The age of the sitter on each occasion was forty-five. Anton Hickel, *Charles James Fox,* oil on canvas, 1794, National Portrait Gallery, London. *(ARTGEN / Alamy Stock Photo)*

The "Saviour of India," Warren Hastings, fends off his tormenters Edmund Burke, Charles Fox, and Frederick, Lord North, whom James Gillray styles "the political banditti." James Gillray, hand-colored etching, 1786, National Portrait Gallery, London. *(Album / British Library / Alamy Stock Photo)*

In consolation for their loss of office in the short-lived Rockingham government, the devil, "Old Orthodox," awards Fox a dice box and Burke a scourge and rosary. James Gillray, "Crumbs of Comfort," hand-colored etching, 1782, Morgan Library and Museum, New York. *(ARTGEN / Alamy Stock Photo)*

Fox cries a puddle as the "wrangling friends" at last part company over the French Revolution. Pitt, at right, rather wishes "they'd cut each other's Throats." Isaac Cruikshank after John Nixon, "The Wrangling Friends or Opposition in Disorder," hand-colored etching, May 1791, British Museum, London. *(Gallery of Art / Alamy Stock Photo)*

Who made off with the Great Seal of England in 1784? James Gillray wildly reimagines the theft as an attack on the Tower of London by Fox, Burke, and Richard Brinsley Sheridan. James Gillray, "Blood & Co, Setting Fire to the Tower, & Stealing the Crown," hand-colored etching, 1788, British Museum, London. (*The Stapleton Collection / Bridgeman Images*)

The king was not the only enemy of the 1783 Fox-North coalition. Gillray's print, featuring the principals in company with a Jesuitical Burke, mocks that improbable alliance as the devil's work. James Gillray, "'Coalition Dance' (Frederick North, 2nd Earl of Guilford; Charles James Fox; Edmund Burke)," hand-colored etching, 1783, National Portrait Gallery, London. (*ART Collection / Alamy Stock Photo*)

A phantasmagorical Burke looms over the shoulder of Richard Price, the imagined author, here, of "On the Benefits of Anarchy Regicide Atheism." James Gillray, "'Smelling out a Rat,' or, the Atheistical Revolutionist Disturbed in His Midnight 'Calculations,'" hand-colored etching, 1790, British Museum, London. (*Library of Congress, Prints and Photographs Division, Cartoon Prints, British*)

The Scotsman William Adam grazes Charles Fox in a 1779 duel. Fox lightheartedly ascribed his escape from serious injury to Adam's use of "government powder." James Gillray, "And Adam Had Power Over All the Beasts of the Earth," hand-colored etching, 1789, National Portrait Gallery, London. (Alto Vintage Images / Alamy Stock Photo)

And ADAM had Power over all the Beasts of the E...

Burke's resignation from office in 1782 as seen through Gillray's unsympathetic eyes. A penniless Irish monk, the orator is supping on potatoes boiled in a chamberpot. Rosary beads, a crucifix, and a cask of whiskey stand at the ready. James Gillray, "Cincinnatus in Retirement, Falsely Supposed to Represent Jesuit-Pad Driven Back to His Native Potatoes," hand-colored print, 1782, Yale Center for British Art, New Haven, CT. *(Library of Congress, Prints and Photographs Division, Cartoon Prints, British)*

Cupid turns up the romantic heat on an already infatuated Burke, as the archenemy of the French Revolution contemplates a vision of Marie Antoinette. Attributed to Frederick George Byron, frontispiece to Edmund Burke, *Reflections on the Revolution in France*, 1790. *(Library of Congress, Prints and Photographs Division, Cartoon Prints, British)*

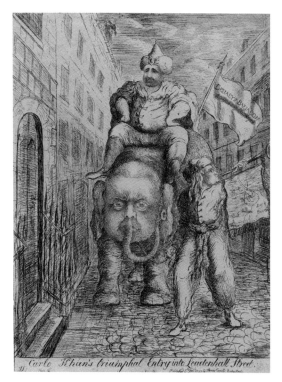

Edmund Burke heralds the arrival on Leadenhall Street, home of the East India Company, of Charles Fox on the back of an elephant bearing an uncanny likeness to Lord North. It's the peak of the fortunes of the ill-omened Fox-North coalition. James Sayers, "Carlo Kahn's Triumphal Entry into Leadenhall Street," etching, 1783, National Portrait Gallery, London. *(Penta Springs Limited / Alamy Stock Photo)*

Frederick, Lord North, 2nd Earl of Guilford, the king's witty, warm, reluctant first minister on the eve of the American war. "Even those who opposed the Minister involuntarily loved the man." Nathaniel Dance-Holland, *Portrait of Frederick North*, oil on canvas, 1773–74, National Portrait Gallery, London. *(The Picture Art Collection / Alamy Stock Photo)*

The young King George III. He would come to detest Charles Fox as the corrupter of the Prince of Wales, his son, but to respect Edmund Burke, who saw the French Revolution exactly as the king did. Studio of Allan Ramsay, *King George III*, oil on canvas, 1761–62, National Portrait Gallery, London. *(Uwe Deffner / Alamy Stock Photo)*

William Pitt the Younger, "something between God and man" to his many admirers. Second-longest-serving British prime minister and Burke's and Fox's bête noire, he had one redeeming feature, the two friends agreed. Pitt was as hopeless with money as they were. John Hoppner, *Portrait of William Pitt the Younger*, oil on canvas, c. 1805, National Portrait Gallery, London. *(Album / Alamy Stock Photo)*

Warren Hastings, governor-general of Bengal, lover of Indian culture and languages and fierce defender of British interests in the subcontinent. Burke pursued him in an eight-year impeachment trial that ended with Hastings's exoneration. Sir Joshua Reynolds, *Warren Hastings*, oil on canvas, 1766–77, National Portrait Gallery, London. *(Album / Alamy Stock Photo)*

In return for money, a parliamentary seat, and political status, Burke gave the horsey, vague, and rich Charles Watson-Wentworth, 2nd Marquess of Rockingham, ideas and the words with which to express them. After Sir Joshua Reynolds, *Portrait of Charles Watson-Wentworth*, oil on canvas, c. 1768, National Portrait Gallery, London. *(ART Collection / Alamy Stock Photo)*

Henry Fox, 1st Baron Holland, Charles Fox's overindulgent father. He was not, contrary to the allegations of his innumerable political enemies, "the public defaulter of unaccounted millions." After Sir Joshua Reynolds, *The Right Honorable Henry Fox (1705–1774), 1st Lord Holland*, oil on canvas, c. 1762, National Portrait Gallery, London. *(ART Collection / Alamy Stock Photo)*

Members of the House of Commons on their best behavior in St. Stephen's Chapel, 1793–94, shortly before Burke's retirement. To a German visitor, many years earlier, the place resembled the choir of a Lutheran church in Prussia, except for the sight of the odd MP "lying stretched out on one of the benches." Karl Anton Hickel, *The House of Commons, 1793–94*, oil on canvas, 1795, National Portrait Gallery, London. *(ARTGEN / Alamy Stock Photo)*

The novelist Frances "Fanny" Burney, marveled of Burke: "Such spirit, such intelligence—so much energy when serious, so much pleasantry when sportive—, so manly in his address, so animated in his Conversation, so eloquent in Argument, so exhilarating in trifling." Edward Francis Burney, *Frances d'Arblay*, oil on canvas, c. 1785, National Portrait Gallery, London. *(ARTGEN / Alamy Stock Photo)*

having at last secured the king's permission to quit, was determined to beat the opposition to the punch.

Having just come from the royal presence, North was in full court dress. The first item on the day's order paper was a motion to evict the ministry. Its author, Charles Howard, Earl of Surrey, rose to speak, but North popped up too, and it was the prime minister whom the speaker of the House recognized. Both the earl and Lord North started talking at once, while MPs on the tightly packed benches cried out encouragement to one man or the other. Intricate arguments over the rules of order ensued, but North put an end to the wrangling by observing that the fact of his retirement rendered the earl's motion unnecessary. Fox objected on the ground that "the House could not place any confidence in the word of the minister."

North took no personal offense at this flagrant imputation on his character—he had heard much worse in the previous dozen years—but he evenly repeated the pledge that "His Majesty's ministry was at an end."

"Before, however, he took leave of his situation entirely," the record reports him as saying,

He felt himself bound to return his most grateful thanks to the House for the very kind, the repeated, and the essential support he had for so many years received from the Commons of England, during his holding of a situation to which he must confess he had at all times been unequal. And it was, he said, the more incumbent on him to return his thanks in that place, because it was that House which made him what he had been. His conduct within those walls had first made him known, and it had been in consequence of the part he had taken in that House, that he became recommended to his sovereign. He thanked the House, therefore, for its partiality to him, on all, and—he would use the phrase—for their forbearance on many occasions. Certainly he could not be pleased at their not thinking him any longer worthy of the confidence of parliament, nor for their wishing to vote his removal, but their general support of him, through a service of many years' continuance, claimed his fullest acknowledgements and his warmest gratitude; and he should

ever hold it in the memory as the chief honour of his life, to have
been so supported.

It would be no difficult thing, North added, to find a more qualified
successor, but "a successor more zealous in the interests of his country,
more anxious to promote those interests, more loyal to his sovereign, and
more desirous of preserving the constitution whole and entire, he might be
allowed to say, could not so easily be found." He concluded by moving "that
the House do now adjourn."

Fox expressed the hope that the new administration would conduct
itself on principles opposite to the debased and corrupting ones of the
ministry it would replace (that is, if North were telling the truth). Burke,
in a very different vein, issued a general warning to the House about
the temptations of power. The present moment, said he, was a "peculiar
period in men's lives, when their ambitious views, that had lain secretly
in a corner of their hearts, almost undiscovered to themselves, were
unlocked, when their prejudices operated most forcibly, when all their
desires, their self-opinions, their vanity, their avarice, and their lust for
power, and all the worst passions of the human mind were set at large and
began to shew themselves."[47]

The members, expecting a long-drawn-out session, had sent their carriages home with instructions not to return for many hours. When North
left the House, his carriage was waiting by the door. Huddled outdoors in
the snow and bitter cold were politicians, including members of the opposition, vainly waiting for their own transportation. "You see, gentlemen,"
North said gaily as he and a few friends stepped into his carriage for the
ride home, "the advantage of being in the *secret*."

"No man ever showed more calmness, cheerfulness and serenity,"
recalled one of North's passengers, the Scottish MP and onetime combat-
ant of Charles Fox, William Adam. "The temper of the whole family was
the same. I dined with them that day, and was witness to it."[48]

CHAPTER 12

Death of Rockingham

The situation of the Prince of Wales was the happiest of any person's in the kingdom, even beyond that of the Sovereign . . . the
enjoyment of hope—the high superiority of rank, without the
anxious cares of government,—and a great deal of power.

—SAMUEL JOHNSON, IN BOSWELL'S *LIFE OF JOHNSON*, APRIL 1783

Along with losing America, King George III had lost Lord North.
There was no replacing America, but there must be a prime minister. George steeled himself for the disagreeable work of summon-
ing the Marquess of Rockingham to form a new government. However, as
if to ensure a fractious, dysfunctional, and short-lived Rockingham administration, the king also sent for Lord Shelburne.

Coming to office in 1770, North had ended a volatile era of annual and
biennial governments; hardly, in that era of starts and stops, did ministers
arrive at their posts before it was time to pack up and leave. North's departure from office, in March 1782, marked the beginning of another such
phase of political instability, one destined to end only with the coming of
the hardy perennial William Pitt the Younger, in 1784. Edmund Burke and
Charles Fox contributed more than their fair share to the political turmoil.

The unstable alliance of the Shelburne and Rockingham parties, not to
mention the impermanent future union of the Foxites and the Northites,
anticipated the yet unspoken dictum of Benjamin Disraeli that "England
does not love a coalition." In fairness, neither England nor Wales nor Scotland had enough time to fall in love with the brand-new Rockingham

coalition. Nominally, the marquess was its leader, the Earl of Shelburne his ostensible number two, with the eleven-man cabinet consisting of five Rockinghams, five Shelburnes, and the unaligned General Henry Seymour Conway. To this disharmonious team would fall the work of negotiating a peace. Fox, as foreign minister, would conduct the talks in sometimes bitter competition with the secretary of state for home and colonial affairs, Lord Shelburne. Burke would occupy the once-lucrative, never-prestigious, subcabinet office of paymaster of the forces.

On paper, Shelburne was the epitome of the eighteenth-century statesman. He was not so in life. "A worthless man" was the young king's verdict in 1763 of Shelburne in his then-capacity as George's aide-de camp.[1] George Rose, a secretary to the Treasury under Shelburne, left office resolving "never to be in a room with him again while in existence." The historian John Cannon records that "no politician who held office with Shelburne wished to do so again."[2]

The nobleman was secretive, uncollegial, and double-tongued. During an exchange with Fox on the floor of the House of Commons in 1782, Shelburne had this to say—"he [Shelburne] made no assertion; he had certainly said, that 'in his opinion,' that was the cause, and the exclusive cause, but he had not asserted it as fact."[3]

For this proneness to casuistry and dissimulation, Shelburne's enemies tagged him with the epithet "Jesuit." Burke was identically abused, though in his case on account of the unsubstantiated rumors of his crypto-Catholicism.[*] Shelburne and Burke likewise shared a common weakness in the business of practical politics. Ideas about public policy were rather their forte—in Shelburne's case, the public debt, administrative reform, and the ambition to retain America in a kind of transatlantic federal union, especially. However, unlike Burke and Fox, Shelburne was at a loss around people. He couldn't read them, couldn't understand what they thought or needed. If Fox was born to be loved, Shelburne came into the world to be misunderstood and, in turn, to misunderstand.

---

[*] Writing to General John Burgoyne on Christmas Eve 1782, Burke tarred Shelburne with the very same slur: he was, charged Burke, "a Jesuit, a prevaricator, a notorious liar." C., 5:56.

But the annoying peer possessed sterling qualities, too, including intelligence, curiosity, and a deep interest in public affairs. Shelburne cultivated and subsidized some of the leading intellectuals of the day, including Richard Price, Joseph Priestly, and Jeremy Bentham. He was an exponent of free trade, parliamentary reform, and a cessation of Britain's perpetual warfare with France. Along with birth and money, such talents propelled him to a position of leadership within the anti-North opposition. Indeed, the king, not much caring for Shelburne but liking the alternatives even less, had first tapped him to head his new government. Lacking the votes to sustain a government, Shelburne wisely declined.

Rockingham, though richer, better born, and more politically powerful than Shelburne, had his own professional deficits. In the House of Lords, he spoke infrequently and unpersuasively, requiring, on one occasion, "a good draft of Madeira" before entering the House and "a comfortable breathing of a vein by Mr. Adair's lancet" after leaving it. He was often unwell and, as Walpole put it, was not so much indolent in business as "trifling and ineffective."* His private virtues and irresistible charm earned him the devotion of his parliamentary followers and the goodwill of his political adversaries. "No man in public life, I believe," again to quote Walpole, "had ever fewer enemies."[4]

So it was the marquess, prompted by Burke, who laid down the conditions under which the proposed new government would consent to serve. The king must consent to Burke's proposed reform of the Civil List, complete with the abolition of numerous pensions and sinecures; he must pledge not to disallow the new government's intended unconditional recognition of American independence; and he must not obstruct bills to exclude from Parliament the government contractors and tax collectors whose financial interests tipped them invariably into the pro-ministerial voting bloc.[5]

---

* It sometimes fell to Burke to light a fire under the marquess. "The question then is," he prodded Rockingham in January 1775, "whether your Lordship chooses to lead, or to be led; to lay down proper Ground yourself, or stand in an awkward and distressing situation on the Ground which will be prepared for you." Quoted in Robinson, *Burke: Life in Caricature*, 26.

Morosely, the king did so pledge,* though not personally to Rockingham, the imminent prime minister, with whom he chose to have no direct
personal contact (so obnoxious were the marquess's principles to His Majesty), but to Shelburne, the designated secretary of state for colonial, home,
and Irish affairs. Rockingham kissed the king's hands—solemnizing his
ascent, for the second time, to the highest political office in the land—on
March 30, 1782.

Not surprisingly, in this arranged political marriage, there was trouble
almost from the altar. Fox, secretary of state for foreign affairs, espoused
the Rockingham line on American independence, not for the sake of magnanimity but to draw America away from France. Shelburne, like the king,
clung to the hope that the colonies might yet be lured back into Britain's
fold. In the matter of economic reform, too, the king and his favored minister saw eye to eye. Neither took to Burke's legislative initiative, and Shelburne did what he could to scuttle it.

Already in April, just as the new government was settling in, Shelburne
was extending hopeful feelers in case "a breach of administration should
happen as to leave him in possession of government."[6] At about the same
time, Fox was contemplating his resignation to protest the impediments
that his colleague was busily laying down to peacemaking. "Shelburne," he
complained to his friend FitzPatrick,

> shows himself more and more every day, is ridiculously jealous of my
> encroaching on his department, and wishes very much to encroach on
> mine.... He affects the [Prime] Minister more and more every day, and
> is, I believe, perfectly confident the King intends to make him so. Provided
> we can stay long enough to have given a good stout blow to the influence
> of the crown, I do not think it signifies how soon we go out after.[7]

Such were the unhappy auguries for the second Rockingham administration. As secretary of state for what was formally known as the Northern

---

* He thought seriously enough about quitting the throne that he wrote a rough draft of a
letter of abdication. Roberts, *Last King of America*, 110.

Department, Fox was responsible for treating with Britain's continental adversaries, France, Spain, and Holland. Shelburne was charged with concluding peace with the "colonists." The two peacemakers almost immediately fell to fighting.

Fox cut an incongruous figure in Parliament, as did all the new Rockingham ministers, seated as they were on the Treasury bench and turned out in court dress, swords, and hair powder, rather than the great coats with boots and spurs that members of the opposition might casually throw on. Fox's transformation, given the low hygienic and sartorial baseline of the secretary's pre-ministerial days, was especially striking.*

Walpole leaves a description of Fox's first waking moments at his rooms on St. James's Street, c. 1782:

> As soon as he rose, which was very late, [Fox] had a levee of his followers, and of members of the gaming club at Brooks's—all his disciples. His bristly, black person and shagged breast, quite open and rarely purified by any ablutions, was wrapped in a foul night-gown, and his bushy hair was disheveled. In these Cynic weeds and with other Epicurean good humour did he dictate his politics, and in this school did the heir to the throne attend his lessons and imbibe them.[8]

Fox would have cause to regret the presence at his levee of the heir to the throne, the Prince of Wales. The future king George IV was a good student, grounded in the classics, instructed in mathematics, and proficient in French. He had studied drawing, fencing, boxing, and—in his own plot at Kew—agriculture. He was making a start in Italian and German. At sixteen, he was accounted amiable, well-mannered, and handsome, if, by his own reckoning, "rather too fond of wine and women."[9]

With George III, as with the old Puritans of Boston, there were no small

---

* Nor did much change during Fox's ministerial days. A witness to his arrival at the House of Commons in July 1783, during the short-lived Fox-North coalition, described him as "as dirty as a scavenger." Cannon, *Fox-North Coalition*, 97.

sins, certainly none concerning his heir in the devilish realm of wine and women. Nor were "Prinny's" lapses anyone's secret.

All the world knew about his devouring love for the actress Mary "Perdita" Robinson (so styled for her memorable performance in Shakespeare's *The Winter's Tale*). He was eighteen, three years from his majority, she in her early twenties. As an earnest of his devotion, he sent her a bond for £20,000, payable on his twenty-first birthday, and many ardent letters. She wisely kept the letters as well as the bond.

The king had had no use for Fox before the prince fell into his exuberant company. Aversion turned darker when the foreign minister became the prince's tutor in the things that seemed to come all too naturally to him.

As for Fox, Walpole had to admit, he appeared to be a changed man. "He is now as indefatigable as he was idle" was Walpole's report in the first week of May. "He has perfect temper, and not only good-humour, but good-nature; and, which is the first quality in a Prime Minister of a free country, has more common sense than any man, with amazing parts that are neither ostentatious nor affected."

The son of England's first and longest-serving prime minister anticipated big things for the foreign secretary. North, Walpole judged, had had "wit and good-humour," if not fellow-feeling or even "good breeding." The elder Pitt, Lord Chatham, was a genius in war but a nullity in peace. "Perhaps I am partial to Charles Fox," Walpole proceeded, "because he resembles my father in a good sense; I wish he had his excellent constitution, too. Yet his application to business may preserve his life, which his former dissipation constantly endangered."[10]

IN MAY 1782, FOX ROSE IN PARLIAMENT TO URGE THE REPEAL OF A LAW that codified England's tyranny over Ireland. The 1719 Dependency of Ireland on Great Britain Act was gall to the Irish and, as Fox contended, an embarrassment to constitutionally minded Englishmen. It subordinated Ireland's Parliament to Britain's and subjected Irish legislation to the threat of veto by the English Privy Council. There had been a particularly highhanded example of this oppression two years earlier when the Irish Parliament sent over to England a bill that would have relieved Irish Catholics and dissenting Irish Protestants of certain civil penalties. The Privy Council allowed Catholic relief but struck down the portion of the bill granting freedom of conscience to nonconforming Protestants.

Moving the repeal of the Dependency Act, Fox contended that it would be better to lose Ireland altogether than to continue to coerce her into hostile union. For Britain to relinquish these arbitrary powers was nothing less than "a sacrifice to justice."

Fox's motion carried without a division and with but a single quibble from the floor. Burke, who felt this partial liberation of Ireland from foreign trammels as if it were his own, rose to memorialize the occasion. "It was not on such a day as that, when there was not a difference of opinion, that he would rise to fight the battle of Ireland," he said;

> her cause was nearest to his heart; and nothing gave him so much satisfaction, when he was first honoured with a seat in that House, as the idea that it might be in his power, some way or another, to be of service to the country that had given him birth; he had always said to himself, that if such an insignificant member as he was could ever be so fortunate as to render an essential service to England, and that his sovereign, or parliament, were going to reward him for it, he would say to them, "Do something for Ireland; do something for my country, and I am ever rewarded." He was a friend of his country; but gentlemen need not be jealous of that; for in being the friend of Ireland, he was of course the friend of England; their interests were inseparable.[11]

As Fox was one of the few commoners in the aristocratic Rockingham cabinet, his was the duty to move the Rockingham government's legislation through the lower house of Parliament. On this occasion, judged Burke, Fox "handled this delicate Business incomparably well."[12]

ONLY POSTERITY IS SURPRISED BY BURKE'S EXCLUSION FROM THE ROCKingham cabinet. The orator's future claims to immortality were less apparent to many of his contemporaries than his living flaws in judgment. The very power and vehemence of his oratory is one key to the mystery of his absence from ministerial office. His long speeches, fits of temper, flights of fancy,* colorful invective, and wounding shafts of ridicule were better calculated to win enemies than friends.

In the years-long impeachment of Warren Hastings, in the parliamentary turmoil attending the Regency crisis of 1788, and of course, during the eruptions over the French Revolution, Burke's rhetorical violence would alarm friend and foe alike. There had been premonitory rumblings during the long, frustrating years of opposition in the American Revolution and in the wake of the fall of Lord North. A nineteenth-century descendant of Shelburne had something to contribute to the puzzle of Burke's subcabinet political career. John Morley, writing at the turn of the twentieth century, tells the story in these words:

> The late Lord Lansdowne,† who must have heard the subject abundantly discussed by those who were most concerned in it, was once asked by a very eminent man of our own time why the Whigs kept Burke out of their cabinets. "Burke!" he cried; "he was so violent, so overbearing, so arrogant, so intractable, that to have got on with him in a cabinet would have been utterly and absolutely impossible."[13]

Burke's persistent money troubles, along with those of his brother Richard and cousin Will, also counted against him. Sir Gilbert Elliot, who revered Burke, marveled that he had come as far as he had in politics with the questionable characters who composed his family circle.

Yet on both of these counts, Fox too was vulnerable. His clever words

---

* "The gay flowers of a brilliant and exuberant fancy were proper for their season, —for hours of jollity and recreation. He should be happy to share in the delights of that fertile imagination which had so long been the wonder and pleasure of that House; but he could not consent to indulge himself in admiring 'the beautiful motes which people the sunbeam,' when his mind was occupied with objects so serious and important as those now before the House." So, in debate in December 1782, did the twenty-three-year-old chancellor of the exchequer, William Pitt, reprove the fifty-three-year-old Burke. PH, 23:272.

† Evidently, Henry Petty-Fitzmaurice, 4th Marquess of Lansdowne (1816–66), Shelburne's grandson.

cut as deeply as Burke's—and as Shelburne's, as far as that goes, whose manner in debate was oftentimes "sneering." As to money, Burke had at least never suffered the indignity of seeing his furniture stacked up on the street in the course of a creditors' squeeze, as did Fox.[14] Nor did Burke ever address his cash flow problems by opening up a faro bank at Brooks's—a spectacle in full public view through the ground-floor windows of the club—as Fox had done. It was the early success of this venture, in 1781, that led Burke erroneously to suppose that his friend was finally solvent.[15]

Fox and Burke by this time were becoming favorites of the newspaper caricaturists. Buyers of the prints of James Gillray and readers of anti-Whig newspapers presently came to know Burke as a bespectacled Catholic monk, subsisting, in one early cartoon, on potatoes boiled in a chamberpot.[16]

It is possible, too, that Burke suffered the social ostracism of the self-made man in a Whig world of landed heirs. He seemed to know about everything except racing, the sport not only of kings but also of Whiggish dukes and marquesses.

"VIOLENT," IN HIS LANGUAGE, BURKE COULD CERTAINLY BE, BUT ALSO quite literally seductive. Fanny Burney fell in love with him, if not at first sight, then at first conversation, at a dinner party at the home of Sir Joshua Reynolds in the spring of 1782: "Such spirit, such intelligence—so much energy when serious, so much pleasantry when sportive,—so manly in his address, so animated in his Conversation, so eloquent in Argument, so exhilarating in trifling." Altogether, as Miss Burney confessed to Hester Thrale, she was "quite desperately and outrageously in love."

Likely her ardor was not quenched by the fan letter that Burke addressed to her about her second novel, *Cecilia*, which appeared in five volumes in July the same year. He had read it in three days (as the Rockinghams' world was falling apart).

"Madam," he addressed the thirty-year-old author,

I might trespass on your delicacy if I should fill my Letter to you with what I fill my conversation to others. I should be troublesome to you

alone, if I should tell you all I feel and think, on the natural vein of
humour, the tender pathetick, the comprehensive and noble moral,
and the sagacious observation, that appear quite throughout that
extraordinary performance. In an age distinguished by producing
extraordinary Women, I hardly dare to tell you where my opinion
would place you amongst them—I respect your modesty, that will not
endure the commendations which your merit forces from every body.

Fanny's father, Dr. Charles Burney, a fellow member with Burke of the
Literary Club, remarked on the friendship between his daughter and his
friend. It was, said he, "an amiable coquetry of smiles, and other symbols,
that showed each to be thinking of the same thing."[17]

"HE WAS NEITHER A MAN WHO HAD PRETENSIONS TO IT FROM RANK IN
the country, or from fortune, nor who aspired to it from ambition," Burke
himself announced to the House of Commons in April 1782, at the start of
the Rockingham-Shelburne coalition. "He was not a man so foolishly vain,
or so blindly ignorant of his own state and condition, as to indulge for a
moment the idea of his becoming a Minister."[18]

Whether Burke was sincere in these conventional expressions of
self-abasement, Rockingham did not choose to contest them. Thus did
the future author of *Reflections on the Revolution in France* come to
occupy "a temporary office of some emolument, considerable expense
and no power,"[19] as Burke described the position of paymaster to James
Boswell, who had asked Burke's help in securing a governmental plum
of his own.

Sir Stephen Fox, the first paymaster, it will be recalled had gotten rich
in office (1661–76 and 1679–80). Fox's son, Lord Holland, became so rich
during his tenure as paymaster (1757–65) that he could afford to pay his
sons' gambling debts. Richard Rigby, Burke's immediate predecessor in
office (1768–82), likewise accumulated enormous wealth, generated, as it
had been since Sir Stephen's time, from the interest accumulated on the
cash he held. Burke was well aware of what £600,000, a typical paymaster's
balance, invested at 4 percent, would produce and how far that £24,000 a

year would go to lift the worry and the mortgages that forever plagued the residents of Beaconsfield.

But dearer to Burke than financial deliverance was his own reputation, which could hardly survive a conventionally gilded career at the Paymaster's Office. Besides, he saw the simple justice of an arrangement whereby the government's cash earned interest for the taxpayers, not for the paymaster. If this is a blindingly obvious insight, it nonetheless eluded most of Britain's leading public financiers for the century and a quarter prior to Burke's accession to the office.

Burke was on his feet in the House of Commons on June 14, 1782, to announce those reforms and to describe the latest version, considerably softened and diluted, of his economic reform proposals of 1780 and 1781. Here was a new Burke, no longer the astringent opposition critic but a respectable exponent of the policies of the government of which he was a member.

The disingenuous words he spoke were as incongruous as the court dress he wore. The reforms were the king's, Burke insisted. The new Civil Establishment Bill, which, in fact, George despised,* was the product of the "transcendent goodness and beneficence of the Crown."

It was indeed, said Burke, "the Crown, to the goodness of which the whole honour was due, his being nothing more than the humble instrument to whose humble lot it had fallen to forward the gracious intention of royalty."[20]

Shelburne, too, hated the final bill, as did Burke's former actual allies in the cause of economic reform. The reformers pointed with disgust to the omission from the legislation of the proposed abolition of a notorious sinecure, the chancellorship of the Duchy of Lancaster, which the Rockingham government had coincidentally settled on John Dunning, the great Whig lawyer. Dunning's stirring resolution of 1780 ("the influence of the crown has increased, is increasing and ought to be diminished") now lost some of its retrospective glory. Nor did the grant to Dunning

---

* "Slovenly constructed," remarked His Majesty, though it would be "best to let it go without much discussion which might render the sting worse." W&S, 4:142.

of a pension in the sum of £4,000 per annum enhance the government's claims to economic purity.

Sir Cecil Wray accosted Burke with the charge that his "famous *Bill of Reform* . . . had now dwindled to a mere NOTHING, so much so, as to be held in contempt by all ranks of people!"[21] Wray, the second member for Westminster who had taken his seat after a by-election only two days earlier, was none other than Fox's new parliamentary colleague. Admiral Rodney, whom Wray succeeded, now covered in glory by his victory in the Battle of the Saintes, was seated in the House of Lords as 1st Baron Rodney.

Though Burke had reformed himself out of a fortune, the opposition attacked him for lining the pockets of his relatives while not forgetting his own. In place of the torrents of investment income that his predecessors had enjoyed, he would settle for a salary of £4,000 a year. His son Richard would become his deputy at £500; his brother Richard, the secretary to the Treasury at £3,000; and his cousin Will, then in India, the deputy to the paymaster of the royal troops on station in India at more than £1,500.

Parrying his critics, Burke declared that he had every intention of reaping a proper and proportional award for his service. To do otherwise "would be to violate the first law of God and Nature, by abandoning the interest of his family for no purpose whatsoever."[22] Of course, there could be no answer to the literally incredible charge, invented by a bought and hostile press, that Burke had provided not only for his family but also for a scrum of imagined Irish supernumeraries to the tune of £35,800 a year.

Yet Burke was perfectly capable of refusing funds that his grateful admirers were prepared to press on him. Thus in 1779 the Catholic Committee of Dublin wrote begging him to condescend to accept a "Small, and Inadequate token of Our Gratitude," the sum of 500 guineas, in appreciation of the "Zeal and Patriotism" that had "So Signally Contributed to Emancipate Us from the Late Severe Penal Laws."

Declining, Burke replied, "If I were to derive any advantage whatsoever, beyond what comes to my share in the general prosperity of the whole, from my Endeavours in this way, I should lose all the relish I find in them; and the whole Spirit which animates me on such occasions. My Principles make it my first, indeed almost my only earnest wish, to see every part of this Empire, and every denomination of men in it happy and contented, and united on one common bottom of equality and justice."[23] Thomas Browne, 4th Viscount Kenmare, who had chaired the Catholic Committee three years earlier, wrote to Burke in March 1782 to reiterate his thanks. "All parties look up to you," Kenmare closed, "as the greatest Ornament of your Country and this Age."[24]

Whatever his formal ministerial status—Kenmare, at least, did not doubt his suitability for high office—Burke retained his self-appointed, unofficial station of advocate for the poor and marginalized. It was indeed his lifelong vocation. Whether to an immigrant down on his luck (Joseph Emin in 1755) or to a poet at the end of his rope (George Crabbe in 1781), Burke freely gave of himself—time, money, hospitality—to vulnerable people. Now, in 1782, he was opening a new chapter in his work for the downtrodden, this time for the people of India. He was in fact, just as Kenmare had styled him in his letter of March, "the Advocate of distrest Humanity."

In some "fragmentary notes of self-justification that seem to date from the early 1780s," Burke identified "one rule with myself—To act as the representative of the people who had no power," Americans, Irish, Catholics, and the people of India, among others. The work had involved him in "labors beyond my strength—feelings beyond my command—and struggles beyond my powers."[25]

RARELY WELL, ROCKINGHAM FELL ILL AND DIED ON JULY 1, 1782, AT THE age of fifty-two. It was barely three months into the life of the coalition. Fox had been champing at the bit to resign in protest over Shelburne's conduct in office. George III's decision to elevate his antagonist to the vacant premiership over Fox's preferred alternative, the Duke of Portland, clinched the foreign minister's decision. Why, he protested, the king had no such constitutional right to name his own senior minister—when in fact, George had every right to do so. To many it appeared that Fox was prepared to subordinate stable government to his personal animus at an especially delicate juncture in British diplomacy.

Fox's uncle, the Duke of Richmond, himself a member of the Rockingham cabinet, tried reasoning with his indignant nephew. "Ld Shelburne may be false, ambitious and cunning," said Richmond; "well, but what then?" He told Fox that Shelburne supported peace, economy in government, and parliamentary reform, all causes dear to the Whigs' hearts. Shouldn't he have a chance to make a mistake before his ministers abandoned him?

It was no use—Fox's mind was made up. "Poor dear Charles," remarked Richmond's sister, Lady Sarah Napier, "is so surrounded with flatterers that tempt him to think that he alone can overset the whole fabric, that it's vain to talk."[26] Neither would Burke serve under Shelburne for reasons that he took two hours to impart to 150 or so members of the Rockingham party at a nine-hour meeting on July 7; it was "the best speech he was ever heard to utter," according to one account.[27]

In the House of Commons, two days later, Burke delivered one of his worst speeches. Met with what he judged to be a disrespectful hubbub from the government side of the House, he issued a kind of blanket challenge to any who dared question his personal integrity—they "knew where to find him."[28] He enumerated Rockingham's merits and contrasted Shelburne's deficiencies. He speculated that the Shelburne administration would prove "fifty times worse" than North's.

Answering some remarks by General Conway, a Rockingham cabinet member who chose not to resign and who defended Shelburne's capacities and achievements, Burke cautioned against taking people at their face value. He next spoke the words that would be thrown back in his face, and mocked in caricaturists' prints, for many years to come.

"He had when young read of a wolf," Burke told the House, "who was mistaken for a simple shepherdess, because dressed like her grandmother, for one quite as gentle and tame as she was."[29] Don't fall into the trap of Little Red Riding Hood, Burke cautioned the middle-aged parliamentarians of the House of Commons, most of whom had never imagined that they would hear a nursery story in the service of a debating point.

Only John Cavendish, Rockingham's chancellor of the exchequer, followed Fox in resigning a cabinet office. Burke and Fox returned to Parliament to take their old places on the opposition benches on July 11. William

Pitt, Shelburne's new chancellor of the exchequer, occupied Fox's former seat on the Treasury bench.[30]

For Burke, Rockingham's death was a calamity. Besides costing him a patron, friend, and advocate, it cut the financial ground out from under his feet. True, Burke might have chosen to remain in the Paymaster's Office, with its blessed salary and sweet perquisites, but for him, as for Fox, office under Shelburne was unthinkable. (Office alongside Shelburne had been bad enough.) Gone, therefore, was the soothing green view from the window of the commodious house on Whitehall Street that the paymaster occupied. Gone, too, was the routine of office, "the busy life" that Burke loved (though he hardly required a government post to keep himself occupied). "He pretended not to great things," Burke was quoted as saying in his moment of loss; "he had been spending all his life in raising a little anthill, but it was all kicked down." He would never have chosen "the cold climes of opposition," Burke went on, but now believed "that he was doomed to spend his whole life in opposition."[31]

As he opened the letters consoling him on Rockingham's death,* Burke wondered what would become of the sinecure that the marquess had been trying to arrange for his son, Richard Jr.† He might equally have wondered about his own finances. Rockingham was his lender of last resort. That his generous creditor had erased those debts in a late codicil to his will was a fact of which Burke may or may not have been aware in his first hours of shock and loss.

TO ALEXANDER WEDDERBURN, THE WHIGGISH LAWYER WITH WHOM HE had once nearly fought a duel, Burke confided another strain of his grief: "To think that all the Labours of his Life, and that all the Labours of my Life, should *in the very moment of their success*, produce nothing better than the delivery to the power of this kingdom into the hands of the E. of

---

* One of the first, dated July 1, was from Adam Smith: "When I first heard of the misfortune my first movement was to run to your house; but I restrained myself for fear of disturbing your sorrow." C., 5:3.

† After much agitation and negotiation, Richard secured his share of the joint receivership of land revenues one year after Rockingham's death, in June 1783. C., 5:53.

Shelburne, the very thing (I am free to say to you and to every body,) the toils of a life ten times longer and ten times more important than mine would have been well employed to prevent—this, I confess, is a sore, a very sore tryal."[32]

Nor did Burke, or for that matter Fox, find much sympathy from Gillray, the caricaturist. A print dating from August 1782 finds the two receiving the devil's consolation for the loss of their respective government posts.[33] Fox, a well-dressed man with a fox's head, is receiving a dice box and dice; Burke, identifiable by his trademark spectacles, is handed a crucifix, scourge, and rosary, the implements of his supposed crypto-Catholicism.

Fox gave no outward sign of grief, political or otherwise, in the wake of his resignation from office. Perdita Robinson and he had become lovers, she having tired of the prince, or vice versa. (He perhaps bored this "woman of undoubted Genius," as Samuel Taylor Coleridge appraised her shortly before her death, in 1800.)[34] James Hare, who at one time shared Fox's house on St. James's Street, hard by Brooks's, left a few lines on Fox's immediate post-ministerial activities:

> Charles passes his whole day with Ms. Robinson, to the utter Exclusion and Indignation of the gallant Col. Tarleton, but not, I believe, of Capt. Craddock, for it is supposed that she has the bad Taste enough to like fucking with him almost as well as with the late Secretary [Fox], whom I never see but at Mrs R's window, unless he comes to Brooks's after she is gone to bed, and gets drunk with Stanhope and Jack Townshend.[35]

SEATED IN JULY, THE SHELBURNE GOVERNMENT HAD ALMOST FIVE months to get its bearings before the December 5 opening of the new parliamentary term. Even so, it was unprepared. In the House of Lords, Shelburne denied that his government unconditionally recognized the independence of the United States. On the same day, in the House of Commons, the new chancellor of the exchequer, William Pitt, asserted the opposite. It would be better, the king admonished Shelburne, if that were the last such embarrassment.

Shelburne required not only the king's support but also the votes of another parliamentary faction. The prime minister's followers, including the loosely defined Friends of the King, numbered 140. Lord North commanded 120 loyalists and Fox a corps of 90. Two hundred members styled "the country gentlemen" voted independently. Attendance rarely approached the theoretical maximum of 550 members, but whatever the turnout, it was clear that Shelburne could not govern alone.

The first order of business of the government was peace, and Shelburne had no easy hand to play. Over the preceding six years, Britain had accumulated much debt, four adversaries, and not one ally. It would fall to the diplomats to sort out competing claims to the islands, fisheries, fortifications, colonies, and peoples across four continents that the contending armies and navies had won and lost.

There would be no popular peace, if precedent held. A calamitous war ended in a humiliating peace, a victorious war in a disappointing one. Before Shelburne lay the ticklish work of yielding just enough to gain the peace, yet not so much as to cost him the king's support or the confidence of the House of Commons.

Lord North, at last freed from the prison of his premiership, acted not at all like a man who had lost a war or who owed more money than he could hope to repay in two lifetimes. If he was "not so fat and more cheerful than ever," as Gibbon found him,[36] it was perhaps because the former prime minister held the balance of power in the House of Commons. The terms of the peace and the composition of the next government were his to influence, if not to command.

Fox told the House that "Great Britain should, in a manly manner, recognize at once that independence, which it was not in her power to check or overturn." He could envision some future day "when by a firm alliance between Great Britain and America, the courts of France and Spain would awake from their idle and illusory dreams of advantage; which they think will follow to them by the separation of America from the mother country;

through that alliance the sun of Britain must rise again and shine forth with dazzling lustre."[37]

North, not anticipating any such special relationship with the former colonies, rather urged that Britain should barter its concession of American independence for an equivalent prize. He wanted, as he informed the House on December 5, "an honourable peace or a vigorous war."[38] He wanted an end to the intramural "suspicions and jealousies" that only emboldened the French, Spanish, Dutchmen, and Americans who seated themselves across the bargaining table from British diplomats in Paris. Above all, said North, he wanted justice for the overly trusting American loyalists who had put their lives and property at hazard for the sake of Great Britain.

North's appeal for national unity was correct and statesmanlike, but no mere words could slake the antipathy of Fox for Shelburne, of young Pitt for North, of the king for Fox, or of Fox for the king. The network of animus considerably narrowed the contenders' possible paths to power. A Shelburne-North coalition was out of the question. (Pitt would never accept it.) One might have assumed that the same dynamic would apply to a Fox-North coalition. However, North's skin, off which had bounced years of Fox's choicest philippics, was thick, and Fox was ambitious for office and power.

Early in February 1783, Lord North sent his son, George, to sound out Fox on the possibility of forging a coalition. By February 13, the former antagonists had shaken hands. (Fox, in the interval, had declined an overture from William Pitt to join the Shelburnes.)

Four days later, as the Commons began to debate the preliminary or (in the case of America) provisional articles of peace,* rumors of a Fox-North alliance had solidified into fact, wanting only official confirmation.

"I have come," Fox told the Commons, after completing his attack on Shelburne's diplomacy, "to take notice of the most heinous charge of all. I am accused of forming a junction with a noble person, whose principles I have been opposing for the last seven years of my life." Fox refused to con-

---

* Dutch negotiations still were at a formative stage.

firm the speculation about a formal coalition, though it was certain that North and he were united in their opposition to the government's peace proposals. However, he proceeded, "if men of honour can meet on points of general national concern, I see no reason for calling such a meeting an unnatural junction. It is neither wise nor noble to keep up animosities for ever. It is neither just nor candid to keep up animosity when the cause of it is no more. It is not in my nature to bear malice, or to live in ill will. My friendships are perpetual, my enmities are not so."[39]

Burke, pointing to the Treasury bench where onetime political adversaries were seated in newfound harmony, denied that there was anything unnatural in the mooted connection of the former antagonists Fox and North (not, he innocently added, that he was aware of any such plan).

Young Pitt declared that the coalition "stretched to a point of political apostacy, which not only astonished so young a man as he was, but apparently astonished and confounded the most veteran observers of the human heart."[40]

A resolution to censure the terms of the peace preliminaries ended in an opposition victory, 224–208. This defeat of the principal work of the administration might have led another man to resign, but the margin was not overwhelming, and Shelburne, characteristically failing to notice that his own government was falling apart, scheduled a second trial for February 21.

Pitt excelled himself on this occasion with a speech defending the treaty, attacking North, and delivering a political funeral oration for Shelburne. Pitt was a boy when his father, Lord Chatham, piled up his great victories against France in the Seven Years' War, but that particular age of British glory was past, as the terms of peace in the recently concluded war must reflect.

Yes, Pitt went on, we have acknowledged American independence, but the events of war, Lord North's "incapacity," and "even a vote of this House," had already granted what "it was impossible to withhold."

And he continued:

We have ceded Florida—We have obtained Providence and the Bahama Islands.

We have ceded an extent of fishery on the coast of Newfoundland—We have established an exclusive right to the most valuable banks.

We have restored St. Lucia, and given up Tobago—We have
regained Grenada, Dominica, St. Kitt's, Nevis, and Montserrat, and
we have rescued Jamaica from her impending danger. In Africa, we
have ceded Gorée, the grave of our countrymen; and we possess Sen-
egambia, the best and most healthy settlement.

In Europe we have relinquished Minorca—kept up at an immense
and useless expense in peace, and never tenable in war. . . .

In the East Indies, where alone we have the power to obtain this
peace, we have restored what was useless to ourselves, and scarcely
tenable in a continuance of the war.

But we have abandoned the unhappy loyalists to their implacable
enemies.

Britain might have done much worse, though Pitt was hardly inclined to
crow. "These," he continued,

are the ruinous conditions which this country, engaged with four
powerful states, and exhausted in all its resources, thought fit to
subscribe, for the dissolution of that alliance, and the immediate
enjoyment of peace. Let us examine what is left, with a manly and
determined courage. . . . Let us feel our calamities—let us bear them,
too, like men.

Pitt devoted his peroration to the political interment of North and Shelburne. The latter, he said, would reclaim his reputation in retirement. As to
North, he said, "whatever appears dishonourable in the peace on your table
is strictly chargeable to the noble lord in the blue ribbon, whose profusion
of the public's money, whose notorious temerity and obstinacy in prosecuting the war, which originated in his pernicious and oppressive policy,
and whose utter incapacity to fill the stations he occupied, rendered peace
of any description indispensable to the preservation of the state."[41]

Thus disposing of Shelburne and North, Pitt narrowed the field of plausible premiers-in-waiting to a small handful. Indeed, the chancellor seemed almost to be nominating himself.

If so, Pitt had reckoned without Fox. Not for Lord Holland's son was the diffidence of Edmund Burke. No more than young Pitt was Fox ashamed to put himself forward. In defending his summertime decision to quit the Shelburne government, Fox declared his ambition for high office. "I will confess," he said, "that I am desirous of enjoying an eminence which must flatter my ambition, promote my convenience and enable me to exert myself in my country's service; and in confessing this desire, I trust that it cannot be termed presumption."[42]

The second vote to censure the peace passed by a vote of 207–190; Shelburne, still not exactly understanding what had happened to him, resigned on February 24. To be succeeded by whom?

Not by a coalition led by Fox and North, George III was adamant. Just the chance of such a deformity was proof of the corruption of the age in which it was his bad luck to reign. For six weeks His Majesty ransacked the alternatives. William Pitt, seeing that he lacked the parliamentary strength to sustain a government, declined the opportunity to form one. Perhaps then the other Pitt, Thomas, son of the late Chatham's elder brother? "Yes," the king replied to that suggestion. "Mr. Thomas Pitt or Mr. Thomas Anybody."[43]

But no Mr. Anybody presented himself. Neither did the business of state, notably the still incomplete work of treaty-making or the indispensable job of raising a revenue, automatically conduct itself.

Despairing, the king again considered abdication. Reconsidering, he steeled himself to the abhorrent Fox and the unspeakable North and to the anodyne Duke of Portland. In titular fashion, the duke would occupy the position of prime minister. Semi-titularly, North would hold the position of secretary of state for home and colonial affairs; literally and figuratively, he would prove a sleeping partner. The younger, more energetic Fox would predominate. "The most unprincipled coalition the annals of this or any other nation can equal," the king remarked to Lord Temple.[44]

To foreshorten the life of this unholy union, George III resolved to withhold from the new ministers the royal gift of peerages and sinecures, those bonding agents of eighteenth-century party loyalty. Other such opportunities for subversion of the new administration would presently suggest themselves.

There would be no ministerial appointment for Burke, who returned to the Paymaster's Office. Few felt so keenly the omission of the Whigs' greatest thinker from the new cabinet as Sir Alexander Dick, a noted Scottish physician. Writing to Boswell on March 21, Sir Alexander proposed that apparently ungovernable Britain take a page from the Roman Republic and install a modern-day triumvirate. In this benevolent dictatorship, Pitt would speak for the Commons, the king for the Crown, and Burke—the unpedigreed, self-made Burke—for the House of Lords. "If there was ever a time for employing a Dictator as in old Rome," the Scotsman urged, "now is the time."[45]

George III—or "Satan," as the king was known in Fox's circle—proved a hard nut to crack. At a royal audience at around the time of the formation of the government in early April, Fox assured His Majesty that he had never uttered a word to the Prince of Wales "which he should not have been glad to have His Majesty hear." The king chose not to respond to this patent untruth.[46]

Neither did dissimulation succeed in the language of courtly self-abasement. "Mr. Fox," the new secretary of state addressed the king on April 16,

> hopes that Your Majesty will not think him presumptuous or improperly intruding upon Your Majesty with professions, if he begs leave most humbly to implore Your Majesty to believe that both the Duke of Portland and he have nothing so much at heart as to conduct Your Majesty's affairs, both with respect to measures and to persons, in the manner that may give Your Majesty the most satisfaction, and that, whenever Your Majesty will be graciously pleased to condescend even to hint your inclinations upon any subject, that it will be the study of Your Majesty's Ministers to show how truly sensible they are of Your Majesty's goodness.

Across the back of the letter George jotted, "No answer."

Perhaps, Fox persisted, the king would welcome a personal briefing on the definitive treaties of peace. His Majesty declined the opportunity: "unnecessary discussions are not my taste." When the treaties were at last signed, sealed, and delivered, and peace was to be proclaimed— virtually the peace that Shelburne had negotiated and that Fox had returned to office by arraigning—the king refused to join in the celebrations. "I think," he told North, "this completes the downfall of the lustre of the Empire."[47]

A controversy over the Prince of Wales's finances laid to rest the admittedly remote possibility that the king would ever warm to Fox and the coalition. The heir to the throne, already a regal spender, would turn twenty-one in August 1783. Unemployed by profession, he had no income except that which the king and the taxpayers, by parliamentary grant, allowed him. The new ministry, eager to stay on the right side of the future king George IV, set to work finding the money for him.

Fox took the lead. Whether or not he had promised the prince £100,000 a year on his imminent majority, it was the figure that Fox and his colleagues proposed to the king. George reluctantly acceded after venting to the prince's treasurer about his son's "neglect of every religious duty . . . and his total disobedience of every injunction I had given."

Paternal submission turned to rejection and rage when the government amended its request to include £29,000 for the prince's previously undisclosed debts. Now the king broadened his attack on his heir's character to encompass the hypocrisy of Whigs' economic reformers: "Believe me, no consideration can ever make me either forget or forgive what has passed, and the public shall know how well founded the principles of economy are in those who have so loudly preached it up."[48]

The coalition retreated, the king relented, and Fox persuaded the prince to accept a compromise: £50,000 a year along with a one-time allowance for debt service of £60,000. Vowing to live within his means, the disappointed prince submitted. While he would presently outdo himself in spending and borrowing, the king would never again commit to paper an invective more cutting* than that which he directed against his son's "shameful extravagance" and the coalition that facilitated it.[49]

THE PAYMASTER'S OFFICE TO WHICH BURKE RETURNED IN APRIL 1783 was not the one he left in July 1782. Gone were John Powell, cashier, and Charles Bembridge, accountant, key employees since the time of Lord Holland almost twenty years earlier. An investigation by the Treasury Board had uncovered evidence that the pair were planning an embezzlement. Powell, under questioning, virtually confessed to it. A prosecution was set in motion, and Isaac Barré, Burke's successor at the Paymaster's Office in 1782, discharged both suspects pending their day in court. Burke, returning to office the next year, rehired them. The decision caused a furor, which Burke's attempts at self-defense only inflamed.

Self-awareness failed the returning paymaster. He regarded Powell and Bembridge as presumably innocent, certainly indispensable, cogs in the Paymaster's Office machinery. They had helped him draft the plan whereby the government's substantial cash balances earned interest at the Bank of England.

Burke knew Powell, too, in his capacity as the Fox family's financial factotum and the chief executor of Lord Holland's estate. It was Powell on whom Charles Fox's distraught father called to sort out his sons' six-figure gambling debts, and it was Powell who stood ready to purchase Holland's seaside retreat in Kent when Charles Fox, who had inherited the property from his father, needed cash. And it was Powell, we may conjecture, who had attended to the details when the minor Burkes, William and Richard, raised a £500 loan from Lord Holland in 1766 during their operations in the shares of the East India Company.

Knowing Powell and Bembridge as he believed he did, Burke refused to prejudge their guilt. "I conceive myself," he wrote to each man in mid-April, "(without reflecting on the Act of my predecessor, who probably proceeded on another turn of things) bound in fairness and equity to continue to

---

* The editor of the king's correspondence called it "the strongest in language I have encountered among the whole of his papers." Cannon, *Fox-North Coalition*, 99.

employ you; informing you at the same time, that if your Conduct should on my own, or on public Enquiry, appear such as admits no just Cause or Alleviation, however disagreeable it may be to me, I shall certainly be obliged to remove you."[50]

At the very least, Burke's decision was questionable, and the opposition availed themselves of the opportunity to prick and probe when the matter came before the House on May 2. Burke was quick to say that he had acted on his own without consulting his colleagues, and that, fortunately, his own reforms of the Paymaster's Office removed the temptation to embezzlement, given that the paymaster's cash was now on deposit at the bank.

James Martin, a well-to-do London banker, retorted that, since the clerks had been dismissed for "gross misbehavior," he could not help "looking upon their restoration as a gross and daring insult to the public."

"Mr. Burke," the parliamentary historian recorded, "rising in a violent fit of passion, exclaimed, '*it is a gross and daring_____*'; but he could proceed no farther, for Mr. Sheridan* by this time had pulled him down on his seat, from a motive of friendship, lest his heat should betray him into some intemperate expression that might offend the House."

Fox, in a similarly supportive vein, said that Burke had only wished to preserve the presumption of innocence and to let justice take its course. As for himself, he could vouch for Powell as "a man of the strictest honour and honesty." Besides, his own family had more to lose than His Majesty's Treasury if Powell turned out to be an embezzler. The sum in contention, £40,000 or so, "was a trifle with regard to the public," something very different in the case of an individual, perhaps an individual named Fox.

Fox's words soothed the House but at the cost of reminding its members that Powell was the acting executor of his father's estate and that he himself, the apple of his father's eye, had so signally contributed to the shambles of his family's finances.[51]

The opposition, unmollified, returned to the attack on May 19. Sir Cecil Wray, Fox's Westminster colleague, led with arguments against a

---

* Richard Brinsley Sheridan, playwright, Whig, and soon-to-be ally of Burke and Fox in the cause of East India Company reform.

motion that the House cease inquiries into the Powell and Bembridge affair to avoid pretrial judgment. Wray demanded, on the contrary, a thoroughgoing House investigation. He characterized Burke's decision as "highly indecent."

These, too, were fighting words, hardly less provocative than Martin's, but now Burke apologized. He regretted not his conduct at the Paymaster's Office but rather his unwonted "warmth" at the House of Commons two weeks earlier. With regard to his reinstatement of the two shady clerks, "he felt such a sunshine of content in his mind, that were the act undone, he was convinced that he would do it again."

"It had ever been, and it ever should be a maxim with him, to compassionate the unfortunate," Burke told the House; "and, if they happened to be connected with him, to protect them, as long as he found them nothing worse than unfortunate." Certainly, Powell and Bembridge were unfortunate men. Powell was going to pieces and had begged to be allowed to resign.

Burke said that the sight of the gray hair of the half-mad Powell had "so far affected and overcome him, that he was scarcely able to come down to the House." He claimed that the two unfortunates "had been committed to his protection by the hand of Providence."

It seemed not to occur to Burke that Powell had a guilty conscience or that Bembridge and Powell might tamper with the books. Neither, evidently, did he wonder how an honest government cashier could raise himself to the happy position of affording the purchase price of Lord Holland's expensively appointed seaside folly, even if the motivated seller, Charles Fox, had been in no position to haggle over the price.

Once more Fox rose to Burke's defense, echoing the paymaster's point that, post-reform, no significant idle funds were left in the office to be stolen. "His worthy friend," said Fox of Burke, "had not, indeed, studied prudence in reinstating the two men, because he must know it would raise a clamour; but as no person attempted to charge him with any bad motives, they must attribute it at the worst, to mistaken humanity, and a desire not to think persons guilty before they were really found so."[52]

The motion to suspend the House's investigation passed by a vote of 161–137, a worrisomely narrow margin from the coalition's vantage point. It was indeed hard to argue with the commonsense objection that "no person under prosecution should, during that prosecution, hold any office of trust."*

On May 21, John Rolle, a Devon landowner who had conceived a deep aversion to Fox during the Admiral Rodney affair,† rose to ask a peremptory question. Did Burke intend to retain the services of Powell and Bembridge? Time was short—the House was eager to take up some India-related business—and Rolle wanted a simple yes or no.

He was to be disappointed over the course of the next two to three hours—just how long Burke spoke is uncertain, as is the kaleidoscopic range of his subject matter. A sense of the range and structure of those remarks is conveyed by a line in the *Parliamentary History*: "Having traveled for a while in the region of allegory, he spoke seriously to the question that had been put to him."

Burke said he would let the House decide the correctness of his decision, that House to which "he would ever bow." He wanted no new vote, rather the sounding of a few of its leading members. In the meantime, he meant to explain himself fully—"Yes or No were short monosyllables to decide so great a question as that which affected his honour in a most intricate business.

"He then entered into a justification of his own conduct from his earliest days," the *Parliamentary History* continues, "the motives that influenced his conduct ever since he began [in] the world; and said, that it was always his maxim to justify the order of providence, and the disposition of the King."

There was a great deal more of this before Rolle interrupted to observe that Burke had wandered from the point. Fox stood up for Burke—as there was no motion before the House, he was perfectly orderly in answering

---

* As Thomas Powys, an independent country gentleman, presently put the matter. PH, 23:923.

† It will be recalled that Fox joined Burke in condemning Rodney for his alleged brutality toward the conquered civilian residents of St. Eustatius, a charge that, following Rodney's victory over the French at the Battle of the Saintes, in April 1782, the admiral's critics were obliged rather to muffle. If this was the reason for Rolle's animus toward Fox, it very likely applied to Burke, too.

as he wished. William Pitt sided with Rolle. The speaker of the House, Charles Wolfran Cornwall, ruled for Burke, who proceeded to explain why he had welcomed Powell and Bembridge back to their respective Paymaster's Office desks.

Without those dutiful assistants, Burke proceeded, there would have been no reform, no saving of some £47,000 a year in public expense, a sum that happened roughly to coincide with that which the suspects were planning to embezzle. "He praised their conduct as men of business and religious integrity; said he ever found them just in their accounts and indefatigable in their duty; that whatever merit he could claim in this reform, he must divide it equally with them."*

"The Pay-office," Burke went on,

> was formerly a very fattening place, into which many a poor man had got, who came out very rich:—men who were weasels when they crept and twisted themselves at entering, but who soon grew so fat, plump and jolly there, that it was a difficult matter to get them out again. To himself he could answer that the allusion was not applicable, for he was still as lean as when he went in, and his determination was to destroy all that steam of fattening in future, which had too long been the custom hitherto.

Only those ignorant of the exacting work of that department would say that it could function without the likes of Powell and Bembridge, said Burke, which point he illustrated with a story about an "arrogant lover" on the morning after his wedding night.

Asked by an intimate friend, "How often?" he replied, "About fifty."

"Then I am certain," says the other, "there was none."[53]

Both the bridegroom and the Paymaster's Office had a duty to perform, Burke explained, and each required "much strength." He supplemented this light blue parable with quotations from the Gospel of Luke,

---

* Early in April 1782 it was reported that Burke had invited the Paymaster's Office clerks out to dinner, so that they might get to know one another "over a bottle." W&S, 4:176.

the *Aeneid*, Shakespeare's *Macbeth* (or Burke's adaptation thereof), his own 1780 "Speech on Economical Reform," and an "abundance of apposite" Latin tags. In closing he burst into tears "two or three times." Newspaper stenographers admitted that he was "utterly impossible" to keep up with.[54]

Rolle, having heard neither yes or no, announced his intention to move that the House vote again. Burke begged his critic's pardon. For the previous two or three hours, he had neglected to mention that Powell had resigned and that Bembridge had offered his resignation. Pitt joined Rolle in demanding that Bembridge, too, be shown the door.

As Lord Holland had fattened himself in the unreformed Paymaster's Office, it's unlikely that Fox enjoyed hearing Burke spin out his weasel story. Still, his friend had talked himself into a jam and needed a way out. Fox gently suggested one: "As so respectable a number of those who composed the minority thought Mr. Bembridge should be dismissed, he wished his right hon. friend to accept the resignation."[55]

Burke would eventually accept Bembridge's resignation. He likewise eventually would testify to Bembridge's good character at the trial at which the suspect would be convicted of conniving in the concealment of £48,799 and for which he would pay a fine of £2,600 and be sentenced to jail for six months. Rather than stand trial, Powell would commit suicide with a penknife.

In 1774, Oliver Goldsmith, poet, playwright, and near-contemporary of Burke's at Trinity College, Dublin, published "Retaliation," some mock epitaphs of his friends in the Johnsonian literary circle. A caricature in verse, Burke's pen portrait did its subject fair, rough justice.

Here lies our good friend Edmund, whose genius was such,
We can scarcely praise it, or blame it too much;
Who, born for the Universe, narrow'd his mind,
And to party gave up, what was meant for mankind:
Tho fraught with all learning, yet straining his throat
To persuade Tommy Townshend to lend him a vote;
Who, too deep for his hearers, still went on refining,
And thought of convincing, while they thought of dining;

Tho' equal to all things, for all things unfit,

Too nice for a statesman, too proud for a wit:

For a patriot too cool; for a drudge, disobedient;

And too fond of the right *to pursue the* expedient.[56]

A variant on Goldsmith's *jeu d'esprit*, shorn of wit, rhyme, and affection, issued from George Johnstone, a blunt-spoken former naval officer and the founding governor of West Florida, in the May 21 House debate. Said Johnstone about Burke, the statesman: "His humanity frequently ran away with him, and rendered him unfit to act with that decision and firmness on great and important occasions, which a consummate statesman ought to have at his command."[57]

And when, in June, the House finally washed its hands of the Powell and Bembridge affair, Lord Sheffield, an Irish peer, heaved a sigh of relief. "Thank God," he wrote, "Burke is quiet."[58]

CHAPTER 13

Fox's India Bill

Fox (added he) is a most extraordinary man; here is a man . . . who
has divided the Kingdom with Caesar; so that it was a doubt
whether the nation should be ruled by the sceptre of George the
Third, or the tongue of Fox.

—SAMUEL JOHNSON, IN BOSWELL'S *LIFE OF JOHNSON*, JUNE 1784

One day in August 1783, Sir Gilbert Elliot sat down to breakfast
with Burke and Fox to discuss Fox's pending bill to reconstitute
the East India Company. "We had a couple of hours of conversation," Sir Gilbert reported to his wife; "but a couple of days would not
exhaust Burke." "Quiet" was not the orator's natural state of being.[1]

Samuel Johnson attributed the gushing flow of Burke's talk to the "ebul-
lition" of his mind—"he does not talk from a desire of distinction, but
because his mind is full."*[2] For the next decade and a half, Burke's mind,
and Fox's too, would be full of India, and of the governor-general of Bengal,
Warren Hastings, and of Hastings's crisis-prone employer, the East India
Company.

---

* Darting from subject to subject, Burke charmed the novelist Frances Burney, though
she felt she could do no justice to his conversation by merely repeating what he said: that
which is "related from him, loses half its effect in not being related by him." Burney, *Diary
and Letters of D'Arblay*, 1:183. Fox, by way of contrast, "never talks in private company,"
said Johnson, or at least, rarely in the lexicographer's intimidating presence. "A man who is
used to the applause of the House of Commons, has no wish for that of a private company,"
Johnson conjectured. "A man accustomed to throw for a thousand pounds, if set down to
throw for sixpence, would not be at pains to count his dice." Boswell, *Life of Johnson*, 857.

It was India that dominated the short life of the improbable governing coalition in which oil and water, Fox and Lord North, made common
cause. And it was in the course of a nobly intended attempt to reform the
East India Company that Burke eulogized Charles Fox in words that have
earned a place among the greatest of all parliamentary orations. Yet that
resounding praise proved no match for the king's popularity, the opposition's guile, or the cartoonists' malice.

The Fox-North coalition was instituted on April 2, 1783, and dissolved
on December 18, 1783. In between, Charles Fox moved his India Bill, which
the Commons enacted but the Lords rejected and, with that vote, doomed
the coalition.

It was Britain's fourth government in little more than a year. The successor to the administrations of North, Rockingham-Shelburne, and
Shelburne-sans-Rockingham, the coalition naturally inherited a backlog
of unfinished business. They could hardly do everything at once. What
they chose to do first was to attack, reform, and rehabilitate the East India
Company: to rewrite its charter and to manage the business themselves.

Or perhaps, as Fox would insist, the company chose them. It was bankrupt, he charged, and its wars, cruelties, and intramural political intrigue
had become a national scandal. The House must hurry to set things right.

Much the same problems had crowded in on the North government
late in the 1770s, but the American war clamored louder than India for the
prime minister's not limitless attention. Neither did the Rockinghams and
Shelburnes choose to grapple with the everlasting Indian problem child
except by stopgap measures. In 1781 a pair of parliamentary committees,
denoted "secret" and "select," attempted to get to the bottom of the Indian
situation, with Burke producing a report that is regarded as the select committee's most authoritative.*

Indeed, Burke knew more about India than most of the Britons who
had lived there. One of the quickest studies in English politics, he had
applied himself to Indian affairs since before he entered Parliament in

---

* *Ninth Report of the Select Committee, Appointed to Take into Consideration the State of
the Administration of Justice in the Provinces of Bengal, Bahar and Orissa*, 1783.

1766. William Burke, leader of the kinsmen's speculative misadventures in East India shares, had subsequently traveled to India to repair the Burkes' finances, and Edmund had allied himself with William's Indian patron, the Raja of Tanjore.

To monitor the company in London, Edmund bought enough East India stock to qualify him to vote at the regular quarterly shareholder meetings.[3] He knew Indian geography, history, and place names, as well as the tongue-twisting proper names of numerous Indian nawabs, rajas, nizams, subahs, sultans, viziers, and begums. Philip Francis, who had gone to India to serve on the Bengal governing council and promptly made a mortal enemy of Warren Hastings, told Burke everything he knew about the company's myriad misdeeds and shortcomings.

The Indian subcontinent stirred Burke's imagination, sympathies, and awe. "Bengal, Bahar, and Orissa, with Benares (now unfortunately in our immediate possession)," he told the Commons, "measure 161,978 square English miles; a territory considerably larger than the whole Kingdom of France," while the "whole of the company's dominion" encompassed a territory "larger than any European dominion, Russia and Turkey excepted," with a population four times greater than Britain's.[4] Ever ready to assist a persecuted individual, Burke now saw 30 million such beings in India, and he dedicated himself to their emancipation.

A decade or so earlier Burke had stood four-square with the loss-making company against the government. Lord North, pleading "necessity," had put forward a bill to restrict the company's dividends, limit the directors to four-year terms, prohibit the servants from accepting presents or trading for their personal gain, and establish, in Bengal, a governing council and a supreme court, the better to regulate corporate operations from London.

Burke, in opposition, had latched on to the word *necessity*, "that grim tyrant." He criticized the government's plans to disenfranchise shareholders owning fewer than one thousand shares and condemned the appointment of parliamentary committees to investigate the company's supposed failings; for his part, Burke could see none. He regretted that the bill had been forced on Parliament "at the end of a fatiguing session, by the unfortunate words, *do something*; that the principle of this bill was an infringement of *national right, national faith and justice*."⁵ Burke defended the swashbuckling Robert Clive and found inspiration in the showy wealth of the returning British nabobs—"I think there is something of a divine providence in it." He judged that the company was capable of producing in India "a system one of the most beautiful ever established in any place."⁶

Certainly, Burke believed what he said, though rare was the occasion when he supported the government on anything. But it was self-directed study, not party politics, that drove him to reconsider his position on the subcontinent. He had decided, by the early 1780s, that the East India Company was bent on the destruction of "a people for ages civilized and cultivated; cultivated by all the arts of polished life, whilst we were yet in the woods."⁷ The "sole author" of these evils, Burke had concluded, was a successor of Clive's in Bengal, Warren Hastings. In Parliament in April 1783, Burke "pledged himself to God, to his country, to that House and to the unfortunate and plundered inhabitants of India to bring to justice as far as in him lay, the greatest delinquent India ever saw."⁸

Fox, though no deep student of India, was likewise committed to the work of saving the company from bankruptcy and the Indian people from the company. The India Bill was "not one of choice," as he would insist in presenting his legislation to the House of Commons, "but of necessity . . . the business forced itself on him, and upon the nation."⁹

The sight of the former enemies fraternally jammed together on the Treasury bench was not one to restore the faith of a political cynic. But the opposition's sardonic reproaches were nothing compared to the explosive power of the caricaturists James Sayers and James Gillray.

Hardly had the coalition kissed hands with the none-too-welcoming king than Gillray issued his drawing titled "Coalition Dance."¹⁰ It depicted North, Fox, and the bespectacled Burke (wearing the Jesuitical cassock, cincture, and biretta), with hands joined, dancing around a term, or bust, of the king, to the music of a demon fiddler. Gillray, thematically borrowing from Sir Joshua Reynolds's masterwork, *Three Ladies Adorning a*

Term of Hymen,* captioned his print, "Let us Dance & Sing—God bless the King—For he has made us merry men all."[11]

In Gillray's "Junction of the Parties," which followed shortly, the devil stirs the contents of a pot into which North and Fox are jointly defecating. Only four weeks of coalition history had passed before Horace Walpole marveled at the sheer quantity of malicious caricature that the government's enemies had called into circulation: "If satiric prints could despatch them, they would be dead in their cradle. There are enough to hang a room."†

The coalition's landmark legislation, though known as Fox's East India Bill, bore the clear marks of Burke's learning and industry. It fell to Fox, as the coalition's motive force, to present the legislation to the Commons, and he knew full well what enemies lay in wait for him.

Fox admitted his forebodings to Burgoyne on the eve of his speech to move the bill, November 17, 1783:

> I have too much reason to think that, upon our India measure . . . we shall meet with great embarrassments and difficulties. The variety of private interests that will militate against us cannot fail of making it a most tempting opportunity to opposition. . . . You will of course consider this as said to yourself only and not let it be known that I am holding croaking language.[12]

Spectators and members filled the House of Commons the next day to hear Fox divulge his plan to serve a "great and glorious cause," the salvation not only of an essential and failing enterprise but also of the people of India and Britain alike; "many, many millions of souls." The essential aim

---

* The Greek god of marriage and fertility.

† "There was great variety in the imagery too. The coalition was a many-headed monster. Fox played Herod to North's Pilate, Cataline to the Vicar of Bray, Cromwell to Charles I. They were lovers, chimney sweeps, jugglers, sharks, and bandits. From the top of the Treasury ladder, they took all the spoils of office. They plundered Liberty and John Bull, made Britannia a prostitute, and as miners, sought to undermine the constitution." Johnson, "Britannia Roused," 24.

was to separate the company's two incompatible missions: sovereign rule and moneymaking.

Fox led off with the disingenuous assertion that there was nothing "visionary or speculative" about his bill. It would, in fact, supplant the Court of Directors with a seven-man commission to be nominated, at the outset, by the House of Commons—that is, by the government of Fox and North—and, after the passage of four years, by the king. The commission, residing in England, "under the very eye of Parliament,"[13] would effectively rule British India. A nine-man subsidiary board, operating under the control of the commission, would manage the commercial operations of the company.

Here, then, was a proposed nationalization, not at once of the company's property but of its brains and management. Wielding vast powers over money and patronage, war, and peace, the commission would be a creature of the coalition. To the historian Andrew Roberts, it looked like "a Brooks's takeover of the wealth of the subcontinent."*[14]

Neither Fox nor Burke was so cynical. To his mistress Elizabeth Armistead, Fox admitted that the bill would cost him heavily in the City, though

> I know I am right and must bear the consequences, though I dislike unpopularity as much as any man. . . . I know I never did act more upon principle than at this moment, when they are abusing me so. If I had considered nothing but keeping my power, it was the safest way to leave things as they are, or to propose some trifling alteration, and I am not at all ignorant of the political danger which I run by this bold measure; but whether I succeed or no, I shall always be glad that I attempted, because I know that I have done no more than I was bound to do, in risking my power and that of my friends when the happiness of so many millions is at stake. I write very gravely . . . but . . . do not fancy from all this that I am out of spirits,

---

* Whose membership now included Burke as well as Fox. Elected in March, the candidate was proposed by none other than the Duke of Devonshire. C., 5:76.

or even that I am much alarmed for the success of our scheme. On the contrary, I am very sanguine.[15]

Fox had invoked the authority and the findings of the parliamentary committees appointed to search for answers to the eternal India question. Both the secret committee, headed by Henry Dundas, and the select committee, which Burke intellectually dominated, agreed "that all the distress and difficulty of the company was ascribable to the disobedience of the orders of the court of directors and the rapacity of the company's servants in India."[16]

It was indeed absurd, Lord North told the Commons, that the Court of Directors, which nominally managed the company, issued orders that the servants in India habitually ignored. "The House had heard that the directors wrote fine letters," said North; "this certainly did them great credit . . . ; but nothing was ever done in consequence, and all the important business of the company ended where it began—in a fine letter!"[17]

In 1776 the directors had recalled Hastings from India, but Hastings's agent, to spare his client the embarrassment of a dismissal, announced that he had chosen to resign instead. Then the client disavowed his agent. Years passed—a letter could spend twelve months at sea before reaching its destination—and Hastings remained in India.

In 1782 there was another attempt to bring Hastings home, this one originating in Parliament. Dundas moved the motion, the House passed it. And the directors, in obedience to the House, gave it their assent—on condition that the proprietors voted their agreement. The proprietors did no such thing but did vote to rescind the recall.* "It was a [corporate] government of anarchy and confusion," as Fox not unreasonably charged.[18]

One could hardly expect anything else, Fox told the House, as the directors "wished not to offend the court of proprietors, to whom they owed their situations; and the proprietors would never be easily persuaded to

---

* To add to the chaos, the government refused to allow official notice of the stockholders' vote to leave the country, so that while the entire subcontinent learned about Hastings's recall, Hastings himself never officially discovered that he was not, in fact, recalled.

sacrifice servants by whom they were enriched: thus, however, the dearest interests of the country were sacrificed, and its honour tarnished, while no power in law existed at present by which the former might be preserved and the latter retrieved."

Even worse than the company's chain of command was its financial position, Fox proceeded. One year before, management had come begging Parliament for £1.5 million. And now the India-based corporate staff was flooding the Home Office with bills—demands for cash—in the sum of £2 million, a sum grotesquely in excess of the allowable maximum set by Parliament of £300,000.

Fox, speaking to the House at his accustomed breakneck speed, said the word *bankrupt*, which, according to the shorthand reporters, he underscored with the modifier *unquestionably*. It was a claim he supported with two figures only, debts of £11.2 million and salable inventory worth £3.2 million. No financial analyst, now or then, could draw such a conclusion from those skimpy facts. When did the debts fall due? Could they not be refinanced? Besides inventory, what liquid assets did the company hold? Fox, no master of personal finance and no student of economics (he judged *The Wealth of Nations* to be an unreadable bore), did not say. But without an emergency cash infusion, he insisted, the company must be ruined, "and the ruin of a body of merchants, so extensive in their concerns, and so important in the eyes of all Europe as the English East India company, must give the national credit a very great shock indeed." Too big to fail, the company must therefore be reconstituted.

The word *nationalization* is not to be found in Johnson's *Dictionary*, but Fox contended that the East India Company was more important to the nation, to which it paid some £1.3 million in annual customs fees, than to its stockholders, to whom it remitted annual dividends of just £256,000. In exchange for the new leaf that his India legislation would compel the company to turn over, said Fox, the Treasury would guarantee its debts, including those £2 million of troubling bills.

Fox promised the House that, in his dedication to the arduous task at hand, he had "left all thoughts of ease, indolence and safety behind him," and he quoted a line of Burke's (which, he noted, was intended "half in jest, half in earnest"), that idleness "was the best gift that God had bestowed upon man."[19]

Rising in rebuttal, the young Pitt ventured a few remarks on indolence (a subject with which North was better acquainted than Fox, he quipped) before turning to the supposed "necessity" of Fox's legislation. Pitt fixed on the word, as Burke had done years earlier: "Was not necessity the plea of every illegal exertion of power, or exercise of oppression? Was not necessity the pretence of every usurpation?"

What Fox proposed, Pitt went on, was the plain usurpation of the company's chartered rights—it was "absolute despotism," complete with "the most gross corruption." Naming his seven commissioners, Fox himself would rule India: "He would have all the power and patronage for which this Bill was principally recommended as tending to eradicate." It was commendable that Fox intended to enact protections for the property rights of the Hindus, "but let him take care that he did not destroy the liberties of Englishmen."[20]

This was preliminary sparring; the issue was drawn in the second reading of the bill on November 27. Whether the modest pullback in the price of the East India Company's shares, from £125 to £120, was in response to Fox's accusations is unclear; certainly the stockholders, meeting at Leadenhall Street on November 21, refused to believe that the business was bankrupt, and they unanimously voted to petition the House of Commons against the threatened "total confiscation" of their property.*

Friends and foes alike could hardly help but admire Fox's pluck in attempting a kind of tutorial in corporate security analysis during the culminating debate over the East India Bill on November 27. Then again, the situation seemed to demand it. He had rushed his bill to the floor, in deepest secrecy, on the ground that the company was at death's door. Having proven no such thing on November 18, he must make good now. To refute him, the company's accountants had submitted

---

* The pro-Fox chairman of the company, Sir Henry Fletcher, retired under the shareholders' censure—after discharging the unwelcome duty of submitting their anti-Fox petition to the Commons.

figures purporting to show that, while perhaps illiquid, the business was unquestionably solvent. It could discharge its debts eventually, if not immediately.

As to this presentation, Fox said, "he found many things inserted, which ought to have been omitted; and many things omitted, which ought to have been inserted." Not that he charged the accountants with positive falsehoods. He would merely identify the shortcomings of their analysis.

Here, then, was a brand-new Fox. The opposition had smiled as he pledged to sacrifice his indolence for the sake of the Indian people. It might well have gasped as the former keeper of the Brooks's faro bank confidently plunged into a line-by-line deconstruction of the East India Company balance sheet. Here, said Fox, probing one entry: Why has not the company marked down the value of its 3 percent government bonds, issued in the sum of £4.2 million, to reflect a subsequent rise in interest rates? Why does the company pretend that its £261,000 claim on the French government for the expense of housing and feeding French prisoners during the Seven Years' War was money good when the French government still refused to pay it? And was it really true, Fox demanded of the House, that the company could dispose of £2.5 million worth of aging inventoried goods at the value claimed? Or that military stores, then on the water to India, could properly be considered the kind of asset with which the company might discharge a debt?

Fox's guided tour through the East India financial statements continued with a swipe at the value of silver presented on the balance sheet ("one solitary thousand pounds") and a query as to the real value of Indian cargoes en route to London from Bengal. Fox found fault with the rupee-sterling exchange rate that the company chose to employ and with the inflated (said he) value at which it marked the debts due from Indian provincial rulers. He read aloud letters attesting to the cruelty of the company's debt collection methods and of the wars that "have constantly been as unproductive of revenue as they were productive of infamy."

Fox favored the House with a reading of a letter from the Subah of Oudh, a princely state in the north of India, protesting the unjust and unpayable debts that the company claimed it owed. Not only Oudh but every such alleged Indian potentate-debtor should be granted remission, Fox said. "And he believed," as the parliamentary reporter quoted him as saying, "that the feelings and the magnanimity of [Great Britain] would go with him in saying, that they would rather be doomed to pay all that the company owed, ill as they could at this time bear it; ill as their sinking-fund could sustain the shock, they would apply to that, rather than wring from the princes of the country, by aiding them in wars on their innocent people." To which the record added, "In this part of his speech, all sides of the House joined in the exclamation of 'hear! hear!' as the testimony of their approbation."[21]

It did not escape the notice of William Pitt that Fox had failed to claim, much less to prove, that the company was bankrupt. The secretary of state had overwhelmed the House with data, but what those figures said, let alone what they meant, was incomprehensible. There were errors, said Pitt—a glance at the balance sheet (a little higher up on the page from which Fox had carelessly quoted) would show that the company in fact held £142,794 in gold and silver, not the "one solitary thousand pounds" that Fox had claimed. Pitt proceeded line by line through the financial statements, correcting here, quibbling there. He landed his most telling blow with the observation that Fox, once more, had ignored the timing of debt maturities, "but had argued as if the whole were due at the present moment." Yes, Pitt acknowledged, the company was "distressed," but it was "by no means insolvent."

Besides, its property was, or ought to be, its own. Its charter, though forcibly amended by the Regulating Act of 1773, was now to be ripped to shreds. There was no "necessity." He hoped, said Pitt, that the House

had too much regard for their own honour and dignity, too scrupulous an attention to justice, and too conscientious an adherence to their duty to their constituents, to support the minister in one of the boldest, most unprecedented, most desperate and alarming attempts at the exercise of tyranny, that ever disgraced the annals of this or any other country.[22]

Pitt's motion for adjournment—just for a day, to allow for a little more scrutiny and debate—fell to defeat at half past four in the morning of November 28, 1783. Fox's India Bill was almost home free.*

IT REMAINED FOR BURKE TO SPEAK HIS PIECE, WHICH HE DID FOR TWO hours on December 1 before a thronged House and gallery. As was to be expected, he flogged the company, catalogued its crimes against the Indian people, pressed for immediate action to forestall its collapse, and pilloried Warren Hastings. He answered the opposition's constitutional arguments† and refuted their claim that the proposed reform was merely the cover, in the first instance, for Fox's outrageous power grab and, in the second, after the selection of the commissioners had shifted from the government to the king, of a mighty accession of the power of the crown. As for himself, "who has supplied a mediocrity of talents by the extreme of diligence, and who has thought himself obliged, by the research of years, to wind himself into the inmost recesses and labyrinths of the Indian detail," his part in the business was hardly worth mentioning.

Notwithstanding his success at defeating the opposition, Burke, by the

---

* To refute Fox, the Court of Directors laid blame for the financial condition of the company on the recently concluded war with America and her European allies. Losses at sea alone ran to £750,000, they asserted. Nor could management repair the financial damage with its own credit; Parliament had prohibited borrowing except from the government. What the company now asked of the government was a fifteen-month suspension of the import duties that it was assessed, "until the trade can be brought back into its regular channel." Meanwhile, the directors promised, the return of peace "opens an immediate prospect of savings from the revenues of India, sufficient to give a very speedy relief to every distress which the war has brought upon the company."

Listening to Fox, his friend General Burgoyne admiringly reported, one might have supposed that the improbable financier "had been educated in the bank. Fox out-argued Pitt, but the directors made stronger financial arguments than either politician." "State of Affairs of the East India Company in England, on the 19th November 1783," PH, 23:141ff.

† Principally that the revocation of the company's charter would subvert the foundations of other chartered British companies, including the Bank of England. "If," countered Burke, "the Bank should by every species of mismanagement, fall into a state similar to that of the East India Company; if it should be oppressed with demands it could not answer, engagements which it could not perform, and with bills for which it could not procure payment; no charter should protect the mismanagement from correction, and such public grievances from redress." W&S, 5:448.

very act of speaking, refuted himself. Never had his "mediocre" talents more closely approached the celestial than in his address on the bill he characterized as the "Magna Carta of Hindostan," and on Fox, whom he insisted on calling its author.[23]

Getting down to cases, Burke observed that Britain was far from the first nation to conquer India, but the Arabs, Tartars, and Persians who had preceded the English were "very soon abated of their ferocity, because they made the conquered country their own."

The English had no such designs. "Our conquest there, after twenty years, is as crude as it was the first day," Burke said.

> The natives scarcely know what it is to see the grey head of an English-man. Young men (boys almost) govern there, without society, and without sympathy with the natives. They have no more social habits with the people, than if they still resided in England; nor indeed any species of intercourse but that which is necessary to making a sudden fortune, with a view to a remote settlement. Animated with all the avarice of age, and all the impetuosity of youth, they roll in one after another; wave after wave; and there is nothing before the natives but an endless, hopeless prospect of new flights of birds of prey and passage, with appetites continually renewing for a food that is continually wasting.

The youth we send to India, Burke went on, are no worse than the boys "whom we are whipping in school or that we see trailing a pike, or bending over a desk at home. But as English youth in India drink the intoxicating draught of authority and dominion before their heads are able to bear it, and as they are full grown in fortune long before they are ripe in principle, neither nature nor reason have any opportunity to exert themselves for remedy of the excesses of their premature power."[24]

Surveying the company's crimes and abuses in India, Burke proceeded, he had recounted not even a quarter of what he had discovered, nor, "I have full reason to believe," had he learned even a quarter of what there was to know. He said he could almost forgive the company its mis-

deeds in the political realm if it had not failed so signally in its commercial dealings.

To buy low and sell high was "the first, the great foundation of mercantile
dealing," but the company had exhibited a "total indifference" to price and
value. It was negligent in the contracts it struck, in the accounts it kept, and
in the supervision of its servants who worked as much for themselves as they
did for the company that paid their salaries. Management was incapable of
coordinating the flow of cash coming in with that of cash going out. No, said
Burke, the war wasn't to blame for the company's myriad shortcomings. "In
its present state," he declared, "the government of the East India Company is
absolutely incorrigible."[25] It did not deserve to govern itself.

Hyperbole was the lingua franca of the eighteenth-century House
of Commons, and Burke was the last member of Parliament to whisper
blame. Thus, as there was no worse criminal than Hastings, so there was
no truer witness, no greater martyr to the truth, than Philip Francis, a onetime Bengal commissioner who had fallen afoul of Hastings and the Court
of Directors and, upon his return to England, became Burke's principal
informant on Indian affairs.

Burke closed his speech with a panegyric to Fox, a justly celebrated tribute that deserves unabridged quotation. "And now, having done my duty to
the Bill, let me say a word to the author," he began.

> I should leave him to his own noble sentiments, if the unworthy and
> illiberal language with which he has been treated, beyond all example
> of parliamentary liberty, did not make a few words necessary; not so
> much in justice to him, as to my own feelings. I must say then, that it
> will be a distinction honorable to the age, that the rescue of the great-
> est number of the human race that ever were so grievously oppressed,
> from the greatest tyranny that was ever exercised, has fallen to the lot
> of abilities and dispositions equal to the task; that it has fallen to one
> who has the enlargement to comprehend, the spirit to undertake, and
> the eloquence to support, so great a measure of hazardous benevo-
> lence. His spirit is not owing to his ignorance of the state of men and
> things; he well knows what snares are spread about his path, from

personal animosity, from court intrigues, and possibly from popular delusion. But he has put to hazard his ease, his security, his interest, his power, even his darling popularity, for the benefit of a people whom he has never seen. This is the road that all heroes have trod before him. He is traduced and abused for his supposed motives. He will remember, that obloquy is a necessary ingredient in the composition of all true glory: he will remember, that it was not only in the Roman customs, but it is in the nature and constitution of things, that calumny and abuse are essential parts of triumph. These thoughts will support a mind, which only exists for honour, under the burthen of temporary reproach. He is doing indeed a great good; such as rarely falls to the lot, and almost as rarely coincides with the desires, of any man. Let him use his time. Let him give the whole length of the reins to his benevolence. He is now on a great eminence, where the eyes of mankind are turned to him. He may live long, he may do much. But here is the summit. He never can exceed what he does this day.

He has faults; but they are faults that, though they may in a small degree tarnish the lustre, and sometimes impede the march of his abilities, have nothing in them to extinguish the fire of great virtues. In those faults, there is no mixture of deceit, of hypocrisy, of pride, of ferocity, of complexional despotism, or want of feeling for the distresses of mankind. His are faults which might exist in a descendant of Henry IV of France,* as they did exist in that father of his country. Henry the Fourth wished that he might live to see a fowl in the pot of every peasant in his kingdom. That sentiment of homely benevolence was worth all the splendid sayings that are recorded of kings. But he wished perhaps for more than could be obtained, and the goodness of the man exceeded the power of the King. But this gentleman, a subject, may this day say this at least, with truth, that he secures the rice in his pot to every man in India.

---

* An allusion to Fox's royal blood. Georgiana Caroline Lennox (1723–74), Fox's mother, was a great-granddaughter of Charles II (1630–85), whose own mother, Henrietta Maria (1606–69), was the daughter of Henry IV of France (1553–1610).

Burke concluded his paean in a crescendo of love:

I confess, I anticipate with joy the reward of those, whose sole consequence, power, and authority, exist only for the benefit of mankind; and I carry my mind to all the people, and all the names and
descriptions, that, relieved by this bill, will bless the labours of this
Parliament, and the confidence which the best House of Commons
has given to him who best deserves it. The little cavils of party will
not be heard, where freedom and happiness will be felt. There is not
a tongue, a nation, or religion in India, which will not bless the presiding care and manly beneficence of this House, and of him who
proposes to you this great work. Your names will never be separated
before the throne of the Divine Goodness, in whatever language, or
with whatever rites, pardon is asked for sin, and reward for those who
imitate the Godhead in his universal bounty to his creatures. These
honours you deserve, and they will surely be paid, when all the jar-
gon, of influence, and party, and patronage, are swept into oblivion.[26]

If, even for Burke, this was going it a bit high, James Sayers brought matters
back down to earth with a thud. The caricaturist's "Carlo Khan's triumphant
Entry into Leadenhall Street," which appeared on December 5, ridiculed all
that Burke had eulogized.[27] There is an elephant, whose face is Lord North's,
on which Fox is riding. Burke is a herald with a trumpet to his lips, though
the stock Papist is without his customary cassock and biretta. Fox, astride
the elephantine North, is fat, happy, and unshaven, tricked out as a grand
mogul, Emperor of the East. The absurdly rendered trio has obvious designs
on the Leadenhall Street headquarters of the East India Company.

Sayers's caricature approximately marked the top of the coalition's fortunes,* published, as it was, three days before the East India Bill cleared
its final hurdle in the House of Commons, by a vote of 208–102. Fox had

---

* Of the fifteen prints published on the East India Bill, thirteen were hostile, only two
sympathetic. "It is difficult to conceive the moral operation and wide diffusion of these
caricatures through every part of the country," recalled the memoirist Nathaniel Wraxall.
Robinson, *Burke: Life in Caricature*, 53.

already nominated the seven commissioners who would succeed to the management of the company in the projected absence of the Court of Directors. "Fox's seven kings,"[28] the opposition mocked the moguls-in-waiting. Oddly enough, Edmund Burke, the Whigs' leading authority on India, was not among them.*

Fox did not doubt the bill's success in the House of Lords. In theory, according to Blackstone, the Lords was a "body of nobility to support the rights of both the crown and the people by forming a barrier to withstand the encroachments of both."[29] In eighteenth-century practice, the upper chamber of Parliament was rather the government's rubber stamp, not least when the government commanded so large a majority as the coalition did in the House of Commons. At three a.m. one early December day at Brooks's, Fox told Burke's friend William Windham about his "great confidence" in the bill's success.[30] As the Lords debated the measure on December 15, one government supporter was overheard assuring another, "I wish I were as sure of the kingdom of heaven as I am of our carrying the Bill this evening."[31]

The Whigs were under no illusion that George III had suddenly warmed to Charles Fox and wished the coalition success. But for all the Whigs' suspicion, they had underestimated their adversaries' cunning.

Edward Thurlow, a powerful opposition voice in the Lords, helped to rouse the king to offensive action. Enactment of Fox's bill would mean the loss of "more than half the royal power," the former lord chancellor assured him.[32] To do nothing, therefore, would make the sovereign a party to the derangement of the constitution.

The bill must be defeated and the coalition dislodged. Discreet and reliable intermediaries, led by Earl Temple, the lord lieutenant of Ireland under Shelburne who had earned the king's confidence with his blistering attacks on the coalition in the House of Lords, would carry out the operation. To him would fall the duty of conveying the king's message to the peers, bish-

---

* The list included Lord North's son, George; Sir Gilbert Elliot, who had huddled with Fox and Burke the prior August; and Lord Fitzwilliam, Rockingham's nephew as well as his financial and political heir.

ops, and sinecurists of the upper chamber, namely: "Whoever voted for the India Bill were not only not his friends, but he should consider them as his enemies; and if these words were not strong enough, Earl Temple might use whatever words he might deem stronger or more to the purpose."[33]

John Robinson, Lord North's political adjutant, entered into the conspiracy to defeat North, his old chief, along with Fox, and to install a successor government when the time was ripe. And who would lead this post-coalition regime? Why, the twenty-four-year-old William Pitt. Or at least, so hoped George III. He was obliged to hope because Pitt had earlier declined the opportunity to form a government that would have spared His Majesty the embarrassment of the coalition which he resolved anew to be rid of.

Since direct negotiations between the king and Pitt were out of the question, a discreet and inconspicuous intermediary must be procured. Lord Clarendon, an aging midlevel diplomat and inveterate place-hunter, filled the bill. Approaching Pitt, Clarendon found the novice receptive on the condition that the king commit himself unequivocally to the project. Royal favor was essential, given that Pitt would begin his prime ministerial career as the leader of a minority. Heavily outnumbered in the House of Commons, he would face, in Burke, Fox, and North, three of the most formidable debaters of the age.

In the Lords on December 9, Thurlow warned that passage of the bill would mean that the crown would "no longer be worthy of a man of honour to wear." In such an event, "The King will, in fact, take the diadem from his own head, and place it on the head of Mr. Fox. Your lordships," Thurlow continued,

have heard much of the ninth report of the select committee [i.e., Burke's *Ninth Report of the Select Committee on India of the House of Commons*]. That extraordinary performance has been in everybody's hands. The ingenious author states that "the East India Company is in possession of a vast empire, with such a boundless patronage, civil, military, marine, commercial and financial, in every department of which such fortunes have been made as could be made no where else." This, my lords, is the true description of that vast and boundless patronage, which this Bill means to throw into the hands of the Minister of the present day.[34]

Dr. Johnson, who admired Fox and revered Burke, held Thurlow in a kind of awe. "I would prepare myself for no man in England but Lord Thurlow," Johnson told Boswell. "When I am to meet with him I should wish to know a day before."* Historians have correctly identified the king's intervention as the decisive factor in the defeat of the bill and of the coalition, but Thurlow's speech was itself a powerful anti-coalition stroke. "In the late war," said Thurlow, "we had been losers in every part of the globe except India, where we now most complain of: there we had supported our honour by the spirited arrangement and amazing talents of Mr. Hastings; we had not only acted on the defensive, but been able to make acquisitions that would repay the expenses of the war in that part of the globe."[35]

Nobody of Thurlow's caliber was available to speak for the coalition in the House of Lords, a fact of which Fox was reminded as he sat helplessly observing the debate on the second reading on the bill on December 15. Not until the close of the proceedings did Earl Fitzwilliam challenge Temple to deny the king's intervention—not the rumor in the newspapers but the now-familiar report that "the noble earl in my eye had declared, that he was empowered by a great person, whose sacred name should never be heard as interfering with the progress of a bill, to say, that that person was hostile to the Bill."

Temple gave him no answer.

The Prince of Wales, loyal to Fox, voted for the bill on the first reading but absented himself from the Lords for the second reading, on December 17; the call of duty to filial authority, higher than that to his boon companion, was not to be ignored. By a margin of nineteen, the bill went down to defeat. Counterattacking in the House of Commons, the coalition challenged the opposition to deny the fact of the king's scandalous intervention. "Mere rumour and hearsay," Pitt shot back, calling it "the lie of the day," but that denial was Pitt's untruth, and he never scrupled to repeat it.[36]

"We are beat in the House of Lords by such treachery on the part of the

---

* Boswell did not discover exactly how his friend would prepare; nor did Thurlow, when Boswell repeated Johnson's praise, offer his biographer a clue: "He smiled, but did not pursue it." Boswell, *Life of Johnson*, 944.

king and meanness on the part of his *friends* in the House of Lords as one could not expect from him or them" was Fox's report on the peers' vote to Mrs. Armistead.

It was the king's prerogative to change his ministers, and this George did at midnight on December 19, his messengers finding Portland, Fox, and North in conference; they were directed to return the seals of office. "I choose this method," the king added, "as audiences on such occasions must be unpleasant."[37]

Burke, the holder of a lesser, noncabinet office, received no messenger but a note from Earl Temple:

Sir,

I have the Kings commands to acquaint you that His Majesty has no further occasion for your service as Paymaster General of His Majesty's Forces. I should be glad of a more agreeable occasion of assuring you of the Truth and respect with which I am, Sir,

Your most obedient,
Humble Servant
Nugent Temple[38]

Burke's final act in office was to secure for Charles Burney (musician, musicologist, and father of Fanny Burney) an appointment as organist to Chelsea Hospital. How the paymaster conveyed the happy news to Burney is best related by his daughter:

One day, after dinner at Sir Joshua Reynolds', Mr Burke drew Mr Burney aside, and "with great delicacy, and feeling his way, by the most investigating looks as he proceeded, said the organist's place at Chelsea College was then vacant: that it was but twenty pounds a year, but that, to a man of Dr. Burney's eminence, if it should be worth his acceptance, it might be raised to fifty."

Shortly thereafter, Burke called at the Burney residence. As the doctor was out, he asked to see Miss Burney, who resumes the narrative:

> He made a thousand apologies for breaking in upon me, but said the business was finally settled at the Treasury. Nothing could be more delicate, more elegant than his manner of doing this kindness. I don't know whether he was most polite or most friendly in his whole behaviour to me. I could almost have cried when he said, "This is my last act in office": he said it with so manly a cheerfulness, in the midst of undisguised regret. What a man he is![39]

BURKE AND FOX WOULD LATER AGREE THAT PITT'S ONLY REDEEMING feature was his irresponsibility with money. It ran through his fingers as it did through theirs. If he had a second human foible, it was an overfondness for port wine. Otherwise, Pitt's life was his work in the House of Commons.

He was a cold fish, no Brooks's material, even if, as his friends insisted, he sparkled in familiar company. To Burke, he was Blifil, the evil, chaste, and oleaginous hypocrite in Fielding's *Tom Jones*.

If Burke's wit, as Dr. Johnson complained, sometimes ran away with him, Pitt's wit was ever under its master's control. And if Fox was "born to be loved," as Burke attested, Pitt, the second-longest-serving British prime minister of all time, at eighteen years and 343 days, was born to be obeyed.

Painfully shy, Pitt hardly looked the part of "something between God and man," the persona that would be ascribed to him by the close of his storied career. In December 1783 he rather resembled the dreamy young man whom his niece, Lady Hester Stanhope, described as "a poet, or some such person, thin, tall, and rather awkward; looking upwards as if his ideas were *en air* and not remarking what was passing around him." His face, she wrote, "was not the kind of face that gave one the idea of a clever man."[40] It was the blazing light in his eyes that announced his ambition and powers.

The Pitt family tutor, the Reverend Edward Wilson, recalled that his brilliant charge seemed "never . . . to learn, but merely to recollect."[41] Like Fox, Pitt was raised to politics in a political home by a political father. He declaimed the works of Milton and Shakespeare to an imaginary House of Commons. However, no stories come down to us about an overindulgent father being incapable of saying no to his precocious statesman-in-training. Perhaps the difference between the two styles of upbringing found expression in the epigram that, whereas Charles was never at a loss for *a* word, William invariably had *the* word. Pitt matriculated at Pembroke College, Cambridge, at fourteen (a tender age even then) and took to mathematics and chemistry, as well as to the classics and history. He is said to have been particularly struck by Newton's *Principia*. Leaving Cambridge in 1779, Pitt went to London to prepare for the bar at Lincoln's Inn, arriving in time to witness the Gordon Riots.

Out in the world, Pitt played neither cards nor horses. He was uninterested in women, lived with his brother, and had a close and loving relationship with his mother. "From the instant that Pitt entered the doorway of the House of Commons," Wraxall recalled in a famous description of the soon-to-be prime minister Pitt,

> he advanced up the floor with a quick and firm step, his head erect and thrown back, looking neither to the right nor to the left, nor favouring with a nod or a glance any of the individuals seated on either side, among whom many who possessed five thousand pounds a year would have been gratified even by so slight a mark of attention. It was not thus that Lord North or Fox treated Parliament, nor from them would Parliament have so patiently endured it; but Pitt seemed made to guide and to command, even more than to persuade or to convince, the assembly that he addressed.[42]

If it's true that Fox's mother, taking the measure of the infant Pitt, predicted that he "will be a thorn in Charles's side for as long as he lives," she did not exaggerate.[43] Fox came to loathe Pitt, as much as he did the king himself.

Obviously, according to Fox, "Master Billy" owed his success to the king's deceit, which the newly minted first lord of the Treasury abetted with his own sturdy lies. It was a galling but temporary situation, Fox had every reason to believe. Did the coalition not still command a hundred-vote majority in the House of Commons? Was it not quite extraordinary that the king and his friends should override the will of the House? Mrs. Crewe, the charming Whig hostess, declared that Pitt presided over a "mince-pie" administration: it wouldn't last beyond Christmas.

Few dreamed that Pitt would survive the next seventeen Christmases. Certainly, Earl Temple was not counting on it, as the new secretary of state laid down the seals of office on December 22, just three days after taking them up. Perhaps Temple feared that Fox's vengeful majority would impeach him. Whatever the reason, the resignation badly rattled Pitt. The news kept him up all night, he told a caller on the morning of December 23. It was said to be the only sleepless night in Pitt's crisis-filled prime-ministerial career.

Fox wasted no time charging Pitt with having skulked into office through "the secret influence of the King" when Parliament reconvened on January 12. Pitt retorted that he "knew of no secret influence, and that his own integrity would be his guardian against that danger."[44] Fox's opposition handily defeated the government in a motion attacking the "unconstitutional abuse of the name of the King" and on a series of motions to prevent a dissolution of Parliament, thus to forestall an early election. This portion of the debate began shortly before three a.m. and ended at about seven a.m.*

The British people, though unpolled, were beginning to express their preference for the king and his minister over Fox and his majority. They expressed themselves in a wave of pro-crown petitions addressed to St. James's Palace. Westminster, Fox's own constituency, contributed more than 8,000 signatures in support of George III and his novice prime

---

* The resolution, which Fox moved, would have been difficult to follow even at high noon. It was surely no easier to grasp in the wee hours. In its entirety: "That it is the opinion of this committee, that any person or persons in his majesty's treasury, or in the exchequer, or in the bank of England, or for any person or persons whatsoever, employed in the payment of public money, to pay, or direct or cause to be paid, any sum or sums of money, for or towards the support of services voted in the present session of parliament, after the parliament shall have prorogued or dissolved, if it be prorogued or dissolved before any act of parliament share have passed appropriating the supplies of such services, will be a high crime and misdemeanor, a daring breach of a public trust, derogatory to the fundamental privilege of parliament, and subversive of the constitution of this country." In other words, the power of the purse—specifically, in this case, the power of Fox's majority to control public spending, and thus to harry Pitt—must remain inviolate. Fox, *Speeches*, 2:323.

minister; Bristol, Burke's former stomping ground, sent almost 5,000; and Glasgow, where Burke was soon to be installed as lord rector of the University of Glasgow, more than 4,000.

Fox's parliamentary majorities were large but vulnerable. When Horace Walpole quipped, "They are crying peerages about the streets in barrows," he meant that the government was offering titles and sinecures by the job lot in exchange for loyalty to Pitt.[45] John Robinson, formerly North's, now the king's, "man of business," was likely the political vendor to whom the pronoun *they* referred.

Sinecures, pensions, and places, "attention and civilities," all in the king's gift, allowed Pitt to make inroads on Fox's majority. The promise of a future peerage might yield a present windfall of votes for Pitt, as it did in the case of the second son of the Duke of Northumberland, Algernon Percy. Because Percy controlled a half-dozen parliamentary seats and the members who occupied them (with only one Foxite exception), Pitt gained seven votes in the House of Commons, including Percy's, with a single promised gift. The king had refused such accommodation to Fox and North. In support of Pitt, the royal fount of honor became a geyser.

Fox and Burke found vindication, if not much else, in this brisk political commerce. For Fox, it confirmed his worst prejudices of the king and Pitt. For Burke, it validated his long-held theory of the secret influence of the crown. North denied that any such "double cabinet" was in operation during his twelve years in office, but he charged that now, under Pitt, the king and his friends were doing business in broad daylight.

It was alien to nature and to the English constitution that Pitt, in the minority, should govern, while Fox, with his majority, should watch, the coalitionists said, and they demanded that the king restore the Commons to its natural, constitutional state. George III, who declared he would rather abdicate than suffer the return of Fox to office, only redoubled his commitment to Pitt.

Not even the well-chosen invective of the greatest Whig orators could pierce the cold, unsmiling exterior of the unseasoned premier. Pitt, said Burke, hadn't lost the confidence of the House; having crept into power "by means the most disgraceful and unconstitutional," he had never earned it.[46] Young Billy's true constituency was King George III.

Burke attacked in a January debate over Pitt's alternative India Bill. Unlike the measure that had sent the coalition packing, Pitt's legislation seemed to offend no one but the wounded coalitionists. In place of Fox's all-powerful governing commission and patronage dispenser was an emollient board of control, appointed by the crown, that would keep watch without looking too deeply. On January 23, the Commons voted down Pitt's legislation, 222–214.

The defeat of their India Bill had cost the Foxites their jobs, but Pitt and his royal constituent were unmovable. In debate, the prime minister was as resourceful as he was tenacious. When General Henry Seymour Conway accused his government of corruption, Pitt coolly asked for the details. As the general unsuccessfully searched his memory, the prime minister quoted a Latin tag attributed to the young Roman commander Scipio in response to a condescending rebuke by the veteran Fabius: *Si nulla alia re modestia certe et temperando linguae adolescens senem vicero.*[*] It was obvious that Pitt could not have prepared this exactly apposite quotation for the unpredictable moment. In Burke fashion, he had simply reached into his brain.

THE COMMONS HAD OTHER OCCASIONS TO TAKE THE MEASURE OF THE king's first minister. Early in January 1784 the death of a younger son of the long-serving Sir Robert Walpole had left vacant a lucrative sinecure. The office was Pitt's to fill, and few could have objected if he had nominated himself[†] since he, too, was a younger son with a private income of only

---

* "If nothing else, though a young man, I shall certainly have shown my superiority over this old man, in modesty the government of my tongue." Courtesy of Layla McDermott.

† "I must acknowledge," Lord Chancellor Thurlow later told the House of Lords, "that I was shabby enough to advise Mr. Pitt to take this office, as it had so fairly fallen into his hands; and I believe I should have been shabby enough to have done so myself, since other great and exalted characters have so recently set me the example." Stanhope, *Life of Pitt*, 1:180. It is possible that Burke was among these "great and exalted characters." A year and a half earlier, he had made a play for the clerkship on behalf of his son, Richard, but had come up empty.

£300 a year. The single substantive duty of the holder of the clerkship of the pells was the pleasant obligation to collect £3,000 a year.

Pitt rather presented the gift to Isaac Barré, the army officer and parliamentarian who had lost an eye at the Battle of Quebec in 1759. Deserving though Barré might have been on account of his war record alone, the politics of the situation made him an even stronger candidate for Pitt's favor. During the debate over economic reform in 1782, Lord Rockingham had indiscreetly granted Barré a pension of £3,200 a year. It was a sum ten times larger than Burke's pending reform measure would allow.

Offered the pells in exchange for his pension, Barré readily agreed. As the sinecure was a permanent drain on the public finances, the exchange lightened the taxpayers' burden by precisely £3,200.

"Sir," said Barré of Pitt, "it is the act of a man who feels that he stands upon a high eminence in the eyes of that country which he is destined to govern."[47]

The Whigs gagged at this hypocritical display of public virtue by the man-child who had lied his way to the premiership. It was an invidious display, too, the coalitionists saw, recalling as it did to the public mind Lord Rockingham's momentary lapse of good judgment in issuing the outsize pension in the first place.

But, countered the king's friends, in the matter of hypocrisy the coalitionists stood alone, a claim they documented with the publication of an anthology of the abuse that Burke and Fox had hurled at Lord North once upon a time. It was a rich trove, and the pamphlet, carefully indexed and replete with a frontispiece depicting Burke, Fox, and North applying a blindfold to the British lion, quickly went through five editions.

Never before in George's reign had the City of London found cause to commend the king's public conduct, but the radical stronghold now made an exception. It voted Pitt, too, its thanks and the Freedom of the City, along with a gold box worth 100 guineas. John Wilkes, of all the improbable royalists, gave a speech commending Pitt for his devotion to "the legal prerogative of the Crown and the constitutional rights of the people."[48] As for the man whom the king, around 1768, had declared to be at the bottom of his list of favorite British subjects, he now saw fit to accept £2,000 from George's electoral fund.*

Come the day appointed to honor Pitt, celebrants unhitched the horses to the prime minister's carriage and dragged it through the London streets themselves. The return route to Pitt's residence in Berkeley Square took the procession by Brooks's on St. James's Street. This was enemy territory, as the pro-ministerialist throng knew full well, and the prime minister's carriage came under attack by persons "among whom—so at least it was at the time asserted and believed—were seen several members of the Club."†49 Pitt and his brother, Lord Chatham, escaped with their lives, as Charles Fox and his brother, Ste, had done many years earlier, when they fell afoul of a London mob of a very different political cast.

Pitt and the king had snatched away Fox's office. Now they were absconding with his darling popularity. To be sure, Fox himself was a party to this loss. No sooner had Parliament returned from the Christmas holidays than the unfrocked foreign secretary demanded that the king reappoint ministers from the majority party—that is, his own. So saying, Fox presented the electorate with the choice that Dr. Johnson famously framed as "whether the nation should be ruled by the scepter of George the Third, or the tongue of Fox?"50

Burke had eulogized the Fox whom he knew and loved. The public could be forgiven for recalling the other Fox, Lord Holland's son, the unchurched gambler and horseplayer, the partner (without benefit of clergy) of Mrs. Armistead, the bankrupt, the traitorous champion of George Washington, and the deep-dyed opponent of Lord North who had suddenly, on a sixpence, turned into North's most expedient ally.

---

* "The King had an election fund; Fox had none; the King had an electoral organization; Fox had to improvise one; the King could offer peerages to borough mongers in return for the nomination to their seats; Fox could only make promises and appeal to past obligations; the King had places to offer Members of Parliament: Fox could only offer places in reversion." Brooke, *King George III*, 257.

† Not including Charles Fox, who brandished the alibi that "I was in bed with Mrs. Armistead, who is ready to substantiate the fact on oath."

During the Wilkes-Middlesex election battle, a not-quite-twenty-two-year-old Fox had declared that the people's civic duty consisted of electing representatives who knew what was good for them. Something of the same aristocratic tone was now resurfacing in the evolved "Man of the People." Thus, Fox accused the Pitt ministry,

> there is an intention in ministers to establish themselves on a foundation unfriendly to the constitutional privileges of this House. They court the affections of the people, and on this foundation, they wish to support themselves in opposition to the repeated resolutions of this House. Is this not declaring themselves independent of Parliament?[51]

FOR A YOUNG MAN IN A HURRY, PITT KNEW WELL HOW TO WAIT. HE HAD neither jumped at the first opportunity to lead the king's government nor, having established himself as a minority prime minister, lunged for the first moment to call a general election. Biding his time, watching Fox's majority dwindle to the vanishing point, he and the king fixed on March 25 as the date for the dissolution of Parliament.

The ensuing general election proved one of the most costly, rancorous, hotly contested, and—in its result—lopsided of the eighteenth century. Sealing the political fate of Edmund Burke and Charles Fox, it consigned them to years of opposing the man they loathed.

In the best of times, a proper Georgian gentleman was quick to defend his honor, if need be with pistols at ten paces. In such a venomous political climate as that of March 1784, the opportunities to give and take offense multiplied. So it happened that in the northeastern city of York, Edmund Burke's son, Richard, exchanged shots with a fellow lawyer over words reflecting on the public character of William Fitzwilliam, financial and political heir to Lord Rockingham, Burke's friend, mentor, and financier.

Richard's opponent, a Mr. Topping, got the ball rolling with a partisan comment over dinner. "Lord Fitzwilliam," said he, "made a damnd blackguard attack on Mr. Pitt and it was received like a blackguard speech in the Lords." Richard, taking offense on behalf of the man who had forgiven his father's debts following Rockingham's death in 1782, retorted, "That was a damn'd lie."

Each demanded that the other take back his words. Neither yielding, they and their respective seconds went out together with pistols on March 12. Topping took aim and missed. Richard fired harmlessly into the air.

"They made us shake hands," Richard reported to his father on the bloodless outcome. "[Topping] then told me [he] meant no insult on Lord Fitz whom he did not even know. I said I would trouble him with a piece of *advice*. The seconds cried out 'no no.' . . . I begged however to recollect that the greatest freedom of speech was perfectly compatible with the greatest decency in language."[52]

It was to Lord Fitzwilliam that Burke owed his secure parliamentary seat, the pocket borough of Malton, but Fox was in for a cliffhanger at Westminster. The largest and most prestigious English constituency, it encompassed the court and the Palace of Westminster, the Parliament buildings, and the residences in which dwelled the most voters of any constituency in the realm. (Every male Westminster householder enjoyed the franchise.) Pitt and the king were determined to spare no effort to ensure that Fox would no longer represent it.

At a Buckingham County meeting on March 20, Burke got a foretaste of what the coalition candidates would be up against. The reading of a proposed address to thank the king for the eviction of the Fox-North ministers and to assure His Majesty of the county's support moved Burke to attempt a rebuttal. The crowd, wanting none of it, hissed and booed, cried "no Burke, no Coalition and no India Bill."

Burke's "very name," according to an account in the *Public Advertiser* newspaper, "disgusted his auditory, and occasioned more tumult and vociferation than ever was remembered in that county meeting before." Nor did things improve when Burke was at last able to say his piece.

What he told the crowd was that they, the people, were unqualified to opine on the India Bill. "The people," after all, "had approved of the American war in the same senseless manner they now disapproved of the India Bill: they had not the capacity to comprehend it."

"He was going into a history of Bengal," the newspaper report continued, "but as the meeting expressed some impatience, he desisted. He protested that he should ever esteem it the pride of his life that he had supported that East India Bill; when every other action of his life was forgotten, he desired that it might be remembered and might descend as a monument to posterity."

The meeting concluded with near-unanimous votes in favor of the king and Pitt and with a succession of toasts at dinner at the George Inn in the village of Aylesbury. "The Fox that attempts to burrough the Constitution may be hunted down by the People" was a sample.[53]

THE WESTMINSTER ELECTION OF 1784 PITTED THREE CANDIDATES IN competition for two seats. Admiral Samuel Hood, a reluctant politician whose presence on the ballot was in obedience to a summons from the king, was a shoo-in. (Horatio Nelson would later appraise Hood as "the best Officer, take him altogether, that England has to boast of.")[54] The two Westminster incumbents, Charles Fox and Sir Cecil Wray, battled it out for the remaining seat.

Speechmaking, drinking, buttonholing, fighting, bribing, and vote-buying amply filled the allotted six or so weeks of voting, from April 1 through May 17. A week in, Fox found himself running a distant third. "I must not give up yet though I wish it," he confessed to Elizabeth Armistead. The celebrity electioneering of the Duchess of Devonshire, a fearless, brainy, beautiful Whig, helped to tilt the race Fox's way, as did Wray's impolitic attacks on Chelsea Hospital, the veterans' home established by Sir Stephen Fox, the grandfather of Wray's now vociferously pro-veteran opponent. Admiral Hood, whose active service had tested him in shot and shell and heavy weather, accounted the Westminster polling experience as "the most arduous and unpleasant business I ever took in hand."[55]

When, finally, the business ended, Fox had 6,233 votes, second to the admiral's 6,694 but ahead of Wray's 5,998. Considering the king's substantial resources,* it was indeed a famous victory, though for Fox alone. Many a Foxite—"Fox's martyrs," as they were quickly known—fell to defeat. A contemporary estimate of the alignment of the new Parliament found 306 members for the ministry, 200 for the opposition and 38 undeclared.

Indeed, Fox himself was not immediately seated, notwithstanding his lavishly choreographed victory procession in which was featured "a State Carriage of their Graces The Duchesses of PORTLAND and DEVONSHIRE drawn by six horses, superbly caparisoned, with six running footmen."[56] Not until March 4, 1785, did the House of Commons vote to suspend a scrutiny of the admittedly broadly corrupted Westminster election results and seat Fox, the man of the people in the meantime having been driven to find parliamentary refuge in a tiny Scottish pocket borough.

There would be few enough such triumphs in the years to come. Burke, arraigned during the campaign as Fox's "evil genius," lamented the fall of an independent Parliament.[57]

"I consider the House of Commons as something worse than extinguishd," Burke wrote to William Baker, who lost his own seat, at Hertford, after seven years in the House of Commons. "We have been labouring for near twenty years to make it independent; and as soon as we had accomplishd what we had in View, we found that its independence led to its destruction. The people did not like our work; and they joind the court to pull it down."[58]

---

* His resources were not infinite, however. Requiring a loan to finance the 1784 general election, George III applied to his banker, Henry Drummond, who in turn inquired about the £23,000 that was still unpaid on the king's advance in 1780. George therefore directed Drummond to touch up Lord North for the £17,000 that, in His Majesty's view, the long-serving prime minister had borrowed on his own credit. North, whose private income amounted to only £5,500 a year, and who had never intended to stand guarantor for such a sum, pleaded incapacity to pay. The king, condemning North's "bare-faced fraud," reluctantly settled up. Thomas, *Lord North*, 144.

CHAPTER 14

The rise and fall of
Warren Hastings

The quintessence of Eastern Despotism.

—WILLIAM JONES, LINGUIST AND ORIENTALIST, CHARACTERIZING

HASTINGS'S APPROACH TO THE GOVERNANCE OF BENGAL

Edmund Burke extolled Robert Clive. He was a national benefactor, said Burke in 1769, contrary to the many who envied Clive his fortune and condemned his means of getting it. "If we make war shall we not conquer?" Burke put it to the House of Commons. "If we conquer, shall we not keep? You are plunged into Empire in the east. You have formed a great body of power, you must abide by the consequence. Europe will envy, the East will envy: I hope we shall remain an envied People."[1]

Yet a commercial enterprise that deployed its own army and navy in the service of turning a profit was a strange and unwieldy organization. Clive, writing to William Pitt the Elder as early as 1759, suggested that "so large a sovereignty may possibly be an object too extensive for a mercantile Company."[2]

Abuses were inherent in the very nature of the business, and iniquity was stamped on the flaunting wealth of the returned nabobs, ran the popular indictment. Perhaps the wonder is not so much that the East India Company periodically veered toward insolvency as that it sometimes turned a profit. When half a world separates middle management from senior executives, when war is an integral part of the business model, and when employees are allowed to compete with, rather than serve, the company that pays their salaries, every drop of black ink is a kind of miracle.*

In 1773, General John Burgoyne, chairman of a committee to investigate the misconduct of the East India Company, moved a series of resolutions to reclaim from Clive the dynastic wealth that, so Burgoyne contended, properly belonged to the British state.

Seconding Burgoyne's motion, Sir William Meredith contended that East India Company–style tyranny—in which "mercantile avarice was the only principle, and force the only means of carrying on a government"— was historically unique. If there was an analogue to Clive in India, Meredith went on, it was Verres in Sicily. Gaius Verres was the crooked and murderous provincial governor whom Cicero prosecuted for corruption and extortion around 70 BC. Quoting Cicero, Sir William asked in so many Latin words if this man of boundless wealth, collected through the most unjust of methods, was not to be brought to justice.

Clive answered his accusers by reading from the many accolades and commendations that awaited him upon his return from Bengal. He mentioned, too, the sword—a "rich sword set with diamonds"—that the company had awarded him for his meritorious service. "Now, Sir," Clive told the House, "Great as my fortune is (and which bears no proportion to what I might have made), yet, to shew that I did not harass, or lay under contribution, those I conquered for my own emolument, I can tell this House, that neither I nor any one in my army received a sixpence from the inhabitants of Murshidabad."

Those I conquered. Clive spoke the words without apology. "I subdued Angria, a very powerful prince. I re-took Calcutta, with an inconsiderable army. Surajah Dowlah had at all times betrayed a disposition to break the treaty; and when an army was sent under the command of M. Duprée, which might have proved fatal to us, I do not hesitate to say, that we bribed the general of that army."[3] Really, Clive told the other members, he did

---

* Financially, there were good years and bad years, but in the twenty-one fiscal years to June 30, 1784, the East India Company showed a cumulative loss of £4,100,219. IOR/ AG/21-24, BL.

nothing that they would not have done in his place, a flattering thought for any armchair general.

Defending Clive on the floor of the House, Alexander Wedderburn, Britain's solicitor-general, sounded rather like the unconverted, pro–East India Company Burke. "When our feuds and animosities are forgotten," he began,

> when our little envies and jealousies of large fortunes are, as they ought to be, buried in oblivion—the recording pen of a candid historian will relate these transactions as they were; and he will not fail to hold forth the admiration of posterity, that in a revolution which acquired to the company a dominion larger, wealthier and more populous than ever Athens possessed—or than Rome itself, when she had conquered the Italian states; larger than France, and in revenues superior to most of the powers of Europe; that in the career of such conquests—of such great events—so few actions are to be discovered by the most inquisitive examination (and a more prying one was never known) so few that reflect dishonour on individuals—none that tarnish the British name.[4]

On May 21, 1773, Burgoyne passed his motion that, in amassing Indian rupees in the equivalent of £234,000, "Robert Lord Clive abused the powers with which he was intrusted." But then again, as dawn was breaking in a debate that had begun at three p.m. the previous day, Wedderburn carried *his* motion, "That Robert lord Clive did, at the same time, render great and meritorious services to this country." Thus did the solicitor-general cut the ground from under Burgoyne's feet. And thus did "Clive of India" keep his fortune and escape parliamentary censure.

There was no such escape for Clive's employer, which, in urgent need of cash, borrowed from His Majesty's government, the only creditor that was willing to lend. It will be recalled that the East India Company had run into stiff consumer resistance in America and that rotting tea was heaped in its stately London warehouses.

Lord North's 1773 Regulating Act, which brought the company under partial government control, alluded, in its preamble, to "various Abuses."

To end them, the legislation established a supreme court to administer British law under British judges, and a four-man executive council effectively to govern Bengal. A majority of the four would decide policy; the governor-general would vote to break a tie.

The company had done nothing to deserve these impositions, said Burke at the time. Still less did the governor-general designate, Warren Hastings, deserve to be smeared with the undefined word "abuses."[5]

Hastings was a very different sort of governor than the conquering Clive. "A plain-looking man like any of us, with a brown coat," John Stewart, secretary to the Bengal Governing Council, said of him.[6] On a short acquaintance, Hastings did indeed appear to be that unassuming figure. He was soft-spoken and gentle-mannered, though steel-willed enough to goad a political enemy into a duel, to preserve British India while others lost America, and to stand up to the invective of Edmund Burke and Charles James Fox during a nine-year ordeal of impeachment.

Like Clive, who settled large sums of money on his friends and relatives, Hastings gave generously. Unlike Clive, however, Hastings's means fell short of the scale of his giving. He wrote ardent love letters to Marian, his wife, and professed that his love for India was greater even than that for his native Britain.[7] To not a few of his East India contemporaries, indeed, Hastings seemed unwisely and unprofitably soft on the natives. His reaction to this criticism we may conjecture from something he once said about European manners. There is a "fierceness" in them, Hastings remarked, "especially among the lower sort, which is incompatible with the gentle temper of the Bengelee."[8]

Four years younger than Burke and sixteen years senior to Fox, Hastings was born at Churchill, Oxfordshire, in 1732. His mother died shortly after his birth, and his father, in holy orders of the Church of England, abandoned him and his elder sister to start a new life for himself and the new Mrs. Hastings in Barbados.

Raised by his grandfather and later by an uncle, young Warren grew up listening to stories about his family's noble lineage and wasted wealth. He yearned to reclaim and restore the ruins of Daylesford, the family ancestral estate, and he eventually did so, in the process becoming almost as land-poor as his nemesis Burke.

Hastings entered Westminster School in 1743, excelled in the classics, and became a King's Scholar, one of a line that included John Locke and John Dryden. But his uncle's death in 1749 consigned him to the care of a guardian who saw no point in the academic career to which the precious boy was evidently pointed. A tug on the right strings rather won Warren an appointment as a "writer," or apprentice, to the East India Company. In January 1750, following a mandatory short course in commercial arithmetic, the aspiring merchant took ship for India, reaching Calcutta eight months later. He was seventeen.

Survival was the first order of business for an Englishman set down in the strange Indian biosphere. A contemporary traveler's description of Calcutta mentions the "scattered and confused chaos of houses, huts, sheds, streets, lanes, alleys, windings, gutters, sinks and tanks, which, jumbled into an indistinguishable mass of filth and corruption, equally offensive to human sense and health."[9]

Having survived, the novice set about learning the rudiments of business: keeping books, copying correspondence, appraising the value of silk and cotton goods for export, trading for his personal account, and picking up a musket in emergencies. By paying novices the pittance of £5 a year, in fact, the company virtually drove them to personal enterprise.* One could triple that compensation, as Hastings appears to have done, by learning Hindustani. The "classical boy," as he was known at Westminster, made a study of Persian and Bengali as well and progressed in his commercial specialty of buying and selling silks.

Hastings was in Cossimbazar, a West Bengal trading center, in 1757, when Siraj ud-Daula, a twenty-something grandson of the nawab, or ruler, of Bengal,[10] swooped down on Calcutta with a force of seventy thousand men. European refugees fled to the fever-ridden village of Falta, and there Hastings met his future wife, Mary Elliott, widow of Captain

---

* "Show me the incentive and I'll show you the outcome," the twenty-first-century epigram of Charles Munger, Warren Buffett's late business partner, retrospectively applies.

John Buchanan, who had been trampled to death in the infamous Black Hole of Calcutta.[11]

Later the same year, Hastings appeared in arms as a volunteer in the British expedition to eliminate Siraj ud-Daula and recapture Calcutta. In the wake of Clive's victory at Plassey, the company chose a figurehead, Mir Jafar, to succeed the vanquished Siraj ud-Daula as the new Nawab of Bengal. By the time the British replaced Mir Jafar with his son-in-law, Mir Qasim, in a 1760 coup, Hastings was the company resident at Murshidabad.

Climbing the corporate ladder, Hastings next repaired to Calcutta to fill a seat on the East India Company management council. Mir Qasim, who regarded himself as no puppet but the company's equal in the joint rule of Bengal, fumed at the Englishmen's repeated trespasses on his revenue and political authority. "They forcibly take away the goods and commodities of the peasants, merchants, &c. for a fourth part of their value," the nawab complained in May 1762; "and by way of violence and oppressions, they oblige the peasants &c. to give five rupees for goods that are worth but one rupee."[12] The personal inland trading activities of the company's servants, conducted free of the customary domestic tariffs, especially rankled him.

"If our people," said Hastings, taking Mir Qasim's side of the argument, "instead of erecting themselves into lords and oppressors of the country, confine themselves to an honest and fair trade, they will everywhere be courted and respected."[13] In defiance of the majority view of his fellow councilors, Hastings held that the moderate Mir Qasim wanted only peace.

Hastings's peace initiative, which he jointly conducted with the governor of Bengal, Henry Vansittart, did not survive Mir Qasim's slaughter of forty-five company servants whom the nawab had been holding hostage. The ensuing war ended with the rout of the nawab's army by a greatly outnumbered British force in the 1764 Battle of Buxar. Militarily the winner but politically the loser, Vansittart made preparations to return home. Hastings, equally discredited, followed him in January 1765, sailing solo. Mary, his wife, had died in 1759, and a daughter born the previous year, Elizabeth, had lived only a month. In 1761 a son, George, had been sent to England, where he too died, in 1764.

It was the dream of the typical bold spirit who risked his life in the

service of the East India Company to return home as rich as Clive. However, such capital as Hastings brought with him was chiefly intellectual.
Sir Joshua Reynolds painted him, a slight figure in his mid-thirties with a
high forehead, thinning hair, and bright eyes, resplendently tailored, seated
with his right hand resting on some Persian manuscripts. Dr. Johnson was
among the recipients of Hastings's proposal to institute a professorship of
Persian languages at Oxford, a post that Hastings himself might have filled
on merit, even in the absence of academic credentials beyond his years
at Westminster. "By the time he became governor"—this was in 1772—he
"spoke not only good Bengali and Urdu but also fluent court and literary
Persian. He even sang 'Hindoostanee airs.'" With the orientalist and philologist William Jones, he would found the "Asiatick Society" and contribute an introduction to the Society-sponsored English translation of the
sacred Hindu text *Bhagavad Gita*.

Called to the first parliamentary hearings into Indian affairs, in 1767,
Hastings testified that the English "have it in our power to make Bengal the
most beneficial spot to this country."[14] Before long, as governor-general of
India's richest province, Hastings would briefly hold that power himself. He
returned to India in 1769 to take up an assignment at Madras, the outbound
voyage proving a happy omen of the success that awaited him ashore. Among
the passengers was Anna Maria Appollonia Chapuset, twenty-two, born to
a Huguenot family in Nuremberg, in company with her husband. Hastings
and she fell in love. They married in due course, with the cuckolded husband,
Baron Carl von Imhoff, a soldier and painter of miniatures, peacefully giving
way to a devoted union that would last forty-one years. In Madras, Hastings
took up the management of the company's commercial interests. He lived
modestly, read widely, and drank moderately.*

THE GREAT FAMINE OF 1770–71 CARRIED OFF HALF OF BENGAL'S RURAL
artisans and, in the worst-hit districts, one-third of its peasants. "The

---

* On the testimony of Sophia Goldborne, a new arrival in Calcutta c. 1780, ranking officials
sat down to a formal dinner at two p.m., by the end of which the gentlemen would each have
drunk three bottles (of unknown size) of claret or two of white wine; "moderate" drinking,
then as always, was a relative term. Bernstein, *Dawning of the Raj*, 72.

husbandmen sold their cattle," in the telling of Sir William Hunter, "they sold the implements of agriculture; they devoured their seed grain; they sold their sons and daughters, till at length no buyers of children could be found. They ate the leaves of the trees and the grass of the field; and in June [1770] the Resident at the durbar affirmed that the living were feeding off the dead."[15]

None of the news reaching London about the calamity was overflattering to the foresight or humanity of the company's servants in Bengal. "Considerations on Indian Affairs," a pamphlet by William Bolts, an embittered former employee who was discharged for illegal trading, had nothing good to say about his erstwhile employer but concluded justly enough: "The Company may be compared to a stupendous edifice, suddenly built upon a foundation not previously examined or secured, inhabited by momentary proprietors and governors, divided by different interests opposed to each other; and who, while one set of them is overloading the superstructure, another is undermining the foundations."[16] In December 1771 the Court of Directors recalled the incumbent governor of Bengal, John Cartier. Hastings was the obvious and popular choice for a successor. His first day of work was April 13, 1772.

As much as Hastings loved India, he regarded Bengal as another branch of the British Empire, like Massachusetts. The nawabs were stripped of their old powers—good riddance, he said—leaving the company as Bengal's de facto ruling power. In Hastings's opinion, the alternative to British rule was indigenous anarchy.

And what a prize was Bengal, Hastings wanted the British people to know, with its 20 million post-famine inhabitants, its £2 million annual tax roll, its nearly £1 million per annum of exports to Britain, and its 25,000-man army. Hastings felt the weight, the responsibility, and the opportunity of these magnitudes. "I have catched the desire for applause in public life," he admitted near the start of what would prove a thirteen-year tenure in Bengal.[17]

But there was no applause in London, where the company's operating losses were mounting, its share price was falling, and its tea inventories were growing. (The rebellious Americans had lost their taste for the

British import.) Under North's 1773 Regulating Act, the governor of Bengal became the governor-general, but the grander title, along with munificent compensation of £25,000 a year, obscured his diminished power.[18] The governor-general now shared the executive function not only with the British state but also with a newly instituted council. Four new English judges, who filled the bench of a new supreme court at Calcutta, would likewise have their say in Bengal's public business. Hastings chaired the council, but three of the five councilmen (counting himself), acting en bloc, could render him a nullity.

Hastings knew only one of his fellow councilmen, the politically dependable, personally dubious Richard Barwell, a Calcutta-born son of an East India Company servant. The remaining three councilors were making their slow, seaborne way to Calcutta; their number did not include Edmund Burke, who had declined an offer to pull up stakes for Calcutta, at a salary of £10,000 a year.[19]

According to advice from Sir Francis Sykes, a friend from their earliest days in India, the trio comprised a pair of fiftyish military men, Lieutenant-General John Clavering, a favorite of the king who would assume the title of commander in chief of the company's forces, and Colonel George Monson, a grenadier who had distinguished himself at the siege of Pondicherry in 1760. The third commissioner was a little-known thirty-two-year-old unemployed former civilian bureaucrat, Philip Francis. "Francis," Sykes advised, "you will find warm and lively, but I think no extraordinary depth of understanding."[20]

Francis indeed proved lively, though anything but warm. His understanding, deeper than Sykes knew, was quick and highly focused. He arrived in Calcutta with the settled belief that the company must not attempt to govern Bengal. No profit-seeking business could, or should, function as a sovereign power. To be sure, Bengal was a conquered British territory, and it should pay the crown an annual tribute on that account, but that was as far as Britain's claim on the Bengali people could extend. A scheme that tried to "draw every principal branch of administration immediately into the hands of Europeans," Francis held, "was defective in its principle and contrary to the nature of things."[21]

Such were Francis's political principles, and he held them sincerely. It was another, narrower conviction, however, that guided his conduct in India and, later, in the impeachment proceedings that played out in Britain's House of Lords. Francis believed that Warren Hastings was guilty of terrible crimes and that he, Francis, by rights, must be governor-general of Bengal in his place.

BORN IN DUBLIN, FRANCIS WAS THE SON OF THE REVEREND PHILIP, WHO had hitched his career to the parents of Charles James Fox: to his father, Lord Holland, and his mother, Lady Caroline Fox, for whom the elder Francis served as private chaplain. Brought to London, young Philip shone at St. Paul's School, which was where his formal education, like Hastings's at Westminster, began and ended.

"He always loved a cosy home," Keith Feiling, Hastings's biographer, observes of Francis. "Women liked him, he had distinction of speech, an agreeable irony and soft hands."[22] Francis read widely and seriously in constitutional law, political economy, and the classics. He wrote incessantly— memoranda, letters, newspaper squibs. Malice was his stylistic watermark.

Almost beyond a doubt, Francis was "Junius," anonymous author of *The Letters of Junius*,* which, over four years, 1769–72, titillated, shocked, and delighted the readers of Henry Woodfall's *Public Advertiser*. Warren Hastings himself was a fan. So coruscating, merciless, malignant, informed, and fluid were these productions that Dr. Johnson (among many others) assumed that Burke alone could have written them, although misanthropy was never Burke's style. Junius attacked the king, the Grafton ministry, and sundry government ministers, including Lord Hillsborough, whom the anonymous Francis accused of goading Massachusetts into rebellion. Just how Francis secured his position on the Bengal council was a mystery fully as deep as the identity of Junius. There is a theory that he laid down his venomous pen in exchange for the India counselor's salary of £10,000 a year. "Junius shall write no more," the king is supposed to have remarked.[23]

---

* Who else but Junius himself would have chosen, as his first gift to the second Mrs. Sir Philip Francis, in 1811, a copy of *The Letters of Junius*?

Lord North briefed the new councilmen before their departure for India. They would, he said, be "armed with extraordinary power to correct enormous abuses."[24] The company itself acknowledged such wrongdoing in an April 1773 demand it made on the president and council at Fort William, the military headquarters of Bengal.

"We wish," the directors led off,

> we could refute the observation, that almost every attempt made by us and our administrations at your Presidency, for the reforming of abuses, has rather increased them, and added to the miseries of the country we are anxious to protect and cherish.

Recently appointed supervisors and chiefs, commissioned to assist "industrious tenants," promote exports, stamp out monopolies, and reduce costs had achieved nothing of the kind, the directors went on.

> Are not the tenants, more than ever, oppressed and wretched? Are our investments [i.e., exports] improved? Have not the raw silk and cocoons been raised upon us fifty per cent in price? We can hardly say what has not been made a monopoly; and as to the expenses of your Presidency, they are at length settled to a degree we are no longer able to support. These facts (for such they are) should have been stated to us as capital reasons why neither our orders of 1771, nor indeed any regulations whatever, could be carried into execution.

London suggested that the Fort William managers had deliberately withheld the damning facts from the directors and stockholders, "for nothing could more plainly indicate a State of Anarchy, and that there was no Government existing, in our servants in Bengal. . . . When oppression pervades the whole country; when youths [i.e., the company's own junior staff] have been suffered with impunity to exercise sovereign jurisdiction over the natives, and to acquire rapid fortunes by monopolizing of commerce, it cannot be a wonder to us, or yourselves, that native merchants do not come forward to contract with the Company; that the manufactures find their way through foreign channels; or that our investments are at once enormously dear, and of a debased quality."[25]

It was to right these wrongs that the directors had looked to a man whose "temperance, economy and application" would set a wholesome example and whose prior achievements in the company's service promised greater success for the future. Warren Hastings was this paragon of character and competence.

Hastings was indeed an accomplished servant. Uniquely among high British officials, he could conduct business in Urdu or Hindi without the aid of a translator. Very much like Burke, he venerated Indian religions and culture. The later arrival in India of William Jones, to fill a place on the supreme court bench, filled Hastings with joy. What conversations, what discoveries, awaited them together.

As governor-general, Hastings was quick to wage war. He was not above accepting lavish gifts from Indian officials with whom he conducted official, putatively arm's-length business. Far from the most venal of the company's ranking servants, he nonetheless occasionally stooped to awarding contracts to his friends. He conducted a lively personal trade in opium, diamonds, and—to sell as turban ornaments—rubies and emeralds.

"If his own brown coat was plain," as his biographer relates, "his horses had silver-plated bits with his crest engraved; he was building a new house in Alipur, begging [Thomas] Motte to send him some Benares marble for its staircase. Captain Price was getting him porcelain and tea from China." No "general reformer" was he, Hastings readily acknowledged to Barwell, whose own reforming interests were even fainter than Hastings's.[26] Less successfully, Hastings scraped and schemed to raise sufficient Bengali revenue to satisfy the stockholders and directors.

To Burke, a lawbreaker earned no leniency because he had sinned in Calcutta or Benares instead of London or Bristol. In particular, natural law—God's law—ran worldwide. Hastings took a more relativistic view. "'Too much stress laid upon general maxims at home' might do terrible damage on Indian frontiers, where sometimes they may do things 'not to be justified on such principles as the public can be judges of'"—so contended Hastings in his own words commingled with those of his biographer. Hastings's "heart was hot against English oppression. . . . To subject Indians to our legal code, he told Lord Mansfield, would be 'wanton tyranny'; we must, rather, found the authority of British Government in Bengal on its ancient laws."[27]

As for the India that Hastings attempted to govern, "Society was set," again to quote Feiling,

> in a complex frame of land revenue, embarrassed by sub-tenures and masked titles, ruled by an aristocracy of Moslem landowners and Hindu bureaucrats and Armenian money-lenders, each living by the profits of office and retailing government patronage. And over all this a few score young Britons, wholly dependent on Indians for the intricacies of the revenue and tolerable administration of justice, not to speak of channels of the private trading whereby nine out of ten of them must live.[28]

THE THREE NEW COUNCILMEN WERE AN ODDLY ASSORTED, UNHARMONIous group. Francis, who appears to have conceived an intense dislike for Hastings in England, had malice to spare for Monson and Clavering besides. Nor, with respect to Calcutta, was it love at first sight: "Since I landed in this Hell I have not known one Moment's Peace of Mind," Francis wrote six weeks after arriving.[29]

Returning to India, Monson found it humiliating to have to deal with field officers whom he had once commanded but who had subsequently been promoted over him. Clavering, who enjoyed the king's special favor and who, under the 1773 regulating act, assumed overall command of the company's armed forces. On the council, he was second in seniority to Hastings but about to be overshadowed by Francis.

The three new arrivals complained that the seventeen-gun salute that greeted them, on October 19, 1774, was four guns shy of their due. They were affronted when Hastings, who had neglected to greet them at dockside, received them for lunch dressed in the eighteenth-century equivalent of business casual. They would learn that pomp—"parade" of any kind, including ruffled shirts—put the governor-general on edge.

On October 24 the newcomers handed Hastings a twenty-eight-point questionnaire. No collegial warmth issued from the peremptory demands for "a general summary State of the Government, under the following heads: i. The Political land Military Department. ii. The success of the [tax] Collections. . . . iii. The actual State of the Treasury. iv. The Administration of Justice."

Hasting was similarly to furnish a "list of the Company's Civil Servants, as well natives as Europeans, with their several Employments, Salaries and Emoluments." Francis et al. laid it down that "all letters on public Business (except those which the Governor General shall receive from the Country Powers) shall for the future be addressed to the Governor General and Council and opened in Council."

Of particular interest to the three new councilmen was the war in the nearby province of Oudh. Why were the company's troops engaged? Should they not be ordered home? Francis et al. wanted all relevant correspondence, including letters between Hastings and the British field commander, Colonel Alexander Champion.

"Rely on what I tell you," Francis wrote home to Clive on November 30. "The foundation is shaken and even Hastings confesses it." And now in cipher: "Mr. Hastings wholly and solely has sold and ruined Bengal. He is the most corrupt of villains. Mr. Barwell is an ignorant, false, presumptuous blockhead."[30]

Voting as a unit, Francis, Clavering, and Monson opposed Hastings and his every work. And when not opposing, they spent their professional hours gathering evidence of Hastings's alleged crimes and reporting those derelictions to London.

There was much to oppose: The newly minted governor-general had built, unified, or reformed, as the respective cases may be, a currency system, postal delivery, public granaries, taxes, and customs. He had set in train the codification of Hindu laws and digests of Muslim legal texts and supported James Rennell's great cartographic survey of India.

A jury of English peers would render its verdict on the impeachment charges that the House of Commons, led by Burke and supported by Fox and others, would bring against Hastings. It is a nice question who had the harder time of it, the prosecution, the defense—or the jurors, to whom Indian place names and proper names, Indian culture, and Indian geography were so much Greek. Hastings's conduct in the so-called Rohilla War, 1773–74, provides a case study in the jurors' difficulty of apportioning guilt or innocence.

THE ROHILLA WAR WAS A WAR OF CHOICE, AND HASTINGS WAS THE ONE, on the company side, who elected it, for financial and strategic reasons alike. The conflict pitted a British brigade under the aforementioned Colonel Champion against the Rohillas, members of an Afghan clan from Rohilkhand, a territory in northeastern India bordering on Nepal.

Hastings had forged an alliance with Shuja-ud-Daula, the Nawab of Oudh. A neighboring state to Bengal, Oudh was essential to Bengal's security, Hastings and the nawab could agree. Besides, this was a financial starving time for the East India Company, and the servants must procure revenue.

Conducting his own personal diplomacy, Hastings set out to treat with the nawab in June 1773. "Foul winds, violent currents and separation of our fleet" notwithstanding, he reached Benares, capital of Oudh, and sat down, alone, with the nawab to negotiate.[31] No translator was needed.

The parties dickered for two weeks. The nawab pressed to acquire the city of Allahabad, which Hastings was happy to relinquish for a fifty-lakh consideration, or the equivalent of £500,000. Both men needed money, Hastings to satisfy the stockholders of the East India Company, the nawab to support his forty-nine children and eight-hundred-strong harem, as well as to meet the usual public expenses. Hastings secured the nawab's pledge to double his contribution to the upkeep of English forces stationed in Oudh.

There was an additional article of agreement. Shuja-ud-Daula, who yearned to annex Rohilkhand, could depend on British support in the event of war between Oudh and the Rohillas. The company, it's true, had no quarrel with the Rohillas, but it welcomed the strategic protection that a defeat of those formidable Afghans might afford it. Hastings's diary records that, in response to the vizier's musing about the possibility of inciting the Rohillas to attack the still-more-menacing Marathas, in a bid to weaken both belligerents, Hastings "commended the project."[32] Here was the purest realpolitik, if not an example of the strain of "Eastern Despotism" that Jones deplored and that Burke and Fox would later hurl back in Hastings's teeth.

The forces of Shuja-ud-Daula indeed invaded Rohilkhand, in February 1774, though by some accounts they followed, rather than led, the expeditionary force of the East India Company into battle, holding their strength in reserve for the subsequent gathering up of plunder. In any case, the company's artillery tore wide swaths through the Rohilla ranks on April 23, 1774, at the Battle of Miranpur Katra. "We have the honour of the day," Colonel Champion, commander of the company's forces, complained, "and these banditti the profit."[33] As far as Francis, Clavering, and Monson were concerned, there was no honor to be acquired, and Hastings was among the foremost of the banditti. Colonel Thomas Pearse, who could generally be found on Hastings's side, deprecated the war as "un-British."

Hastings was under instructions from the Home Office to seek peace as well as revenue. "We [the Court of Directors]," the directive read, "also utterly disapprove and condemn offensive wars, distinguishing, however, between offensive measures unnecessarily undertaken with a view to pecuniary advantages and those which the possession of our honour, or the protection of safety of our possessions, may render absolutely necessary."[34]

Hastings, who himself abjured offensive war, regarded the financial and strategic considerations of the treaty as inseparable. Oudh bordered on Bengal, while the Rohillas, some fifty to sixty thousand strong, bordered on Oudh. To the east of all three territories lay Maratha, a powerful confederacy that, from Hastings's vantage point, presented the company with its principal strategic risk. The stability of Oudh would surely be tested if the Marathas and the Rohillas joined forces to make the mischief of which they were more than capable.

Even later arrivals in India than the British, the Rohillas were fierce enough to establish themselves as the overlords of one to two million Hindus. Fox and Burke would later characterize the conquerors of Rohilkhand as an ancient and long-settled people; Hastings corrected the record with the image of a ferocious army that "quartered themselves upon the people."[35]

In Burke's subsequent telling, Hastings was guilty of the "extermination" of the Rohillas, "where that humane governor spared neither man, woman, nor child; where the heads of the unfortunate men were torn from their bodies, while the famished women were crawling through the British camp, to implore the comfort of a little rice."[36] Nothing of the kind seems to have happened.[*] The Rohilla War was a grubby little frontier affair, entered into for reasons that many criticized at the time and that most, perhaps, would condemn today.[†] Francis was soon reporting back to London that Bengal was the "seat of a corruption unparalleled in the history of mankind."[37]

Voting as one, the three new arrivals effectively took command of Bengal, reducing Hastings and Barwell to a permanent minority of two. Rich in the flamboyant nabob fashion, Barwell entertained lavishly, gambled for high stakes, and scoffed at the fancy ideas of the newly landed commissioners. In 1775 he fought a duel with General Clavering, the father of the girl he had hoped to marry, over the general's accusation that he had embezzled company funds. There was no bloodshed and no wedding.[‡] The

---

[*] Claims of atrocities primarily originated from Colonel Champion, who proved an unreliable and biased witness. The report of company servant Nathaniel Middleton found that "there had been much distress and inconvenience" but no "extermination," the reports of which were "due in some part to our army's soreness in being deprived of any share in the spoil." Feiling, *Hastings*, 119.

[†] "I own," Hastings recalled, "that such was my idea of the Company's distress, at home, added to my knowledge of their wants abroad, that I should have been glad of any occasion to employ their [i.e., the company's] forces, which saves so much of their pay and expenses." Hastings, *Memoirs*, 1:359.

[‡] "What distance do you choose, Sir?" Barwell demanded of his prospective father-in-law when the two met one morning to settle matters with pistols. "The nearer the better," the soldier retorted. Francis, for one, was astounded that the general, hero of the 1759 British assault on the island of Guadeloupe, missed his mark. Feiling, *Hastings*, 143.

Court of Directors, too, later came to suspect Barwell of dipping his hand in the company till.

But it was a British court, with British judges and a British jury, that featured in a second collision between Hastings and his three tormenters. The conflict played out in two superficially unrelated court proceedings, both involving a crooked elderly Brahmin tax collector named Nandakumar.

Early in March, Nandakumar accused Hastings of taking a 350,000-rupee bribe. This was, of course, music to the ears of the anti-Hastings troika, who convened a meeting of the council to hear evidence against the governor-general. Nandakumar's evidence was a letter, evidently forged, whose supposed signatory would deny having written it. Naturally, Hastings was outraged, the more so because Clavering moved that Hastings's personal servant, or banyan, named Cantoo, be placed in stocks for allegedly facilitating his master's crime.

Hastings refused to acknowledge the legitimacy of the sham judicial proceeding—"shall I sit at this Board to be arraigned in the presence of a wretch whom you all know to be one of the basest of mankind?" Neither would he accept the inevitable verdict when it came, nor the order to repay the bribes that he denied having taken. He warned that if Cantoo wound up in stocks, the two of them, Clavering and Hastings, would meet with pistols. (The colonel retreated.) "The meanest drudge enjoys a condition of happiness compared to mine," Hastings cried out by post to Lord North.[38]

In May, Nandakumar himself was arrested and charged with forgery. It was alleged that the defendant had signed his name to a false claim against the estate of a deceased Indian banker. A civil proceeding against Nandakumar had stalled in the Mayor's Court at Calcutta. Now presented as a criminal matter, the case would come before the newly instituted Supreme Court, whose chief justice, Elijah Impey, happened to be an old Westminster School friend of Hastings's.

Nandakumar's trial began in June. The courtroom was an oven, but the only concession that the wig- and gown-clad justices made to the weather was a thrice-daily change of their dripping linen. Solemnity was indeed appropriate to the occasion, as forgery was a capital offense under English law. The trial ended a week after it started with a verdict of guilty and a sentence of death.

Though few could defend Nandakumar's character, many wept at his hanging. Hastings fell under suspicion.* Who else had both the means and motive to procure the defendant's death? "If it be observed that [Nandakumar] is the principal evidence against the Governor-General," the troika insinuated in a London-bound message, "the measures taken to compass his destruction may be easily accounted for."³⁹

No matter where one stood concerning the internecine struggles of the East India Company, there was something shocking in the hanging of a Brahmin in a British court, before an all-British jury, on a capital offense that, in India, was in no way punishable by death. Robert Chambers, one of four British judges to hear Nandakumar's case, urged that the felony charge be dismissed. The economic conditions that supported such severity in England were hardly present in India, Chambers reasoned. His argument went nowhere.

The East India directors subsequently criticized its servants for failing to show Nandakumar mercy. As to Hastings, even if he had had the authority to intervene, it's not clear that he would have chosen to do so. "Nandakumar has met with a miserable fate, which he has deserved ever since I knew him," the governor-general confided on August 7, two days after the hanging. But Hastings had no such authority, as the troika had rendered him powerless.⁴⁰

Neither Francis nor Clavering nor Monson responded to the prisoner's repeated petitions for mercy. Clavering produced an unopened envelope from the prisoner at a council meeting on August 14. Inside was Nandakumar's final petition dated August 4, the day before the execution.

* Properly so, according to archival research by Lucy S. Sutherland. Certain references in the papers of George Vansittart, the historian concludes, point to the "almost inescapable conclusion . . . that Hastings was covertly involved in the prosecution, and that his denials employ 'an economy of truth.'" Sutherland, "New Evidence," 438–65; Derrett, "Nandakumar's Forgery," 223–38.

Only "idiots and biographers" could doubt that Hastings himself was the cause of Nandakumar's death, Thomas Babington Macaulay would later pronounce.[41] Burke anticipated the great historian by accusing Hastings in the House of Commons of judicial murder "at the hands of Elijah Impey."*

HASTINGS SHOWED FEW OUTWARD SIGNS OF THE SUFFERING HE BORE under the aggressive, and passive-aggressive, assault of Francis, Monson, and Clavering. George Bogle, the diplomat and adventurer who, as a young company writer, had served as Hastings's personal assistant, marveled to his father in March 1776:

> Mr. Hastings bears this attack with calmness and equanimity, which raises his character in the eyes of everybody; and although to pay court to him is the sure way to give umbrage to his opponents, who are possessed of all power, yet the respect that is felt for his character preserves his levees, now when he is stripped of power, as crowded as ever.[42]

"He is more tough than any of us, and will never die a natural death," said Francis of Hastings.[43] It was one of the nicest things that Francis is known to have said about anyone, though it proved only half-true. (Hastings would slip away naturally at the age of eighty-six.) Accused, insulted, and ignored, the governor-general stubbornly remained in office. In August 1776 news reached Calcutta that the directors had voted to recall him by a vote of 11–10, but that the stockholders had overridden them by a majority of 107. Hastings exulted as Francis despaired.

By this time, both Monson and Clavering had fallen ill. Monson resigned in August and died in September. Hastings, holding the governor-general's

---

* Of note is that Judge Chambers, friendly with Francis and sympathetic to Nandakumar, privately opined of the accused that "he certainly was guilty of uttering the writing in question, knowing it to be forged." Feiling, *Hastings*, 151.

tie-breaking vote, now returned to the authority he had wielded before the newcomers' arrival in 1774. Clavering's death in 1777 further isolated Francis, in no way improving his disposition and setting up a decisive personal confrontation with Hastings.

Hastings's newfound authority was hostage to the votes in the executive council of the eventual successors to Monson and Clavering. Edward Wheler, the first of the new arrivals, in December 1777, instantly gravitated to Francis. The second, Lieutenant-General Sir Eyre Coote, the new commander in chief, who landed in March 1779, gravitated to himself; impartially vain, hostile, and venal, he made himself insufferable to Francis and Hastings alike. At this precarious juncture, Barwell's young wife died; he begged to be allowed to go home to England. In the absence of Hastings's ally, the balance of power in council would once more tilt to Francis.

It was not the best time for intramural company upheaval. France, having recognized American independence in February 1778, was once more at war with Britain, and a French fleet was soon expected in India. On the ground, company forces tangled with the Marathas to the west and with the fierce Hyder Ali, Nawab of Mysore, to the south. Hastings, doing his best to move the geopolitical chess pieces, faced constant resistance from the Francis faction, which favored a defensive posture in Bengal, with the absolute minimum number of expeditionary distractions outside it. Hastings, his eye fixed on the security of the British Empire in toto, demanded a forward strategy against the French and the insubordinate Indian princes.

Was there no room for compromise? Hastings opened negotiations with Francis in January 1780. An agreement of sorts was reached—not, Francis insisted, an alliance or union but "more like an armed truce." Hastings could fight his wars, while Francis could hire, and promote, his corporate protégés.

But when Francis reverted to his outspoken opposition to military action outside Bengal, Hastings resolved to be done with him or to die trying. "I judge of his public conduct by my experience of his private," wrote the governor-general in an official message to the council, "which I have found to be void of truth and honour." Fighting words, they goaded Francis, who had never fought a duel, perhaps had never fired a pistol, into a sunrise meeting on August 17, 1780.

At a distance of fourteen paces, Francis missed his mark; Hastings, firing almost simultaneously, did not, and Francis toppled to the ground. "Good God! I hope not," said Hastings in response to Francis's self-refuting cry that he was a dead man.

Before long, Francis was sitting up with pen and paper. "I consider this event as a quietus to all personal hostility between Mr. H. and me," he wrote to his friends in England,

> and I desire that you and all my friends will speak and act accordingly. This injunction goes to everything. It would be irregular and unbecoming in me now, as well as useless in every respect, to suffer the public quarrel to lead me into anything that could bear the appearance of personal animosity to him. Let him be condemned or acquitted by the evidence that exists of his whole conduct. As I lay bleeding on the ground and when I thought the wound was mortal, I gave him my hand in token of forgiveness. From that moment to the end of my life, I am neither his friend nor his foe.[44]

Only a month passed before Francis was back to criticizing Hastings's military strategy, though by now it was a strategy that met with the approval of Wheler and Coote. There was nothing for it, the former Junius realized, but to resign (warning the directors while he was at it that Hastings was wrecking the peace that Clavering and he had so carefully wrought) and to resume his attack on Hastings with his pen.

THE FIRST THING TO SAY ABOUT THE REVERSAL OF EDMUND BURKE'S thinking about the East India Company, from devoted booster to arch critic, is that neither the hapless Will Burke, nor the perennially unbalanced finances of the extended Burke family, can explain it. Some suspected otherwise.[45] William went to India in 1776 to repair his net worth. He returned in 1778 as British agent of the Raja of Tanjore, a major city in Madras at the southeastern tip of the Indian subcontinent, whose civilian governor had been ousted in a company-sponsored military coup. The "King of Tanjore," as Will styled the raja in memorials to Lord North, sought the protection of the British Crown. It was a cause that Edmund eagerly took up. It appears that Will dreamed of becoming the royal governor of Tanjore in case the raja woke up one morning deciding to cede his territory to George III. Nothing of the kind happened, though Edmund, when briefly returned to the Paymaster's Office in 1782 with the second Rockingham government, appointed Will a deputy paymaster for British forces in India. It was a newly created post that Lord Cornwallis, a Hastings successor as governor-general, characterized as "most unnecessary."

Such allegiances and interests, important as they seemed to Edmund and Will, did not change the course of Anglo-Indian events. Edmund Burke rather changed his mind about India, because the facts, as he understood them, had changed. "Burke almost certainly knew more about India than did any other man in public life who had not actually been there," the editors of Burke's papers observe.[46] The qualification is important. Not having lived in India, Burke depended on Philip Francis.

Burke had appealed to Francis in 1777 to take cousin Will under his protection. By the time Francis returned to England, in 1781, Burke had become deeply immersed in India, especially Tanjore, and the affairs of the East India Company. A leading member of the Commons' Select Committee on India, he was the principal author of the committee's first, ninth, and eleventh reports, which appeared between 1782 and 1783. Each document bore the characteristic mark of Burke's tireless, self-directed study, but the author did not stint in acknowledging Francis's help to the House of Commons during his speech urging passage of Fox's India Bill.

No doubt Francis was a key informant, but Burke's own study had already activated the powerful engine of his sympathy. The Indian people, borne down by the East India Company, called out for help. If he alone heard their cries, he alone would have to answer them. Perhaps India would one day pay a political dividend—for a time in 1783, as Fox's bill cleared the House of Commons, it appeared that the day was at hand. But when the bill failed in the Lords, and the Fox-North coalition failed almost in unison, Burke only redoubled his efforts to bring the agents of Indian misgovernance to justice.

Not the least of the obstacles in Burke's path was the sheer strangeness of India to his English-speaking political contemporaries. The country gentlemen of the House of Commons could hardly tell a nawab from a nizam or a Hindu from a Muslim. Indeed, Burke acknowledged in the *Ninth Report of the Select Committee,** the subject left most of the members "fatigued" unto "Despair."

Burke, never flagging, condemned the company for its impossible mission, the very concept of a "mercantile sovereign" being a non sequitur. To put commercial matters right, there must be an end to administered prices and company-controlled monopolies. But Burke did not intend to impeach the company's business model. In April 1783 he announced his intention of bringing to book "the greatest delinquent that India ever saw."[47]

Francis and he were now united in the anti-company, anti-Hastings cause. Dine with him at his home on Harley Street, Francis urged Burke in April 1784, for the opportunity to meet people "who are unfashionable enough to think this a proper time to shew their Attachment to the Cause, and their esteem of the Men who support it. Every Man who loves me, loves you. They are not great Men, but they are better."[48]

With Burke regarding Hastings, or later in respect to revolutionary France, one was either with him or against him. It enraged William Jones, as a sitting judge on the bench of the British Supreme Court in Calcutta, to hear through the grapevine that Burke had dared to threaten him: "If I *hear, that Jones sides with Hastings*, I will do all in my power to have him recalled."[49] Whether or not Burke said it, he might have thought it, and Jones saw fit to remind the statesman of a judge's duty to remain aloof from political controversy.[50]

---

* The committee's full name continues: "Appointed to take into Consideration the State of the Administration of Justice in the Provinces of Bengal, Bahar and Orissa."

ON JULY 30, 1784, BURKE MOVED FOR PAPERS—THAT IS, EVIDENCE—
concerning the conduct of Warren Hastings in the matter of Almas Ali
Khan. Almas was a wealthy Indian revenue officer whom Hastings had
marked for death for a suspected criminal offense. Hastings instructed John
Bristow, the company's resident in Lucknow, in the province of Oudh, to
determine what if any law Almas had broken. If a crime had been committed and if the suspect were tried and found guilty, he must be put to death,
"as a necessary to deter others from the commission of the like crimes."
Take care, Hastings admonished Bristow, to avoid fraudulent or treacherous methods of police work lest Hastings become vulnerable to charges "by
those who may hereafter be employed in searching our records for cavils
and informations against me." And now, Burke asserted, Almas was dead.[51]

"Eastern Despotism" indeed! Nor was this scandalous episode anything other than standard corporate operating procedure. "The same
wild and outrageous policy prevailed, and threatened an utter extermination of all our settlements in that part of the world," said Burke. "Every
district in India almost daily exhibited marks or specimens of the same
inhumanity and disclosed scenes of misery and degradation, by means
of our mismanagement, of which few Europeans have any conception."[52]

Just how Burke had come to know about these events on the other side
of the world was a bit of a mystery. Almas, in fact, was alive and kicking,
but Hastings's threat to that rich functionary was real enough; and the
governor-general did write the memorandum from which Burke quoted.

Hastings was guilty of many other enormities, Burke went on—"ravaging
countries, depopulating kingdoms, reducing the gardens of the universe to
a desert, plundering opulent towns,"[53] and despicably relieving a pair of old
ladies from Oudh of their jewels in the sum of £550,000.[54]

If the loss of Fox's India Bill meant the indefinite postponement of
relief for the suffering Indian masses, said Burke, God would not forget it.
"A cry for vengeance had gone forth and reached his ears, who never could
be inattentive to the distresses of his creatures," he warned the House;
"and we could expect as little mercy from him as we had shewn to them."

The fast one that the kings' friends had pulled in the House of Lords to defeat Fox's bill and topple the coalition dealt the English constitution a shock from which it would "never" recover. "The empire was mutilated, and its very credit tottered to the foundation. These were symptoms of a dissolution at hand. The decree was fixed."

Pointing to the Treasury bench, Burke proceeded, "What are these men? Are they not the Ministers of vengeance to a guilty, a degenerated and unthinking nation? Yes.—They are literally the executioners of that aweful and irreversible verdict which is registered in Heaven against us."

It could not have been surprising that Burke, believing such things, tossed and turned at night. What was a little out of the ordinary was the candor with which he described the agonies he felt on behalf of a people he had never seen. "The cries of the native Indians were never out of his ears," Burke told the House; "their distresses rouses his whole soul, and had kept him busy when those who now sneered at his earnestness and sensibility were much more agreeably engaged." He had read the relevant damning parliamentary documents on those victims at a cost to his sleep. The facts they contained had resolved him to put a stop to the "tyranny," "robberies," and "assassinations" of the East India Company. He was "fully committed; his character was before the Public: he risqed all the little popularity which his labours had procured him from a grateful Public—It was in hopes of breaking the spirit, or checking the operations of that inhumane system, that he had so frequently and so patiently submitted to the scorn and derision of the House and of the world."

Burke, though famously shortsighted, could make out the laughing, mocking faces of Macnamara, Rolle, Grenville, and many others. So be it. "Millions of individuals had been made the victims of our indiscretion," he said; "and, what reason had he to complain being made the butt of juvenile statesmen?"*[55]

---

* The younger generation of parliamentarians, in general, had little patience with Burke's speechmaking. In debate on June 16, according to the parliamentary report, "some of the young members vociferat[ed] so loudly as to prevent Mr. Burke from being distinctly heard," to which the statesman replied: "He saw he was among a parcel of rocks, the sides of which resounded with the intemperate lashing of a roaring surge, and therefore, though he was past, and had got the better of those feelings, which they were so stupidly clamorous hoped to oppress him with, he thought it more prudent at the moment to bow to the storm."

WARREN HASTINGS RESOLVED TO GO HOME. MARIAN, UNWELL, HAD
returned to England in 1784. He desperately missed her and would have
felt bereft even if his workaday life had not become a drudgery. "I am now
without power," he complained to his British agent, Major Scott—"and am
alone responsible."[56]

Others, including General Burgoyne, the defamer of Lord Clive, had
lost America. Hastings had kept India and would leave it in a rare condition of peace. At Benares, the governor-general took time to begin writing
the preface he had promised to Charles Wilkins's translation of *Bhagavad
Gita*, or Song of God, the sacred Hindu scriptural text. The book would
live, wrote Hastings, "when the British dominion in India had long ceased
to exist, and when the sources it once yielded of wealth and power are lost
to remembrance."[57]

He appealed to the directors with a late addendum to his expense
account. In support of Indian painting, literature, and music, he wrote, he
had spent freely of his own funds. Would the company see its way clear to
reimburse him, if not out of generosity, then out of justice? "Improvident
for myself," Hastings jotted to the higher-ups, "zealous for the honour of
my country—I seldom permitted my prospects of futurity to enter into the
views of my private concerns."

Saying his goodbyes, Hastings had heard himself hailed as "Pillar of
Empire, Fortunate in War." There were presents of horses and armor,
crowds to cheer him at Murshidabad, and even a friendly welcome from
Munni Begum, whose jewels he had once ordered seized.[58]

Reports from England suggested that a rather cooler welcome awaited
him there. While Fox's India Bill, with its imputations against both the
company and himself, had properly been defeated, Pitt's successor India
Bill, with its similarly insulting aspersions, had become law in August 1784.
The problem ran deeper than mere insinuation, Hastings confided to Marian. The new law stripped the stockholders of their veto power over the
directors and installed a Board of Control to second-guess the company's
decisions in India. Altogether, Hastings charged, an act more damaging

"to the national honour could not have been devised, though fifty Burkes, Foxes and Francises had clubbed to invent one."[59]

Hastings stepped aboard the *Indiaman Barrington*, bound for Plymouth on February 7, 1785. A week later Burke rose in the House of Commons to propose an inquiry into "the conduct of certain persons, lately returned from India."

"If no other persons undertook the business," added Burke, "he himself would at some future period."[60]

CHAPTER 15

A "prejudged case" before a "bribed tribunal"

I impeach him in the name of human nature itself.

—BURKE IN HIS OPENING SPEECH AT THE TRIAL OF WARREN HASTINGS

Calcutta was slowly slipping from view of the homebound *Indianman* when Warren Hastings started at the memory of an old bureau that he had neglected to empty before leaving. Where it was he had no inkling, but he well knew what it contained. It plagued him to imagine "all my most secret papers" falling into "strange, and possibly scoundrel hands."[1]

The governor-general's mind wandered to the reception he was likely to meet in England. Burke, Fox, and of course Francis had their knives out for him, he was well aware. Pitt too had made shocking accusations against him, albeit at a lower rhetorical volume than the others. In moving his own India reform legislation in January 1784, in the wake of Fox's defeated bill, the prime minister had spoken as if it were a judicially established fact that the East India Company was a corporate outlaw. He had singled out the government of Bengal for its supposed proclivity for "conquest" and "bloodshed." Enactment of his bill, Pitt promised the House, would "prevent the Government [of Bengal] from being ambitious and bent on conquest. Propensities of that nature have already involved India in great expenses and cost much bloodshed. Ambition and trouble are companions but too often; and they have proved particularly hurtful to our interests in India."[2]

Hastings judged the prime minister's slanders no less odious than Burke's or Fox's, and it was small consolation that Pitt, unlike his Whig assailants, did not speak the name "Warren Hastings" out loud. There was only one governor-general of Bengal, and everyone knew his name.

Hastings seems never to have doubted his own innocence, the mysterious contents of that lost bureau notwithstanding. He knew, better than anyone, his own worth, success, and purity of purpose. *Innocence*, perhaps, is the wrong word for the confidence that steeled him. By rights, he knew that he should never have fallen under suspicion. His noble record was sufficient armor against suspicion, let alone an indictment.

Perhaps, too, Hastings drew confidence from the very extravagance of Burke's accusations. Whatever peccadilloes the governor-general might have committed in the process of saving British India from the French and sundry hostile Indian princes, he had not exactly reduced "the gardens of the Earth to a desert."

In the opinion of Hastings's devoted London agent, Major John Scott, MP, the governor-general deserved much more than a clean legal bill of health. As Lord Clive was ennobled upon his return to Britain, so should Hastings be. And if no English title were available, an Irish barony, like Clive's, would do.

At a court reception in September 1784 in honor of Marian Hastings, Scott took up the matter with Pitt. What could be done to honor the returning governor-general?

Pitt replied as if, nine months earlier, a different prime minister than he had imputed criminal deeds to the East India Company and to its Bengal governor-general.

"I look upon Mr. Hastings to be a very great and indeed a wonderful man," said Pitt now, as Scott reported his words back to Hastings. "He has done very essential services to the state, and has a claim upon us for everything he can ask. My only difficulty, and I confess it appears to me to be a material one, is, the resolution of the House of Commons standing upon our journals."[3]

Pitt's allusion was to a parliamentary motion of censure, dated May 28, 1782, directing the East India Company to recall Hastings. It was an ambiguous black mark, harsh though its language.* Burke had demanded punishment for the company's servants, Hastings included, who had brought Great Britain into "such disgrace," but Fox, no student yet of Indian affairs, spoke of Hastings's "unimpeached integrity." Henry Dundas, chairman of the Commons' Secret Committee on Indian Affairs, was content to recall Hastings, not to prosecute him.[4]

Pitt continued, telling Scott: "For though I admit that the charges against Mr. Hastings were ridiculous and absurd, and were, as I really think, fully refuted, yet until the sting of those resolutions is done away by a vote of thanks [in the House of Commons] for Mr. Hastings' great services, I do not see how I can with propriety advise his Majesty to confer an honour on Mr. Hastings."[5]

Even so, Hastings returned in June 1785 to the warmest of welcomes from, among others, the king and queen. The directors of the East India Company unanimously voted him their gratitude, the unanimity of the ballot adding luster to the commendation. From the celebratory dinner that followed the presentation of thanks, the light-drinking former ruler of Bengal returned home late, "much enflamed."

"Indeed," Hastings wrote to his private secretary, George Nesbitt Thompson, "I find myself everywhere and universally treated with evidences, apparent even to my own observation, that I possess the good opinion of my country."[6]

Perhaps Hastings, prompted by the always optimistic Scott, remembered that Burke had failed to follow through on his threatened

* The motion condemned the conduct of Hastings and William Hornby, governor of Bombay, as "repugnant to the honour and policy of this nation, and thereby brought great calamities on India, and enormous expences on the East India Company." It ordered the directors "to pursue all legal and effectual means" for their removal "and to recall them to Great Britain." The directors complied, only to be overruled by the Court of Proprietors. Voting 428–75, the stockholders countermanded the directors' orders and added a separate vote of thanks to the governor-general. W&S, 5:438–39.

impeachment of Lord North.* Politicians had been known to change their minds.

However, no mere exercise in opposition research or parliamentary nose counting can explain Hastings's unwavering belief in his innocence of criminal charges or in the substantively unblemished record of his service. It was his bad luck to match up with a prosecutor, in Edmund Burke, who was no less certain of Hastings's guilt than the defendant was of his innocence.

THE REUNION WITH MARIAN WAS A JOY, AND HASTINGS BEGAN TO plan for their life together in retirement. He sent to India for things that were not readily available in England: shawl goats (the ones he had taken on board had died at sea) and seeds with which to grow lychee, cinnamon, Bhutan turnips, and custard apples. The animals† and the seeds were destined for Daylesford, the Hastings family estate, now tumbledown, which he was determined to buy and restore, even at twice the prevailing market price.[7]

Where would the money come from? Hastings returned with about £70,000. It was a modest fortune—Clive had disembarked in England fairly dripping with wealth, and even Francis brought home from the East enough to procure him a "noble mansion in St. James's Square."[8] If

---

* Nathaniel Wraxall (1751–1831), the memoirist, onetime East India Company paymaster, and later a Pittite member of Parliament, left an interesting, if finally unpersuasive, psychofinancial speculation on what impelled Burke to pursue Hastings for more than a decade. What was lacking in the famed opposition orator, Wraxall proposed, was the "complacency and suavity which office, prosperity and wealth are formed to produce. If the Coalition Administration had retained possession of the Government, and of course Burke had continued to occupy the [Paymaster's Office], with its splendid emoluments, Hastings would undoubtedly have been recalled with marks of Ministerial censure; but I greatly question whether the Paymaster of the Forces would, in opposition to the King's opinions, have drawn up and presented articles of impeachment against him. We have seen how easily Burke was induced to lay aside his intentions of impeaching Lord North in 1782 as soon as that nobleman relinquished his place." What Wraxall overlooks is the depth of Burke's sympathy for the oppressed Indian masses and his determination to free them from the clutches of Englishmen like Hastings. Would £4,000 a year at the Paymaster's Office have damped his rage? It seems unlikely. Wraxall, *Historical Memoirs*, 4:301.

† His prize Arabian horse, which survived the voyage hale and hearty, turned Londoners' heads.

conservatively invested in consols and mortgages, Hastings's £70,000 would yield on the order of £3,000 a year, not quite half of the £7,000 that Hastings felt he needed to lead a life of genteel peace and comfort.

Marian had money of her own, though sons to raise as well. She likewise had diamonds,* and exotic Indian dresses, which she wore well and on which envious eyes fastened. A divorcee, she was nonetheless twice received by the queen. She kept a coach, which bore the Hastings coat of arms, and rented a house, properly staffed, on St. James's Park.

The Britain that Hastings left in 1769 was only just beginning to industrialize; the Trent and Mersey Canal, destined to transform Josiah Wedgwood's pottery business and to revolutionize the economics of inland transport, was still under construction. By the time Hastings returned, sixteen years later, the Industrial Revolution was in full stride.[9]

If, to the long-absent Hastings, the new economic landscape of Britain seemed unfamiliar, its politics might have been unrecognizable. Lord North had come to power in 1770 and retired from office in 1782. Yet he had returned in 1783 in an improbable coalition with Charles Fox and Edmund Burke, two of North's former implacable enemies.

To top it off, Fox, North, and Burke were defeated over Fox's India Bill, legislation that would have shifted managerial authority over British India from Bengal to London. And who should have succeeded that ill-fated coalition but the absurdly young son of William Pitt, the great Earl of Chatham, who, in 1757, had denoted Robert Clive his "heaven-born general"?[10]

Small wonder that Hastings had not yet taken the measure of the younger Pitt. Then again, neither had the Whigs. The 1784 elections, as we have seen, were a triumph for Pitt and a reciprocal disaster for the coalition. Fox, at least, had won in Westminster, after a long-drawn-out and certainly bipartisanly corrupt contest and an arduous scrutiny of the results.

---

* There were jewels to spare as gifts for their royal highnesses, though "these splendid offerings of Oriental respect" soon recoiled on the donor and recipients alike. Londoners in 1786 stopped and stared at the spectacle of "the miraculous stone-eater" of Cockspur Street chewing and swallowing small rocks. It wasn't long before shopwindows were filled with caricatures of the king, dressed as the "Great Mogul," gulping down the diamonds that Warren Hastings was tossing into his open mouth. Wraxall, *Historical Memoirs*, 4:254.

Three candidates had contested for the two Westminster seats. Admiral Lord Hood, a hero of the Battle of the Saintes, was a shoo-in for the first. Fox had won the second, defeating his Pittite rival, Sir Cecil Wray, by a vote of 6,234–5,998.

But Wray, protesting the outcome, demanded a scrutiny, which the high bailiff, Thomas Corbett, readily granted. In the attempt to deny Westminster to Fox, the government party had expended perhaps one-quarter of its national election budget. The tortoise pace of the work of authenticating each and every ballot in the seven parishes of Britain's largest and most democratic borough provided some consolation, at least, to Pitt.

For as long as it dragged on, Westminster was denied parliamentary representation and its hopeful candidates their places. Pending an end to the stalemate, as we have seen, Fox secured a seat in an obscure constituency at the northernmost fringe of Scotland. In the opening debates of the new Parliament, Pitt sarcastically congratulated the Whig leader on "the extent of his fame, which, spreading to the remotest corner of Great Britain, had procured his election for the Orkney and Shetland Islands."[11]

Fox now discovered that it was possible to hate Pitt even more than he had in the wake of the twenty-four-year-old's underhanded rise to power in 1783. "To the honourable gentleman over against me (Mr. Pitt)," Fox told the House of Commons at the start of the scrutiny, in June 1784, "I will beg leave to offer a little advice. . . .

> Let him well weigh the consequences of what he is about, and look to the future effect of it upon the nation at large. Let him take care, that when they see all the powers of his administration employed to overwhelm an individual, men's eyes may not open sooner than they would if he conducted himself within some bounds of decent discretion, and not thus openly violate the sacred principles of the constitution. A moderate use of his own power might the longer keep people from reflecting upon the extraordinary means by which he acquired it.[12]

Fox affected a heavy heart in telling the House what a talented and, at one time, principled rival Pitt had been. Chatham's son would, perhaps, "leave [his father] far behind in the pursuit of glory; but he never could have expected that he would have descended so low, to be the prosecutor of any man."

On paper, the younger Pitt's majority was impregnable, but he had taxed the members beyond their endurance. "Where," Fox demanded of the bored parliamentarians, "could he find a man who would not tell him he was sick of his scrutiny?"[13]

On March 3 the House ordered an end to the tedious, vindictive affair. It proved one of Pitt's few parliamentary defeats. To mark the occasion, Whigs illuminated their houses for three nights in a row, and strong-backed partisans, unhitching the horses from Fox's carriage, drew the now officially victorious member for Westminster to the House of Commons. Fox sued the bailiff responsible for his unwanted tenure as the representative of Orkney and Shetland, collected a £2,000 judgment, and distributed the winnings among the charities of Westminster.[14]

WHAT FOX DID NOT DO WAS RETURN TO THE HOUSE OF COMMONS. AS Pitt's position was unshakable, so was opposition to his power futile. Besides, the majority was not so much for Pitt as against Fox, Fox acknowledged—many of the new members had been elected specifically for the purpose of sending Lord Holland's son packing. In the circumstances, "lying by for a little while," as Fox advised the Duke of Portland, was the wisest course of action.[15]

On October 10, 1784, the fourth anniversary of Fox's first victory at Westminster, some five hundred Whigs turned out at the Shakespeare's Head Tavern, Covent Garden, to salute their leader. They were a happy and loyal lot, Burke judged, but their leaders, even Fox himself, were without a plan. "Nor does it seem to occur to them that any such thing is necessary," Burke advised a protégé, William Windham, MP. "Accordingly every thing is left to accidents; and I thought Fox had great faith in the Chapter of that Scripture."[16]

There was something else besides politics and indolence that kept Fox away from the opposition benches of St. Stephen's Chapel. Elizabeth Armistead and he had met in the early 1770s when Fox, in company with a visiting French nobleman and George Wyndham, 3rd Earl of Egremont, kicked in the door of a bedroom in a high-grade whorehouse to surprise their friend, Lord Bolingbroke.[17] The woman in Bolingbroke's arms turned out to be the love of Fox's life.

Born Elizabeth Bridget Cane in 1750, Mrs. Armistead was just beginning her career in prostitution and (intermittently) on the London stage. She had much to offer besides her beauty, as Fox ardently attested, but her professional attainments, too, are well documented. By 1776, according to *Town and Country*, she could claim "the conquest of two ducal coronets, a marquis, four earls and a viscount."[18] Politically, she favored Whigs, including Lord George Cavendish and the Prince of Wales. Two of her patrons bought her an annuity.

By 1784 Fox and she were head over heels in love, living together, unmarried, in Elizabeth's small house on St. Anne's Hill in Chertsey, in the borough of Runnymede, Surrey, twenty miles southwest of London. She played the harpsichord, he read Ariosto. Charles told her he had never been so happy; perhaps he was becoming healthier, too. Brooks's was inaccessible, and it was "dear Liz," and not his own ungovernable appetite, that determined the daily menu. "Quietly and unobtrusively, the prostitute was setting about the reform of the rake."[19]

Both made sacrifices. Elizabeth relinquished her income and Fox his reputation, or what little remained of that reputation in the eyes of respectable London. Proud to be seen with her in public, he shocked the sensibility of even so progressive a reformer as Richard Price. "Immoral and indecent conduct," huffed the mathematician and Unitarian divine at the scandalous sight of the statesman in company with the formerly vendable beauty.[20]

She was in Paris in 1787 when Fox wrote with assurances that, no matter how absurd the Parisian fashion, "I dare say I shall like it upon Liz as I do everything else. Come home soon and be kind and good to old one, as it does not *sig* [signify] how you are drest. If you did but know the sort of longing I have to see you, you would not stay long; & the more I receive of your letters the more I long."

He had made a good speech in the House opposing Pitt's Anglo-French commercial treaty, but the effort tired him, so out of practice at speaking had he become during his tactical boycott of Parliament. "Thirty-eight years have I lived most of them very happy," he continued, "and I do not know any thing at all serious that I have to reproach myself with; the remaining half of my life whether it is to be happy or otherwise depends entirely upon you, indeed it does. I never can be happy now that I have known you but with you."[21]

FOX RETURNED TO THE COMMONS IN FEBRUARY 1785 TO CONDEMN THE avaricious British financers who were plundering the southeast India presidency of Madras. The East India Company, though not (for once) Hastings personally, had facilitated predatory lending practices. Crippling debts at usurious rates of interest were bankrupting the admittedly corrupt local government, under the Nawab of Arcot, that had contracted them. How much better this bad situation would be, Fox told the House, if his India Bill, not Pitt's, were the law of the land.

Fox approached India, the East India Company, and Warren Hastings as political questions. Burke treated them as moral certainties. Fox was not unmindful of the Indian people nor Burke of the alignment of forces within the House of Commons, and the two made common cause until, by Fox's reckoning, the cause became both futile and politically harmful.

Burke took up the great cause of India expecting to lose. Misjudging Pitt and Dundas, he doubted that the House would ever vote to impeach Hastings (it did); or that the peers would ever vote to convict (it did not). All he could hope for was the opportunity to "acquit and justify [himself] to those few persons and to those distant times, which may take a concern in these affairs."[22]

Burke's great speech on the Nawab of Arcot's debts, in February 1785, exposed shocking lapses in British conduct and financial management, and it put Burke and Fox on the road to achieving one part of the impossible. This signal achievement, moreover, would come courtesy of the king's first minister himself, the detested Pitt.

Pitt's India Bill had instituted a new Board of Control to direct and oversee the company from London. Pitt himself was a member. Its chairman was Henry Dundas, who also led the House of Commons' Secret Committee on Indian Affairs. The Whigs rose up in protest when the board voted to nullify the directors' order to investigate the validity of the enormous debts of Muhammad Ali Khan, also known as the Nawab of Arcot. Never mind that the majority of the directors had found the debts to be, at the very least, suspicious. Pitt, Dundas, et al. summarily ruled them bona fide.

To what had the directors objected? Fox supported a motion to lay those findings before the House. Burke followed with a speech that neither Demosthenes nor Tully could have "exceeded in energy, eloquence or animation," according to a member who heard it and disagreed with most of it. Certainly, Burke had no contemporary peer in his mastery of the facts about India, in his zeal to bring the company's delinquents to justice and in "his beautiful and allegorical language, which borrowed its allusions by turns from every source, sacred or classic, as they suited his purpose," again to quote the admiring and skeptical eyewitness.[23]

Burke charged, first, that the debts were fictitious, "every debt for which an equivalent of some or other is not given, is on the face of it a fraud." He alleged that the Board of Control's refusal to investigate represented prima facie evidence of a corrupt bargain between the money men and the Pitt government. And he predicted that the debts, in their immensity, would crush the impoverished taxpayers who could never hope to discharge them. There was merit, in varying degrees, in each allegation.

Indian place names, monetary values, and geography drew a blank from not a few members of the House of Commons. If he was to persuade them, he must first engage them, and to this end, he encouraged them: "you are just as competent to judge whether the sum of four millions sterling ought, or ought not, to be passed from the public treasury into a private pocket."[24]

Burke reminded the backbench squires that rich returning English nabobs were buyers of social status and parliamentary seats as well as of acres and houses. For how many years, he mused, had "all England, Scotland and Ireland . . . been witness to the immense sums laid out by the servants of the [East India] Company in stocks of all denominations, in the purchase of lands, in the buying and building of houses, in the securing quiet seats in parliament, in the tumultuous riot of contested elections . . . which sometimes have excited our wonder, sometimes roused our indignation;

that after all India was four millions still in debt to *them*? India in debt to *them*! For what?"

The criminally incompetent borrower, the Nawab of Arcot, had incurred an overall debt of £4,440,000, Burke related, a sum that, at the implied 14 percent interest rate, yielded an income of £623,000 a year, a sum "a good deal more than one third of the clear land-tax of England, at four shillings in the pound; a good deal more than double the whole annual dividend of the East India Company."[25]

Burke did not come unprepared to these subjects. He, and later cousin Will, were the friends—and in Will's case, the London agent—of the Raja of Tanjore, a rival of the Nawab of Arcot. The Burkes' enemies readily imputed the statesman's condemnation of the nawab's tangled finances as the pleading of an interested party, but Edmund took no money for championing the cause of the oppressed masses.

His famous speech went on for hours—for five hours, Wraxall reckoned, "an intolerable length."[26] It began late in the evening and ended, on notes of deep purple, early in the morning.

"It is difficult for the most wise and upright government to correct the abuses of remote delegated power," said Burke, "productive of unmeasured wealth, and protected by the boldness and strength of the same ill-got riches. These abuses, full of their own native wild vigour, will grow and flourish under mere neglect."

Burke's speech has succeeded better with posterity than it did with the sleepy members. The cry of "Question!" short for "Prior question," the parliamentary demand that debate be brought to a close, or in this case, the very specific demand that Burke stop talking, echoed in St. Stephen's Chapel. When Burke did finally finish, the ministerial benches sat mum, "Pitt disdaining to refute allegations which his character sufficiently repelled." The opposition mustered 69 votes to investigate the Board of Control's complacency in the face of the directors' suspicions; the government tallied 164.[27]

PERHAPS, IN THE ABSENCE OF MAJOR SCOTT AND PHILIP FRANCIS, THERE would have been no impeachment, at least not one to span nearly a decade. One man goaded the defendant, the other the prosecution. Scott never failed to remind Hastings of his perfect innocence; Francis, to let Burke forget Hastings's irredeemable guilt. Contrary to Francis, however, the Rohilla War did not "extirpate" the vanquished Afghan enemy; nor did Hastings arrange for the "judicial murder" of poor, crooked Nandakumar. And contrary to Scott's ill-judged counsel to Hastings in the summer of 1784, "we" had not "fully and effectually confounded all your enemies . . . by reason and argument."[28]

Burke was not wrong that Hastings was a kind of oriental despot. There was indeed a strong moral case against him, especially if, as Burke insisted, right and wrong are invariable across the world's geographies. Whether that case rose, in law, to the extremities of evil that Francis and he so vehemently contended is doubtful; certainly the House of Lords, after hearing eight years of evidence, decided it did not.

As for the hopeful Scott, it would have been better had he not portrayed Burke to Hastings as a figure of parliamentary ridicule or, worse, as "that reptile."[29] As he badly underestimated Burke's devotion to the interests of the Indian people, so he reciprocally overestimated the strength of his client's case.

On January 24, 1786, the first day of the new Parliament, Scott noticed Burke making a late arrival into the House. Did the member for Malton, Scott asked, intend to proceed with the motion concerning "a gentleman lately returned from Bengal," that he announced his intention to move six months earlier?

Burke did not reply but parried with a story about Henry IV of France refusing to oblige an enemy with the information as to which day and place he, the king, would choose to do battle with him. For Burke, the opening salvo roared on February 13 with a notice of intention to begin his campaign against Hastings. He followed on the seventeenth with a motion for papers.

IMPEACHMENT, A CONSTITUTIONAL ARTIFACT LAST DEPLOYED IN 1746, was a political impossibility, Burke was quite certain. He therefore set about laying the groundwork for a court of his own creation, of which the newspaper- and pamphlet-reading public in the present, and readers of the journals of the House of Commons in the future, would form the jury. He would convict Hastings on the strength of the documents he would open and the witnesses he would call.

"I undertake," Burke told the House, "the task devolved on me by the natural death of some in their graves, by the civil death of others and by the worst kind of death, to principle and consistency, who have left me to assert the dignity of the House of Commons and vindicate the justice of the nation."[30]

The Whigs, showing a united front, eagerly joined him in bringing specific charges against Hastings. They numbered twenty-two, beginning with the 1774 Rohilla War, a conflict that Dundas's own Secret Committee on Indian Affairs of the House of Commons had denounced in its *Fifth Report* of 1782. The evidence supporting Burke's claim that Hastings had hired out British forces for profit to wage a genocidal war against a noble people had little basis in evidence at the time and still less with the subsequent accumulation of historical research. With that allowed, there was an unbridgeable gulf between Hastings's and Burke's views of the legitimate uses of British power in India. Hastings, though he disavowed waging war for money alone, saw nothing amiss in employing "our Army" for the purpose of making fiscal ends meet.[31] Burke recoiled from it.

Reading and debating the charges filled April and May. Hastings heard himself described as a warmonger, a persecutor of rajas, a receiver of bribes, a dispenser of inflated contracts, a conductor of monopolies, a suppressor of evidence, and a receiver of stolen property. Would he be allowed the opportunity to defend himself?

Unhappily for Hastings, he would. On May 1 the defendant appeared before the bar of the House to refute the accusations against him. Clive, summoned to the House in 1773 to answer the charges against *him*, had spoken for an hour, sometimes in stirring phrases ("leave me my honour, take away my fortune"). Hastings, thirteen years later, rather chose to speak forgettably and at length. The House was brimful of members when he began reading his text at 3:45 p.m. on May 1, 1786. There were many fewer when he stopped at 10:30 p.m. Attendance continued to dwindle as he resumed the next morning and persisted throughout the day and into the evening of May 2.

Hastings was seated—the Commons had extended him the courtesy of a chair. A slight figure, he nonetheless projected the authority of a man who was accustomed to obedience.[32] The text from which he read was a narrative of his career in India and a point-by-point refutation of the charges against him. From time to time, he paused to turn over the reading to William Markham, son of the Archbishop of York, or the clerk of the House, though if the reader varied, the message remained the same.

Hastings had refused to take the position that his achievements overshadowed the mistakes he might admittedly have made. Thurlow, it will be recalled, had helped to rescue Clive from parliamentary attack by moving that the hero of Plassey, whatever his flaws, "did at the same time render great and meritorious service to the nation."[33]

There would be no such invocation of "at the same time" for Hastings. He asserted his "general Claim to the approbation of this Honourable House, and of my Country, for my Services; but I neither desire, nor will admit, of their being placed in Balance against my faults, if I have Faults to stand in opposition to them." Not many members on either side of the aisle had ever encountered a perfect person before.[34]

The Whigs were in no hurry to deliver the impeachment motion to the House for an up-or-down vote. The longer the debate, the greater the accumulation of evidence and the richer the record of criminality. Nor was Pitt ready to divide the House over the single question of whether to impeach. Better, he determined, to hold separate votes on each count, beginning on June 1 with the Rohilla War.

Burke, repeating his accusations of despotism, extortion, and genocide, enjoined the House to consider that something greater than Hastings's undoubted guilt was at stake: "They were this day to vote on a set of maxims and principles to be the rule and guide of future governors in India; what they determined, therefore, would decide the world as top their opinion of British justice and British policy."[35]

Dundas, responding for the government, found much to approve in the conflict that he had previously decried and in the governor-general who prosecuted it; Hastings was now "the Saviour of India." Burke hotly rejoined but his resolution—that the charge warranted impeachment for high crimes and misdemeanors—lost by 119–67.

The Whigs, who had hardly expected victory, found consolation in the friends whom they collected in the course of defeat. Open-minded independent members like William Wilberforce had weighed the evidence and, in some cases, reached the anti-Hastings conclusions. A contemporary of Pitt's at the University of Cambridge, Wilberforce had won election to the Commons from Yorkshire, England's largest county, at the age of twenty-four. He was an evangelical Christian determined to do God's work, if he could find that work.

The opportunity presented itself on June 13 when Fox moved a resolution on the second count against Hastings. Benares, a sacred Hindu city along the Ganges in northern India today called Varanasi, was the sovereign property of the East India Company. It had entered the company's fold in 1775 under terms that reserved to the wealthy raja, Chait Singh, perfect freedom of action so long as he paid the company its annual tribute and bent to the authority of British rule.

Perhaps the raja was too wealthy. Certainly the company was short of cash. In any case, the company issued new demands—arbitrarily, Fox told the House. "Mr. Hastings," said Fox,

> after stipulating that no more demand of any kind than the annual tribute should be made upon the raja, demanded first five lacks of rupees, which were paid, but with some murmuring; he next demanded five lacks more, which were also paid, though with some murmuring; he again demanded a third five lacks, and these again were paid.[36]

Next came a demand for two thousand cavalry, which, Chait Singh protested, he did not possess. The five hundred horsemen he offered instead seem never to have materialized. Nor were the final five lakhs of rupees produced to the company's satisfaction. If such lapses were the murmurs to which Fox alluded, Hastings treated them as a "direct charge of disaffection and infidelity," and as a prelude to "open revolt, waiting only for a proper reason to declare it." He ordered that Chait be fined to the tune of fifty lakhs.*

"I was resolved to draw from his guilt," Hastings later wrote, "the means of relief to the company's distresses, and to exact a penalty, which I am convinced he was able to bear. . . . In a word, I had determined to make him pay largely for his pardon, or to exact a severe vengeance for his past delinquency."[37]

Hastings set out to confront Chait Singh. Guarded by European officers commanding six companies of Indian sepoys, he traveled to Benares to arrest the raja and exact the fine. A showdown between Hastings's escort and Chait Singh's troops ended in a bloodbath. Every company officer died, and Chait Singh escaped into exile.

The successor raja, Mahip Narain, now confronted a new demand. The company would henceforth charge annual rents of forty lakhs, up from twenty-two lakhs. No 82 percent rent rise has ever redounded to the prosperity of a tenant, and farmers in droves abandoned the land.[38]

Appealing to the "honour and justice of the House," Fox declared that the members must choose to be the "avengers of those oppressed by Mr. Hastings or his accomplice."[39]

A short exchange between Pitt and Wilberforce occurred behind the speaker's chair during the subsequent debate.

"Does not this look very ill to you?" Pitt asked his friend.

"Very bad, indeed," Wilberforce answered.[40]

Pitt had taken the time to brief himself thoroughly about the facts, law, and political context of the Benares charge, and he attended to Fox's speech. Hastings and his friends had expected the prime minister's support, and Pitt, as he began to speak, suggested that they had it.

Contrary to Fox, Pitt contended, Chait Singh was a vassal whose

---

* "It is difficult to believe," as a modern scholar sums up, "that such draconian measures would have been undertaken against Chait Singh in 1781 if the Company's need for money had not been quite so urgent." Marshall, *Impeachment*, 103.

sovereign had every right to demand "extraordinary aids to meet extraordinary emergencies"; in this case, the danger was France, and the sovereign was the East India Company. Nor was Hastings out of bounds in jailing the raja for the purpose of investigating him. However, Pitt continued, the fine that Hastings "determined to levy was beyond all proportion exorbitant, unjust and tyrannical . . . admitting the supposed guilt of the Raja in delaying to pay an additional tribute demanded of him, the punishment was utterly disproportionate, and shamefully exorbitant."[41]

The prime minister's support of the Benares count, qualified though it was, made it possible to imagine that the impeachment could go forward. Fox's motion passed, with Dundas, too, voting aye, 119–79.*

Hastings reported the news to Thompson in India:

> I have been declared guilty of a high crime and misdemeanor in having *intended* to exact a fine too large for the offense, the offense being admitted to merit a fine, from Chait Singh. This has given consequence to my accuser, who was sinking into infamy, and had every reason to expect punishment for the baseness and falseness of his charges against me.[42]

The goats that Thompson had put on a ship for England had died at sea, like the previous brace, Hastings continued; would he please send more? "And not forget the turnip seeds," which, if they could grow in Bhutan, could certainly take root in England. There was no news about the chest of drawers.

His lost papers still tormented him. "It pains me to recur to the subject of my bureau," Hastings closed. "I have not yet received any intelligence from you or [William] Larkins about it. You cannot conceive my anxiety about it."[43]

---

* George Dempster, MP, a former East India Company director, replied to Pitt with the claim that, during the prior war, the French so esteemed Hastings that "they rested their hopes of success in India on the chance of his being recalled. In short, if the late governor-general deserved impeachment at all, it certainly was for that foolish disinterestedness which would not suffer him to bring home a larger fortune." PH, 26:113.

AS THE 1787 SESSION OF PARLIAMENT OPENED, THE FATE OF THE PROSE-
cution's case rested with the celebrated playwright-turned-politician
Richard Brinsley Sheridan. It fell to the author of *The School for Scandal*
to carry the article of charge relating to confiscation of the wealth of the
begums of Oudh, a pair of noble Indian widows. Hastings's shifting version of events along with the unpersuasive testimony of supposed eyewit-
nesses afforded Sheridan wide scope for the display of his rhetorical and
dramatic gifts.

The essence of the charge was that Hastings seized private property on
the trumped-up pretext that the victims, as in Benares, were in league with
enemies of the East India Company. However, whether the begums held
bona fide title to wealth in their possession was not entirely clear. Nor
was it cut and dried that Hastings had overstepped in seizing it or that the
begums were plotting a revolt.

Sheridan began his speech with a promise to trust "nothing to declamation," but to prove every fact. Five and a half hours later, however, many
facts remained hazy, but there was nothing wrong with the declamation.
Never had the members heard such a speech.

"They could not behold," Sheridan said of his fellow members of
Parliament,

the workings of the hearts, the quivering lips, the trickling tears, the
loud yet tremulous joy of the millions whom their vote of this night
would for ever save from the cruelty of corrupted power. But though
they could not directly see the effect, was not the true enjoyment
of their benevolence increased by the blessing of being conferred
unseen? Would not the omnipotence of Great Britain be demonstrated to the wonder of nations, by stretching its mighty arm across
the deep, and saving by its fiat distant millions from destruction?
And would the blessings of the people thus saved dissipate in empty
air? No! If I might dare (said Mr. Sheridan) to use the figure—we
shall constitute Heaven itself our proxy, to receive for us the blessings
of their pious gratitude, and the prayers of their thanksgiving—It is

with confidence, therefore, Sir, that I move you on this charge, "That Warren Hastings, esq., be impeached."

As Sheridan sat down, "the whole House, members, peers and strangers, involuntarily joined in a tumult of applause, and adopted a mode of expressing their approbation, new and irregular in that House, by loudly and repeatedly clapping with their hands."[44]

In debate the next day, Pitt remarked on the defects in Hastings's defense and the "unprovoked severity" of his administration. He again revealed, as he had done in the Benares matter, deep knowledge of the details and the broad setting of the alleged crime. For a second time the House voted for the motion to impeach, and by a larger margin than on the first, 175–68.

If Burke had had his way, the House would immediately have voted on a resolution to notify the Lords of its intention to bring its case, but Pitt wanted more evidence of Hastings's guilt and a stronger sense of the House's commitment to act. More articles of charge therefore made their way to the floor. By April 2, six had passed, and on May 10, the House of Commons formally directed Burke to impeach Warren Hastings at the bar of the House of Lords. The movers of this improbable enterprise, Burke most of all, had achieved the seemingly impossible.

On May 21, Hastings was arrested, escorted to the bar of the House of Lords by the Black Rod, and made to post £2,000 in bail money.[45] He shrugged off such humiliations, "except the ignominious ceremonial of kneeling before the House of Lords, though I think it a usage that reflects more dishonour on that assembly for permitting the continuance of so iniquitous a form, than on those who are compelled to submit to it, and on whom it is inflicted as a punishment not only before conviction, but even before the accusations against them are read." Ready for his trial, Hastings said he hoped it would end before the close of the "next sessions of Parliament."[46]

There had been twenty-two original articles of charge, of which few were fit for court. Many consisted, in Pitt's words, "of facts incapable of proof, or which if proved, could not be imputed to Mr. Hastings as delinquencies."[47] The work of reducing those sometimes sprawling narratives to proper articles of impeachment fell to Burke, Fox, et al. in company with a professional solicitor and counsel.

French Laurence, a young lawyer who later assisted Burke with this kind of work, described the trials of legal collaboration with a literary and oratorical genius. "I must observe in confidence," related French, "that [Burke] does so ride up and down, backwards and forwards, so trot, canter, and gallop now on the high road, now on the turf and sometimes by a short cut, till he is stuck in the mire or lost in the wood; that we are not in truth very far distant from the place where we set out."[48]

Philip Francis seems not to have won the affection of the House of Commons. Certainly, he did not earn the trust of the ministerial bench, expert on India though he undoubtedly was. So it confused and enraged Burke, and Fox, too, when the House, in December 1787, voted 97–23 to exclude their right-hand man from the managers' committee to prosecute Hastings in the House of Lords.

Pitt seemed to want the impeachment neither to fail nor, exactly, to succeed. He had nothing to gain by identifying the government as a friend of the controversial Hastings nor, for that matter, by fully embracing the prosecution; the Whigs could have that rabbit hole all to themselves.[49]

At last, in May 1788, the Commons approved seven principal articles of impeachment, reduced from the original twenty-two, and conveyed them to the Lords. Accusations ranged from "a wicked and malicious design to harass, oppress and ruin Chait Singh" to the numerous depredations allegedly committed against the state of Oudh and its inhabitants, including the aforementioned begums.

The Commons—that is, the "Knights, Citizens, and Burgesses in Parliament assembled, in the Name of themselves and of all the Commons of *Great Britain*"—charged the defendant with concluding fraudulent treaties and exacting excessive taxes and tributes, including the ones that Hastings allegedly refused to reduce, for humanity's sake, in the wake of the 1770 Bengal famine.

Still other articles charged Hastings with mismanaging company revenue, issuing grossly overpriced contracts to favored vendors "in pursuance of a System of Profusion and Prodigality,"[50] and extorting money from vulnerable Indian princes while calling those rupees, diamonds, or securities "presents" (though the receipt of unexhorted gifts was itself illegal).[51] The articles and subdivisions of articles filled 125 printed pages.

February 12, 1788, the day before the opening ceremonies and preliminary legalities, found Burke with a heavy cold and a hoarse voice. He was besieged by requests for tickets to the next day's spectacle, even by the deaf Sir Joshua Reynolds.[52] It was obligatory to see and be seen (if not to hear and be heard) at Westminster Hall on the thirteenth.

At noon the managers of the prosecution made their entrance. Fanny Burney, at least, had no trouble getting in; the queen herself, whom Burney served as second keeper of the robes, pressed tickets on her. Seated in the grand chamberlain's box, she watched Burke in the vanguard: "He held a scroll in his hand, and walked alone, his Brow knit with corroding Care and deep labouring Thought." It was the brow that had once captivated her, and "how did I grieve to behold him now, the cruel Prosecutor—such to me he appeared—of an injured and innocent man!"[53]

Next came Fox, followed by Sheridan, Wyndham, William Adam (with whom Fox had fought his duel), Sir Gilbert Elliot, Charles Grey, General Burgoyne, and other leading Whigs. Next entered the House of Commons at large,* followed by a grand procession of clerks, lawyers, peers, bishops, and officers, each in his coronation robes, concluding with the princes of the blood, including the Prince of Wales. Lord Chancellor Thurlow, "his train borne," brought up the rear.

Hastings, to Burney's nearsighted eyes, looked gaunt and pale, and her heart went out to him after he spoke his few words to the court: "My Lords—Impressed—deeply impressed—I come before your Lordships— equally confident in my own integrity, and in the Justice of the Court before which I am to clear it."[54]

An interminable monotone reading of the bill of charges, spanning

---

* Frances, Lady Clermont, seated next to Burney, remarked of the rank-and-file MPs, "All those creatures that filled the Green Benches, looking so little like Gentlemen, and so much like Hair-Dressers." Burney, *Diary and Letters of D'Arblay*, 4:258.

two full days, gave some of the spectators reason to rue the money they had spent, or the favors they had had to call in, to secure a seat. Burke, "full dressed" in "dark brown," began his opening remarks on Friday, February 15; they lasted two hours and forty minutes. He resumed on Saturday and picked up where he had left off on Monday, February 18. By the time he finished, on Tuesday, he had held forth for eleven hours and ten minutes.[55] He had never before spoken longer, and never would again.

It was a great speech—even some Hastings loyalists so esteemed it— beginning with a two-day survey of the scope of the charges, followed by an examination of the principles of arbitrary government and moral relativism on which, by Burke's conjecture, Hastings had fallen into crime and error. Venality, too, Burke contended, was a thread in the criminal's skein: "Money is the beginning, the middle and the end of every kind of act done by Mr. Hastings."[56]

Not every crime that Burke mentioned was encompassed in the articles of impeachment. Indeed, Hastings had played no part in alleged atrocities that the company had supposedly committed or condoned while collecting taxes in Rangpur, northern Bengal, in February 1783. Unsubstantiated reports of killings there had reached Burke shortly before he spoke. He did not, perhaps could not, corroborate them in time, but nonetheless he chose to incorporate the gory details in his speech. Much of the story proved baseless.[57]

Burney despaired as she listened to him: "My eyes dreaded a single glance towards a man so accused as Mr. Hastings." But as Burke shifted gears to invective from supposed fact, her spirits rose. "In short," she recorded, "so little of proof, to so much of passion, that, in a very short time, I began to lift up my Head."[58]

"I impeach him," said Burke in his peroration, "in the name and by virtue of those eternal laws of justice which he has violated.

"I impeach him in the name of human nature itself."[59]

Burney, her opera glass raised to her eye, similarly took the measure of Charles Fox, who charged Hastings with the Benares count on February 22. Like Burke, Fox was vehement, but at the same time—and wholly unlike

Burke—he appeared emotionally detached from his work. "He looked all good humour and negligent ease," Burney wrote of Fox,

> the instant before he began a speech of uninterrupted passion and vehemence; and he wore the same careless and disengaged air the very instant he had finished. A display of talents in which the inward man took so little share, could have no powers of persuasion to those who saw them in that light; and therefore, however their brilliancy might be admired, they were useless to their Cause; for they left the mind of the hearer in the same state that they found it.[60]

"We know that we bring before a bribed tribunal a prejudged case," Burke remarked to Francis in December 1785. But then, what of it? "In that situation all that we have to do is to make a case strong in proof and in importance, and to draw inferences from it justifiable in logick, policy and criminal justice. As to all the rest, it is vain and idle."

Fox was in a different position, Burke acknowledged. As the leader of a party, his ambitions were necessarily political. Yet, "in a party-light, and as a question to draw numbers," one could hardly have picked a worse cause.[61]

As a party matter, the impeachment was already a losing cause. Fox soon lost interest in it, as did, at a rather more rapid rate, Sheridan. Fox's attendance at the managers' meetings became sporadic. Burney, in watching Fox's face at Westminster Hall, had also read his mind.

Burke's face was likewise a window on his thoughts. The panegyric on Fox that Burke had spoken in his famous India Bill speech of 1783 now rather more closely fit Burke himself than the putative author of the legislation. "It will be a distinction honourable to the age," Burke had then said of Fox, "that the rescue of the greatest number of the human race that ever were so grievously oppressed, from the greatest tyranny that was ever exercised . . . has fallen to the lot of abilities and dispositions equal to the task."

Certainly, Burke had the abilities, the disposition, and not least the devotion to the task. And it was Burke, most of all, who—even at that early hour of the impeachment—had "put to hazard his ease, his security, his interest, his power . . ."* for the benefit of a people whom he has never seen."[62]

STORIES OF THE DEATH OR MORTAL ILLNESS OF KING GEORGE SEEPED from Windsor to the City of London and into the market for British sovereign debt. "The stocks" fell by 2 percent on November 3, the same day as the king confessed to his brother, the Duke of York, "I wish to God I might die for I am going mad!"[63] George was coherent one moment, babbling and delirious the next. He assaulted the Prince of Wales. He mistook an oak tree for the King of Prussia, attempting to shake hands with the former. The sovereign was a functional, essential element of the English constitution. In the absence of George III, who might that sovereign, or more likely regent, be? And who would lead the government under him?

Charles Fox was in Italy with Mrs. Armistead when the king's rumored illness exploded into an acknowledged public fact. Fox was not only the leader of the opposition but also a friend of the Prince of Wales (once, indeed, a close friend). If the prince was to be the regent with the associated sovereign power to form a government, Fox would almost certainly become prime minister.

It was no certain proof of insanity that the king had battered his son's head against a wall. Deadbeat, liar, and lecher, the prince could be said to have had it coming. As to Prinny's roistering, spending, and drinking, Fox was a mentor and confessor, as the king would not forget.

All depended on the king's medical prognosis. There were many doctors. There were government doctors, those politically aligned with Pitt, who were prone to optimism, and there were Whig doctors, sympathetic to Fox and his friends, who inclined to pessimism.

Fox did not return from the Continent until November 25. (The *Morning Post*'s report of three weeks earlier that he had retired from politics to

---

* The ellipsis replaces the phrase, "even his darling popularity," of which political attribute Fox had much and Burke little.

live on his gambling winnings proved baseless.)[64] "It does seem a sort of a phenomenon," Sir Gilbert Elliot mused to his wife,

> to think of Fox lost for months to England in countries where the post goes twice a week, and England is totally lost to him; and that one on whom a nation seems at present altogether to depend should not know or inquire how the world wags, from September to November.[65]

In Fox's absence, enterprising Whigs positioned themselves for a political upheaval. Sheridan, anticipating a Whiggish regency, set about ingratiating himself to the prince. The Duchess of Devonshire recorded the playwright's sour response to a report that Burke resented his neglect of his impeachment duties: "Sheridan, who is heartily tired of the Hastings trial, and fearful of Burke's impetuosity says that he wishes Hastings would run away and Burke after him."[66] Questions about the mounting cost of the prosecution had already been raised in the House of Commons.

Pelting home from Italy, Fox contracted dysentery. Once returned, he was on his back. What should he say, and what should the Whigs do? Burke advised him that the prince should take the initiative, snatching it away from Pitt. He should address the Commons and Lords, briefing them on his father's condition and seeking their counsel on next steps. By so doing, the prince would raise himself in the public's estimation and "stiffle an hundred Cabals, both in Parliament and elsewhere, in their very Cradle."[67]

"But I am going further than intended; God bless you," Burke diffidently added to his onetime protégé; nobody knew better than he that he had lost Fox's ear. Indeed, the supremely confident Whigs who were drawing up plans for their supposedly imminent return to power made no room for Burke in any policymaking position, not even on the India board. The idea of Burke in everyday discussion and correspondence with the directors of the East India Company was one that Fox judged "impossible."[68]

Burke's marginalization, in fact, was discouragingly bipartisan. Alone among the Whigs, he held that the regency issue was a constitutional one in which no compromise was acceptable. For his colleagues, office was the prize and political flexibility the means to obtaining it. On the government side of the aisle, Pitt took an almost sadistic delight in excluding Burke from a bipartisan, twenty-one-man committee to question the doctors on the king's health.* Neither did the king have a kind word. In a lucid moment in mid-December, His Majesty impugned the rhetoric of the greatest orator of his realm as "flowry."[69]

HASTE WAS THE WHIGS' STRATEGY, DELAY THE GOVERNMENT'S. PITT, ON medical advice, believed that the king would recover eventually, but he knew not when. On December 10, 1788, he moved for the appointment of a committee to examine the precedents for the temporary indisposition of the sovereign. Fox rose to oppose.

There were no relevant precedents, Fox protested. The search would waste time and find nothing. It was the prince's inalienable right "to assume the reins of government, and exercise the power of sovereignty, during the continuation of the illness and incapacity with which it had pleased God to afflict his majesty." There must be no delay.

Pitt was delighted. Had the leader of the Whigs not just espoused something very like the divine right of kings? Had the champion of the prerogatives of the House of Commons in 1784 now denied the lower House a voice in setting the terms of a regency? Pitt countered that the prince, the heir apparent, "had no more right . . . to the exercise of the executive power than any other subject in the kingdom." It rather fell to the Commons and the Lords, "in behalf of the people," to make such a determination. Fox's doctrine, Pitt contended, was "little less than treason against the constitution."[70]

"Mr. Pitt," the Whig poet Samuel Rogers jotted in his commonplace book,

* The prime minister announced his selections on the floor of the House, pausing after the twentieth. Who would be the twenty-first? Shouts of "Burke" welled up from the opposition benches. Pitt said nothing, "and Burke's name was repeated still more loudly. All this time he sat erect. . . . When Pitt kept us all in suspence for a couple of minutes, he very quietly proposed Lord Gower. Burke threw himself back in his seat, crossed his arms violently, and kicked his heels with evident marks of discomposure." James Bland Burges, MP (1752–1824), quoted in Lock, *Edmund Burke*, 2:209. A Hastings man, Burges had felt the lash of Burke's temper when he questioned the cost of the impeachment.

"conceives his sentences before he utters them. Mr. Fox throws himself into the middle of his, and leaves it to God Almighty to get him out again."[71]

Burke conceived his sentences, facts, and philosophical touch points before speaking, while allowing full scope for improvisation after he was on his feet. He read deeply in the history of Europe's lunatic royals and favored the House with a long speech on the subject. Impatient with Richard Warren's ambiguous pronouncements of the king's condition, he inspected a madhouse in Hoxton to see for himself how patients close to the king's age of fifty responded to treatment.

In the House, he spoke often and so vehemently as to invite the remark that he, not the king, ought to be in a straitjacket. But what was he to do? Pitt was on the high road to despotism. The prime minister would, if he could, name his own regent, defining and circumscribing the powers of that puppet to aggrandize his own.

On December 22, Burke declared his simple proposal to resolve the regency dispute. Like Fox, he urged that the Prince of Wales assume the regency. Unlike Fox, he argued not from the apparent high Tory position of kingly succession but from the fundamental tenets of the English constitution. Neither, he said, perhaps unnecessarily, was he angling for a ministerial post in a new government.

"Whether his sentiments would be considered as favouring of Whig or Tory principles," said Burke,

> he was very indifferent; and what the opinions of others, as to the degree of desire he had for employment, he gave himself no uneasiness to discover. He indeed knew as little of the inside of Carlton-House [the prince's London residence] as he did of Buckingham-House [the king's preferred London residence]; he only hoped he should be understood as he really meant, to deliver his sentiments as a plain citizen.

Burke reminded the House that Britain was governed by a hereditary monarchy; "it was so by the written and by the unwritten law; it was so by the very essence of our excellent, our at present matchless Constitution. . . . It was our inheritance," he went on:

it was our strong barrier, our strong rampart against the ambition of mankind. It held out an excellent lesson to the most aspiring; it said, "Thus far shalt thou go, and no further;" it sheltered the subject from the tyranny of illegal tribunals, bloody proscriptions, and all the long train of evils attendant upon the distractions of ill-guided and unprincipled Republicks.[72]

And yet the prime minister had declared that any citizen had as strong a claim to the throne as the Prince of Wales, or, perhaps, as the House of Hanover. "Was it possible for such monstrous opinions to be entertained?" Pitt had proposed them, and Burke now denounced them.

"Here," according to the parliamentary record,

Mr. Burke broke out with astonishing power, and said, "I disclaim all allegiance, I renounce all obedience and loyalty to a King so chosen, and a Crown so formed"—(a great cry of hear! hear! hear!) "I have, said he, given my allegiance already to the House of Hanover to possess the power given by the Constitution. I worship the Gods of our glorious Constitution, but I will not worship *Priapus* [the Roman god of licentiousness]."[73]

Even so, Pitt won his motion to begin work on legislation to define the terms on which the prince might hold the regency. The Whigs, in Fox's weakened and distracted state, lacked the mettle to oppose—and, except for Burke, the fire. His colleagues had become strangers to him.

Burke fought on, drawing no praise from Pitt (as Fox had done) for the moderation of his discourse. On February 6, he again attacked Pitt's measure to withhold sovereign powers from the prospective regent, especially the power to bestow honors. "By the Bill," said Burke,

responsibility was given to the Prince of Wales, but the whole House of Brunswick, who were to be *outlawed, excommunicated*, and *attainted*, as having forfeited all claim to the confidence of the country! [Some Gentlemen smiling at the extent of this doctrine, and the vehemence of emphasis with which it was delivered] Mr. Burke burst out into a most violent passion, and with a degree of warmth that we scarcely ever before witnessed, reprobated the conduct of the other side of the House, and in language that was not sufficiently articulate for us to collect distinctly the whole of what Mr. Burke had said, charged them with degrading the Royal Family, sowing the seeds of future distractions and disunion in that family, and with proceeding to act TREASONS, which the justice of their country would one day overtake them for, and bring them to trial—

Mr. Burke was interrupted by a loud and general cry from the other side of the House, of "ORDER, ORDER!"[74]

The king's recovery, in March, closed debate, completed the rout of the Whigs, and brought joy to Fanny Burney and to all at Windsor. "I could not keep my Eyes dry all Day long," she recorded. "A scene so reversed! Sadness so sweetly exchanged for thankfulness and delight!"[75]

WARREN HASTINGS SAT IN THE PRISONER'S DOCK IN THE HOUSE OF LORDS listening to the impeachment managers condemn a man he didn't know. Hastings bore the accusations with a remarkable placidity, but he drew the line at murderer.

In the course of accusing Hastings with the corrupt receipt of money, Burke added that "he had murdered that man by the hands of Sir Elijah Impey."[76] Nandakumar was the man, and Sir Elijah, chief justice at the British supreme court in Calcutta, was the judge who had sentenced him to death.

By all we know, Hastings did no such thing, nor did the bill of impeachment so charge him. Burke, believing Philip Francis's version of the Nandakumar affair, had seen fit to accuse the defendant out of the juridical blue. The accusation went unchallenged in the Lords, but Major Scott, acting on behalf of Hastings, filed a protest in the House of Commons. Either, Scott petitioned, charge Hastings formally with these heinous crimes that were nowhere laid in the articles of impeachment (thus affording the accused and his attorneys the right to vindicate his innocence) or grant suitable redress. "Mr. Hastings' Petition, Complaining of Words Spoken by Mr. Burke at Westminster Hall," came up for debate at the end of April 1789.

The idea that the culprit could become an accuser was an absurdity, Fox argued. It inflamed him that Pitt would accept the petition. Did the House not understand what the managers were up against? For one thing, a "most powerful criminal, a man who, for fourteen years possessed all the patronage of India." For another, "all the corruption of the East and all the powers of the bar."[77] He trusted, said Fox, that the hard-pressed managers would never lose the confidence of the House.

The debate resumed in early May, with Burke choosing to weigh in by letter. "Neither hope, nor fear, nor anger, nor weariness, nor discouragement of any kind," he pledged, "shall move me from this trust—nothing but an act of the House, formally taking away my commission, or totally cutting off the means of performing it. I trust we are all of us animated by the same sentiments."[78]

On May 4 the Marquis of Graham moved a motion that the words spoken by Burke in regard to the judicial killing of Nandakumar "ought not to have been spoken." Colonel Phipps, in seconding, complained that the managers were out of control, so indulged by the House as to turn them, almost, into "spoilt children."[79]

Before an exchange of pleasantries with Phipps that led to the clearing of strangers from the galleries (so close to a challenge to a duel had the verbal combatants hurled themselves), Fox wondered "with what face" the managers could return to Westminster Hall to resume the trial knowing how little the Commons supported them.

For himself, Fox said, if the motion of the Marquis of Graham passed the House, he feared "he could not be a useful servant to the public." Burke, his right honorable friend, "had done justice to God and man and deserved no censure."[80]

The vote of censure passed, 135–66, while a countermotion, to thank Burke and his fellow managers and to urge them on in their arduous work, went down to defeat. Not a few of the managers were discouraged. The trial, just as Hastings complained, seemed destined to go on forever— Burke's poor health had forced a recent postponement. Fox planned to move a motion to the Lords for still another adjournment and to use the expected rejection of that initiative as a pretext for abandoning the impeachment altogether. However, Fox failed to appear at the appointed hour on May 5 for a decision on whether to persist. In his absence, Burke carried the argument—the impeachment would go on and on and on.

Writing Fox to patch up hard feelings a week later, Burke noted that the two of them hardly saw each other anymore.[81]

CHAPTER 16

"Their friendship was at an end"

"Mr. Fox whispered that there was no loss of friendship." Burke
replied, "Yes, there was—he knew the price of his conduct—he
had done his duty at the price of his friend."

—COBBETT'S PARLIAMENTARY HISTORY

The dust from the fallen Bastille had hardly settled when Charles
Fox passed judgment on the opening act of the French Revolution.
"How much the greatest event it is that ever happened in the world,"
he exclaimed to his friend FitzPatrick in July 1789, "& how much the best."[1]

To the same event, Edmund Burke would later supply the superlative
"most astonishing,"[2] but he was content for now to join his fellow countrymen in gazing "at a French struggle for Liberty and not knowing whether
to blame or applaud." There was something "paradoxical and Mysterious"
about the business, Burke allowed. "The spirit is impossible not to admire;
but the old Parisian ferocity has broken out in a shocking manner."[3]

By February 9, 1790, when Burke uttered his first parliamentary words
on what by then had indisputably become a revolution, the ancien régime
had defaulted on a portion of its debts,* and Louis XVI had effectively been

---

* On August 16, 1788, the cash-strapped government had found it necessary to pay the
holders of certain maturing public loans in IOUs rather than gold and silver. Harris,
"French Finances," 254.

deposed. Monasteries had been sacked, feudalism abolished, the Declaration of the Rights of Man and the Citizen proclaimed, a new paper currency conjured, and the vast properties of the Catholic Church nationalized.[4] The center of French political power, uprooted from Versailles, rested now with the National Assembly and the hungry Parisian masses.

The spirit of the thing was indeed infectious, and many cheered the tidings of a long-overdue French emancipation. A decrepit monarchy, a too-worldly Catholic Church, and an entitled aristocracy were institutions exactly unfit for the Age of Reason. "I say nothing of french News but if I were to begin I should never finish," Fox wrote to Thomas Grenville in August.[5]

Frenchmen of a Whiggish sort were reenacting, with a century's lag, the stirring scenes of 1688, Fox asserted. They had rendered their despotic king a cipher and committed their devotion to freedom to parchment. "Liberty, Property, Safety and Resistance to Oppression" had become the natural and timeless basis of French civil society.

The Declaration of the Rights of Man and the Citizen condemned arbitrary arrest and asserted the right to the presumption of innocence. It announced a progressive system of general taxation "equally distributed among all citizens," including the formerly lightly burdened aristocracy. The representatives of the French people, formed into the National Assembly, declared that "ignorance, forgetfulness or contempt of the rights of man [were] the only causes of public misfortunes and the corruption of Governments." Hopeful, ringing words! Small wonder that at what might be reckoned the first anniversary of the revolutionary movement, France was broadly approving of its upheaval.[6] Could a British friend of liberty be any less so?

Burke had supported Irish Catholics against the British penal laws, the American colonists against King George III, the Corsicans against a French invasion, and the Indian people against Warren Hastings. He had stood with the Jews of St. Eustatius against Admiral Rodney, African captives against the English slave traders, and defaulting London debtors against the laws that nonsensically locked them up where they could earn no money. In the light of this record, many wondered, how could Burke not take sides with the National Assembly against Louis XVI?

Arthur Young, the agricultural reformer with whom Burke had engaged in friendly consultations on the finer points of experimental farming, had traveled widely in France between 1787 and 1790. Having seen for himself the inequities of the French feudal system, Young could see every justification for the revolution. And if the oppressed had too often repaid their oppressors with violence, such evils were "surely . . . more imputable to the tyranny of the master, then to the cruelty of the servant." Not that the English public was sufficiently informed to judge the situation on its merits: "The murder of a seigneur, or a chateau in flames, is recorded in every newspaper; the rank of the person who suffers, attracts notice; but where do we find the register of that seigneur's oppressions of his peasantry, and his exactions of feudal services, from those whose children are dying around him for want of bread?"[7]

Besides, once upon a time, the British themselves had deposed one king, James II, and installed another, William III, along with his queen, Mary II, eldest daughter of James II. This was the Glorious Revolution of 1688, and every good Whig revered it. A "conservative" by twenty-first-century standards of political assortment, Burke was rather a popular reformer in his own day.

What Burke would not reform was the English constitution. He loved it just the way it was, rotten boroughs (one of which he happened to represent in Parliament) and all. In his point-blank resistance to constitutional innovation and parliamentary reform, Burke parted company with Fox, Sheridan, the Duke of Richmond, and Lord John Cavendish, among others who would widen the franchise, redraw the electoral map, increase the frequency of elections, and otherwise adapt the House of Commons to the changing times.

And when, in March 1782, Burke's own party took up the reforming cause, he wrote to stop it. This was the moment when the Rockingham Whigs had at last emerged from opposition to lead the king's government. The marquess himself, the new first lord of the Treasury, pledged to give the reformers a fair hearing.

Burke prepared a speech to close that debate before it could start. He wanted the innovators to understand that England was not theirs to improve. It was nobody's invention but had grown organically, like a tree. Time had sanctioned it.

The "ground of authority" of the constitution, Burke went on, was no party platform, no single election. "Prescription" was rather the fount of legitimacy. By prescription, he meant the validity conferred by the passage of time. Long-settled customs and institutions owed their authority to prescription. Better then, as a rule, "any settled scheme of government against any untried project." It is a constitution, he wrote, "made by what is ten thousand times better than choice, it is made by the peculiar circumstances, occasions, tempers, dispositions, and moral, civil and social habitudes of the people, which disclose themselves only in a long space of time."[8]

Perhaps Burke saw how long were the odds against his success, or the risks he ran in shattering the unity of a party that had finally achieved ministerial office. In any case, he discreetly left his speech unspoken and its text unpublished.[9]

By 1790, however, he was prepared to avow the differences between his view of the Whiggish legacy and that of the Foxite reformers—not least in the nature and significance of the founding Whig revolution.

"What we did was in truth and substance, and in a constitutional light," said Burke, speaking of 1688,

> a revolution not made, but prevented. We took solid securities; we settled doubtful questions; we corrected anomalies in our laws. In the stable parts of our constitution we made no revolution, no; nor any alteration at all. We did not impair the monarchy. Perhaps it might be shown that we strengthened it very considerably.[10]

That the French were up to something very different he perceived almost immediately. On October 5, 1789, protests over the high price of bread in a Parisian market were the prelude to the gathering up of knives, truncheons, pikes, cannon, bayonets, and the movement of those weapons under the motive power of thousands of women and their male auxiliaries, on foot, in a driving rain, to confront the king at Versailles. They invited themselves into the National Assembly, demanding bread. The deputies were happy to pass the soggy intruders on to the king, who was under the protection of a twenty-thousand-man relief force, led by Lafayette. The next morning, a melee at the palace left many dead, including two guards-men, whose heads were paraded on pikes. The unmanned king meekly agreed to return to Paris in a procession now grown to sixty thousand and that included wagonloads of flour from the royal stores as a gesture of goodwill and submission. Louis XVI would never see Versailles again.

"This day," Burke marveled on October 10 in a letter to Richard Jr., "I heard from [French] Laurence, who has sent me papers confirming the portentous state of France—where the elements which compose Human Society seem all to be dissolved, and a world of Monsters to be produced in the place of it—where Mirabeau presides as the Grand Anarch and the late Grand Monarch makes a figure as ridiculous as pitiable."[11]

Before long, Burke was denouncing the "pillage of the Church,"[12] the imprisonment of the king, and the political extinction of the nobility and the clergy. He marked the deepening crisis of public finance (people had simply stopped paying their taxes) and of the new paper currency, the assignat. "It was created by necessity," a French observer remarked of the stopgap money issued to service the unwieldy public debt, "as we throw a wooden bridge over a foaming flood, and as we must pass over the trem-bling bridge, we pass with our eyes shut."[13]

November 4, 1789, was, for Burke and the French and for generations of readers yet unborn, a red-letter day. It was the day when a young French admirer of Burke's wrote to ask his British mentor to offer an opinion—a favorable one, perhaps?—on the French Revolution. And it was the day when Richard Price, an English dissenting minister and moral philoso-pher, gave the revolution his imprimatur with a Whiggish allusion to 1688.

Burke responded to his young French friend, Charles-Jean-François Depont, as he answered Richard Price, each in the pages of his master-piece, *Reflections on the Revolution in France*. It was Depont to whom Burke addressed that magnificent essay and against Price's arguments that he hurled his anathemas. "You may easily believe," wrote Burke to Depont, "that I have had my Eyes turned with great Curiosity to the astonishing scene now displayed in France. It has certainly given rise in my Mind to many Reflexions."[14] They presently became *the Reflections*.

"You may have made a Revolution, but not a Reformation," Burke's letter to Depont, the seedling of *Reflections*, said. "You may have subverted a Monarchy, but not recover'd freedom."[15] Burke, who had not yet resolved his own questions on the French situation, struck a searching, inquisitive tone in his draft to Depont. Apologizing for such argumentative liberties as he might have taken, he remarked on the paradox that "I, whose opinions have so little weight in my own Country, where I have some share in a Publick Trust, should write as if it were possible they should affect one Man, with regard to Affairs in which I have no concern."[16]

British politics had indeed, by 1789, seemed to pass Burke by. The regency affair had cast the leading Whigs, Burke included, even deeper into the outer darkness of opposition in which they had found themselves in 1784. Newspaper caricaturists continued to render him in spectacles, priestly cassock, and biretta. They mocked him for his verbosity and condemned him for his vindictiveness toward Warren Hastings, which they contrasted with the stout defense he had made on behalf of John Powell and Charles Bembridge, the crooked clerks of the Paymaster's Office, in 1783.

A new Burke debuted in caricature late in 1790. No longer a monk, he was a clown running the gauntlet, and suffering the lash, of the leading British friends of the French Revolution. Price, prominent among those progressive thinkers, is sarcastically crying, "Cut the Jesuitical Monster in pieces, cut him to the bone! Oh what a glorious sacrifice to true religion and the rights of Humanity!"

The point of the unsheathed sword of Lady Justice is touching his midsection, while Burke, addressing his erstwhile impeachment colleague and revolutionary fellow traveler Richard Brinsley Sheridan, pleads, "For God's sake, Sherry, be merciful!"[17]

On November 4—the birth date of William III and therefore, by proxy, of the Glorious Revolution—Price delivered a sermon to the Revolution Society in London. Price was no ordinary dissenting Protestant minister, though he regarded his pastoral duties as the most important work of his life, not excluding his contributions in the fields of demographics, public finance, actuarial science, and the theory of probability. With the sponsorship of, among others, Benjamin Franklin, he was elected a fellow of the Royal Society. His bold support of the cause of American independence made him a celebrity in the United States. His opposition to the Test and Corporation Acts, which codified the establishment of the Church of England, was adamant.[18]

"A Discourse on the Love of Our Country," Price's November 4 text, took a more-than-welcoming line toward the French Revolution. A worthier object of love than one's country, Price said, was that of the "citizens of the world," a universal benevolence. And what might promote this constructive reorientation of patriotic devotion? Why, the shucking off of "that gloomy and cruel superstition . . . which has hitherto gone under the name of religion."

Price, as an Englishman, had partaken of the blessings of 1688. He had lived to witness the glories of 1776 and 1789 (and both revolutions, he assured the Revolution Society, were indeed glorious). "And now, methinks," he said, "I see the ardour for liberty catching and spreading; a general amendment beginning in human affairs; the dominion of kings changed for the dominion of laws, and the dominion of priests giving way to the dominion of reason and conscience."

If, as Burke believed, the trouble with French ideas was their communicability, what Price said next threatened a political pandemic.

> Be encouraged all ye friends of freedom, and writers in its defense! The times are auspicious. Your labours have not been in vain. Behold kingdoms, admonished by you, starting from sleep, breaking their fetters, and claiming justice from their oppressors! Behold the light you have struck out, after setting AMERICA free, reflected to FRANCE, and there kindled into a blaze that lays despotism in ashes, and warms and illuminates EUROPE![19]

On February 5, 1790, Fox went on record in the House of Commons to support a reduction in British military spending. "It was now universally known throughout all Europe," he declared, "that a man, by becoming a soldier, did not cease to be a citizen." Louis XVI's troops were laying down their arms in solidarity with the rampaging Parisians.[20]

Burke, fresh from reading Price's sermon, listened uneasily to Fox and to Pitt, too—the prime minister expressed confidence that the French tumults would terminate in "harmony and general order."

How busy the French had been since the previous summer, Burke dryly remarked on February 9 as the debate continued. They had shown themselves "the ablest architects of ruin that had hitherto existed in the world." In just a few months "they had completely pulled down to the ground, their monarchy; their church; their nobility; their law; their revenue; their army; their navy; their arts; and their manufactures."

In the bad old days of Louis XIV (1638–1715), France had set the pace in despotism. Tricked out though the Sun King's governance might have been in manners, gallantry, splendor, and the like, it was "nothing better than a painted and gilded tyranny: in religion, an hard stern intolerance." Nor were Britain's contemporaneous sovereigns, James II and Charles II, impervious to the lure of French absolutism, so flattering was that regime "to the pride of Kings."

Though political fashions had changed, France was once more in the avant-garde. Now it was exporting anarchy, or more exactly, as Burke put it, an "irrational, unprincipled, proscribing, confiscating, plundering, ferocious, bloody, and tyrannical democracy."

In the seventeenth century, intolerance was the exportable French religious doctrine. In the eighteenth century, under the teachings of Voltaire and Rousseau, the French learned atheism, "a foul, unnatural vice, foe to all the dignity and consolation of mankind, which seems in France, for a long time, to have been embodied into a faction, accredited and avowed."* And it, too, was primed for export.[21]

* Gouverneur Morris, American minister to France in the fall of 1789, attended a performance of *Charles neuf,* an anti-Catholic tragedy based on the St. Bartholomew's Day massacre of 1572. In the play, a cardinal incites the king to the murder of his Huguenot subjects, then consecrates the assassins' daggers and absolves the killers of their sins, "all this," as Morris relates in his diary, "with the Solemnities of established Religion. A murmur of Horror runs through the Audience. There are several Observations calculated for the present Times and I think this Piece, if it runs thro the Provinces as it probably will, must give a fatal blow to the Catholic Religion. . . . Surely there never was a Nation which verged faster towards Anarchy. No Law, no Morals, no Religion, no Principles." Morris, *Diary of French Revolution,* 1:295.

For all the world, it had seemed as if French Catholics believed in the mass, in transubstantiation, and in the rest of the body of Catholic dogma. "But," recorded the French journalist Louis-Sébastien Mercier, "the people did not believe in them at all. All the sarcasms of Voltaire against the priests, all the pleasantries of the author of the Pucelle [Voltaire's ribald and profane retelling of the story of Joan of Arc], had reached them." Corruption within the church played its part in subverting religious faith, as did the laity's new freedom to think and write. Most remarkable, however, Mercier concluded, was not the fact of the overthrow of the church, but the speed at which it happened, "with all the circumstances of the most profound contempt or hatred."[22]

Burke, too, was stunned by the speed of events. He mourned France as he might have done an acquaintance who took his own life with a pistol shot. It was over and done with in a trice, and there was no going back. He regretted that Fox had dropped even one word about these terrible goings-on, though he was prepared to ascribe the error to Fox's devotion "to the best of all causes, liberty." That his friend and he should find themselves on opposite sides of the French argument filled him with an "inexpressible" pain, said Burke, and again he quoted Virgil: *"Quae maxima semper censatur nobis, et erit quae maximas semper"*—"which is always thought greatest by us, and will ever be greatest."

"His confidence in Mr. Fox," Burke continued, "was such and so ample, as to be almost implicit." He was not ashamed to admit that he treated Fox's brain as an annex of his own, a marvelous accession that he wouldn't give up. "He wished, on all occasions," Burke went on,

> that his sentiments were understood to be conveyed in Mr. Fox's words; and that he wished, as amongst the greatest benefits he could wish the country, an eminent share of power to that right honourable gentleman; because he knew that, to his great and masterly understanding, he had joined the greatest possible degree of that natural moderation, which is the best corrective of power; that he was the most artless, candid, open, and benevolent disposition: disinterested

in the extreme; of a temper mild and placable, even to a fault; without
one drop of gall in his whole constitution.[23]

Burke, in private, had had some sharp words about Fox's disengagement
from the impeachment. Sheridan, too, who had alienated Burke during
the regency crisis, was neglecting his Hastings duties—in March, Burke
had had to appeal to the playwright's wife to secure his presence at an
important meeting of the prosecution managers.[24]

Fox, Burke said, was his "best friend," and he only reluctantly marked
their disagreement on the French Revolution. However, he wanted the
House to know that no friendship would sway him from his determination to bar the importation of French democracy. In that essential service,
he would, if he had to, "abandon his best friends and join with his worst
enemies." He would resist all such radical innovation, "so distant from all
principles of true and safe reformation; a spirit well calculated to overturn
states, but perfectly unfit to amend them."[25]

Fox returned Burke's panegyric. He had "learnt more from his right
honourable friend than from all the men with whom he had ever conversed." No more than Burke did Fox support "any dangerous innovation to our excellent constitution," though he "would not run the length
of declaring, that he was an enemy to every species of innovation. That
constitution, which we all revered, owed its perfection to innovation; for,
however admirable the theory, experience was the true test of its order
and beauty."

Burke and he, said Fox, "could never differ in their principles, however they might differ in their application." Fox deplored "the scenes of
bloodshed and tyranny" in France, but better those disturbances than
the despotic order of Louis XVI that had heretofore suppressed them.
It would prove a boon on both sides of the Channel that France had
"regained her freedom."[26]

There were no such emollient words from Sheridan, who charged that
Burke had "come forward as the advocate of despotism." It was forgiv-
able that Fox might fall into error of judgment. It was too much to bear
when Sheridan topped off the same mistake with an absurd personal

insult. Burke announced to the House that Sheridan and he "were sep-arated in politics."*

It could not have gone unnoticed that, as one Whig quarreled with another, William Pitt paid Burke a most handsome compliment. "The sentiments that the Rt. Hon. Gentleman had that day professed concerning the Constitution, had inspired him with a most sincere and lasting gratitude," said the prime minister.

LISTENING TO BURKE ON FEBRUARY 9, 1790, FOX WAS ASTONISHED "AT such a mixture of superior Sense & Absurdity."[27] He found little sense and much absurdity in Burke's performance three weeks later in debate over the proposed repeal of the hundred-year-old laws that reserved British civil offices and degrees from the universities of Oxford and Cambridge for conforming members of the Church of England.

The civil disabilities under which English dissenting Protestants labored were codified in the Corporation Act of 1661 and the Test Act of 1673. Like the Irish Catholic penal laws, the dissenting Protestant laws were less for-midable in everyday life than they were on paper, but the nonconformists resented them along with the petty everyday fibs that they inveigled from the lips of their honest victims.

Might, therefore, the congregants of three dissenting congregations in the city of Bristol depend on their old friend, Edmund Burke, to support a motion to repeal parts of those noxious laws, which were set to be intro-duced on Friday, May 8, 1789? Of course, Burke replied at once, if his health allowed. "If I should find myself able to attend I shall certainly Vote for the Bill, in conformity with my known principles."[28] In the event, Burke's health did not allow, but Fox spoke long and eloquently in support of the repeal motion, which failed by a vote of 102–122.[29] "I hear that Fox dis-tinguished himself," Burke reported to his Bristol correspondent, Richard Bright, "as he does on all occasions."[30]

---

* "The attempted reconciliation of the principal protagonists was, according to reports reaching the Duchess of Devonshire, 'perfectly irish, for they are now on worse terms than ever.'" Mitchell, *Fox and Disintegration*, 156.

Ten months later Fox moved his own motion to repeal of the laws by which the holders of offices of trust under the crown must receive the sacrament of communion according to the rites of the Church of England. Nothing about those controversial laws had changed. What was new was the French Revolution and the warmth with which the leading dissenters, Richard Price and Joseph Priestly among them, had cheered it on.

Before the Bastille and the women's march on Versailles, Burke had assured Bright, "There are no Men on Earth to whom I have been more attached, and with a more sincere Esteem and Affection, than to some amongst the Dissenters."[*][31] Then Price preached; the women, cannons in tow, marched; and Burke, on February 9, made his anti-revolutionary declaration. Would Burke, "in conformity with his known principles," now join Fox in supporting the repeal of the Test and Corporation Acts?

Yes, many assumed, true to his principles, Burke would indeed join Fox in relieving the disabilities of the Dissenters, but Fox knew his friend better. Moving his motion, he anticipated Burke's arguments against risking reform in a time of revolutionary ferment.

France's only bearing on the matter, Fox therefore objected, was by way of inverse example. He invited the House to recall the Edict of Nantes in 1598, Henry IV's enlightened, freedom-bestowing gift of toleration to the previously proscribed French Protestants. And recall, especially, Louis XIV's revocation of that measure in 1685. "By that rash measure," said Fox,

> liberality and toleration were thrown away; the arts and manufactures were driven into other countries, to flourish in a more genial soil and under a milder form of government. This should serve as a caution to the church of England. Persecution might prevail for a time, but it generally terminated in the punishment of its abettors.

---

* Relations between the Whigs and the Dissenters had cooled considerably since 1784 when, as both Fox and Burke complained, the nonconforming Protestants had voted en masse to oust the coalition and install William Pitt; Fox congratulated himself on March 2 for "having been selected by men who had rather acted as his enemies than friends, to fight their battles." C., 5:471; Fox, *Speeches*, 4:75.

Fox now turned to Richard Price, whose sermon, spoken from the pulpit of the Old Jewry Church on the centenary of the Glorious Revolution, "had delivered many noble sentiments, worthy of an enlightened philosopher." The trouble, said Fox, lay not in Price's sentiments but in the pulpit itself. Neither pulpit, nor altar, nor sacramental table was a fit place for political discourse—"religion and politics ought ever to be kept separate."[32]

Burke countered that the time, and the Dissenters, had changed. Dr. Priestly, scientist and Unitarian minister, with whom Burke had formerly been on the friendliest of terms, was now looking forward to the destruction of the Church of England. It was coming—the fulminating priests were bringing it on themselves—"perhaps as suddenly, as unexpectedly, and as completely, as the overthrow of the late arbitrary Government of France."[33]

Burke produced a letter from his pocket from a Mr. Fletcher, a Dissenter, which reported on the shocking things that Fletcher had recently heard at a meeting of Dissenting ministers at Bolton, in Lancashire. Some of the more radical participants were angling for the repeal, not only of the Corporation and Test Acts, but also of tithes and liturgy. If they could, they would disestablish the Church of England.

Burke said he wished that Fox had moved his motion ten years earlier, when he could have supported it (though, as we have seen, Burke professed to stand ready to vote for repeal in March 1789). "But at present," he said, "if the Test and Corporation Acts were repealed, some other Test ought to be substituted." Indeed, he had drafted one himself.* "He professed himself ready to grant relief from oppression to all men, but unwilling to grant power."[34]

Even so, Burke would not vote against Fox's motion. He would yield to

---

* Burke's proposed substitute read, in part: "I A.B. do in the presence of God, sincerely profess and believe that a religious establishment in this state is not contrary to the law of God, or disagreeable to the law of Nature or to the true principles of the Christian religion, or that it is noxious to the community; and I do sincerely promise and engage, before God, that I never will . . . attempt, or abet others in any attempt to subvert the constitution of the church of England." Far better this, said Burke, than the Sacramental Test, the sacrament being "too solemn an act for prostitution." W&S, 4:317.

the House, though "he did not think this a fit moment for such a Motion to be put."

Fox was unmollified. What he had heard from Burke had "filled him with grief and shame," but there was consolation, on the one hand, in the knowledge that he, Fox, had fashioned his arguments with fidelity to the principles that his mentor had taught him.

Burke, on the other hand, had

> taken pamphlets, private letters, anecdotes, conjectures, suspicions, and invectives, for the materials of his speech; which he had worked up with all the charms of fancy and the embellishments of oratory, for which his right honourable friend was so eminently distinguished.

Fox closed not by reproaching his friend but by praising him to the skies, much as Burke had eulogized Fox three weeks earlier. To what could one ascribe Burke's strange lapse from his former principles? Why, to his very "benevolence and mercy." The miseries that the French political upheaval had dragged in its wake were normal revolutionary growing pains.

"The imagination of his right honourable friend," Fox continued,

> had eagerly caught hold of such objects, and, in contemplating the ruin of the government, the desolation of the church, the misery of the beggared ecclesiastics, and the general distresses of the inhabitants, he had actually lost the energy of his natural judgment, through the exquisite acuteness of his feelings; otherwise, a person of his great good sense could never have been so led astray into enmity against the just cause of the dissenters, as a body, merely because Dr. Priestly, Mr. Palmer, and Mr. Robinson* happened to differ from him in their speculative opinions.[35]

Burke had mentioned the Gordon Riots of 1780 as a cautionary tale in mob violence. To Fox, it seemed that he had insinuated an analogy

---

* Samuel Palmer (1741–1813) was the author of *The Protestant Catechism*; Robert Robinson (1735–90) was the author of *Political Catechism*. Burke condemned both volumes. C., 4:83.

between the decidedly non-mobbish dissenters of 1790 and the drunken firebrands of 1780. If a likeness was to be drawn, Fox retorted, it was between the bigoted anti-Catholics of 1780 and the prejudiced anti-nonconformists of 1790.

But again, Fox fell back on panegyric. "He remembered with pleasure," he said, "the conduct of [Burke] upon that occasion." Burke, it will be recalled, had waded into the crowd to debate all comers; in a sense, he had risked his life for the sake of Catholic emancipation. "The mob then," said Fox, "were illiberally insisting on a repeal of a good law; the members of the established church were now as illiberally objecting to the repeal of a bad law."

AT THE CLOSE OF HIS SPEECH OF FEBRUARY 9, BURKE DECLARED HIMSELF "weak and weary" and "little disposed to controversies."[36] He was soon to regain strength and zeal. As for controversy, he was born to contend and could hardly stop, even if he wanted to. His greatest contentious work, his bequest to the ages, *Reflections on the Revolution in France*, lay just ahead of him.

The first thing to be said about the book is that its author was deeply informed—even such critics as James Mackintosh admitted it.* Characteristically, Burke gathered up everything there was to read about France, from the journals of the National Assembly to the private correspondence he cultivated with knowledgeable Frenchmen to newspaper reports and official documents. Fox, just as characteristically, conducted little research. It is not quite true that the downfall of Louis XVI was enough to win him over, but it set him on the pro-revolutionary course from which he never veered far.

In form, *Reflections* was a 356-page letter. "Dear Sir," Burke began, nom-

---

* Mackintosh, the author of *Vindiciae Gallicae: A Defense of the French Revolution*, published in 1791, subsequently changed his mind about the revolution and *Reflections*. Visiting Burke at Beaconsfield in 1796, Mackintosh found him "minutely and accurately informed, to a wonderful exactness, with respect to every fact relative to the French Revolution." He remembered "the astonishing effusions" of Burke's conversation, "the sublimest images mingled with the most wretched of puns." Burke, *Reflections*, 49; Finlay, "Mackintosh, Sir James."

inally addressing Charles-Jean-François Depont. It was not only a standard epistolary salutation but also (minus the "Dear") the convention by which, in the House of Commons, a member formally addressed his remarks to the speaker.

There are no chapters, sections, headlines, or other devices to segment *Reflections* by theme or subject; the composition is "loose," as the author himself admitted. It reads like one of Burke's parliamentary stemwinders. To the reader is left the pleasure of following Burke's mind as it sifts facts, assigns causations, weighs historical analogies, forms distinctions, and identifies cross-Channel differences in society, politics, and religion.

Depont had fished for Burke's approval of the Revolution—in vain! "But am I so unreasonable as to see nothing at all that deserves commendation in the indefatigable labours of this [national] assembly]?" Burke does finally get around to asking four paragraphs from the end. His answer might be imagined: "The improvements of the national assembly are superficial, their errors, fundamental."

The nature of man divided Burke and Price most fundamentally. Believing that he was perfectible, Price was anxious to get on with the work of deposing kings, breaking chalices, and reforming parliaments. Burke, proceeding from the contrary assumption, defended the institutions, habits, customs, and prejudices that saved us sinners from ourselves.

The book's first focus is properly on England, whose internal enemies Burke is writing to defeat. He attacks Price with Hastings-grade invective, denouncing, as he goes, the people's supposed right to cashier their governors or "to form a government for ourselves." As to the right to revolt against a despot, Burke advises extreme caution:

> Times and occasions, and provocations, will teach their own lessons. The wise will determine from the gravity of the case; the irritable from sensibility to oppression; the high-minded from disdain and indignation at abusive power in unworthy hands; the brave and bold from the love of honourable danger in a generous cause: but, with or

without right, a revolution will be the very last resource of the thinking and the good.

To forestall their own quite unnecessary revolution, Burke continues,
the French might have mended their ancient and excellent constitution.
Instead, they overfilled a new national assembly with country lawyers, "the
fomentors and conductors of the petty war of village vexation. . . . Who
could flatter himself that these men, suddenly, and, as it were, by enchant-
ment, snatched from the humblest rank of subordination, would not be
intoxicated with their unprepared greatness?" Naturally, the revolution
was doomed.[37]

Man, Burke wrote, is a "religious animal," and atheism is abhorrent to
him, not only to his reason but also to his instincts. In Britain, church
and state were one, to the advantage of both. An atheistic officeholder—in
England, for the time being, a contradiction in terms—would govern only
for the moment, unlike the godly politician who, with his eye on immortality, would strive for "a permanent fame and glory."[38]

Burke compared contemporary England with the new France. Observe,
on one side of the Channel, a national church rich in wealth and status; on
the other, a church stripped of both. Since, to Burke's mind, religion was
the very basis of civil order, irreligion would serve French society no better
than country lawyers had served the National Assembly.

As to the basis of French irreligion, Burke pointed his finger at the *phi-
losophes*, the "political men of letters," who had conceived and carried out
"something like a regular plan for the destruction of the Christian religion." Richard Jr. added the observation that the "atheistical fathers have a
bigotry all their own; and they have learnt to talk against monks with the
spirit of a monk."[39]

Epigrams ornament *Reflections*; open the book almost at random to
find one. Thus, on the wisdom of moderate reform (and the trap of revolutionary action): "I cannot conceive how any man can have brought
himself to that pitch of presumption, to consider his country as nothing
but carte blanche, upon which he may scribble whatever he pleases. . . . A

disposition to preserve, and an ability to improve, taken together, would be my standard of a statesman. Every thing else is vulgar in the conception, perilous in the execution."

Or on the costly temptation to blame society's ills on "kings, priests, magistrates," rather than on the human propensity for sin: "A certain quantum of power must always exist in the community, in some hands, and under some appellation. Wise men will apply their remedies to vices, not to names, to the causes of evil which are permanent, not to the occasional organs by which they act, and the transitory modes in which they appear."⁴⁰

On full display in these pages is the encyclopedic range of Burke's learning. Classical allusions, Latin tags, and lines of English poetry jostle with deeply informed analyses of political, religious, and economic affairs. Burke had not objected to the American colonists' experiments with paper money, but he reprobated the French assignat.

What stood behind the new French banknotes was the confiscated real estate of the Catholic Church. A "dishonest, perfidious and cruel" confiscation, the stolen collateral conferred no honest value on the new paper money.

Burke examined the volatile trading patterns of the Church properties which the revolutionary government had put up for sale. Why such violent swings in quoted value? He ascribed them to the superabundance of new currency. The assignats had "volatized"* the real estate market, which "assumes an unnatural and monstrous activity." The "worst and most pernicious part of the evil of a paper circulation [was] the greatest possible uncertainty in its value."⁴¹

Burke rather glossed over the ancien régime's money troubles. He failed to mark the default of August 1788 and uncritically credited the overly optimistic fiscal forecasts of his friend, the king's finance minister, Jacques Necker.⁴²

A friend and correspondent of Adam Smith, Burke was usually to be found contending on the side of free markets and sound money. He seemed

---

* The word *volatized* is unmentioned in Johnson's *Dictionary*. If a Burke coinage, it makes one more contribution by the political philosopher to the budding field of economics.

to see no paradox in his defense of an economic and aristocratic system that, in its power to disrupt the established social, economic, and political order, was arguably more revolutionary than Robespierre. Some twenty years earlier a young nobleman had asked Dr. Johnson what had become "of the gallantry and military spirit" of the old English aristocracy. "Why, my Lord, I'll tell you what is become of it," Johnson replied; "it is gone into the city to look for a fortune."[43]

As perfectible man needed no religion or king, the new thinking had it, neither did he require gold. The assignat would do in place of the expensive, unwieldly, and now ostensibly obsolete monetary metal. Indeed, according to cleric and politician Jean-Baptiste Royer, the assignat would presently render gold worthless.[44]

Burke, correctly taking the opposite side of the argument, identified coercion as the essential element of the French monetary system. The assignat was legal tender; the creditor had no choice but to accept it in payment for a debt.

The British banknote, by contrast, was not money but the promise to pay money, the pound being defined as a weight of gold (113 grains to be exact). It was an Englishman's right to demand the gold in exchange for the paper representation of gold.

"Not one shilling of paper-money of any description is received but of choice," Burke wrote.

> The whole had its origin in cash [gold] actually deposited; and it is convertible, at pleasure, in an instant, and without the smallest loss, into cash again. Our paper is of value in commerce, because in law it is of none. It is powerful on [the Exchange] because in Westminster-hall it is impotent. In payment for a debt of twenty shillings, a creditor may refuse all the paper of the bank of England. Nor is there among us a single public security, of any quality or nature whatsoever, that is enforced by authority.[45]

The French recoiled at comparisons between their assignats and the paper money of John Law, the error-plagued genius of the Mississippi

Bubble of 1719–20. Burke rather contended that it was an injustice "to that great mother fraud, to compare it with their degenerate imitation." Law, at least, aimed for an increase in French commerce rather than of "feeding France with its own substance."

If Burke idealized the operation of the British gold standard and the prerevolutionary French church, a great inflation and the guillotine did presently make their appearance in France. Sound money would have forestalled the first evil, while Christian charity could have mitigated the second.

THE WOMEN'S MARCH ON VERSAILLES OF OCTOBER 5–6, 1789, THE BLOOD-shed in the palace, and the intruders' attempt on the life of the queen, Marie Antoinette, moved Burke to write the most quoted passages in *Reflections*. In his telling, the royals fled a palace "swimming in blood, polluted by massacre and strewed with scattered limbs and mutilated carcasses." It was nothing so bad, English friends of the revolution protested, though *The Times*, "on an accurate return," counted 107 dead on both sides.[46]

Burke had sent his manuscript to Philip Francis for comment. As "Junius," twenty years earlier, Francis's style had been the envy of literary London, and he had previously edited some of Burke's writing. Nor was he afraid to wield a corrective pencil on the master's prose. "I am the only friend," as Francis was bold enough to tell Burke, "and many there are, who ever ventures to contradict you or oppose you, face to face, on Subjects of this nature."

Francis warned against going forward with publication of the manuscript. It was "very loosely put together." In places, it lacked the gravity appropriate to the author and the topic. And was Burke sure he wanted to get into a pamphlet war with Dr. Price? "Remember," Francis cautioned, "this is one of the most singular, that it may be the most distinguished, and ought to be one of the most deliberate acts of your life."[47]

Francis especially marked, as innumerable other contemporaries and generations of future readers would do, Burke's paean to Marie Antoinette. He had caught a glimpse of the then-dauphiness some sixteen years earlier, "and surely," the readers of *Reflections* were informed, "never alighted on this orb, which she hardly seemed to touch, a more delightful vision. I saw her just above the horizon, decorating and cheering the elevated sphere she just began to move in,—glittering like the morning-star, full of life, and splendor, and joy. Oh! What a revolution! And what a heart must I have, to contemplate without emotion that elevation and that fall!"[48]

Far from emotionless, Burke wept as he wrote those words,[49] and Marie Antoinette, subsequently reading them in a French translation supplied by John Wilkes's daughter, Polly, broke into sobs.[50]

"Little did I dream," the famous passage continued,

> that I should have lived to see such disasters fallen upon her in a nation of gallant men, in a nation of men of honour and of cavaliers. I thought ten thousand swords must have leaped from their scabbards to avenge even a look that threatened her with insult.—But the age of chivalry is gone.—That of sophisters, oeconomists, and calculators has succeeded; and the glory of Europe is extinguished forever.

"Pure Foppery" was Francis's verdict. "If she be a perfect female character you ought to take your ground upon her virtues," but Burke had said nothing of them. No one believed she possessed them, "which you know."

Francis left Burke with the prediction that "the mischief you are going to do to yourself, is, to my apprehension, palpable. It is visible. It will be audible. I snuff it in the wind. I taste it already."[51]

Returning home late on February 19 from a supper and ball hosted by the Prince of Wales, Burke found Francis's letter. He read it and lay awake all night. In his reply next day, he yielded no point, and neither did Richard Jr. who, writing under his own name and enclosing his letter in Edmund's, ordered Francis to cease from distracting his father from "the many and great labours he has on hand, by any further written communications of this kind."

"Are you so little conversant with my father," Richard closed, "or so inslaved by the cant of those, who call themselves his friends only to injure *themselves* through time, as to feel no deference for his judgment, or to mistake the warmth of his manner for the heat of his mind? Do I not know my father at this time of day? I tell you, his folly is wiser than the wisdom of the common herd of able men."[52]

Meanwhile the Hastings trial dragged on. The managers chafed under a lack of witnesses[53] and under rules of evidence that excluded much of the incriminating material they had hoped to bring forward.[54] Gouverneur Morris, the wryly observant American diplomat who was on hand to watch the session of April 29, 1790, conveys a sense of the painfully slow tempo of the proceedings, still five years away from a verdict.

> We wait till past two before the Lords come down and then, after a Decision against the Managers upon a former Question, much Time is consumed in Complaints against that Decision. A Witness being then called up and a Question proposed to him, an Objection is raised by the Counsel as being within the Decision just delivered. A long Argument on this Subject from the Managers, which the Counsel very properly reply to with their Silence, and the Opinion of the Lords being clear the Question is given up without a formal Declaration of that Opinion. Shortly after another question is proposed to the Witness, which is objected to. And hereupon arises a serious Argument.

Burke and Fox spoke for the manager, he continued. "The former," Morris judged,

> has Quickness and Genius but he is vague, loose, desultory and confused. . . . Mr. Fox has not the needful self-possession to make a Great Speaker. But he is acute and discerns well. He does not sufficiently convey to others the Distinctions which he feels. His Mind appears like a clouded Sun, and this I believe results from the Life he leads. Temperance, Application and the Possession of Competence, with Moderation to enjoy it, would render him very great, if happily his faculties be not at that Point where a Continuation of former Habits becomes necessary to keep them alive.[55]

ON JULY 14, 1790, THE FIRST ANNIVERSARY OF THE FALL OF THE BASTILLE, 652 well-wishers of the revolution, including Dr. Price but excluding Charles Fox, gathered for a celebratory dinner at London's Crown and Anchor Tavern.

Price raised a toast to "an Alliance between France and Great Britain, for perpetuating peace, and making the world happy." Sheridan, also on hand, moved "that this meeting do sincerely rejoice in the establishment of the Revolution in France, and at the cordiality which subsists between the two nations."[56]

At the end of August, *The Times* playfully speculated on how Burke was passing his summer. No doubt the literary farmer was engaged in experimental animal husbandry at Beaconsfield. "He sits upon a plough tail, and translates Virgil's Bucolics to the Farmers," the paper imagined—"but they do not understand the gentleman." In fact, the gentleman was racing *Reflections* to the press.[57]

It went on sale on November 1, three weeks before the opening of Parliament, but a year after Dr. Price had said his provoking piece. By year end, 17,500 copies, at the fancy price of five shillings, were in print. Quotable excerpts filled newspaper columns. The Burkes had a bestseller on their hands.

Just as Francis predicted, the Marie Antoinette material sparked discussion, controversy, and raillery. It took the caricaturist William Holland just twenty-four hours to produce a sketch of Burke, a cherub hovering over his bewigged head, kneeling before a sublime Antoinette; his hands are clasped in adoration while the cherub's torch heats Burke's amorous brain. Two weeks later Burke reappeared in shop windows as Quixote returning to Antoinette after a prolonged absence (sixteen years, in fact, exactly corresponding to Burke's first sighting of the dauphiness); a thought bubble reveals his regrets for the years that he wasted in the company of his visibly decrepit aged wife, Jane, who weeps in the background.[58]

Critical reaction to the book divided along party lines, though not as those lines had previously been drawn. The Whig press, which like most of the Whig party had welcomed the French Revolution, condemned Burke as an apostate and his book as a Tory apologia. Conducting an imaginary chemical analysis of the *Reflections*, the *Gazetteer* anticipated Thomas Paine, author of the forthcoming *Rights of Man*, by finding elements of despotism, priestcraft, and other such wicked substances in Burke's pages.[59] "Once and for all," said Francis, who acknowledged the book's "rich[ness] and "flavour" while rejecting its anti-revolutionary thesis, "I wish you would let me teach you to write English."[60]

The Times, which supported the government and opposed the revolution, found it easy to praise *Reflections*, notwithstanding its author's many prior offenses against the paper's editorial line: "this work may be truly said to redeem them all."[61] Edward Gibbon likewise approved: "I admire his eloquence, I approve his politics, I adore his chivalry and I can even forgive him his superstition." Fanny Burney, who had taken Hastings's side in the impeachment, was in raptures, calling *Reflections* "the noblest, deepest, most animated, and exalted work that I think I have ever read."[62]

Sir Gilbert Elliot, in a single winding, luxuriant sentence, reminded Burke of all that he had achieved: "Every Scholar, and every man who without deserving that name, has any relish for mental pleasures, and finds any gratification in works of genius, whether his taste may point particularly to Letters, to composition and Eloquence, to Philosophy or Politicks whoever in short is delighted with the view of Excellence, abstracting even from the great subjects and still greater objects of the work, must make this book his companion and his constant resource."[63]

In February, George III sought out Burke at a court levee (rather than, as was customary, waiting for Burke to appear before him in his turn) to thank the author for calling the attention of the readers of *Reflections* to the importance of the idea of the gentleman. The next day His Majesty, regretting that he had not said more, let it be known how grateful he was to the former chronic opposition thorn in his side. "Here," Jane Burke reported to William Burke, "we are in high fame."[64]

Dr. Price did not soak up Burke's time in a pamphlet war, as Francis had feared, but dozens of other dissenters, democrats, republicans, and radicals took up their pens. Thomas Paine, the most powerful and successful of these challengers, was the oil to Burke's water. "When we survey the wretched condition of man under the monarchical and hereditary systems of Government," Paine summed up his argument, "dragged from his home by one power, or driven by another, and impoverished by taxes more than by enemies, it becomes evident that those systems are bad, and that a general revolution in the principle and construction of Government is necessary."[65]

Rights of Man had been in print for just a month when members of the Unitarian Society thronged the Kings Head Tavern, on April 14, to toast the book and the man who made it possible. A participant in the evening's festivities, Henry Wisemore, wrote to Burke to send him backhanded thanks. "If you had not written," said Wisemore, "we should not have been blessed with Payne's Magnificent answer to you, which is a book that must open the eyes of the People of England." If, Wisemore advised, Burke should care to renounce his former "treason against liberty" and join the celebration of the glorious revolution in France scheduled for next July 14, he should reserve his seat now, as the stewards were expecting a big crowd.[66]

Predicting trouble, a Cassandra requires validation, and the sooner it happens the better for the reputation of the gloomy prophet. It enhanced neither the sales of *Reflections* nor the predictive standing of Edmund Burke that the news from France took a mild turn in 1791. No sign yet of war, regicide, the guillotine, the Committee of Public Safety, hyperinflation, the Terror, or Napoleon. Besides, the opposition was busy with other crises. Russia's occupation of the fortress of Oczakov in Crimea threatened to upset the international balance of power and therefore the peace of Europe, the government contended. To hold a belligerent Russia at bay, Pitt applied to the Commons for money with which to rearm. The opposition denied that British interests were involved and argued against the unnecessary public expense. Far from preventing a war, Fox accused Pitt of trying to start one.

The balance of power was once a cause for which he strongly advocated, Fox told the House of Commons on April 15, 1791. But now that France had a government "from which neither insult nor injustice was to be dreaded by her neighbours, he was extremely indifferent to the balance of power,"[67] and he would so remain until some other nation came along to make trouble.

Fox had issued no public comment on *Reflections*; privately he regretted its existence.[68] He judged, as well, that it was better not to risk intra-Whig dissension by provoking its volatile author.

Forgetting himself on the floor of the House, Fox now did just that. Comparing the new France with the old one, he contended that even the enemies of the principles of the revolution had "reason to rejoice in its effects." Not stopping there, "he praised the new government of France, in its internal relation, as good, because it aimed to make those who were subject to it happy." Some held a different opinion, Fox acknowledged, but "he for one admired the new constitution of France, considered altogether, *as the most stupendous and glorious edifice of liberty which had ever been erected on the foundation of human integrity in any time or country.*"

"As soon as Mr. Fox sat down," records the parliamentary record, "Mr. Burke rose, in much visible emotion, but the cry of 'Question!' being general, he unwillingly gave way."[69]

Along with his accession of fame, Burke had earned his quotient of infamy. The hostility was palpable within his own party, even among its grandest and richest people (who might have been expected to warm to Burke's stout defense of property rights), never mind within the councils of the Unitarian Society. *"How the Devil could your friend Burke publish such a Farrago of Nonsense?"* the Prince of Wales inquired of Lord Inchiquin at around the time *Reflections* appeared.[70]

In some respects then, as Burke's young admirer William Windham remarked, Burke was "a man decried, persecuted and proscribed; not much being valued, even by his own party, and by half the nation considered as little better than an ingenious madman."[71]

To a new generation of backbenchers, who valued brevity more than eloquence, Burke seemed a relic. When he rose to speak, they coughed, and if they couldn't silence him, they fled. Perhaps they stayed to listen, even to enjoy, that portion of a speech of Burke's on March 1 in which the defender of Catholic civil liberties raised a "hearty laugh" by contending that the pope, politically speaking, "was as dead as Julius Caesar" (and continuing in a kind of roll call of the emperors of Rome, considering each as a pope). But the House might have thinned, as Burke, "at some length, entered into the history of past ages, and the progressive state of different governments, down to the present."[72]

"How finely he has spoken!" Fanny Burney exclaimed of a virtuosic performance of Burke's at the Hastings trial the year before—"with what fullness of intelligence, and what fervour!" With this, Windham eagerly agreed. "Yet,—so much, so long!" she added.

"True, Windham responded ingenuously, yet concerned—'What a pity he can never stop.'"[73]

On April 21, Burke announced plans to take up the question of the French Revolution at some undetermined future date. Denied the opportunity to respond to Fox's pro-revolutionary ardor on April 15, he looked forward to his next opening.

May 6 proved the momentous date; the occasion was a bill in the House of Commons concerning the government of Quebec. The scheduled business was a clause-by-clause consideration of the text of the legislation. The actual business, well tipped to all, was the likely explosive airing of differences between Fox and Burke over the great disturbances some three thousand miles east of the Canadian province.

Burke would tax the House with his loquacity. He now risked exasperating it with an overly large conception of the relevance of French politics to North American colonial management. The press, however, knowing its Burke and its Fox, correctly reckoned that no shouted calls of "Order" would silence either the author of *Reflections on the Revolution in France* or his dearest friend and, on this matter, ablest adversary. Rarely do newspaper publishers reallocate space to news coverage at the expense of precious advertising, but the looming great debate was one of those rare occasions in London journalism.[74]

No sooner had the chairman of the Committee of the Whole House announced that "the clauses of the Bill be read paragraph by paragraph" than Burke rose to correct him. Parliament must take an enlarged view of the situation, he said. Was Canada to be governed by the "law of nations or the Rights of Man?"

Burke said a few mildly approving words about the new American constitution. He pivoted to the English one, then to the French. "It was," he said of the latter, "in all its parts abominably bad, vicious and impracticable; it could not have been grafted on the English Constitution. It was as distant from it as Heaven from Earth, as Vice is from Virtue, and Wisdom from Folly."

As Burke described the situation of Louis XVI, who was then under house arrest by "the Chief Jailer of Paris, M. de la Fayette," he was called to order by a fellow member of the opposition, William Baker. Thinking, perhaps, of William Pitt, Baker alleged that Burke was "the unwitting tool of those who wished to sow the seeds of dissension among Friends." To this, Fox added the charge that Burke was claiming a right "to abuse the Government of every country as much as he pleased and in as gross terms as he thought proper, whether it had any reference or not to the point."*[75]

Burke was again called to order by a fellow Whig. Cries of "Order!—Order!" and "Go on!—Go on!" interrupted him. Resuming, Burke said that he wouldn't have had to say anything if the French had minded their own business, but they were as committed to proselytizing as Louis XIV was to conquering.[76]

Now a colleague from the Hastings impeachment, John Anstruther, called Burke to order. If he really believed that the constitution was in danger, said Anstruther, he should bring forward a measure to save it, not stymie debate on the Quebec Bill.

Burke said he would abide by the judgment of the House; was he out of order? He said he felt ill-used by his former friends. It was unfortunate to be "hunted by one party, and sometimes by another." When the shouting abated, he promised to "proceed in the account he was going to give of the

---

* "The friends of Burke," according to the London *World* of April 25, "who really wish him well, appear to consider him as a coal that flies out of the fire upon a carpet. The moment he rises to speak in the House, somebody gets up and—*puts him out.*"

horrible and nefarious consequences flowing from the French Idea of the Rights of Man."

Lord Sheffield moved that Burke was out of order. Fox seconded it; Pitt refused to support it.[77]

Now Fox spoke. He said that Burke had come looking for a quarrel, evidently to confirm the obvious untruth that he, Fox, had republican designs on the English constitution. Burke and he differed on the French Revolution, but what of it? To the House, in the business at hand, it was a matter of "theoretical contemplation" only. He would never recant his first opinion of the French Revolution, that it was "one of the most glorious events in the history of mankind." An arbitrary government was toppled, and a new one, dedicated to the happiness of the people, was rising in its place. None of this touched the English constitution.[78]

If the House decided to allow Burke to proceed on his tangent, Fox continued, he would leave until relevant debate resumed.* So saying, he said he intended no disrespect to Burke, whom he once again credited with teaching him all he knew about politics. Among these lessons was one, during the American crisis, that the "revolt of a whole people must have been provoked." With that great principle in mind, said Fox, he could not help but exult in a new French constitution founded on the rights of man, just as—yes—the English constitution was founded. "To deny it, was neither more nor less than to libel the British constitution; and no book his right honourable friend could cite, no words he might deliver in debate, however ingenious, eloquent and able—as all his writings and all his speeches undoubtedly were—could induce him to change or abandon that opinion; he differed upon that subject with his right honourable friend *toto caelo*."[79]

"Mr. Burke," recorded a witness, "commenced his reply in a grave and governed tone of voice." He said that Fox knew full well what he was going

* Having promised to walk out if Burke continued in the same irrelevant vein, Fox got up from his seat and—as Burke resumed speaking—stepped outside for a light refreshment. Some twenty or thirty of Fox's devoted followers mistook that insignificant errand for a political statement, and they followed their leader out of the hall. The misunderstanding did not help to sweeten Burke's temper. Fox, *Speeches*, 4:220.

to say. (The two of them had gone over it together at Fox's home on April 21 before walking to the House together.) There was no surprise except in the perfidy of Fox's attempt to impugn and misrepresent his entire political career. Such was the gratitude, said Burke, of one "whom he always considered his warmest friend; but who after an intimacy of more than twenty-two years, had at last thought proper, without the least provocation, to commence a personal attack on him."[80]

Had he not been interrupted, said Burke, he would have proved why those purportedly glorious events across the Channel were the prelude to disaster, immediately in France and eventually in Britain.

Turning again to Fox, he charged him with ripping up "the whole course and tenour of his public and private life." Again he was called to order, now for questioning the motives of a fellow member of Parliament. Differ though they had at times, said Burke, Fox and he had never let even one difference for one moment interrupt their friendship.

"It certainly was indiscreet at his time of life to provoke enemies, or give his friends occasion to desert him," Burke went on, but if that were the cost of his duty—of exclaiming, with his last breath, "Fly from the French constitution!"—so be it.

"Mr. Fox whispered that there was no loss of friendship," the Parliamentary History records. "Mr. Burke replied, Yes, there was—he knew the price of his conduct—he had done his duty at the price of his friend—their friendship was at an end."

Perfection must be left to God, Burke closed, "while to us poor, weak, incapable mortals, there was no rule of conduct so safe as experience."[81]

Fox was in tears, and minutes passed before he continued. Even then "frequent effusions of tears, choaked and embarrassed his utterance for a great part of his speech."[82] At one point, Fox protested against the insults that, he said, Burke had just hurled at him. Burke, seated—he, too, by some accounts, had wept—responded in a voice loud enough to be heard that he had no recollection of insulting Fox.

"My right honourable friend," answered Fox, "does not recall the epithets: they are out of his mind: then they are completely and for ever out of mine. I cannot cherish a recollection so painful, and, from this moment, they are obliterated and forgotten."[83]

It enraged Burke that Fox would quote his own words against him to prove a purely fictitious inconsistency in Burke's long-held opinions. Thus in 1780, Fox had pointed out, Burke joined the majority of the House in subscribing to Dunning's famous 1780 resolution "that the influence of the crown had increased, was increasing and ought to be diminished." It was therefore obvious, Fox concluded, that the English constitution was in fact deserving of the periodic amendment that Burke himself had prescribed. Burke found no solace in Fox's assurance that he quoted only those sentiments of Burke's that "redounded to his right honourable friend's honour, and to the glory of his character. And where could he find the incident that did not?"

It stung Burke that his onetime protégé had denounced *Reflections* "both in publick and in private and in every one of the doctrines it contained." If hate is a first cousin to love, Burke's raging words, like Fox's tears, effaced any doubt about the affection that the two friends had felt for one another. "The whole tenor of his argument proves," said Burke,

> that my friendship is unworthy of his acceptance. I feel the misfortune, but I feel it like a man! The torrent of odium which has been produced, and the reprobation of all mankind, will not make me swerve from my duty by the smallest alteration of sentiment! To his representation of me as a fool, he opposes his compassion and tenderness, but my character is paramount to every consideration, and I will abide by the consequence!!![84]

Pitt, closing the debate at 12:30 a.m. on May 7, assured Burke that he, if nobody else, was grateful for the able and eloquent defense of the constitution that he had made. When debate resumed on the clauses of the Quebec Bill on May 11, however, Burke insisted that he was quite literally alone. A member of Parliament for twenty-five years, he would count that time wasted if the House "would at last countenance a most insidious design to ruin him and crown his age with infirmity."

"After a great deal of remark and complaint, on the ground of matter

personal to himself," the *Parliamentary History* relates, "Mr. Burke eventually came to consider the subject of the clause before the House."[85]

PARLIAMENT HAD RARELY SEEN ANYTHING QUITE LIKE THE SET-TO OF
May 5. Even so cynical a connoisseur as Horace Walpole was amazed: "It
was the most affecting scene possible, and undoubtedly *an unique* one, for
both the commanders were in earnest and *sincere.*"[86] *The Times* couldn't
decide which contestant was more admirable, the one who sacrificed a
friendship to principle or the other who refused.

In any case, the Whigs were broken in two. Burke, it is true, boasted
no faction, but he had his pen, and his version of the Whigs' creed would
henceforth compete with Fox's. Looking back from a distance of four years,
Robert Adair, a Fox loyalist, judged May 6 a disaster for the Whigs and
their party: "Men of their size could not break company without dividing
the world between them."[87]

Burke, in the May 11 debate, had twice announced his intention to
retire. The next day *The Morning Chronicle*, trying to help hurry the plan
along, announced that on the authority of the "great and firm body of the
Whigs of England," Fox was the winner of the debate, and "Mr. Burke
retires from Parliament."[88]

Burke said he would have liked nothing better—indeed, he would have
declined to stand in the general election of 1790 except for the overhang-
ing impeachment.[89] The May 11 proceedings had confirmed him in his
determination to be done with the men who had so little use for him. Not
a single supposed political ally had said a single conciliatory word to him.
Perhaps, he mused, he was to blame for his isolation, "but be that as it
may, it is when people fall into mistake that they stand in need of friends
and apologists."

A quarter-century in the House, Burke bitterly reflected—and not one
friend. "I confess it forms a presumption against my whole Life."

Epilogue

Fox veered to the left and Burke clung to the right, and that was that. The former friends rarely spoke, though they did not stop listening. What they heard, each from the other, left them both exasperated, often angry, and sometimes incredulous.

Revolutionary France declared war on the Habsburg monarchy in 1792 and added Great Britain to its list of enemies in 1793. Burke retired from Parliament and buried both his brother Richard and his only living child, Richard Jr., in 1794. The Hastings business at last concluded, with a resounding acquittal for the "greatest delinquent,"[1] and Burke, oppressed by his debts and fearing imprisonment for them, secured a government pension in 1795.

In 1796, in *Two Letters on a Regicide Peace*, Burke exhorted the Pitt government to greater efforts in the war against the atheistic, anarchistic, proselytizing enemy. He founded a boarding school near Beaconsfield for the sons of aristocratic French émigrés, subsidizing it at the start with his own threadbare resources,[2] and he lent his moral support to the foundation of an Irish national seminary. It continues to this day as St. Patrick's Pontifical University Maynooth.[3]

Charles Fox remained in Parliament, leading his close-knit corps of anti-Pitt Whigs against the war with France and opposing the government's suppression of civil liberties. He secured, with the Libel Act of 1792, the empowerment of juries to determine what was libel and the guilt or innocence of the accused libeler (judges having formerly wielded such powers). He attacked the slave trade and, at length, moved the motion that abolished it. He attested that, if he had done nothing else in his almost forty years in Parliament, that achievement would have been enough.[4]

Like Burke, Fox won a temporary late-in-life reprieve from his money troubles. Remarkably, it came to light that Burke was among Fox's major creditors, to the tune of £7,000.[5] Mrs. Armistead and Charles were secretly married in 1795 but said not a word about it until 1802, when Mr. and Mrs. Fox, still head over heels, traveled to France together and saw Talleyrand— "with whose wife," the former courtesan Catherine Worlée Grand, "Mrs. Fox had many interesting recollections to compare."[6]

Fox lived long enough to return to power, again at the Foreign Office, in 1804, to try but fail to make peace. In Britain's struggles with the American colonies, he had contended that the North ministry could do no right. Nor, by his lights, could the Pitt administration do anything right in the contest with France. It was the French revolutionaries whom Britain goaded into war, and it was Bonaparte, not Pitt, who pined for peace. Peace at any price was Fox's essential policy.

It was a world of bad choices, he allowed: "While the French are doing all in their power to make the name of liberty odious to the world, the Despots are conducting themselves to shew that Tyranny is worse." For him, for now, the choice was liberty, even of the force-fed French variety.[7]

No more than Burke could Fox defend mass slaughter, universal suffrage, domestic surveillance committees, or the guillotine. But what was the alternative? To Fitzwilliam, the Whig magnate, in March 1792, he described the Foxites' predicament:

> *You* seem to dread the prevalence of Paine's opinions (which in most part I detest as much as you do) while *I* am much more afraid of the total annihilation of all principles of liberty and resistance, an event

which I am sure you would be sorry to see as I. We both hate the two extremes equally, but we differ in our opinions with respect to the quarter from which the danger is most pressing.[8]

In April some young friends of Fox's organized the Society of the Friends of the People to promote parliamentary reform; a London Corresponding Society and a Society for Constitutional Information promoted a similarly radical political agenda.[9] Fox tried to call off the idealists with the objection that the present was no time for political tinkering. Even so, Gillray's pencil reimagined Fox and Sheridan wearing slogans of the French Revolution and taking potshots at a fence post sculpted to resemble George III's head.[10]

Fox was caught between the left and right wings of his fractured party. The September Massacres shocked him, but so did Prussia's avowed aim of restoring Louis XVI to the throne. About the French, he lamented, "There is a want of dignity and propriety in everything they do." And yet, as to the coalition of Austria and Prussia, now united against France, he condemned it as an alliance "against Liberty in general."

Fox balked, as well, at the improbable new political alliance of Pitt and the Duke of Portland, sealed to move a motion in May 1792 for a royal proclamation against seditious practices. There was no such risk as English republicanism, Fox told the House. The danger was rather that of "a high church spirit and an indisposition to all reform."[11]

When the invading Prussians and Austrians retreated before the élan and cannon fire of the French army at Valmy on September 20, 1792, Fox was as joyous as the victors. "No public event not excepting Saratoga and York Town, ever happened that gave me such delight," he told his nephew, Lord Holland. "You know," he added to Elizabeth Armistead, "I have a natural partiality to what some people call rebels."[12]

For Fox, the political clock had stopped with the defeat of his India Bill in 1783 at the conniving hands of the king and his twenty-four-year-old first minister. Perhaps even in the absence of this career-wrecking event, the sometime man of the people would have taken the revolutionaries' side in 1789. As it was, his cause and duty were clear. Hatred of Pitt was his eternal flame, and he saw the world by its glowing light.

In December 1792, at a meeting of the Whig Club, Fox made bold to toast "Equal Liberty to All Mankind." In the same month, responding to the king's speech, he ridiculed the "idiotic clamour" over an imagined popular insurrection. The great question, he said, was rather whether the Commons was prepared to grant the executive government "complete power over our thoughts." Pitt and Portland carried their motion, 290–50.[13]

Louis XVI was beheaded in January. It was an example, Fox remarked, of the "wild, extravagance and unthinking cruelty" that "stained the noblest cause that ever was in the hands of Men."[14]

Pitt's tightening of the laws against seditious speech (as extremely broadly defined) led Fox to contend that, as between the French Committee of Public Safety and what passed for due process in Britain, there was little to choose from. "Every thing in the world seems to be taking a wrong turn," he mused in the summer of 1793, "and strange as it sounds, I think the success of the wretches who now govern Paris is like to be the least Evil of any that can happen."[15]

In a decree of November 19, 1792, the regime, now denoted the Convention, declared "in the name of the French Nation: that it will accord fraternity and help to all peoples who wish to recover their liberty." Another declaration on December 15 authorized conquering French generals to graft French political doctrine on the statute books of the countries they occupied and to set afloat, in the monetary channels of those conquests, the new French currency, the assignat. "If the [liberated] people do not have the means to carry out the Revolution by their own efforts," declared Pierre-Joseph Cambon, a member of the National Convention, "then it will be necessary for the liberators to supplement them and to act in their own best interests by exercising temporarily the revolutionary power." It was in service of the coming of a Universal Republic.[16]

It had been only two years since the French democrats had renounced foreign aggression. "War on the castles, peace to the cottages!" was the new revolutionary cry.[17] France was "the natural political enemy" of Britain, Fox had asserted while Louis XVI was still on his throne, but no more than Thomas Paine could Fox easily imagine a belligerent republic.[18] It was kings who made war.

BY THE AUTUMN OF 1793, BURKE HAD COLLECTED HIS COMPLAINTS against Fox, committed them to paper, and dispatched them to the Duke of Portland and Earl Fitzwilliam, the aristocratic heads of the Whig party. *Observations on the Conduct of the Minority* is a near fifty-page bill of indictment of Charles Fox's political conduct, principally involving France.*

Burke charged Fox with willful ignorance of the weighty underlying reasons for the war with France. No mere riparian contretemps, such as those relating to navigation on the River Scheldt, had lit the fire of European war (as concerning as the conduct of the French government in that affair was to the Pitt government). England was fighting not over boundaries or borders but against an armed ideology.

"Mr. Fox well knew," complained Burke, "that not one man argued for the necessity of a vigorous resistance to France, who did not state the war as being for the very existence of the social order here, and every part of Europe; who did not state his opinion, that this war was not at all a foreign War of Empire, but as much for our Liberties, Properties, Laws, and Religion; and even more so than any we had ever been engaged in."[19]

It angered Burke, too, that Fox was playing to the envy and ignorance of the English poor, stirring them up against this most necessary war. Certainly, such people know that they would suffer from it; that was a matter of feeling. "The *causes* of war," Burke went on, "are not matters of feeling, but of reason and foresight, and often of remote considerations, and of a very great combination of circumstances, which *they* are utterly incapable

---

* The first of the charges, of which there are fifty-five, accuses Fox of dispatching Robert Adair, a personal emissary equipped with a cipher book, to Russia during the Oczakov crisis of 1791 to frustrate the hard-line diplomacy of the Pitt government and the war that, in Fox's opinion, it would certainly provoke. Here, Burke contends, was a "most unconstitutional act, and an high treasonable misdemeanor." W&S, 8:409. In any case, there was no war, and Catherine the Great, Empress of Russia, in gratitude and admiration of Fox, sent a message to the Russian ambassador in London desiring him to send her the "very best bust" of the eloquent statesman, which she would place in her gallery between Cicero and Demosthenes. Mitchell, *Fox*, 117.

of comprehending; and, indeed, it is not every man in the highest classes who is altogether equal to it."

As to a reunion with Fox, Burke wrote, "The Duke of Portland knows how much I wished for, and how much I laboured [for it], and upon terms that might every way be honourable and advantageous to Mr. Fox—His conduct in the last session has extinguished these hopes forever."[20]

Burke closed with a plea to redirect the Whig agenda to principles and away from individuals: "Mr. Pitt may be the worst of men, and Mr. Fox may be the best; but, at present, the former is in the interest of his country, and of the order of things long established in Europe: Mr. Fox is not. I have, for one, been born in this order of things, and would fain die in it."

To which he added, "I write this with pain, and a heart full of grief!"[21]

PITT HAD NO PREVISION OF THE COMING TROUBLES WITH FRANCE. IN presenting his ninth budget to the House of Commons in February 1792, he ventured a long-range speculation, which he prefaced with a nod to the limits of human foresight. "Unquestionably," he boldly continued, "there never was a time in the history of this country, when, from the situation of Europe, we might more reasonably expect fifteen years of peace, than we may at the present moment."[22]

"Much to admire and nothing to agree with," Pitt famously quipped about Burke, but in his *Reflections*, the verbose statesman gave back human foresight its good name.[23] A war of ideology financed by paper money and sustained by mass conscription—he had anticipated not only the French Revolution but also the modern age itself.*

Burke, though he now had no party, held firmly grounded principles. Fox had his party but no firm ground of principle. After 1784, his principal political objective was to return to power, passing Pitt, descending, as he rose. Burke, with his adamant ideas of national danger and his under-

---

* Arthur Young had come around to agree. In February 1793, the former defender of the Revolution had published his pamphlet called *The Example of France, a Warning to Britain.* C., 7:356.

standing of the dynamics of the French Revolution, inevitably entered Pitt's orbit. Fox would prefer almost any other.

When, on May 16, 1794, Pitt moved a bill to suspend habeas corpus, thereby granting His Majesty the right to detain any subject on the mere suspicion of "conspiring against his person and government," Fox jumped up to denounce "an abuse of the power of government, an abuse of law, an abuse of justice, an outrage to humanity." Said Burke in support of the measure: "it was withholding, for a short time, the liberty of the country to preserve it forever."[24] At three in the morning on Sunday, May 18, 1794, the bill passed, 147–28.

Fox was not wrong that Pitt had exaggerated the risk of domestic insurrection. The loyal members of the Association for the Preservation of Liberty and Property against Republicans and Levellers soon far outnumbered those of the so-called corresponding societies, friendly to the revolution.[25] It was an "intolerable calumny on the people" to suppose that they would abandon their country, Fox had said on an earlier occasion.[26] He could see no insurrection, only innocent publicans "threatened with the loss of their licenses if they shall suffer any newspapers to be read in their houses that they shall think seditious. Good God! Where did the justices find this law?"[27]

AT LAST THE HASTINGS TRIAL ENDED, AND IT ENDED FITTINGLY, WITH Burke in full cry against the devil. Having opened the trial in 1788 with a four-day speech, Burke closed it in 1794 with a nine-day speech. Only conceive of the absurdity of installing such a criminal as Warren Hastings to reform the government at Bengal (as the East India Company did in 1773), Burke said; "My Lords, you might as well as expect a man to be fit for a Perfumer's Shop who has lain for a month in a Pig's stye."[28]

In 1788 celebrities had thronged the galleries, and the cause of justice had united the nineteen managers of the prosecution. By 1794 it was the curious public who sometimes showed up to watch, while the ranks of the managers had dwindled to Burke and two or three others.

Burke's famous motion for conciliation with America on 1775 had prompted one of the orator's admiring listeners, Henry Flood, an Irish MP, to speculate that Burke was perhaps too brilliant for his own good.

"I don't mean to join with the cry which will always run against shining parts," Flood explained,

> when I say that I sincerely think it interrupts him so much in argu-
> ment, that the house are never sensible that he argues as well as he
> does. Fox gives a strong proof of this, for he makes use of Burke's
> speech as a repertory, and by stating crabbedly two or three of those
> ideas which Burke has buried under his flowers, he is thought almost
> always to have had more argument.[29]

The profusion of Burke's rhetorical flowers did nothing to quicken the pace of the proceedings, but there were other reasons for the extraordinary length of the trial. Judges were away on the circuit, the defense and prosecution contended over the admissibility of evidence, or the Commons contended with the Lords over the details of parliamentary procedure. Once Lord Derby moved for a three-day adjournment to accommodate his spectating at the Newmarket races. Only in 1788 did the trial fill more than thirty days of the twelve-month calendar. In 1790, the year of a general election (with some dispute over whether the impeachment should continue under a new government), it occupied only fourteen days; in 1793, the year of the outbreak of war between Great Britain and Revolutionary France, it ran for twenty-two days. The prosecution rested its case in 1791; the defense, in 1793.[30]

Spectators, as the defendant described his ordeal, gawked at Hastings, some with opera glasses, or they trained their eyes on Burke or Fox or Sheridan and applauded those oratorical liars (with Burke, to top it all, mangling the pronunciation of Indian proper names)[31] as one might do at the theater. All the while, Hastings's legal bills mounted. He would have pleaded guilty if only he had caught a glimpse of the hellish future, the defendant sighed.[32]

But the end was in view on May 28, 1794, as Burke rose to parry the defense's case, to restate the prosecution's, to demonize the accused, and not least, to remind the noble jurors of their obligations under God and the law. Sometimes, in his raging, Burke forgot his flowers and buried his arguments under ordure. He described a forgetful witness as a man whose memory "passes through him like a diarrhoea" and Hastings as "a Tyrant," "a Robber," "a Thief, "a Cheat," "a Sharper," "a Swindler,"[33] and an Egyptian plague, which "covered the land with vermin and locusts, and spread over it all the calamities of distress, of misery, and sore disease."[34]

The landscape painter and diarist Joseph Farington, visiting the trial on June 3, observed that Hastings was "writing or reading the whole time and appeared to pay no direct attention to Burke."[35] Even so, the accused had no choice but to hear. Eight days later, his reservoir of self-control exhausted, Hastings looked up from his desk to charge his accuser with lying.

In return, Burke demanded that "this wicked wretch" be silenced. And to the judges, he said, "your Lordships will reckon with him for it, or the world will reckon with you."[36]

On May 25, 1793, the Archbishop of York, John Markham, a member of the House of Lords, accused the managers of treating the witness, James Peter Auriol, former secretary to the supreme council in Bengal, as a common pickpocket. "If," charged the archbishop, "Robespierre and Marat were in the Managers Box they could not say any thing more inhumane and more against all sentiments of honor and morality."[37]

Burke, too, was prepared to invoke comparisons with the ferocious French Jacobins. Hastings's turpitude was as deep-dyed as theirs, he charged. "My Lords," Burke addressed the jury, "your House yet stands. It stands as a great edifice, but let me say it stands in the midst of the ruins that have been made by the greatest moral earthquake that has ever convulsed and shattered this globe of ours."

Burke invited the highborn jury to imagine themselves in the position of the members of the Parliament of Paris, men of rank, fortune, and learning, not so different from themselves: "It is but the other day that they submitted their necks to the axe but not their honour."[38]

One hundred and sixty-four peers had attended the opening day of the trial and 230 had attended at least one session, but only twenty-nine deemed themselves sufficiently well informed to cast a vote to acquit or convict.[39] The result, on April 23, 1795, was the acquittal to which Burke had long ago resigned himself. Of the twenty-nine, five found the defendant guilty on a majority of counts, but nineteen voted not guilty on all counts. Hastings, sixty-three years old, was a free man. He distributed £100 to the court attendants.[40]

Hastings had run up legal bills of £78,932, of which £40,000 remained unpaid. His lawyers invited him to name his terms: over how many years would he care to pay, and what rate of interest, if any, would he prefer to bear? They seemed to feel sorry for him.*[41]

Others felt duty-bound to help. The next year the East India Company, with the blessing of the Pitt government, granted Hastings an annuity of £4,000 a year over forty years along with an interest-free loan of £50,000. Burke was livid, but the former defendant was spending money much faster than the company was dispensing it. The restoration of Daylesford, Hastings's ancestral estate, complete with landscaping, plantings, wine cellar, lake (including bridge, islands, and cascade), etc. cost him £54,000, and "his bankrupt hand was open as ever" to needy friends. By 1799, his wife and he were annually taking in less than £3,000 a year, while spending almost £4,700. Hastings's debts towered at £71,000.[42]

Lord Thurlow, sympathetic to Hastings during the trial, regarded the defendant's dealings with money as "the weak point of his character." Fox, perhaps recognizing more than a little of himself in Hastings's chaotic finances, remarked, "though in no friendly sense, [that] on all money subjects, there was something 'peculiarly magnificent' about him."[43]

Public reputation was another matter. In 1801, Hastings had written to Lord Nelson to assure the naval hero of the "love and veneration of his country." The admiral replied that no man's praise could mean more to him than that of he who had "been the chief of an empire nearly as large as Europe."[44]

The Prince of Wales sought out Hastings's company, Oxford gave him an honorary degree (to the accompaniment of the undergraduates' exultant whoops), and the ex-governor-general, in 1808, launched an East Indiaman bearing the once-disgraced name *Warren Hastings*.

---

* In 1795, Burke wrote to the speaker of the House, Henry Addington, to advise that the Treasury was £19,411 10s 9 d. in arrears on payments to the solicitors for the prosecution, and that those lawyers had received not a penny since 1790. C., 8:177.

In 1813, after lengthy testimony before the House of Commons about potential changes in the charter of the East India Company, Hastings pulled back his chair to depart. As he rose, the members spontaneously stood and uncovered their heads. It was a mark of respect, as the honoree's wife, Marian, was proud to observe, usually "only shown to Kings and Princes." Said Hastings, "The colours of my setting sun are too vivid."[45]

FINANCIALLY, CHARLES FOX LIVED FROM BANKRUPTCY TO BANKRUPTCY. Of ordinary collateral, he possessed little, but to the member for Westminster, the love of his solvent friends was as good as a vaultful of government securities.

Those friends gathered at the Crown and Anchor Tavern on June 4, 1793, to pool their money to endow him with lifetime financial security. Philip Francis, the main speaker, sang Fox's praises and summoned the generosity of the crowd. The Fox fund ultimately topped £61,000, of which £21,000 was earmarked to relieve the beneficiary from his outstanding debts. The balance, his friends allowed themselves to imagine, would support the gambling orator, along with Mrs. Armistead, in suitable comfort for the rest of their days.

"You will hear by others of what has been done & is doing for me," Fox apprised Lord Holland. "I may perhaps flatter myself but I think it is the most honourable thing that has ever happened to any Man."[46]

With regard to Burke, it might well have been one of the most extraordinary things. Francis Russell, 5th Duke of Bedford, a major donor to the fund and one of its volunteer administrators, identified £7,000 that Fox owed to Edmund Burke. "It was contracted at a time when poor Charles was very much distressed," reported the duke, a fast friend of Fox's and a believer in his avant-garde politics,* "and tho I do not wish to take from Mr.

---

* Sympathetic as Fox was to the French Revolution, he stoutly defended orthodox monetary arrangements (opposing Pitt's decision to abandon the gold standard in 1797) and stood sentinel over the unregulated market in credit. In response to a government emergency proposal in April 1793 to advance £5 million to traders and manufacturers against the illiquid collateral of goods and property, he sensibly asked why the Bank of England, then a for-profit, stockholder-owned institution, hadn't chosen to lend to those needy borrowers on a commercial basis. To intrude the government into the business of lending and borrowing presented a grave threat to the constitution, Fox protested. Fox, *Speeches*, 5:91–93.

Burke (who is the creditor) merit in not requiring payment yet I am sure you will agree with me in thinking him one of the last men Fox should owe money to."[47]

Where Burke found a spare £7,000 to lend is a mystery. That he chose not to press Fox for repayment is remarkable, as Burke's own financial position was hardly less dire than Fox's.

Since, with a rare exception, the House of Commons paid its members no salary, office or corruption were the ways to political wealth. Burke, partaking only intermittently of the first and not at all of the second, lived on the loans and gifts of his aristocratic patrons, first Rockingham and later Fitzwilliam. Burke was land-poor and almost as inattentive to the details of income and outgo as Fox or, for that matter, Hastings or Pitt. His friendly creditors and he built a small mountain of obligation.

Burke retired from Parliament in June 1794, shortly after a contentious debate on whether to extend to the managers of the impeachment the House's customary thanks for arduous work. The vote in favor was 50–21, with not a few of the nays withholding approval on account of Burke's abusive language to the defendant.[48] How would Hastings's chief prosecutor make ends meet in retirement? Something must be done for Burke, the grand Whigs agreed.

"CASTING A ROOT" AT BEACONSFIELD WAS BURKE'S FOND HOPE AS HE strained to buy the estate in 1768. Richard Jr. would inherit the land and succeed him in the House of Commons. Perhaps, if a peerage could be arranged, his beloved heir would ascend to the Lords. And when, in July 1793, Richard was duly elected to Parliament from the borough of Malton (Fitzwilliam had waved him through), Edmund Burke called it "The Happiest day of his Life."[49]

Richard, thirty-six years old, was chronically unwell, but his death, of tuberculosis, only two weeks later, was the more terrible for being unexpected. His anguished parents wondered how they could go on or indeed, in their desolation, whether they should. His father's heart was "torn to pieces."[50]

Burke mixed self-reproach with sorrow in the draft of a reminiscence that he prepared after Richard's death. "My affairs," he confessed, "were always in a State of embarrassment and confusion. But he and his mother contrived that this should rarely be visible to the world. . . . They kept from me personally every thing that was fretful, teizing and disgusting, so that in Truth I had but a kind of loose general knowledge of several things, which if they had during so many years of other contention and close application to Business have come to my knowledge in detail, I am perfectly sure I never borne up against them."[51]

Something *should* be done for Burke. What could be done? Ideal would be a grant from the Commons, free from any imputation that Burke had sold out to the government of the man who, in league with the king, had smashed the Fox-North coalition. In fact, the Commons dithered, Pitt acted, and the Civil List furnished a pair of grants, £1,200 each, to Edmund and Jane Burke.

But it was far from enough, and creditors closed in on Beaconsfield. By the end of June 1795, Burke was writing to Walker King, his secretary and assistant, about his dread of debtors' prison.

King forwarded that alarming letter to Pitt, who sprang back into action. The result was the grant of a set of annuities with a cash value of £27,760 as well as a pair of pensions in the annual sum of £2,630. Richard Burke, Jr., had estimated his family's gross debt at £30,000. It appeared that the Burkes could liquidate those claims and live comfortably on their income.

But the two mortgages that encumbered Beaconsfield in 1794 were still running when Jane sold the property in 1812. Richard had underestimated his father's debts, while the father continued to spend much more than he took in. The result, if not misery, was unrelieved anxiety.*

Burke's pension elicited some criticism in Parliament, including, in November 1795, from the Duke of Bedford, who said it ill-suited the progenitor of economic reform. Burke, in fact, had never opposed royal preferment for meritorious service, and he wasted no time in responding to the thirty-year-old heir to thousands of acres of English agricultural land and

---

* Brooks's was dunning Jane for £109, three shillings and six pence for unpaid club fees as late as January 1802. Morgan Library, MA 693.30.

119 urban acres in the very heart of London. No scholar, the nobleman had been reluctant to speak in the House of Lords, "for fear of not expressing himself in correct English."[52] Burke now became his tutor.

"The Duke of Bedford," wrote Burke, immortalizing his victim in a *Letter to a Noble Lord*, "is the Leviathan among all creatures of the Crown. He tumbles about his unwieldy bulk; he plays and frolicks in the ocean of the Royal bounty. Huge as he is, and whilst 'he lies floating many a rood,' he is still a creature. His ribs, his fins, his whalebone, his blubber, the very spiracles through which he spouts a torrent of brine against his origin and covers me all over with the spray—every thing of him and about him is from the Throne. Is it for *him* to question the dispensation of the Royal favour?"[53]

Burke contrasted his own hard-won place in the world to the duke's happy accident of birth: "At every step of my progress in life (for in every step was I traversed and opposed), and at every turnpike I met, I was obliged to shew my passport, and again and again to prove my sole title to the honour of being useful to my Country, by a proof that I was not wholly unacquainted with it's laws, and the whole system of it's interests abroad and at home."[54] It fell to Burke, a principled advocate of government by the property-holding classes, to instruct those aristocrats in how to conduct themselves.

Only in the technical sense of his absence from the House of Commons was Edmund Burke retired. He wrote public essays, including his *Letters on a Regicide Peace*, built and administered his sixty-boy school for the sons of loyalist French officers who were serving with British forces, and conducted a lively private correspondence on political subjects. Burke wrote *Thoughts and Details on Scarcity*, a searching treatise on the virtues of the unregulated interplay between supply and demand that won plaudits from a scholarly economist as recently as the year 2020.* Adam Smith attested that Burke "was the only man, who, without communication, thought on these topics exactly as he did."[55]

---

* Collins quotes one of Burke's most characteristic propositions: "The 'laws of commerce' . . . are the 'laws of nature, and consequently the laws of God.'" Collins, *Commerce and Manners*, 2.

We find Burke, in March 1795, "overwhelmed with Grief, shame and anguish," at the failure of Earl Fitzwilliam, newly appointed Viceroy of Ireland, to secure the right of Catholics to serve in Parliament (a quest perhaps premature and certainly impolitic) and at Fitzwilliam's humiliating recall from Dublin less than two months after he took up his viceroyalty.[56]

We find him, his fires unbanked, in July 1796, boiling over with rage at the plans to grant Hastings a pension. "Let my endeavours to save the Nation from that Shame and guilt be my monument," he writes to French Laurence, a Whig MP who instantly sided with Burke in the party's division between him and Fox; "The only one I will ever have. Let every thing I have done, said, or written be forgotten but this."[57]

And we find him, in March 1797, writing to William Windham, by then Pitt's secretary at war (an administrative position inferior to that of secretary *of* war), bemoaning the prime minister's reluctance to bring the fight to the French. "He cannot make peace because he will not make war."[58]

What Pitt could not seem to grasp were the stakes, "the system of Europe, taking its laws, manners, religion and politics in which I delighted so much. My poor son was called off in time—*'ne quid tale videret.'*"*[59]

Burke, who was rarely ill, suffered an attack of stomach pain in the summer of 1796. The strongest corroborating evidence that his stomach was indeed, as he himself predicted, "irrecoverably ruind,"[60] was the onset of weakness that, starting in November, left him too weak to lift his pen.

In company with Jane, he spent months taking the curative waters at Bath. He tried opium and purging and a physician's diet of meat alone. He grew better and worse and better again, but the underlying morbid trend was unshakable. Happily, his mind was spared, and his conversation delighted and amazed Charles Henry Parry, the son of his physician, who kept him company toward the end.

"In the beautiful Evenings of June," Parry recorded, "he has sometimes walked, leaning on my arm, to his Farm . . . & made frequent pauses to admire the beauties of the Scene. After the turbulent Season of political life, he quietly enjoyed the tranquility of the Country. He had a particular

* "Lest he should see anything of the kind." Virgil, *Aeneid*, bk. 11, l. 417.

pleasure in watching his Cows quietly chewing the Cud. That animal, said
he, gives me a more complete idea of Repose, than any other object in
nature."[61]

Fox, whose enmities, as he once told the House of Commons, were not
forever, had heard of Burke's decline and sent a message asking for the
opportunity to say goodbye. In reply came this note:

> Mrs. Burke presents her compliments to Mr. Fox, and thanks him
> for his obliging inquiries. Mrs. Burke communicated his letter to
> Mr. Burke, and, by his desire, has to inform Mr. Fox that it has cost
> Mr. Burke the most heart-felt pain to obey the stern voice of duty
> in rending asunder a long friendship, but that he deemed this sac-
> rifice necessary; that his principles remained the same; and that in
> whatever life yet remained to him, he conceives that he must live
> for others and not for himself. Mr. Burke is convinced that the prin-
> ciples which he has endeavoured to maintain are necessary to the
> welfare and dignity of his country, and that these principles can be
> enforced only by the general persuasion of his sincerity. For herself,
> Mrs. Burke has again to express her gratitude to Mr. Fox for his
> inquiries.[62]

Fox had likely not forgotten this rebuff as, three years later, he replied
to a request to contribute to a fund to raise a national memorial to his
onetime friend. "The truth is, that, though I do not feel any malice against
Burke," Fox began, "I must own that there are parts of his conduct that I
cannot forgive so entirely as perhaps I ought," notably Burke's attempt to
"destroy" him in the opinion of his political allies, particularly Earl Fitzwilliam. "This was surely not only malice, but baseness in the extreme; and if I
were to say that I have quite forgiven it, it would be boasting a magnanimity which I cannot feel."[63]

"Obstinacy," Burke had said, was the fault, of all the political faults, of
which the House of Commons was least tolerant, and perhaps the great
man had forgotten his own maxim. But in his greatness he had taken it

upon himself to save the world from evil, not from every evil but from those evils which it was in his power to resist.

Now Hastings had his pension and the sansculottes their Revolution but he, Edmund Burke, would never yield—not even for the sake of a man who, as he himself once put it, was "born to be loved."

AT BREAKFAST ON JANUARY 24, 1799, HIS FIFTIETH BIRTHDAY, FOX PRE-sented his wife with some lines of verse:

Of years I have now half a century passed,
And none of the fifty so blessed as the last,
How it happens my troubles thus daily should cease,
And my happiness thus with my years should increase,
This defiance of Nature's more general laws,
You alone can explain, who alone are the cause.[64]

Fox by then was an absentee member of Parliament. He had seceded in 1797 in protest over the stranglehold of Pitt and the king over the no-longer-independent House of Commons. He returned to Parliament in 1801, after Pitt, quite without warning, resigned over his failure to enact a Catholic relief bill. And he returned to office for a second term as foreign secretary in a new coalition government, a Fox-Grenville alliance, in January 1806, on a program of peace and Catholic emancipation.

Fox by now was beginning to feel the effects of the disease that would kill him. For his reputation in statecraft, it might have been better if he had died sooner. Talleyrand and he, Fox had been certain, could settle a permanent peace in an hour's sit-down together. It laid him low to discover that Talleyrand and Napoleon wanted not peace but the rest of Europe.

On September 13, 1806, Fox lay dying at Chiswick House, west of London, which the Duke of Devonshire had loaned him during his illness. Elizabeth's diary records his gently rebuking words as she sat crying at his bedside: "Oh, fie, Liz, is this your promise?"

"We had agreed some years ago," the diary entry goes on, "that whichever was likely to die first the other should stay by all the time and try to look gay and cheerful but my God who could do it."

"He had hold of my hands bid me kiss him looked at me with a heavenly smile said 'I die happy but pity you.'"

At length, "seeing that I was unhappy he made an effort and said it don't signify my dearest dearest Liz."[65] They were his last words.

PITT'S DEATH, SOME NINE MONTHS BEFORE, HAD RAISED THE POLITICAL question of whether a state funeral should be granted to Britain's longest-serving prime minister but one, just behind Robert Walpole. Fox opposed the measure, not on party grounds, still less on personal ones, he assured the House, but because the motion to bury Pitt at public expense in Westminster Abbey had contained the phrase "that excellent statesman."

Fox allowed his rival "the brilliancy of [his] expression, and the electricity of his elocution" but refused to consent to the excellence of his statesmanship. He condemned Pitt for lending his gifts to the system of royal dominion over Parliament. "I cannot but accuse the late minister of having, I will not say criminally, for the expression might sound, in some ears, too harsh, but most unfortunately, lent his brilliant talents and his commanding eloquence, to support of it."

William Windham, though he had abandoned the Whigs to serve in Pitt's government, also rose to object. Burke had been granted no state funeral, he pointed out, "and yet Mr. Burke was inferior to no man in the splendour of his talents, nor in the purity of his mind, nor in genuine and disinterested patriotism, nor in long experience and devotion to the public service."[66] It could not be that Burke's failure to hold high office disqualified him. He was Pitt's equal in everything but his employment.

Burke, in keeping with the instructions in his will, was buried in the Beaconsfield churchyard next to his son, Richard Jr., and brother, Richard Sr. He had stipulated that his funeral be on no grander scale than that of his brother and that no monument, "beyond a middle-sized tablet, with a small and simple inscription on the church-wall, or on the flag-stone, be erected. I say this, because I know the partial kindness to me of some of my friends. But I have had, in my life-time, but too much of Noise and compliment."[67]

Pitt, in February 1806, got his state funeral, but Fox upstaged him in October with an enormous, privately financed outpouring of veneration and grief. The procession to Westminster Abbey from Fox's final residence in Stable Yard was ninety minutes in passing. Among the mourners were 174 members of the Whig Club; more than one hundred MPs; fifty-seven poor men, "with badges of the crest of the deceased, the number corresponding with his age"; the cabinet; the chief mourner, Lord Holland, Fox's nephew; a half-dozen grand Whigs serving as pallbearers; twenty gowned divines; the High Constable of Westminster; and musicians playing over and over Handel's "Dead March" from *Saul*. Observers marked, especially, the order and solemnity of the vast crowds.[68]

Burke lives still in the canon of Western political thought; noise and compliments from admiring politicians and adoring readers have rarely subsided since his death. A cult of Charles Fox began to form almost from the time the underage MP first strode into the House of Commons. It persisted through the nineteenth century and lingers in the amiable gatherings of the Fox Society at Brooks's.

As to monuments, a white marble sculpture of Fox in the west end of the nave at Westminster Abbey depicts the dying statesman, recumbent, with the figure of Liberty cradling his head and shoulders, a black slave praying at his feet, and a figure representing Peace resting her head on his knee. Burke's collected works, his writings and speeches and letters, constitute his monument, marble in its own right.

ACKNOWLEDGMENTS

My thanks, first, to James Robertson, Jr., who contributed facts, enterprise, organization, motive power, and much more to this volume. Hired as a research assistant, he has become my intellectual partner.

Edward Short, Edward Chancellor, and Robert Messenger generously and critically read the manuscript. The copy editor Janet Biehl "made the rough places plain and the crooked things straight." (For all remaining blemishes, I claim credit.)

Every author owes a debt to the teachers who helped him on his way. In grateful memory, therefore, I wish to acknowledge Jacques Barzun, Robert E. Ferrell, Henry F. Graff, H. Scott Gordon, and John Snyder.

The bibliography accompanying this text is but meager thanks to the scholars of Britain's Georgian age—and, especially, to the editors of Edmund Burke's correspondence and writings and speeches—who make possible the work of a journalistic interloper.

Declan Hurley made valuable contributions to this project, as did Koen van der Blij, who searched archives in the U.K. and the Netherlands. Jeff Kattenhorn and Karen Stapley at the British Library kindly lent assistance. So did Sarah Bridges at the Northamptonshire Archives and Heritage

Service, Polly Cancro at the Morgan Library and Museum, and Terre Murphy at the William L. Clements Library of the University of Michigan. Layla McDermott translated Latin passages. My thanks to all.

Covid forced the closing of airports, archives, and museums, but dedicated staff at the National Archives of the United Kingdom scanned and forwarded material that would otherwise have been unobtainable. Special thanks to the Derbyshire Record Office and the Sheffield City Archives.

And what is an author without an editor and publisher? For his patience and encouragement, John Glusman, vice-president and executive editor at W. W. Norton, has my gratitude.

APPENDIX:

VALUE OF MONEY

1 shilling (s) = 12 pence
1 pound (£) = 20 shillings
1 guinea (gn.) = 21 shillings

1 penny	Enough gin to get drunk on
3 pence	Meal of bread, cheese, and beer
6 pence	Fee for shaving and dressing of a wig
1 shilling	Postage for a letter from London to New York
10 shillings	Price of Samuel Johnson's *Dictionary*
£1 15s	Monthly pay for an East India Company seaman
£30	Annual rent paid by James Boswell for two rooms in a London townhouse
£100	Annual salary for an Oxford fellow
200 gn.	Price for a full-length portrait painted by Joshua Reynolds
£500	Minimum value of East India Company shares needed to cast a vote
£750	Annual salary of Edward Gibbon for his sinecure at the Board of Trade

£900	Sum Charles James Fox lost in a single game of billiards
£1,400	Lord North's annual salary in the 1760s
£6,000	Annual housekeeping expenses for Lord Holland
£20,000	Purchase price of Burke's Beaconsfield estate
£78,932	Warren Hastings's legal bills for his impeachment defense
£140,000	Charles James Fox's gambling debts as of 1776
£300,000	Net worth of Robert Clive on his return from India
£800,000	Amount provided annually to King George III by Parliament
£11 million	Market capitalization of the East India Company in 1769
£132.6 million	National debt of Britain at the end of the Seven Years' War[*]

---

[*] Picard, *Dr. Johnson's London*; Hume, "Value of Money"; Boswell, *London Journal*, 59.

NOTES

Abbreviations

C.   Correspondence of Edmund Burke
Burke, Edmund. *The Correspondence of Edmund Burke.* Edited by Thomas W. Copeland, Lucy S. Sutherland, George H. Guttridge, John A. Woods, P. J. Marshall, Alfred Cobban, Robert A. Smith, and R. B. McDowell. 10 vols. Cambridge, UK: Cambridge University Press, 1958–78.

W&S   Writings and Speeches of Edmund Burke
Burke, Edmund. *The Writings and Speeches of Edmund Burke.* Edited by T. O. McLoughlin, James T. Boulton, William B. Todd, P. J. Marshall, Donald Bryant, L. G. Mitchell, Paul Langford, and Warren M. Elofson. 9 vols. Oxford: Oxford University Press, 1981–2015.

M&C   Memorials and Correspondence of Charles James Fox
Fox, Charles James. *Memorials and Correspondence of Charles James Fox.* Edited by John Russell. 4 vols. London: Richard Bentley, 1853–57.

PH   Parliamentary History
William Cobbett, ed. *Cobbett's Parliamentary History of England from the Norman Conquest in 1066 to the Year, 1803.* 36 vols. London: R. Bagshaw, 1806–20.

BL   British Library
British Library, London.

NA   National Archives
National Archives, Kew, United Kingdom.

Preface

1. James Boswell, *The Life of Samuel Johnson* (New York: Penguin, 2008), 504, 926.
2. Leslie George Mitchell, *Charles James Fox* (Oxford: Oxford University Press, 1992), 41.
3. W&S, 3:510.
4. Edward Gibbon, *Miscellaneous Works of Edward Gibbon* (Dublin: P. Wogan, 1796), 1:157.
5. C., 5:377.
6. Mitchell, *Fox*, 20.
7. *Morning Chronicle* (London), May 2, 1798.
8. W&S, 5: 449–51.
9. George III and Frederick North, *The Correspondence of King George the Third with Lord North: From 1768 to 1783*, ed. William Bodham Donne (London: John Murray, 1867), 2:90.
10. Loren Dudley Reid, *Charles James Fox: A Man for the People* (London: Longmans, Green and Co., 1969), 268.
11. W&S, 3:132.
12. M&C, 1:145–47.
13. W&S, 6:304.
14. Mitchell, *Fox*, 111.
15. Mitchell, *Fox*, 115.

Chapter 1

1. Ireland, Parliament of Ireland, *An Act to Prevent Papists Being Solicitors*, 10 Will III c.13, 1698.
2. Richard Mant, *History of the Church of Ireland: From the Revolution to the Union of the Churches of England and Ireland, January 1, 1801* (London: John W. Parker, 1840), 482.
3. Conor Cruise O'Brien, *The Great Melody* (Chicago: University of Chicago Press, 1992), 12.
4. James Prior, *Life of the Right Honourable Edmund Burke* (London: Henry G. Bohn, 1854), 32.
5. C., 1:274.
6. Edmund Burke, *The Early Life Correspondence and Writing of the Rt. Hon. Edmund Burke*, ed. Arthur P. I. Samuels (Cambridge, UK: Cambridge University Press, 1923), 97.
7. Burke, *Early Life Correspondence*, 274.
8. James McGuire, "Nagle, Sir Richard (1635/6–1699)," *Oxford Dictionary of National Biography*.
9. Burke, *Early Life Correspondence*, 97–98.
10. Prior, 3.
11. Constantia Maxwell, *Dublin Under the Georges* (London: Faber & Faber, 1956), 123, 148.
12. O'Brien, 19.
13. O'Brien, 19–20.
14. O'Brien, 21.
15. Prior, 9.
16. Prior, 5.
17. C., 1:1.

18. C., 1:86.
19. Longinus, "On the Sublime," in *Aristotle: Poetics. Longinus: On the Sublime. Demetrius: On Style*, trans. W. Hamilton Fyfe (Cambridge, MA: Harvard University Press, 1995), 171.
20. Longinus, 125.
21. Burke, *Early Life Correspondence*, 117.
22. C., 1:36.
23. C., 1:32–33.
24. C., 1:39.
25. C., 1:65–66.
26. Samuel Johnson, *Lives of the Poets* (London: J. M. Dent, 1925), 1:56.
27. Frederick P. Lock, *Edmund Burke* (New York: Oxford University Press, 1998), 1:41.
28. C., 1:xv.
29. C., 1:89.
30. C., 1:74.
31. Burke, *Early Life Correspondence*, 221.
32. C., 1:25.
33. Burke, *Early Life Correspondence*, 227–28.
34. Burke, *Early Life Correspondence*, 228.
35. Burke, *Early Life Correspondence*, 229.
36. Burke, *Early Life Correspondence*, 230.
37. Burke, *Early Life Correspondence*, 253.
38. Burke, *Early Life Correspondence*, 252.
39. C., 1:101.
40. C., 1:86.
41. Burke, *Early Life Correspondence*, 303.
42. James Kelly, "Harvests and Hardship: Famine and Scarcity in Ireland in the Late 1720s," *Studia Hibernica*, no. 26 (1992): 66.
43. W. E. H. Lecky, *England in the Eighteenth Century* (New York: D. Appleton, 1878), 2:233.
44. Burke, *Early Life Correspondence*, 219.

Chapter 2

1. Henry Fox to Ilchester, January 24, 1749, quoted in Giles Stephen Holland Fox-Strangways, *Henry Fox, First Lord Holland* (New York: Charles Scribner's Sons, 1920), 1:174.
2. George Otto Trevelyan, *The Early History of Charles James Fox* (London: Longmans, Green, 1880), 43.
3. Stanley Ayling, *Fox: The Life of Charles James Fox* (London: John Murray, 1991), 15–16.
4. Trevelyan, *Early History of Fox*, 42.
5. Christopher Clay, *Public Finance and Private Wealth: The Career of Sir Stephen Fox 1627–1716* (Oxford: Clarendon Press, 1978), 197.
6. Clay, 117.
7. Clay, 1.
8. Clay, 333.
9. Michael J. Braddick, "Fox, Sir Stephen (1627–1716), Financier and Government Official," *Oxford Dictionary of National Biography*.
10. Abel Boyer, *The History of the Reign of Queen Anne* (London: A. Roper, 1703), 320.

11. Trevelyan, *Early History of Fox*, 7.
12. Peter Luff, "Fox, Henry, First Baron Holland of Foxley (1705–1774), Politician," *Oxford Dictionary of National Biography*.
13. Edward Lascelles, *The Life of Charles James Fox* (Oxford: Oxford University Press, 1936), 3.
14. Emily Fitzgerald, *Correspondence of Emily Duchess of Leinster (1731–1814)*, ed. Brian Fitzgerald (Dublin: Dublin Stationery Office, 1949), 1:251.
15. Ayling, 11.
16. Fitzgerald, 251.
17. Ayling, 13.
18. *London Chronicle*, September 17–19, 1761.
19. John Russell, *The Life and Times of Charles James Fox* (London: Richard Bentley, 1866), 1:32.
20. Henry Fox, "Memoir on the Events Attending the Death of George II and the Accession of George III," in *The Life and Letters of Lady Sarah Lennox* (London: John Murray, 1902), 1:76.
21. Luff.
22. Fox, "Memoir on the Events," 71.
23. Fox, "Memoir on the Events," 41.
24. Lucy Sutherland and J. Binney, "Henry Fox as Paymaster General of the Forces," *English Historical Review* 70, no. 275 (1955): 235.
25. Sutherland and Binney, 236.
26. Sutherland and Binney, 245.
27. Clay, 313.
28. Sutherland and Binney, 243.
29. Fox, "Memoir on the Events," 72.
30. Trevelyan, *Early History of Fox*, 30.
31. Thad W. Riker, *Henry Fox, First Lord Holland: A Study of the Career of an Eighteenth-Century Politician* (Oxford: Oxford University Press, 1911), 1:303.
32. Sutherland and Binney, 249.
33. Riker, 2:288.
34. Russell, 1:6.
35. Mitchell, *Fox*, 9.
36. Christopher Hobhouse, *Fox* (London: Constable, 1947), 4.
37. Mitchell, *Fox*, 8.
38. Russell, 1:42.
39. Mitchell, *Fox*, 6.
40. Russell, 1:42.
41. Russell, 1:41.
42. Russell, 1:55.
43. Lascelles, 25.
44. Russell, 1:41.
45. Mitchell, *Fox*, 10.
46. Mitchell, *Fox*, 12.
47. Mitchell, *Fox*, 12.
48. Russell, 1:59.
49. Mitchell, *Fox*, 11.
50. Sutherland and Binney, 252.

Chapter 3

1. Lock, 1:65.
2. Lock, 1:69.
3. Lock, 1:67.
4. C., 1:111.
5. C., 1:113.
6. C., 1:113.
7. Lock, 1:74.
8. C., 1:117.
9. Prior, 44.
10. C., 1:119–20.
11. Joseph Emin, *Life and Adventures of Joseph Emin* (Calcutta: Baptist Mission Press, 1918), 48.
12. Emin, 49–52.
13. Lock, 1:85.
14. W&S, 1:173.
15. W&S, 1:176.
16. Prior, 45.
17. W&S, 1:215.
18. W&S, 1:228.
19. Clement Carlyon, *Early Years and Late Reflections* (London: Whittaker, 1835), 1:56.
20. W&S, 1:216.
21. W&S, 1:273.
22. W&S, 1:275–76.
23. W&S, 8:126.
24. W&S, 1:299.
25. W&S, 1:318.
26. W&S, 1:185–87.
27. Boswell, *Life of Johnson*, 305–6.
28. W&S, 1:271.
29. W&S, 1:59–61.
30. Lock, 1:89.
31. C., 1:107.
32. George C. McElroy, "Burke, William (1728/30–1798)," *Oxford Dictionary of National Biography.*
33. C., 1:154.
34. C., 1:140.
35. McElroy.
36. Lock, 1:165.
37. Prior, 57.
38. Edmund Burke, "Preface," *Annual Register*, 1759, v.
39. Burke, *Annual Register*, 1759, 5.
40. Burke, *Annual Register*, 1759, 4.
41. Burke, *Annual Register*, 1759, 445–49.
42. C., 1:129.
43. C., 1:123.

44. C., 1:131.
45. *Corke Journal*, May 4, 1762.
46. Thomas P. Power, "Nicholas Sheehy (1728/9–1766)," *Oxford Dictionary of National Biography*; Luke Gibbons, *Edmund Burke and Ireland: Aesthetics, Politics, and the Colonial Sublime* (Cambridge, UK: Cambridge University Press, 2004), 22.
47. C., 1:147–48.
48. C., 1:165.
49. C., 1:200.
50. C., 1:195–96.
51. Boswell, *Life of Johnson*, 252.
52. Patrick Woodland, "Verney, Ralph, Second Earl Verney (1714–1791)," *Oxford Dictionary of National Biography*.
53. C., 1:223–25.
54. C., 1:223.
55. C., 1:223.

Chapter 4

1. John L. Bullion, "'To Know This Is the True Essential Business of a King': The Prince of Wales and the Study of Public Finance, 1755–1760," *Albion* 18, no. 3 (1986): 436–37.
2. John C. Miller, *Origins of the American Revolution* (Stanford, CA: Stanford University Press, 1962), 84–85.
3. Miller, *Origins*, 113.
4. William Tudor, *The Life of James Otis, of Massachusetts* (Boston: Wells & Lilly, 1823), 144.
5. Miller, 89.
6. Carl Van Doren, *Benjamin Franklin* (New York: Viking Press, 1961), 322.
7. Thomas Hutchinson, *The History of the Colony and Province of Massachusetts-Bay*, ed. Lawrence Shaw Mayo (Cambridge, MA: Harvard University Press, 1936), 3:85.
8. Miller, *Origins*, 90.
9. Miller, *Origins*, 116.
10. John Adams, *Papers of John Adams*, ed. Robert J. Taylor (Cambridge, MA: Belknap Press, 1977), 1:133.
11. Miller, *Origins*, 123.
12. Miller, *Origins*, 126.
13. Miller, *Origins*, 130.
14. Miller, *Origins*, 113.
15. Miller, *Origins*, 150.
16. Edmund Burke, *Annual Register* 8 (1766): 37.
17. Arthur H. Cash, *John Wilkes: The Scandalous Father of Civil Liberty* (New Haven, CT: Yale University Press, 2006), 5, 52.
18. Cash, 71.
19. Cash, 68.
20. Trevelyan, *Early History of Fox*, 27.
21. Jeremy Black, *Pitt the Elder* (Cambridge, UK: Cambridge University Press, 1992), 257.
22. John Wilkes, *The North Briton* (London: W. Bingley, 1769–71), 1:155–56.
23. Peter D. G. Thomas, "Wilkes, John (1725–1797)," *Oxford Dictionary of National Biography*.

24. Thomas, "Wilkes, John."
25. Cash, 192.
26. Cash, 192.
27. Cash, 194.
28. C., 1:230–31.
29. Cash, 194.
30. J. V. Beckett and Peter D. G. Thomas, "George Grenville (1712–1770)," *Oxford Dictionary of National Biography.*
31. Andrew Roberts, *The Last King of America: The Misunderstood Reign of George III* (New York: Viking, 2021), 157.
32. C. P. Moritz, *Travels in England in 1782* (London: Cassell, 1886), 43.
33. George Otto Trevelyan, *George the Third and Charles Fox: The Concluding Part of the American Revolution* (London: Longmans, Green, 1912), 1:50.
34. C., 1:233; Lock, 218.
35. W&S, 2:50.
36. W&S, 2:46.
37. C., 1:233.
38. C., 1:245.
39. C., 1:239.
40. C., 1:237.
41. W&S, 2:53.
42. W&S, 2:49.
43. W&S, 2:52.
44. W&S, 2:54.
45. Miller, *Origins*, 159–60.
46. James Grant, *John Adams: Party of One* (New York: Farrar, Straus & Giroux, 2005), 123–24.
47. Augustus Henry Fitzroy, *Autobiography and Political Correspondence of Augustus Henry, Third Duke of Grafton*, ed. Sir William Anson (London: John Murray, 1898), 108.
48. Gregory M. Collins, *Commerce and Manners in Edmund Burke's Political Economy* (Cambridge, UK: Cambridge University Press, 2020), 232.
49. W&S, 2:54–57.
50. C., 1:286.

Chapter 5

1. M&C, 1:62.
2. Ayling, 27–28.
3. Peter Durrant, "FitzRoy, Augustus Henry, Third Duke of Grafton (1735–1811)," *Oxford Dictionary of National Biography.*
4. W&S, 2:224–26.
5. W&S, 2:228.
6. Cash, 254.
7. Trevelyan, *Early History of Fox*, 167–68.
8. A. F. Blackstock, "Luttrell, Henry Lawes, Second Earl of Carhampton (1737–1821)," *Oxford Dictionary of National Biography.*
9. Trevelyan, *Early History of Fox*, 170.

10. *Middlesex Journal* (London), March 26, 1771.

11. A. A. Hanham, "Parsons, Anne (c. 1735–1814/15)," *Oxford Dictionary of National Biography.*

12. John Noorthouck, *A New History of London Including Westminster and Southwark* (London: R. Baldwin, 1773), bk. 1, chap. 25.

13. M&C, 1:64.

14. M&C, 1:63–64.

15. Robert Bisset, *The Life of Edmund Burke* (London: G. Cawthon, 1800), 1:63–64.

16. Susan Grace Schroeder, "The Personal and Public Relationship between Edmund Burke and Charles James Fox: Its Evolution and Significance," master's thesis, Loyola University, 1961, 21.

17. Grant, 81.

18. M&C, 1:68.

19. Ayling, 44.

20. Russell, 69.

21. George Rudé, Wilkes *and Liberty: A Social Study* (London: Lawrence & Wishart, 1983), 135.

22. Henry, 276.

23. Fitzroy, *Autobiography*, 238–39.

24. Rudé, 136–37.

25. Russell, 1:32.

26. Hobhouse, 28.

27. Charles James Fox, *The Speeches of the Right Honorable Charles James Fox, in the House of Commons* (London: Longman, Hurst, Rees, Orme & Brown: 1815), 1:xlviii.

28. M&C, 1:74.

29. W&S, 2:236.

30. Noorthouck, bk. 1, chap. 25.

31. W&S, 237–41.

32. Lock, 1:268.

33. Fitzroy, *Autobiography*, xxxii.

34. Lock, 1:289–90; C., 2:127.

35. W&S, 2:261.

36. W&S, 2:269.

37. W&S, 2:260.

38. W&S, 2:314.

39. W&S, 2:321.

40. Cash, 278.

41. George III and North, 1:64.

42. Fox, *Speeches*, 1:6–11.

43. *London Evening Post*, March 28, 1771.

Chapter 6

1. Woodland, "Verney, Ralph, Second Earl Verney."

2. C., 154.

3. H. V. Bowen, *Revenue and Reform: The Indian Problem in British Politics 1757–1773* (Cambridge, UK: Cambridge University Press, 1991), 19.

4. H. V. Bowen, "Clive, Robert, First Baron Clive of Plassey (1725–1774)," *Oxford Dictionary*

of National Biography.

5. William Dalrymple, *The Anarchy* (London: Bloomsbury, 2019), 127.
6. Bowen, "Clive, Robert."
7. Nick Robins, *The Corporation That Changed the World* (London: Pluto Press, 2012), 75.
8. Peter D. G. Thomas, *George III: King and Politicians, 1760–1770* (Manchester: Manchester University Press, 2002), 159.
9. Dalrymple, 210.
10. Dalrymple, 208.
11. Dalrymple, 208.
12. Bowen, *Revenue and Reform*, 9.
13. H. V. Bowen, "Lord Clive and Speculation in East India Company Stock, 1766," *Historical Journal* 30, no. 4 (1987): 910.
14. Bowen, "Lord Clive and Speculation," 909.
15. Lucy Sutherland, "Lord Shelburne and East India Company Politics, 1766–1769," *English Historical Review* 49, no. 195 (1934): 457.
16. Sutherland, "Lord Shelburne," 457.
17. Sutherland and John A. Woods, "The East India Speculations of William Burke," in *Politics and Finance in the Eighteenth Century* (London: Hambledon Press, 1984), 332.
18. Bowen, "Lord Clive and Speculation," 912.
19. Bowen, *Revenue and Reform*, 13.
20. Sutherland, "Lord Shelburne," 458.
21. Sutherland and Woods, 345.
22. Bowen, *Revenue and Reform*, 16.
23. Sutherland, "Lord Shelburne," 465.
24. Ross J. S. Hoffman, *Edmund Burke, New York Agent with His Letters to the New York Assembly and Intimate Correspondence with Charles O'Hara, 1761–1776* (Philadelphia: American Philosophical Society, 1956), 362.
25. Sutherland and Woods, "East India Speculations," 336–37.
26. Lauchlin Macleane, "Account of the Revenue and Charges Shewing the Net Receipts and Net Income for Six Years, from August 1765–April 1777," Box 99, 149–52, Shelburne Papers, Clements Library, University of Michigan.
27. Sutherland and Woods, 337.
28. Sutherland and Woods, 338.
29. John Nicholls, *Recollections and Reflections, Personal and Political, as Connected with Public Affairs, During the Reign of George III* (London: James Ridgway, 1820), 1:54–55.
30. Sutherland, "Lord Shelburne," 464.
31. "Protest Against Rescinding the East India Dividends," *Gentleman's Magazine*, July 1767, 350.
32. W&S, 2:65–66.
33. C., 1:351.
34. Lock, 1:256.
35. Lock, 1:250.
36. Lock, 1:252.
37. Lock, 1:254.
38. Dixon Wecter, "Edmund Burke and His Kinsmen," *University of Colorado Studies: Studies in the Humanities* 1, no. 1 (February 1939): 50.
39. Locke, 1:251.
40. Lock, 1:250.

41. Bowen, *Revenue and Reform*, 13, 105.
42. Bowen, *Revenue and Reform*, 117.
43. Bowen, *Revenue and Reform*, 117.
44. W&S, 2:219–20.
45. W&S, 2:221.
46. Bowen, *Revenue and Reform*, 23.
47. W&S, 220–22.
48. Sutherland and Woods, "East India Speculations," 339.
49. Robins, 92.
50. C., 2:26.
51. C., 2:26–29.

Chapter 7

1. C., 2:140.
2. Wecter, "Burke and Kinsmen," 39, 68.
3. C., 2:149.
4. Wecter, "Burke and Kinsmen," 56.
5. Wecter, "Burke and Kinsmen," 57.
6. *Public Advertiser* (London), March 20, 1771.
7. P. J. Marshall, *Edmund Burke and the British Empire in the West Indies: Wealth, Power, and Slavery* (Oxford: Oxford University Press, 2019), 75.
8. Wecter, "Burke and Kinsmen," 58.
9. C., 2:227.
10. Wecter, "Burke and Kinsmen," 49.
11. Wecter, "Burke and Kinsmen," 61.
12. Marshall, *Burke and Empire*, 58.
13. Henry Cavendish, *Sir Henry Cavendish's Debates of the House of Commons, During the Thirteenth Parliament of Great Britain, Commonly Called the Unreported Parliament* (London: Longman, Orme, Brown, Green & Longmans, 1841), 1:378.
14. Hobhouse, 26.
15. George III and North, *Correspondence*, 1:89.
16. Fox, *Speeches*, 1:15.
17. George III and North, *Correspondence*, 1:89.
18. W&S, 2:362.
19. W&S, 2:362n1.
20. W&S, 2:361.
21. W&S, 2:370.
22. W&S, 2:368.
23. Peter Whiteley, *Lord North: The Prime Minister Who Lost America* (London: Hambledon Press, 1996), 23.
24. Sir Nathaniel William Wraxall, *Historical Memoirs of My Own Time* (Philadelphia: Carey, Lea & Blanchard, 1897), 1:363.
25. *Maria, Duchess of Gloucester when Lady Waldegrave (1736–1807)*, Royal Collection Trust, https://www.rct.uk/collection/420247/maria-duchess-of-gloucester-when-lady -waldegrave-1736-1807.
26. Fox, *Speeches*, 1:16.

27. Roberts, 219.
28. Letter from George III to Lord North on a debate in the House of Lords, February 26, 1772, Royal Archives GEO/Main/1270.
29. Luff.
30. W. M. Elofson, "The Rockingham Whigs in Transition: the East India Company Issue 1772–1773," *English Historical Review* 104, no. 413 (1989): 956.
31. C., 2:309.
32. Mitchell, *Fox*, 21.
33. Fox, *Speeches*, 1:13–14.
34. M&C, 1:85–87.
35. Trevelyan, *Early History of Fox*, 447.
36. Trevelyan, *Early History of Fox*, 40.
37. Trevelyan, *Early History of Fox*, 454–55.
38. Ayling, 38.
39. Ayling, 38.
40. Trevelyan, *Early History of Fox*, 455.
41. Trevelyan, *Early History of Fox*, 460–61.
42. George Selwyn, *George Selwyn: His Letters and His Life*, ed. E. S. Roscoe and Helen Clergue (London: T. Fisher Unwin, 1899), 68.
43. P. M. Geoghegan, "Frederick Howard, Fifth Earl of Carlisle (1748–1825)," *Oxford Dictionary of National Biography*.
44. Selwyn, 69.
45. Andrew I. M. Duncan, "A Study of the Life and Public Career of Frederick Howard, Fifth Earl of Carlisle, 1748–1825," dissertation, University College, Oxford, 1981, 8.
46. Duncan, 14.
47. Mitchell, *Fox*, 102.
48. Fox-Strangways, 2:352.
49. Ayling, 42.
50. Wecter, "Burke and Kinsmen," 65.
51. Mitchell, *Fox*, 272.
52. C., 2:450.
53. Wecter, "Burke and Kinsmen," 65.
54. C., 2:450–51.
55. Marshall, *Burke and Empire*, 65.
56. Marshall, *Burke and Empire*, 81.
57. C., 2:462.
58. C., 2:460–61.
59. Lowell Joseph Ragatz, *The Fall of the Planter Class in the British Caribbean, 1763–1833: A Study in Social and Economic History* (New York: Century, 1928), 116.
60. C., 2:462.
61. Wecter, "Burke and Kinsmen," 65.
62. Marshall, *Burke and Empire*, 79.
63. Wecter, "Burke and Kinsmen," 66–67.
64. Wecter, "Burke and Kinsmen," 66.
65. Wecter, "Burke and Kinsmen," 67–68.
66. Marshall, *Burke and Empire*, 64.
67. Trevelyan, *Early History of Fox*, 474.

68. W&S, 2:390.
69. Sutherland, *East India Company in Eighteenth-Century Politics* (Oxford: Clarendon Press, 1952), 221.
70. Sutherland, *East India Company*, 222–23.
71. Bowen, "Clive, Robert."
72. W&S, 2:396.
73. W&S, 2:396.
74. W&S, 2:390.
75. Ayling, 49.
76. Ayling, 40.
77. Trevelyan, *Early History of Fox*, 471–72.
78. *Treasury Board Minute Books, January 14, 1773–February 22, 1774*, Records Created or Inherited by H. M. Treasury, Collection 29, bks. 42–43, NA.
79. *Treasury Board Minute Books, January 24–May 6, 1773*, bks. 42–43, NA.
80. Ayling, 41.
81. *Treasury Board Minute Books*, bk. 43, pp. 252–53, 271, NA.
82. Russell, 1:101.
83. Luff.

Chapter 8

1. Whiteley, 7.
2. Whiteley, 8.
3. Richard Cumberland, *Memoirs of Richard Cumberland* (London: Lackington, Allen & Co., 1806), 1:437.
4. Trevelyan, *George III and Fox*, 1:59.
5. Whiteley, 14.
6. Charles Daniel Smith, *The Early Career of Lord North the Prime Minister* (London: Athlone Press, 1979), 168.
7. Whiteley, 74.
8. Smith, *Early Career of Lord North*, 114.
9. Whiteley, 82.
10. Whiteley, 88.
11. PH, 16:845.
12. Wraxall, 1:376.
13. Cavendish, *Debates*, 1:441.
14. Cornelius P. Forster, *The Uncontrolled Chancellor: Charles Townshend and His American Policy* (Providence: Rhode Island Bicentennial Foundation, 1978), 123.
15. Bernard Bailyn, *The Ordeal of Thomas Hutchinson* (Cambridge, MA: Harvard University Press, 2006), 36.
16. Van Doren, 383.
17. David C. Hendrickson and Robert W. Tucker, *The Fall of the First British Empire* (Baltimore: Johns Hopkins University Press, 1982), 258–59.
18. Hiller B. Zobel, *The Boston Massacre* (New York: W. W. Norton, 1970), 77.
19. Andrew David Struan, "An Englishman and a Servant of the Publick: Major-General Thomas Gage, 1763–1775," master's thesis, University of Glasgow, 2006.
20. Zobel, 99.

21. John C. Miller, *Sam Adams: Pioneer in Propaganda* (Stanford, CA: Stanford University Press, 1936), 197.

22. Miller, *Sam Adams*, 201.

23. Francis Bowen, "Life of James Otis," in *The Library of American Biography*, ed. Jared Sparks (Boston: Charles C. Little & James Brown, 1846), 2:162.

24. Miller, *Sam Adams*, 126.

25. Miller, *Sam Adams*, 224.

26. Miller, *Sam Adams*, 223.

27. Cavendish, *Debates*, 1:486–89.

28. Cavendish, *Debates*, 1:550–51.

29. Hoffman, 64.

30. W&S, 2:46.

31. W&S, 2:49.

32. Hoffman, 56.

33. Cavendish, *Debates*, 1:191, 200.

34. Hoffman, 57.

35. Hoffman, 61.

36. W&S, 3:374–75.

37. W&S, 2:324–34.

38. Miller, *Sam Adams*, 135.

39. W&S, 2:329.

40. W&S, 2:329.

41. PH, 16:469–70.

42. C., 2:165.

43. C., 1:166.

44. Hoffman, 497.

45. C., 2:233.

46. Carl B. Cone, "Edmund Burke, the Farmer," *Agricultural History* 19, no. 2 (145): 68.

47. Hoffman, 503.

48. Hoffman, 101.

49. C., 2:229–330.

50. C., 2:524.

51. PH, 17:178–86.

52. W&S, 2:407.

53. W&S, 2:429.

54. W&S, 2:432–33.

55. W&S, 2:453–55.

56. W&S, 2:463.

57. Miller, *Origins*, 385.

58. Miller, *Origins*, 384.

Chapter 9

1. Patrick Woodland, "Dowdeswell, William (1721–1775)," *Oxford Dictionary of National Biography*.

2. Woodland, "Dowdeswell, William."

3. W&S, 2:462.

4. C., 3:168.
5. W&S, 3:57–60.
6. W&S, 3:69.
7. PH, 18:168–89.
8. PH, 18:190–93.
9. C., 3:383.
10. George III and Lord North, 2:215.
11. PH, 18:322.
12. PH, 18:330–38.
13. W&S, 3:104.
14. Collins, 293.
15. W&S, 3:114.
16. W&S, 3:118–39.
17. W&S, 3:157.
18. W&S, 3:130.
19. W&S, 3:131.
20. PH, 18:538.
21. "Petition to George III, King of Great Britain, 1775," Manuscripts and Archives Division, New York Public Library Digital Collections, https://digitalcollections.nypl.org/items/af2242e0-7f2b-0132-7d52-58d385a7b928.
22. *Address of the Gentlemen, Clergy, Merchants, Manufacturers, and principal Inhabitants of the Town and Neighbourhood of Manchester in the County Palatine of Lancaster, to the King* (Manchester: C. Wheeler, 1775).
23. Hobhouse, 69.
24. Fox, *Speeches*, 1:50–52.
25. Mitchell, *Fox*, 25.
26. *The Parricide: A Sketch of Modern Patriotism*, May 1, 1776, print, Lewis Walpole Library, Yale University.
27. Grant, 175.
28. Whiteley, 74.
29. M&C, 1:145–47.
30. C., 3:294.
31. C., 3:290.
32. PH, 18:1397.
33. C., 3:299.
34. Boswell, *Life of Johnson*, 329.
35. C., 3:384.
36. PH, 18:1443–44.
37. *London Gazette*, November 2, 1779.
38. PH, 18:1444.
39. E. A. Reitan, "The Civil List in Eighteenth-Century British Politics: Parliamentary Supremacy Versus the Independence of the Crown," *Historical Journal* 9, no. 3 (1996): 322.
40. Fox, *Speeches*, 1:74–6.
41. PH, 19:213.
42. PH, 19:230.
43. PH, 19:228–32.

44. C., 3:339.
45. George III, *The Correspondence of King George III, 1760–1783* (London: Macmillan, 1928), 3:450.
46. Whiteley, 170.
47. Lascelles, 65.
48. C., 3:380.
49. Wraxall, 2:277–79.
50. M&C, 1:162.
51. C., 3:408.
52. Mitchell, *Fox*, 29.
53. Trevelyan, *George III* and *Fox*, 2:84.
54. Wraxall, 2:260.
55. PH, 19:672–83.

Chapter 10

1. John Grainger and Daniel Clark, Trial, July 1768, in *Proceedings of the Old Bailey, 1674–1913*, online, https://www.oldbaileyonline.org, Ref. no. t17680706-46.
2. Rudé, 97.
3. Horace Walpole, *The Yale Edition of Horace Walpole's Correspondence*, ed. W. S. Lewis (New Haven, CT: Yale University Press, 1967), 23:39.
4. W&S, 3:376.
5. C., 4:85.
6. W&S, 3:426.
7. W&S, 3:483–84.
8. W&S, 3:471.
9. W&S, 3:487–90.
10. Matthew Kilburn, "Association Movement (act. 1780–1785)," *Oxford Dictionary of National Biography*.
11. *Cambridge Chronicle*, January 15, 1780, quoted in H. Butterfield, "The Yorkshire Association and the Crisis of 1779–80," *Transactions of the Royal Historical Society* 29 (2007): 82.
12. W&S, 3:447.
13. W&S, 3:497–513.
14. W&S, 3:528.
15. W&S, 3:545.
16. W&S, 3:502.
17. W&S, 3:510.
18. PH, 21:36.
19. PH, 21:237n1.
20. Garland Cannon, "Sir William Jones and Edmund Burke" *Modern Philology* 54, no. 3 (1957): 170–71.
21. Michael J. Franklin, *Orientalist Jones: Sir William Jones, Poet, Lawyer, and Linguist, 1746–1794* (Oxford: Oxford University Press, 2011), 103.
22. C., 4:274.
23. PH, 1395–406.
24. *Morning Chronicle* (London), February 28, 1780.

25. W&S, 3:584–86.
26. W&S, 3:588–90.
27. W&S, 3:563.
28. PH, 21:347.
29. W&S, 3:593.
30. W&S, 3:590–96.
31. William C. Lowe, "Lennox, Charles, Third Duke of Richmond (1735–1806)," *Oxford Dictionary of National Biography*.
32. Christopher Hibbert, *King Mob* (London: Longmans, Green, 1958), 38.
33. PH, 668–69.
34. Hibbert, 107.
35. C., 4:246n.
36. Hibbert, 102.
37. Hibbert, 87, 121.
38. W&S, 3:614.
39. W&S, 3:614.
40. Colin Haydon, "Gordon, Lord George (1751–1793)," *Oxford Dictionary of National Biography*.
41. Hibbert, 149.
42. Hibbert, 132–33.

Chapter 11

1. N. C. Phillips, "The British General Election of 1780: A Vortex of Politics," *Political Science* 11, no. 2 (1959): 3–22.
2. Whiteley, 187–88.
3. P. T. Underdown, "Edmund Burke, the Commissary of His Bristol Constituents, 1774–1780," *English Historical Review* 73, no. 287 (1958): 253.
4. C., 4:268, 274.
5. C., 4:272, 277.
6. C., 4:273.
7. W&S, 3:627.
8. W&S, 3:664.
9. C., 4:277–78.
10. C., 4:278.
11. W&S, 3:665–67.
12. C., 4:299.
13. *London Courant and Westminster Chronicle*, September 16, 1780.
14. *London Courant and Westminster Chronicle*, September 18, 1780.
15. C., 4:283.
16. *Public Advertiser* (London), September 8, 1780.
17. C., 4:283.
18. C., 4:299–302.
19. C., 4:314–15.
20. W&S, 4:66.
21. W&S, 4:71.
22. PH, 22:247.

23. C., 4:339.
24. Dixon Wecter, "Four Letters from George Crabbe to Edmund Burke," *Review of English Studies* 14, no. 55 (1938): 298–99.
25. Moritz, 3.
26. C., 4:368.
27. C., 4:364–65.
28. C., 4:378.
29. C., 4:385.
30. PH, 22:398–405.
31. W&S, 4:97–98.
32. John C. Miller, *Triumph of Freedom 1775–1783* (Boston: Little, Brown, 1948), 558–62.
33. Wraxall, 2:435.
34. PH, 22:636–38.
35. PH, 22:680.
36. Mitchell, *Fox*, 43.
37. Fox, *Speeches*, 1:423–38.
38. Peter D. G. Thomas, "North, Frederick (1732–1792)," *Oxford Dictionary of National Biography*.
39. PH, 22:715–23.
40. J.P.W. Ehrman and Anthony Smith, "Pitt, William (1759–1806)," *Oxford Dictionary of National Biography*.
41. PH, 22:746–48.
42. PH: 22:853–65.
43. C., 4:419.
44. Whiteley, 199.
45. Peter D. G. Thomas, *Lord North* (London: Allen Lane, 1976), 130–33.
46. Whiteley, 201–3.
47. PH, 22:1213–24.
48. Whiteley, 204.

Chapter 12

1. John Cannon, "Petty [formerly Fitzmaurice], William, Second Earl of Shelburne and First Marquess of Lansdowne (1737–1805), Prime Minister," *Oxford Dictionary of National Biography*.
2. John Cannon, *The Fox-North Coalition: Crisis of the Constitution 1782–1784* (Cambridge, UK: Cambridge University Press, 1969) 59.
3. Cannon, "Petty, William."
4. Paul Langford, "Walpole, Horatio [Horace], Fourth Earl of Orford (1717–1797)," *Oxford Dictionary of National Biography*.
5. Roberts, 40.
6. Cannon, "Petty, William."
7. M&C, 1:252–53.
8. Ayling, 104–5.
9. King George III, *The Later Correspondence of George III*, ed. A. Aspinall (New York: Cambridge University Press, 1963), 5:22.
10. M&C, 1:319–20.
11. Fox, *Speeches*, 2:66.

12. C., 4:454.
13. John Morley, *Edmund Burke: A Historical Study* (New York: Alfred A. Knopf, 1924), 141.
14. Mitchell, *Fox*, 100.
15. C., 4:377.
16. Nicholas K. Robinson, *Edmund Burke: A Life in Caricature* (New Haven, CT: Yale University Press, 1996), 39.
17. C., 5:25–26.
18. PH, 22:1228.
19. C., 4:445.
20. W&S, 4:143.
21. W&S, 4:149.
22. W&S, 4:145.
23. C., 4:117–21.
24. C., 4:422.
25. W&S, 4:29.
26. Lady Sarah Lennox, *The Life and Letters of Lady Sarah Lennox*, edited by Countess of Ilchester and Lord Stavordale (London: John Murray, 1901), 2:19–20.
27. C., 5:9.
28. W&S, 4:151.
29. Lock, 1:516.
30. C., 4:9.
31. W&S, 4:154.
32. C., 4:20.
33. James Gillray, *Crumbs of Comfort*, August 1782, National Portrait Gallery, London.
34. Samuel Taylor Coleridge, *Collected Letters*, ed. Earl Leslie Griggs (Oxford: Oxford University Press, 1956), 1:562.
35. Mitchell, *Fox*, 97.
36. Edward Gibbon, *The Autobiography and Correspondence of Edward Gibbon, the Historian* (London: Alex Murray & Son, 1869), 274.
37. PH, 23:233–36.
38. PH, 23:249.
39. PH, 23:487.
40. PH, 23:491.
41. PH, 23:549–53.
42. Fox, *Speeches*, 2:136.
43. Roberts, 426.
44. Roberts, 442.
45. Lock, 1:522.
46. Horace Walpole, *The Last Journals of Horace Walpole During the Reign of George III, from 1771–1783* (London: J. Lane, 1910), 2:509–10.
47. Cannon, *Fox-North Coalition*, 85–90.
48. Cannon, *Fox-North Coalition*, 95–96.
49. George III, *Correspondence*, 4:400.
50. Wecter, "Burke and Kinsmen," 97.
51. PH, 23:803–5.
52. PH, 23:901–6.
53. PH, 23:911–18.

54. W&S, 4:167–76.

55. PH, 23:920.

56. Oliver Goldsmith, *Retaliation: A Poem* (London: G. Kearsly, 1776), 8–9.

57. PH, 23:922.

58. Cannon, *Fox-North Coalition*, 96.

Chapter 13

1. C., 5:107n7.

2. Boswell, *Life of Johnson*, 339.

3. C. H. Philips, *The East India Company, 1784–1834* (Manchester: University of Manchester Press, 1940), 2.

4. W&S, 5:389.

5. W&S, 2:393–96.

6. W&S, 5:2–3.

7. W&S, 5:389.

8. W&S, 5:194.

9. Fox, *Speeches*, 2:197.

10. James Gillray, *Coalition Dance*, April 5, 1783, National Portrait Gallery, London.

11. Robinson, 46.

12. Cannon, *Fox-North Coalition*, 114.

13. Fox, *Speeches*, 2:207.

14. Roberts, 456.

15. Ayling, 20.

16. Fox, *Speeches*, 2:198.

17. PH, 23:1284.

18. Fox, *Speeches*, 2:199.

19. Fox, *Speeches*, 2:200–12.

20. PH, 23:1209–10.

21. Fox, *Speeches*, 2:223–29.

22. PH, 23:1277–81.

23. W&S, 5:386.

24. W&S, 5:400–3.

25. W&S, 5:431–32.

26. W&S, 5:449–51.

27. James Sayers, *Carlo Khan's Triumphant Entry into Leadenhall Street*, December 1783, Lewis Walpole Library, Yale University.

28. Horace Twiss, *Public and Private Life of Lord Chancellor Eldon* (London: John Murray, 1844), 1:163.

29. Cannon, *Fox-North Coalition*, 125.

30. William Windham, *The Windham Papers* (London: Herbert Jenkins, 1912), 1:54.

31. William Hague, *William Pitt the Younger* (New York: Knopf Doubleday, 2004), 125.

32. Cannon, *Fox-North Coalition*, 126.

33. Cannon, *Fox-North Coalition*, 133.

34. PH, 24:126.

35. PH, 24:133.

36. Hague, 125.

37. Cannon, *Fox-North Coalition*, 138–44.

38. C., 5:119.

39. C., 5:120.

40. Hester Stanhope, *Memoirs of the Lady Hester Stanhope* (London: Henry Colburn, 1846), 2:161.

41. Hague, 8.

42. Hague, 110.

43. Mitchell, *Fox*, 3.

44. PH, 24:274–94.

45. Hague, 133.

46. PH, 24:355.

47. Henry Stanhope, *Life of the Right Honourable William Pitt* (London: John Murray, 1879), 1:180.

48. Roberts, 468.

49. Stanhope, *William Pitt*, 1:152.

50. Boswell, *Life of Johnson*, 926.

51. Leslie George Mitchell, *Charles James Fox and the Disintegration of the Whig Party, 1782–1794* (Oxford: Oxford University Press, 1971), 85.

52. C., 5:130ff.

53. W&S, 4:178–80.

54. Daniel A. Baugh and Michael Duffy, "Samuel Hood, First Viscount Hood," *Oxford Dictionary of National Biography*.

55. Baugh and Duffy.

56. Ayling, 137.

57. Thomas Northcote, "To the Right Hon. Mr. Fox," *Public Advertiser* (London), April 21, 1784.

58. C., 5:154.

Chapter 14

1. Cavendish, *Debates*, 1:244–46.

2. George Forrest, *Life of Lord Clive* (London: Cassell, 1918), 2:175–77.

3. PH, 17:857–77.

4. PH, 17:861.

5. W&S, 2:395–96.

6. Keith Feiling, *Hastings* (Hamden, CT: Archon Books, 1967), 158.

7. Dalrymple, 239–40.

8. Feiling, 41.

9. Jeremy Bernstein, *Dawning of the Raj: The Life and Trials of Warren Hastings* (Chicago: Ivan R. Dee, 2000), 10.

10. Dalrymple, 82.

11. Bernstein, 48.

12. Henry Vansittart, *A Narrative of the Transactions in Bengal, From the Year 1760 to the Year 1764, During the Government of Mr. Henry Vansittart* (London: J. Newbery, 1766), 99–100.

13. Dalrymple, 168.

14. P. J. Marshall, "Hastings, Warren (1732–1818), governor-general of Bengal," *Oxford Dictionary of National Biography*.

15. Dalrymple, 216–17.
16. Dalrymple, 228.
17. Marshall, "Hastings, Warren."
18. Robins, 112.
19. Bernstein, 82.
20. Francis Sykes to Warren Hastings, March 20, 1774, in Sophia Weitzman, *Warren Hastings and Philip Francis* (Manchester: Manchester University Press, 1929), 213–14.
21. Weitzman, 56.
22. Feiling, 128.
23. Feiling, 127.
24. Philip Francis, *Memoirs of Sir Philip Francis*, ed. J. Parkes and H. Merivale (London: Longmans, Green, 1867), 1:367.
25. James Mill, *History of British India* (London: Baldwin, Cradock, Joy, 1826), 3:362–63.
26. Feiling, 84–87.
27. Feiling, 86.
28. Feiling, 138.
29. Weitzman, 222.
30. Weitzman, 222.
31. Feiling, 113.
32. Feiling, 115.
33. Mill, 3:402.
34. Bernstein, 93.
35. Feiling, 111.
36. W&S, 5:458.
37. Weitzman, 25.
38. Feiling, 145.
39. Feiling, 149.
40. Feiling, 152.
41. Thomas Babington Macaulay, "Warren Hastings," *Edinburgh Review* 74 (October 1841): 160–255.
42. Bernstein, 101.
43. Feiling, 156.
44. Bernstein, 132–37.
45. Feiling, 286.
46. W&S, 5:1.
47. W&S, 5:194–97.
48. C., 5:142–43.
49. Garland Cannon, *Life and Mind of Oriental Jones* (Cambridge, UK: Cambridge University Press, 1990), 210.
50. C., 5:142–44.
51. C., 5:253.
52. W&S, 5:464.
53. W&S 5:461.
54. W&S, 5:410.
55. W&S, 5:468–71.
56. Feiling, 304.
57. Feiling, 322.

58. Feiling, 314–15.
59. Bernstein, 170.
60. W&S, 5:618.

Chapter 15

1. Warren Hastings, *Memoirs of the Life of the Right Hon. Warren Hastings, First Governor-general of Bengal* (London: Richard Bentley, 1841), 3:239.
2. Hastings, 3:225.
3. Hastings, 3:174.
4. P. J. Marshall, *The Impeachment of Hastings* (Oxford: Oxford University Press, 1965), 19.
5. Hastings, 3:174.
6. Hastings, 3:241.
7. Hastings, 3:242–43.
8. Wraxall, 4:304.
9. Martin Hutchinson, *Forging Modernity: Why and How Britain Got the Industrial Revolution* (Cambridge, UK: Lutterworth Press, 2023), 241.
10. Bowen, "Clive, Robert."
11. Hague, 154.
12. Fox, *Speeches*, 2:489.
13. Fox, *Speeches*, 3:26–37.
14. Mitchell, *Fox and Disintegration*, 99.
15. Mitchell, *Fox and Disintegration*, 101.
16. C., 5:177.
17. Add MS 51725, 128–29, BL.
18. *Town and Country Magazine* (London: A. Hamilton), July 1776.
19. I. M. Davis, *The Harlot and the Statesman: The Story of Elizabeth Armistead and Charles James Fox* (Bourne End: Kensal Press, 1986), 81.
20. Mitchell, *Fox*, 73.
21. Davis, 90.
22. W&S, 6:1.
23. Wraxall, 4:86–88.
24. W&S, 5:488.
25. W&S, 5:493.
26. Wraxall, 4:82–86.
27. Wraxall, 4:89.
28. Hastings, 3:172–73.
29. Hastings, 3:170.
30. W&S, 6:48.
31. W&S, 6:82.
32. Wraxall, 4:315.
33. Bowen, "Clive, Robert."
34. W&S, 4:8.
35. PH, 26:39.
36. PH, 26:94.
37. Marshall, *Impeachment*, 101–3.

38. Marshall, *Impeachment*, 106.
39. PH, 26:97.
40. Hague, 198.
41. PH, 26:111.
42. Hastings, 3:295.
43. Hastings, 3:297.
44. PH, 26:273–94.
45. Hastings, 3:328.
46. Hastings, 3:335.
47. PH, 26:877.
48. Marshall, *Impeachment*, 69.
49. C., 5:362.
50. W&S, 6:133, 164.
51. W&S, 6:182.
52. C., 5:378.
53. Frances Burney, *Diary and Letters of Madame D'Arblay*, 7 vols. (London: Henry Colburn, 1854), 4:47.
54. Burney, 4:50.
55. W&S, 6:266.
56. W&S, 6:268.
57. C., 5:386.
58. Burney, 4:99.
59. W&S, 6:459.
60. Burney, 4:99–100.
61. C., 5:241–44.
62. W&S, 5:449.
63. Thomas Moore, *Life of Richard Brinsley Sheridan* (London: Brown & Green, 1825), 2:21–31.
64. John Derry, *The Regency Crisis and the Whigs, 1788–1789* (Cambridge, UK: Cambridge University Press, 1963), 207.
65. Mitchell, *Fox*, 80.
66. Mitchell, *Fox and Disintegration*, 125.
67. C., 5:429.
68. C., 5:438.
69. C., 5:430n2.
70. Fox, *Speeches*, 3:402–3.
71. Mitchell, *Fox and Disintegration*, 133.
72. PH, 27:819.
73. PH, 27:822.
74. PH, 27:1173–74.
75. Burney, 5:10.
76. Fox, *Speeches*, 3:465.
77. PH, 27:1351.
78. C., 5:468.
79. PH, 27:1411.
80. PH, 27:1412–22.
81. C., 5:473.

Chapter 16

1. Mitchell, *Fox and Disintegration*, 154.
2. Burke, *Reflections on the Revolution in France*, ed. J. C. D. Clarke (Stanford, CA: Stanford University Press, 2002), 154.
3. Burke, *Reflections*, 61.
4. William Doyle, *Oxford History of the French Revolution* (Oxford: Oxford University Press, 1980), 435.
5. Mitchell, *Fox*, 110.
6. Doyle, 135.
7. Arthur Young, *Travels During the Years 1787, 1788 and 1789, Undertaken More Particularly with a View of Ascertaining the Cultivation, Wealth, Resources, and National Prosperity of the Kingdom of France* (Dublin: R. Cross, 1793), 2:515.
8. Burke, *Reflections*, 55.
9. Burke, *Reflections*, 56.
10. Burke, *Reflections*, 39.
11. C., 6:30.
12. C., 6:36.
13. Louis-Sébastien Mercier, *New Picture of Paris* (Dublin: N. Kelly, 1800), 1:184.
14. C., 6:41.
15. C., 6:46.
16. C., 6:50.
17. Robinson, 144.
18. D. O. Thomas, "Price, Richard (1723–1791)," *Oxford Dictionary of National Biography*.
19. Burke, *Reflections*, 64.
20. Fox, *Speeches*, 4:34.
21. W&S, 4:286.
22. Mercier, 2:43–44.
23. W&S, 4:280–87.
24. C., 4:454, 6:55.
25. W&S, 4:288.
26. W&S, 4:294n.
27. Mitchell, *Fox and Disintegration*, 157.
28. C., 5:470.
29. Fox, *Speeches*, 4:10.
30. C., 5:471.
31. C., 5:471.
32. Fox, *Speeches*, 4:68.
33. W&S, 4:314n.
34. W&S, 4:317.
35. Fox, *Speeches*, 4:74.
36. W&S, 4:293.
37. Burke, *Reflections*, 196.
38. Burke, *Reflections*, 257.
39. Burke, *Reflections*, 276.
40. Burke, *Reflections*, 328.
41. Burke, *Reflections*, 360.

42. Burke, *Reflections*, 284n.
43. Boswell, *Life of Johnson*, 327.
44. Andrew Dickson White, *Fiat Money Inflation in France* (New York: D. Appleton, 1912), 31.
45. Burke, *Reflections*, 401.
46. Burke, *Reflections*, 233.
47. C., 6:86.
48. Burke, *Reflections*, 238.
49. C., 6:91.
50. Burke, *Reflections*, 240n.
51. C., 6:86–87.
52. C., 6:90.
53. Marshall, *Impeachment*, 73.
54. Marshall, *Impeachment*, 74.
55. Morris, 493.
56. *Times* (London), May 15, 1790.
57. Burke, *Reflections*, 31n.
58. Robinson, 141–43.
59. Lock, 2:333.
60. C., 6:151.
61. Lock, 2:334.
62. Burney, 2:278.
63. C., 6:155.
64. C. 6:239.
65. Thomas Paine, *The Rights of Man* (London: J.S. Jordan, 1791), pt. 1, 166.
66. C., 6:247.
67. PH, 29:218.
68. Mitchell, *Fox and Disintegration*, 158.
69. Fox, *Speeches*, 4:198–200.
70. C., 6:273n.
71. Windham, 1:6.
72. W&S, 4:322–23.
73. Burney, 3:263.
74. W&S, 4:324.
75. PH, 29:364–401.
76. PH, 29:371–75.
77. PH, 29:376.
78. Fox, *Speeches*, 4:215.
79. Fox, *Speeches*, 4:217.
80. Fox, *Speeches*, 4:218.
81. PH, 29:387.
82. W&S, 4:345.
83. Fox, *Speeches*, 4:223.
84. W&S, 4:350.
85. W&S, 4:353–57.
86. Horace Walpole to Mary Berry, May 12, 1791, Horace Walpole Collection, Lewis Walpole Library, Yale University.

87. Mitchell, *Fox and Disintegration*, 166.
88. C., 6:271.
89. C., 6:276.

Epilogue

1. PH, 23:800.
2. Lock, 2:552–53.
3. O'Brien, 521.
4. Mitchell, *Fox*, 249.
5. Milton MSS, Box 45, Duke of Bedford, December 13, 1793, Northamptonshire Record Office.
6. Hobhouse, 239.
7. Mitchell, *Fox*, 131.
8. Mitchell, *Fox*, 119.
9. Hague, 267.
10. James Gillray, *Patriots Amusing Themselves; - or - Swedes Practising at a Post*, hand-colored etching, National Portrait Gallery, London.
11. Mitchell, *Fox*, 122–24.
12. Mitchell, *Fox*, 124–25.
13. Mitchell, *Fox*, 127–28.
14. Mitchell, *Fox*, 130.
15. Mitchell, *Fox*, 131.
16. W&S, 9:424n.
17. Doyle, 199.
18. Mitchell, *Fox*, 108.
19. W&S, 8:429.
20. W&S, 8:407.
21. W&S, 8:452.
22. Hague, 260.
23. William Pitt quoted in Auckland, *The Journal and Correspondence of William, Lord Auckland* (London: Bentley, 1862), 3:320.
24. PH, 31:505, 518.
25. Doyle, 200.
26. PH, 30:13–14.
27. Fox, *Speeches*, 4:460.
28. W&S, 7:619.
29. James Caulfeild, *The Manuscripts and Correspondence of James, First Earl of Charlemont, Vol. 2, 1784–1799* (London: His Majesty's Stationery Office, 1894), Thirteenth Report, app., pt. 8.
30. Feiling, 351–52.
31. W&S, 7:228.
32. Feiling, 351, 359.
33. W&S 7:228.
34. *Times* (London), May 29, 1794.
35. Joseph Farington, *Diary* (London: Hutchinson, 1802), 1:51.
36. W&S, 7:517.

37. E. A. Bond, ed., *Speeches of the Managers and Counsel in the Trial of Warren Hastings* (London: Longman, Brown, Green, Longmans, & Roberts, 1859), 3:xxiv.
38. W&S, 7:692–94.
39. W&S, 7:696.
40. Feiling, 366.
41. Add MS 29224, BL; Add MS 29205, ff.370, BL; P. J. Marshall, "The Personal Fortune of Warren Hastings: Hastings in Retirement," *Bulletin of the School of Oriental and African Studies* 28, no. 3 (1965): 547.
42. Feiling, 372–82.
43. Feiling, 367–68.
44. Feiling, 385.
45. Feiling, 393–94.
46. Mitchell, *Fox*, 105–6.
47. Milton MSS, Box 45, Duke of Bedford, December 13, 1793, Northamptonshire Record Office.
48. Lock, 2:470.
49. Lock, 2:476.
50. C., 7:568.
51. C., 7:591.
52. E. A. Smith, "Russell, Francis, Fifth Duke of Bedford," *Oxford Dictionary of National Biography*.
53. W&S, 9:164.
54. W&S, 9:160.
55. Bisset, 2:429.
56. O'Brien, 517.
57. C., 9:62.
58. C., 9:300.
59. C., 9:307.
60. C., 9:61.
61. Lock, 2:576.
62. C., 9:372.
63. Mitchell, *Fox*, 115.
64. Hobhouse, 229.
65. Davis, 170; L. G. Mitchell, "Fox, Charles James (1749–1806), Politician," *Oxford Dictionary of National Biography*.
66. Parliament of the United Kingdom, *Hansard Parliamentary Debates*, cc. 41–73, vol. 6 (1806).
67. C., 9:375.
68. Samuel Parr, *Characters of the Late Charles James Fox* (Birmingham: J. Mawman, Poultry, 1809), 1:72.

BIBLIOGRAPHY

Adams, John. *Papers of John Adams*. Vol. 1. Edited by Robert J. Taylor. Cambridge, MA: Belknap Press, 1977.

Address of the Gentlemen, Clergy, Merchants, Manufacturers, and Principal Inhabitants of the Town and Neighbourhood of Manchester in the County Palatine of Lancaster, to the King. Manchester: C. Wheeler, 1775.

Auckland, William, Lord. *The Journal and Correspondence of William, Lord Auckland*. London: Bentley, 1862.

Ayling, Stanley. *Fox: The Life of Charles James Fox*. London: John Murray, 1991.

Bailyn, Bernard. *The Ordeal of Thomas Hutchinson*. Cambridge, MA: Harvard University Press, 2006.

Baugh, Daniel A., and Michael Duffy. "Hood, Samuel, First Viscount Hood (1724–1816), Naval Officer." *Oxford Dictionary of National Biography*. Online ed., https://doi.org/10.1093/ref:odnb/13678.

Beckett, J. V., and Peter D. G. Thomas. "Grenville, George (1712–1770), Prime Minister." *Oxford Dictionary of National Biography*. Online ed., https://doi.org/10.1093/ref:odnb/11489.

Bernstein, Jeremy. *Dawning of the Raj: The Life and Trials of Warren Hastings*. Chicago: Ivan R. Dee, 2000.

Bisset, Robert. *The Life of Edmund Burke*. 2 vols. London: G. Cawthon, 1800.

Black, Jeremy. *Pitt the Elder*. Cambridge, UK: Cambridge University Press, 1992.

Blackstock, A. F. "Luttrell, Henry Lawes, Second Earl of Carhampton (1737–1821), Army Officer and Politician." *Oxford Dictionary of National Biography*. Online ed., https://doi.org/10.1093/ref:odnb/17223.

Bolts, William. *Considerations on India Affairs*. London: J. Almon, 1772.

Bond, E. A., ed. *Speeches of the Managers and Counsel in the Trial of Warren Hastings*. London: Longman, Brown, Green, Longmans & Roberts, 1859.

Boswell, James. *The Life of Samuel Johnson*. New York: Penguin, 2008.

———. *London Journal, 1762–3*. New York: McGraw-Hill, 1950.

Bourke, Richard. *Empire and Revolution: The Political Life of Edmund Burke*. Princeton, NJ: Princeton University Press, 2015.

Bowen, Francis. "Life of James Otis," in *The Library of American Biography*. Edited by Jared Sparks. Boston: Charles C. Little & James Brown, 1846.

Bowen, H. V. "Clive, Robert, First Baron Clive of Plassey (1725–1774), Army Officer in the East India Company and Administrator in India." *Oxford Dictionary of National Biography*. Online ed., https://doi.org/10.1093/ref:odnb/5697.

———. "Lord Clive and Speculation in East India Company Stock, 1766." *Historical Journal* 30, no. 4 (1987).

———. *Revenue and Reform: The Indian Problem in British Politics 1757–1773*. Cambridge, UK: Cambridge University Press, 1991.

Boyer, Abel. *The History of the Reign of Queen Anne*. London: A. Roper, 1703.

Braddick, Michael J. "Fox, Sir Stephen (1627–1716), Financier and Government Official." *Oxford Dictionary of National Biography*. Online ed., https://doi.org/10.1093/ref:odnb/10043.

Brooke, John. "Fox, Hon. Charles James (1749–1806)," *The History of Parliament: The House of Commons, 1754–1790*, ed. L. Namier and J. Brooke (1964), https://www.historyofparliamentonline.org/volume/1754-1790/member/fox-hon-charles-james-1749-1806#footnote14_8fnkf67.

———. *King George III*. London: Constable, 1972.

Bullion, John L. " 'To Know This Is the True Essential Business of a King': The Prince of Wales and the Study of Public Finance, 1755–1760." *Albion* 18, no. 3 (1986): 429–54.

Burke, Edmund. *Annual Register* 1–9 (1760).

———. *The Early Life Correspondence and Writing of the Rt. Hon. Edmund Burke*. Edited by Arthur P. I. Samuels. Cambridge, UK: Cambridge University Press, 1923.

———. *Reflections on the Revolution in France*. Edited by J. C. D. Clarke. Stanford, CA: Stanford University Press, 2002.

Burke, Peter. *The Public and Domestic Life of the Right Hon. Edmund Burke*. London: Nathaniel Cooke, 1854.

Burney, Frances. *Diary and Letters of Madame D'Arblay*. 7 vols. London: Henry Colburn, 1854.

———. *The Early Journals and Letters of Fanny Burney: 1782–1783*. 5 vols. Quebec: McGill-Queen's University Press, 1988.

Butterfield, H. "The Yorkshire Association and the Crisis of 1779–80." *Transactions of the Royal Historical Society* 29 (2007): 82.

Cannon, Garland. "Sir William Jones and Edmund Burke." *Modern Philology* 54, no. 3 (1957): 165–86.

———. *Life and Mind of Oriental Jones*. Cambridge, UK: Cambridge University Press, 1990.

Cannon, John. *The Fox-North Coalition: Crisis of the Constitution 1782–4*. Cambridge, UK: Cambridge University Press, 1969.

———. "Petty [formerly Fitzmaurice], William, Second Earl of Shelburne and First Marquess of Lansdowne (1737–1805), Prime Minister." *Oxford Dictionary of National Biography*. Online ed., https://doi.org/10.1093/ref:odnb/22070.

Carlyon, Clement. *Early Years and Late Reflections*. 2 vols. London: Whittaker, 1835.

Cash, Arthur H. *John Wilkes: The Scandalous Father of Civil Liberty*. New Haven, CT: Yale University Press, 2006.

Caulfeild, James. *The Manuscripts and Correspondence of James, First Earl of Charlemont, Vol. 2, 1784–1799*. London: His Majesty's Stationery Office, 1894.

Cavendish, Henry. *Sir Henry Cavendish's Debates of the House of Commons, During the Thirteenth Parliament of Great Britain, Commonly Called the Unreported Parliament*. London: Longman, Orme, Brown, Green & Longmans, 1841.

Cavendish, Richard. "Daniel Defoe Put in the Pillory." *History Today* 53, no. 7 (2003).

Clay, Christopher. *Public Finance and Private Wealth: The Career of Sir Stephen Fox 1627–1716*. Oxford: Clarendon Press, 1978.

Coleridge, Samuel Taylor. *Collected Letters*. Edited by Earl Leslie Griggs. Oxford: Oxford University Press, 1956.

Collins, Gregory M. *Commerce and Manners in Edmund Burke's Political Economy*. Cambridge, UK: Cambridge University Press, 2020.

Corley, T.A.B. "Chudleigh, Elizabeth [married names Elizabeth Hervey, countess of Bristol; Elizabeth Pierrepont, duchess of Kingston upon Hull] (c. 1720–1788), Courtier and Bigamist." *Oxford Dictionary of National Biography*. Online ed., https://doi.org/10.1093/ref:odnb/5380.

Cumberland, Richard. *Memoirs of Richard Cumberland*. London: Lackington, Allen & Co., 1806.

Dalrymple, William. *The Anarchy*. London: Bloomsbury, 2019.

Davis, I. M. *The Harlot and the Statesman: The Story of Elizabeth Armistead and Charles James Fox*. Bourne End: Kensal Press, 1986.

Derrett, J. Duncan M. "Nandakumar's Forgery." *English Historical Review* 75 (1960): 223–28.

Derry, John. *The Regency Crisis and the Whigs, 1788–9*. Cambridge, UK: Cambridge University Press, 1963.

Dille, Catherine. "Dyer, Samuel (bap. 1721, d. 1772), Translator." *Oxford Dictionary of National Biography*. Online ed., https://doi.org/10.1093/ref:odnb/8352.

Doyle, William. *Oxford History of the French Revolution*. Oxford: Oxford University Press, 1980.

Duncan, Andrew I. M. "A Study of the Life and Public Career of Frederick Howard, Fifth Earl of Carlisle, 1748–1825." PhD diss., University College, Oxford, 1981.

Durrant, Peter. "FitzRoy, Augustus Henry, Third Duke of Grafton (1735–1811), Prime Minister." *Oxford Dictionary of National Biography*. Online ed., https://doi.org/10.1093/ref:odnb/9628.

Ehrman, J.P.W., and Anthony Smith. "Pitt, William [Known as Pitt the Younger] (1759–1806), Prime Minister." *Oxford Dictionary of National Biography*. Online ed., https://doi.org/10.1093/ref:odnb/22338.

Elofson, W. M. "The Rockingham Whigs in Transition: The East India Company Issue 1772–1773." *English Historical Review* 104, no. 413 (1989): 947–74.

Emin, Joseph. *Life and Adventures of Joseph Emin*. Calcutta: Baptist Mission Press, 1918.

Farington, Joseph. *Diary*. London: Hutchinson, 1802.

Feiling, Keith. *Warren Hastings*. Hamden, CT: Archon Books, 1967.

Ferishta, Mahomed Kasim. *History of Hindostan*. Translated by Alexander Dow. 2 vols., 2nd ed. London, 1770.

Finlay, Christopher J. "Mackintosh, Sir James, of Kyllachy (1765–1832), Political Writer and Politician." *Oxford Dictionary of National Biography.* Online ed., https://doi.org/10.1093/ref:odnb/17620.

Fitzgerald, Emily. *Correspondence of Emily Duchess of Leinster (1731–1814).* Edited by Brian Fitzgerald. Dublin: Dublin Stationery Office, 1949.

Fitzroy, Augustus Henry. *Autobiography and Political Correspondence of Augustus Henry, Third Duke of Grafton.* Edited by William R. Anson. London: John Murray, 1898.

———. *Hints &c. Submitted to the Serious Attention of the Clergy, Nobility and Gentry, Newly Associated.* London: B. White & Son & J. Deerett, 1790.

Forrest, George. *Life of Lord Clive.* London: Cassell, 1918.

Forster, Cornelius P. *The Uncontrolled Chancellor: Charles Townshend and His American Policy.* Providence: Rhode Island Bicentennial Foundation, 1978.

Fox, Charles James. *The Speeches of the Right Honorable Charles James Fox, in the House of Commons.* 6 vols. London: Longman, Hurst, Rees, Orme, & Brown, 1815.

Fox, Henry. "Memoir on the Events Attending the Death of George II and the Accession of George III." In *The Life and Letters of Lady Sarah Lennox.* London: John Murray, 1902.

Fox-Strangways, Giles Stephen Holland. *Henry Fox, First Lord Holland.* 2 vols. New York: Charles Scribner's Sons, 1920.

Francis, Philip. *Memoirs of Sir Philip Francis.* Edited by J. Parkes and H. Merivale. 2 vols. London: Longmans, Green, 1867.

Franklin, Michael J. *Orientalist Jones: Sir William Jones, Poet, Lawyer, and Linguist, 1746–1794.* Oxford: Oxford University Press, 2011.

Geoghegan, P. M. "Howard, Frederick, Fifth Earl of Carlisle (1748–1825), Politician and Diplomat." *Oxford Dictionary of National Biography.* Online ed., https://doi.org/10.1093/ref:odnb/13899.

George III. *The Correspondence of King George III, 1760–1783.* Edited by Sir John Fortescue. London: Macmillan, 1928.

———. *The Later Correspondence of George III.* Edited by A. Aspinall. Cambridge, UK: Cambridge University Press, 1963.

George III and Frederick North. *The Correspondence of King George the Third with Lord North: From 1768 to 1783.* Edited by William Bodham Donne. London: John Murray, 1867.

Gibbon, Edward. *The Autobiography and Correspondence of Edward Gibbon, the Historian.* London: Alex Murray & Son, 1869.

———. *Miscellaneous Works of Edward Gibbon.* Dublin: P. Wogan, 1796.

Gibbons, Luke. *Edmund Burke and Ireland: Aesthetics, Politics, and the Colonial Sublime.* Cambridge, UK: Cambridge University Press, 2004.

Goldsmith, Oliver. *Retaliation: A Poem.* London: G. Kearsly, 1776.

Grainger, John, and Daniel Clark. Trial, July 1768. *Proceedings of the Old Bailey, 1674–1913.* Online, https://www.oldbaileyonline.org. Ref. no. t17680706-46.

Grant, James. *John Adams: Party of One.* New York: Farrar, Straus & Giroux, 2005.

Hague, William. *William Pitt the Younger.* New York: Knopf Doubleday, 2004.

Hanham, A. A. "Parsons, Anne [Nancy] [married name Anne Maynard, Viscountess Maynard] (c. 1735–1814/15), Courtesan and Political Mistress." *Oxford Dictionary of National Biography.* Online ed., https://doi.org/10.1093/ref:odnb/75617.

Harris, Robert D. "French Finances and the American War 1777–1783." *Journal of Modern History* 48, no. 2 (June 1976): 233–58.

Hastings, Warren. *Memoirs of the Life of the Right Hon. Warren Hastings, First Governor-general of Bengal.* 3 vols. London: Richard Bentley, 1841.

Haydon, Colin. "Gordon, Lord George (1751–1793), Political and Religious Agitator." *Oxford Dictionary of National Biography.* Online ed., https://doi.org/10.1093/ref:odnb/11040.

Hendrickson, David C., and Robert W. Tucker. *The Fall of the First British Empire.* Baltimore: Johns Hopkins University Press, 1982.

Hibbert, Christopher. *King Mob.* London: Longmans, Green, 1958.

Hobhouse, Christopher. *Fox.* London: Constable, 1947.

Hoffman, Ross J. S. *Edmund Burke, New York Agent with His Letters to the New York Assembly and Intimate Correspondence with Charles O'Hara, 1761–1776.* Philadelphia: American Philosophical Society, 1956.

Hume, Robert D. "The Value of Money in Eighteenth-Century England: Incomes, Prices, Buying Power—and Some Problems in Cultural Economics." *Huntington Library Quarterly* 77, no. 4 (2015): 373–416.

Hutchinson, Martin. *Forging Modernity: Why and How Britain Got the Industrial Revolution.* Cambridge, UK: Lutterworth Press, 2023.

Hutchinson, Thomas. *The History of the Colony and Province of Massachusetts-Bay.* Edited by Lawrence Shaw Mayo. 3 vols. Cambridge, MA: Harvard University Press, 1936.

Ireland. Parliament of Ireland. *An Act to Prevent Papists Being Solicitors.* 10 William III c.13. 1698.

Jenkinson, Hilary C. "Exchequer Tallies." *Archaeologia,* 2nd ser., vol. 12 (1911): 367–380.

Johnson, David. "Britannia Roused: Political Caricature and the Fall of the Fox-North Coalition." *History Today* (June 2001).

Johnson, Samuel. *A Dictionary of the English Language.* London: J. & P. Knapton, et al., 1755, https://johnsonsdictionaryonline.com/1755/job_ns.

———. *Lives of the Poets.* London: J. M. Dent, 1925.

Kelly, James. "Harvests and Hardship: Famine and Scarcity in Ireland in the Late 1720s." *Studia Hibernica,* no. 26 (1992): 66–105.

Kilburn, Matthew. "Association Movement (act. 1780–1785)." *Oxford Dictionary of National Biography.* Online ed., https://doi.org/10.1093/ref:odnb/9780198.

Klinge, Dennis Stephen. "Edmund Burke, Economical Reform and the Board of Trade, 1777–1780." *Journal of Modern History* 51, no. 3 (1979).

Langford, Paul. "Walpole, Horatio [Horace], Fourth Earl of Orford (1717–1797), Author, Politician, and Patron of the Arts." *Oxford Dictionary of National Biography.* Online ed., https://doi.org/10.1093/ref:odnb/28596.

Lascelles, Edward. *The Life of Charles James Fox.* Oxford: Oxford University Press, 1936.

Lecky, W.E.H. *England in the Eighteenth Century.* New York: D. Appleton, 1878.

Lennox, Lady Sarah. *The Life and Letters of Lady Sarah Lennox.* Edited by the Countess of Ilchester and Lord Stavordale, 2 vols. London: John Murray, 1901.

Literary Club, London. *Annals of the Club, 1764–1914.* London: Oxford University Press, 1914.

Lock, Frederick P. *Edmund Burke.* 2 vols. New York: Oxford University Press, 1998–2006.

Longinus. "On the Sublime." In *Aristotle: Poetics. Longinus: On the Sublime. Demetrius: On Style.* Translated by W. Hamilton Fyfe. Cambridge, MA: Harvard University Press, 1995.

Lowe, William C. "Conway, Francis Seymour-, First Marquess of Hertford (1718–1794), Courtier and Politician." *Oxford Dictionary of National Biography.* Online ed., https://doi.org/10.1093/ref:odnb/6121.

———. "Lennox, Charles, Third Duke of Richmond, Third Duke of Lennox, and Duke of Aubigny in the French Nobility (1735–1806), Politician." *Oxford Dictionary of National Biography.* Online ed., https://doi.org/10.1093/ref:odnb/16451.

Luff, Peter. "Fox, Henry, First Baron Holland of Foxley (1705–1774), Politician." *Oxford Dictionary of National Biography.* Online ed., https://doi.org/10.1093/ref:odnb/10033.

Macaulay, Thomas Babington. "Warren Hastings." *Edinburgh Review* 74 (October 1841): 160–255.

Mant, Richard. *History of the Church of Ireland: From the Revolution to the Union of the Churches of England and Ireland, January 1, 1801.* London: John W. Parker, 1840.

Marshall, P. J. *Edmund Burke and the British Empire in the West Indies: Wealth, Power, and Slavery.* Oxford: Oxford University Press, 2019.

———. "Hastings, Warren (1732–1818), Governor-general of Bengal." *Oxford Dictionary of National Biography.* Online ed., https://doi.org/10.1093/ref:odnb/12587.

———. *The Impeachment of Hastings.* Oxford: Oxford University Press, 1965.

———. "The Personal Fortune of Warren Hastings: Hastings in Retirement." *Bulletin of the School of Oriental and African Studies* 28, no. 3 (1965): 541–52.

Matthew, Nicholas. *Sterling: The History of a Currency.* New York: John Wiley & Sons, 1999.

Maxwell, Constantia. *Dublin Under the Georges.* London: Faber & Faber, 1956.

McElroy, George C. "Burke, William (1728/30–1798), Political Writer and Administrator in India." *Oxford Dictionary of National Biography.* Online ed., https://doi.org/10.1093/ref:odnb/4030.

McGuire, James. "Nagle, Sir Richard (1635/6–1699), Lawyer and Jacobite Politician." *Oxford Dictionary of National Biography.* Online ed., https://doi.org/10.1093/ref:odnb/9780.

Mercier, Louis-Sébastien. *New Picture of Paris.* Dublin: N. Kelly, 1800.

Mill, James. *History of British India.* London: Baldwin, Cradock, Joy, 1826.

Miller, John C. *Origins of the American Revolution.* Stanford, CA: Stanford University Press, 1962.

———. *Sam Adams: Pioneer in Propaganda.* Stanford, CA: Stanford University Press, 1936.

———. *Triumph of Freedom 1775–1783.* Boston: Little, Brown, 1948.

Mirowski, Philip. "The Rise (and Retreat) of a Market: English Joint Stock Shares in the Eighteenth Century." *Journal of Economic History* 41, no. 3 (1981): 559–77.

Mitchell, Leslie George. *Charles James Fox.* Oxford: Oxford University Press, 1992.

———. *Charles James Fox and the Disintegration of the Whig Party, 1782–1794.* Oxford: Oxford University Press, 1971.

———. "Fox, Charles James (1749–1806), Politician." *Oxford Dictionary of National Biography.* Online ed., https://doi.org/10.1093/ref:odnb/10024.

Moore, Thomas. *Life of Richard Brinsley Sheridan.* London: Brown & Green, 1825.

Moritz, C. P. *Travels in England in 1782.* London: Cassell, 1886.

Morley, John. *Edmund Burke: A Historical Study.* New York: Alfred A. Knopf, 1924.

Morris, Gouverneur. *A Diary of the French Revolution.* Boston: Houghton Mifflin, 1939.

Nicholls, John. *Recollections and Reflections, Personal and Political, as Connected with Public Affairs, During the Reign of George III.* London: James Ridgway, 1820.

Noorthouck, John. *A New History of London Including Westminster and Southwark.* London: R. Baldwin, 1773,

North, Lord, Seventh Earl of Guilford. "Lord North the Prime Minister." *North American Review* 176, no. 558 (1903): 778–91.

O'Brien, Conor Cruise. *The Great Melody.* Chicago: University of Chicago Press, 1992.

Paine, Thomas. *The Rights of Man.* London: J. S. Jordan, 1791.

Parliament of the United Kingdom. *Hansard Parliamentary Debates* (1806).

Parr, Samuel. *Characters of the Late Charles James Fox*. Birmingham: J. Mawman, Poultry, 1809.

Philips, C. H. *The East India Company, 1784–1834*. Manchester: University of Manche, 1809ster Press, 1940.

Phillips, N. C. "The British General Election of 1780: A Vortex of Politics." *Political Science* 11, no. 2 (1959): 3–22.

Picard, Liza. *Dr. Johnson's London*. London: Phoenix, 2003.

Power, Thomas P. "Sheehy, Nicholas (1728/9–1766), Roman Catholic Priest." *Oxford Dictionary of National Biography*. Online ed., https://doi.org/10.1093/ref:odnb/25287.

"Protest Against Rescinding the East India Dividends." *Gentleman's Magazine*, July 1767.

Prior, James. *Life of the Right Honourable Edmund Burke*. London: Henry G. Bohn, 1854.

Ragatz, Lowell Joseph. *The Fall of the Planter Class in the British Caribbean, 1763–1833: A Study in Social and Economic History*. New York: Century, 1928.

Reid, Loren Dudley. *Charles James Fox: A Man for the People*. London: Longmans, Green and Co., 1969.

Reitan, E. A. "The Civil List in Eighteenth-Century British Politics: Parliamentary Supremacy Versus the Independence of the Crown." *Historical Journal* 9, no. 3 (1996): 318–37.

Riker, Thad W. *Henry Fox, First Lord Holland: A Study of the Career of an Eighteenth-Century Politician*. 2 vols. Oxford: Oxford University Press, 1911.

Roberts, Andrew. *The Last King of America: The Misunderstood Reign of George III*. New York: Viking, 2021.

Robins, Nick. *The Corporation That Changed the World*. London: Pluto Press, 2012.

Robinson, Nicholas K. *Edmund Burke: A Life in Caricature*. New Haven, CT: Yale University Press, 1996.

Rudé, George. *Wilkes and Liberty: A Social Study*. London: Lawrence & Wishart, 1983.

Russell, John. *The Life and Times of Charles James Fox*. 3 vols. London: Richard Bentley, 1866.

Schroeder, Susan Grace. "The Personal and Public Relationship between Edmund Burke and Charles James Fox: Its Evolution and Significance." Master's thesis, Loyola University, 1961.

Selwyn, George. *George Selwyn: His Letters and His Life*. Edited by E. S. Roscoe and Helen Clergue. London: T. Fisher Unwin, 1899.

Smith, Adam. *An Inquiry into the Nature and Causes of the Wealth of Nations*. New York: Modern Library, 1937.

Smith, Charles Daniel. *The Early Career of Lord North the Prime Minister*. London: Athlone Press, 1979.

Smith, E. A. "Russell, Francis, Fifth Duke of Bedford (1765–1802), Agriculturist and Politician." *Oxford Dictionary of National Biography*. Online ed., https://doi.org/10.1093/ref:odnb/24308.

Stanhope, Hester. *Memoirs of the Lady Hester Stanhope*. 2 vols. London: Henry Colburn, 1846.

Stanhope, Philip Henry. *Life of the Right Honourable William Pitt*. London: John Murray, 1861.

Struan, Andrew David. "An Englishman and a Servant of the Publick: Major-General Thomas Gage, 1763–1775." Master's thesis, University of Glasgow, 2006.

Sutherland, Lucy. *The East India Company in Eighteenth-Century Politics*. Oxford: Clarendon Press, 1952.

———. "Lord Shelburne and East India Company Politics, 1766–9." *English Historical Review* 49, no. 195 (1934).

———. "New Evidence on the Nandakuma Trial." *English Historical Review* 72 (1957): 438–65.

Sutherland, Lucy, and J. Binney. "Henry Fox as Paymaster General of the Forces." *English Historical Review* 70, no. 275 (1955): 229–57.

Sutherland, Lucy, and John A. Woods. "The East India Speculations of William Burke," in *Politics and Finance in the Eighteenth Century*. London: Hambledon Press, 1984.

Thomas, D. O. "Price, Richard (1723–1791), Philosopher, Demographer, and Political Radical." *Oxford Dictionary of National Biography*. Online ed., https://doi.org/10.1093/ref:odnb/22761.

Thomas, Peter D. G. *George III: King and Politicians 1760–1770*. Manchester: Manchester University Press, 2002.

———. *Lord North*. London: Allen Lane, 1976.

———. "North, Frederick, Second Earl of Guilford [known as Lord North] (1732–1792), Prime Minister." *Oxford Dictionary of National Biography*. Online ed., https://doi.org/10.1093/ref:odnb/20304.

———. *The Townshend Duties Crisis: The Second Phase of the American Revolution 1767–1773*. New York: Clarendon Press, 1987.

———. "Wilkes, John (1725–1797), Politician." *Oxford Dictionary of National Biography*. Online ed., https://doi.org/10.1093/ref:odnb/29410.

Trevelyan, George Otto. *The Early History of Charles James Fox*. London: Longmans, Green, 1880.

———. *George the Third and Charles Fox: The Concluding Part of the American Revolution*. London: Longmans, Green, 1912.

Tudor, William. *The Life of James Otis, of Massachusetts*. Boston: Wells & Lilly, 1823.

Twiss, Horace. *Public and Private Life of Lord Chancellor Eldon*. London: John Murray, 1844.

Underdown, P. T. "Edmund Burke, the Commissary of His Bristol Constituents, 1774–1780." *English Historical Review* 73, no. 287 (1958): 252–69.

Van Doren, Carl. *Benjamin Franklin*. New York: Viking Press, 1961.

Vansittart, Henry. *A Narrative of the Transactions in Bengal, From the Year 1760 to the Year 1764, During the Government of Mr. Henry Vansittart*. London: J. Newbery, 1766.

Walpole, Horace. *The Last Journals of Horace Walpole During the Reign of George III, from 1771 to 1783*. London: J. Lane, 1910.

———. *The Yale Edition of Horace Walpole's Correspondence*. Edited by W. S. Lewis. New Haven, CT: Yale University Press, 1967.

Wecter, Dixon. "Edmund Burke and His Kinsmen." *University of Colorado Studies: Studies in the Humanities* 1, no. 1 (February 1939).

———. "Four Letters from George Crabbe to Edmund Burke." *Review of English Studies* 14, no. 55 (1938): 298–309.

Weitzman, Sophia. *Warren Hastings and Philip Francis*. Manchester: Manchester University Press, 1929.

White, Andrew Dickson. *Fiat Money Inflation in France*. New York: D. Appleton, 1912.

Whiteley, Peter. *Lord North: The Prime Minister Who Lost America*. London: Hambledon Press, 1996.

Wilkes, John. *The North Briton*. London: W. Bingley, 1769–71.

Windham, William. *The Windham Papers*. London: Herbert Jenkins, 1912.

Woodland, Patrick. "Dowdeswell, William (1721–1775), Politician." *Oxford Dictionary of National Biography*. Online ed., https://doi.org/10.1093/ref:odnb/7959.

———. "Verney, Ralph, Second Earl Verney (1714–1791), Politician." *Oxford Dictionary of National Biography*. Online ed., https://doi.org/10.1093/ref:odnb/28234.

Wraxall, Nathaniel William. *Historical Memoirs of My Own Time*. Philadelphia: Carey, Lea & Blanchard, 1897.

Young, Arthur. *Travels During the Years 1787, 1788 and 1789, Undertaken More Particularly with a View of Ascertaining the Cultivation, Wealth, Resources, and National Prosperity of the Kingdom of France*. Dublin: R. Cross, P. Wogan et al., 1793.

Zobel, Hiller B. *The Boston Massacre*. New York: W. W. Norton, 1970.

INDEX

Note: Footnotes are indicated by *n* after the page number.